OF SHEEP AND OTHER THINGS

A farming odyssey of the Campbells in Australia
1846–2013

Alex Campbell AM

THE AUTHOR

Alex spent his childhood on Lake Violet, an isolated sheep station east of Wiluna in WA, before completing his schooling at Christ Church Grammar School in Perth. He commenced his farming career at Kulin in the WA wheatbelt, before being allocated a virgin mallee block at Borden. After fully developing the land with wife Jenn, they moved to Narrikup, a mixed farming area to the north of Albany.

Alex represented the farm sector at State and National level, firstly as State President of the WA Farmers Federation and serving on the National Farmers Federation executive, then through a number of Landcare and research related organisations. His greatest contribution was in dryland salinity, chairing the National Dryland Salinity Program, WA State Salinity Council and the Co-operative Research Centre for Salinity.

Alex retired to Perth in 2013, but has retained an interest in agriculture, with his daughter farming at Dandaragan on WA's west coast, and son managing sheep stations in the Riverina region of NSW.

Jenn and Alex, 2006

Published in 2017 by Alex Campbell
© Alex Campbell 2017
ISBN 978-0-646-97740-9

All rights reserved. No part of this publication may be reproduced, stored in a retrieval system or transmitted in any form or by any means, electronic, mechanical, photocopying, recording or otherwise, without the prior written permission of the publisher.

A catalogue record for this book is available from the National Library of Australia

COVER CAPTIONS
Front cover top: Evelyn Campbell at Micalago in 1903 (See page 49)
Front cover bottom: Lake Violet woolshed, 1933 (See page 88)
Back cover top: Mustering plant, Lake Violet, 1930s (See page 101)
Back cover bottom: Front view of the homestead and front garden, 2006 (See page 297)

To Mum and Dad, Jenn, Anna and Jock

CONTENTS

	Preface	8

PART I: BUSHRANGERS, SHEARERS AND SQUATTERS

1	The Danish Connection	14
2	David – Goimbla and Bushrangers	19
3	David – Cunningham Plains and Merino Sheep	30
4	The Powells of Turalla and Lake George	41
5	Nat – Trackside and Shearing Teams	44
6	The Ryries of Micalago and the Monaro	62
7	Don – Cricket, Koonoona and Millstream	67
8	Don – Lake Violet, Wiluna and the Goldfields	85
9	The Roses of Mount Anderson and the West Kimberley	109
10	Don – Goldsbroughs and Wydgee Past Co	113

PART II: A PRODUCT OF THE MENZIES ERA

11	Lake Violet, Through a Boy's Prism	126
12	The Perth Schoolboy	132

PART III: FROM A MALLEE BLOCK TO LANDCARE

13	The Would-be Farmer	149
14	Tillgaree, the Mallee Block	165
15	The Mallee Bride	183
16	From Mallees to Redgums	207
17	Crystal Brook – Bracken to Vineyards	221
18	Farmer Politics	232
19	Parallel Lines of Endeavour	250
20	The War on Salinity	259
21	Put Out to Pasture	289
	Appendix I: Property Details	300
	Appendix II: The Campbells	311
	Appendix III: Timeline for Alex Campbell	319
	Acronyms	321
	Endnotes	323
	Acknowledgements	334
	Index of People and Places	337

PREFACE

My father asked, 'Now are you sure about farming as your future career?' The conversation way back in 1959 was the beginning of a fulfilling life on the land and, later, in representing farmers at the state and national level. Having sold the farm in 2013, I had cause to reflect not only on my own time in agriculture, but also to earlier generations stretching back to 1846.

There have been many powerful influences that have dominated our family and Australian agriculture over the years: the relentlessly variable climate – 'a sunburnt country, of drought and flooding rains';[1] the rise and decline of the mighty Merino wool industry; state and federal politics as experienced by those of us 'in the bush'; challenges as diverse as dingoes, rabbits, bush fire, salinity and now climate change; benefits of strong rural communities as demonstrated by the support of local fire brigades, sporting facilities and Landcare; all faced under the ever-present constraints of isolation and distance. It brings to mind the well-tested grazier adage: 'It's 20 per cent breeding and 80 per cent feeding.'

That's not to deny the enormous contribution of the sheep and cattle stud industries over the years, but rather to highlight the much bigger gains or losses made through the husbandry and care of animals and the land we farm. In the Australian context, the response to drought would have to be the most critical management decision to influence sustainable farming and profitability, alongside a host of lesser issues to test our mettle.

It's my contention that the same adage holds true for humans. On the 'breeding' side, random selection would have to be the governing criterion! However, the 'feeding' of our offspring through the example we set, the stories we tell and the education we provide is far more telling in determining the success or otherwise of the next generation. Parents may be the greatest influence, though grandparents' stories of earlier generations also help to develop the family picture.

And so it is for the Campbells in Australia and the contribution we have made to agriculture. The stories and records have come down through government and church sources, newspaper articles, family scrapbooks and photo albums, together with word of mouth. In many ways they are similar to the rock art of ancient Aboriginal cultures, with physical images gaining life and meaning as stories are retold about them. I guess I've reached the stage of life that compels me to also leave a handprint at the back of the cave!

I will outline the 'breeding and feeding' of the Campbells, with increasing detail as the generations progress. While the emphasis is on agriculture, you will find the large family has also played its part in many other spheres of Australia's development.

The book is written as a yarn, supported by accurate detail where needed. As such, I have included the conversation and thoughts of various people as appropriate to the time and, unless showing attribution, they are of my own making. The first part covers the family and the development of agriculture through to my father's generation and is written in the third person, while the remaining two parts are a personal story of my own life, written in the first person. Two appendices give further detail of our family and the properties they nurtured to become the homes for future generations. I tell the story up to my generation as the next are still living their stories – it's not for me to second-guess the issues that motivate them.

The defining role of the women who married into the Campbell family will be spelt out. Without exception, they have been innovative, courageous, loyal and of strong personal character. Many of them were also of pioneering pastoral families, equally deserving of mention in this farming odyssey.

Readers will note that I haven't imposed today's political correctness on past generations. For example, I refer to Aboriginals as Natives, blacks or blackfellas, as was done in that time and context. Imperial measures are used through to decimalisation in February 1966.

To aid the reader, here is a simplified family tree (see Appendix II for further details).

> **John** Campbell: 1766–1826 (Ireland–Denmark–England)
> **Thomas** Campbell: 1804–1872 (Denmark–England–India)
> **David Henry** Campbell: 1829–1885 (India–NSW)
> **Nathaniel Powell** Campbell: 1874–1952 (NSW–SA–WA)
> **Donald Henry Alexander** Campbell: 1907–1987 (SA–WA)
> **Alexander David** Campbell: 1941–present (WA)
> **Anna** and **Jock** Campbell: 1971–present and 1972–present (WA–NSW).

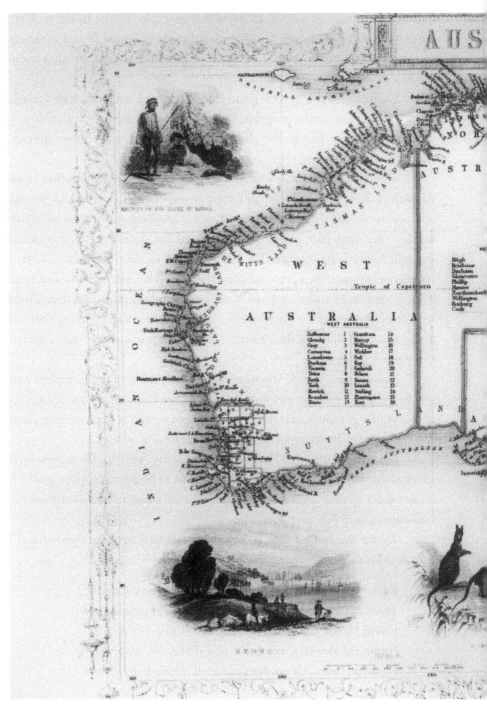

Original engraving by John Tallis and Company 1850. Note the extent of New South Wales and the 19 counties clustered around Sydney

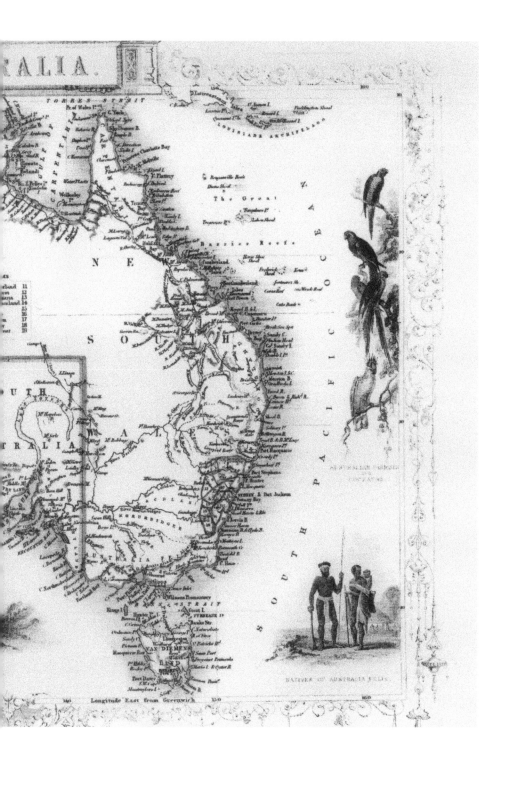

PART ONE

BUSHRANGERS, SHEARERS AND SQUATTERS

How can you tell where you are going if you don't know where you have come from?

Old Irish saying

1 THE DANISH CONNECTION

I don't believe the few drops of Danish or Scottish blood still pulsing through our veins has very much influence on the present generation, though I'm convinced attitudes, personalities and beliefs are passed down the line. Many people consider the Scots and Danes are similar, as being reserved and self-sufficient, or (less kindly) stubborn and aloof – either way, not very talkative and taking a while to gain their trust and confidence. So, how can the Campbells have such a strong Danish connection?

As with all family histories, delve far enough and you will find villains, Royalty and a few from t'other side of the blanket. The Campbells are no exception, and they do lay claim to a Royal connection through an annulled marriage – and a Danish one at that! Stories have been handed down through the generations, becoming less clear as the years pass, to the point of becoming a legend. Interest resurfaced in the early 1980s, when Anne Campbell was looking into the family background.[2] She chanced upon a distant cousin, Madeline Few,[3] who was also delving into the family's past and was intrigued when she received the following information:

> Thomas Campbell, b. 1804 at Kronborg Castle, according to my records, and according to the family legend, was not the son of John Campbell at all. It was told to us by our father when we were young, one of the Saltings referred to it in a letter to the family, so when I found that cousin Tom Fraser[4] had also heard the story from his father, I really began to think there must be something to it.
>
> When Dad left NSW for WA in about 1900, his mother told him that his grandfather was the son of a Danish Prince, who later became King, and his grandmother, a French lady-in-waiting at the Danish Court – a Lady Elizabeth de Burgh.

There was supposed to have been a morganatic marriage[5] when the Prince was very young and at the time was not heir to the throne. However, as soon as it looked as if he could be next in line, his family had the marriage annulled. The child was taken off to England and brought up by the Campbells, who allowed him to take their name. If the story is true, the only Prince of Denmark who could possibly fill the bill would be King Christian VIII – historically, he matches the legend beautifully. Grandma told Dad 'no matter what he did or where he went, he must never forget he had Royal blood in his veins'. Delicious, don't you think?[6]

My mother played her part in keeping the legend alive by giving me a photograph of Kronborg Castle many years ago, with the following wording:

Don's great-grandfather was born at Kronborg Castle, supposedly of Royal birth. People used to say how like Prince Philip, Don was. Well, Philip's grandfather, the ex-King of Greece, was originally a Danish Prince.

Kronborg Castle, Denmark (image from widely distributed postcards; source Wikipedia)

These stories from the 1980s posed more questions than answers, but sowed the seed for further research. Madeline Few came to the rescue some 30 years later, having engaged a Danish archivist to help in her work, which unearthed further information – short of any definitive answers regarding the 'Royal connection'.

The earliest recorded reference to our line of Campbells, is of John, born in Dublin in February 1767. At the time, Ireland was under British rule and Catholics were forbidden to own or inherit land, resulting in many wealthy English and Scottish people moving there. It's known the fifth Duke of Argyle (also known as John Campbell) spent considerable time in Ireland, while many others bearing the Campbell name are recorded as owning property and living there. There's no record of John's birth certificate, or any direct connection to the Duke, but family silverware has been passed down the line, showing the Campbell crest (a boar's head) and the motto *Ne Obliviscaris* (forget not).

John's family moved to Denmark when he was very young. The first documented evidence we have is of him being granted his master mariner's 'ticket' on 19 November 1785: 'completed satisfactorily in faultless Danish'. He was also described as being: '18 years old, born in Dublin, of medium stature with black hair'. From 1786 to 1791, he is recorded as the second mate and then first mate on ships plying between Copenhagen and the Danish West Indies. He is later described as captain of various ships on the same trade route from 1792 to 1806.

John married Elisabeth Sophie Berg on 21 October 1796 with the reception held at 'The House', Bredgade, Copenhagen. Her birth date is recorded as 1777, born at Lyngby near Copenhagen, the daughter of a wealthy innkeeper. Elisabeth was one of a large family and in the employ of the royal household.

John and Elisabeth had eight children, seven having full documentation of their births: John Christian born 1798, Copenhagen; Robert 1800, London; Henry 1802, Copenhagen; Thomas 1804, no birth details; Julia 1806, London; Louisa Anne 1808, Copenhagen; Augustus 1809, London; and Phillip, 1811, London. These records show the family travelled freely between Copenhagen and London.

John's successful career with the Danish merchant navy was brought to an abrupt end as a result of the Napoleonic wars, when Britain became concerned the Danish fleet could be lost to the French. Denmark refused to cede to the British, ships were destroyed and they were to remain at war from 1808 to 1814 in a naval, rather than military, capacity. Though John was all but Danish, other than by birth, life was too difficult in Denmark under these circumstances so he moved his family to Chatham Place, Hackney (a London suburb), in 1808 and set himself up as a merchant.

John must have retained the support of the Royal Court, however, for he was appointed acting Consul in 1816 following the discharge of Consul General Hornemann owing to bankruptcy, then appointed Royal Consul in London from 1821 through to his death in 1826.

Finally, the archivists noted Christian VIII (the Prince in question, who ruled as King in old age, 1839–1848) had 10 extramarital children, 'for whom he carefully provided'. Thomas was not among those listed, but they also noted there has been persistent rumour and mention of an unknown male child resulting from a morganatic marriage. Therefore, for such a rumour to persist in Denmark for nearly 200 years, one has to wonder if there may be more to the Campbell legend than at first meets the eye?

The Campbells would have been ideally placed to take in an inconvenient Royal offspring, and family belief is that Elisabeth had a stillborn child in 1804, before taking Thomas in as her own. There are no records regarding Elisabeth giving birth (stillborn or otherwise), just as there is no record of Thomas's birth.

Considering the authority of the Royal Court at the time, they could have ordered all references to the marriage and male child be removed from the records – 'a wiping of data', to use current terminology. It's also reasonable to assume there may have been a behind the scenes 'nod and a wink' of approval for the John Campbells to take the child and move off to London, away from the prying eyes and gossip of the court. Perhaps the Consulate positions were a reward for services rendered?

If the above scenario has any merit, then who was Thomas's mother? There has been continued speculation in Denmark as to possible contenders as it's well known the Prince had many and varied dalliances – 'the sowing of wild oats' being a socially accepted pastime for nobility of the day. One of the contenders, without any supporting documentary evidence, could be Elisabeth's younger sister. When baby Thomas seemed to be in danger because of Royal accession speculation, it might well have been arranged for John and Elisabeth to take him in as their own and assume the Campbell name, as who could be better placed to help out than the mother's own sister? Irrespective of who the mother was, in today's parlance, Thomas would be the adopted son of John and Elisabeth.

So after all the facts and conjecture, what do we really know of great-great-grandfather Thomas Campbell? He was certainly half Danish on his mother's side, irrespective of whether it was a Berg sister, and may have been half Danish of Royal birth on his father's side, if the family and Danish legends have any credence.[7]

The Danish connection continues, for he moved to India as a cadet in the Danish East India Company, based in Serampore, West Bengal.[8] Perhaps being sent off to India was part of the 'nod and a wink' arrangement entered into by John, to ensure Thomas's anonymity? When in India, Thomas married Helena Maria Elizabeth Fiellerup (known as Maria). Her parents were born in Denmark and were now working for the same company, which further develop the Danish connection. Thomas and Maria lived in India until their deaths, Maria in 1863 and Thomas in 1872. It's their second-eldest child, David Henry Campbell, who really is the beginning of the Australian story.

We should spare a thought for Maria, as she was born in India, isolated from her Danish heritage, and had 12 children before her death at 53 years of age (see Appendix II for further details). This has to be one of the most heroic contributions to the Campbell story.

Before leaving India and the Danish connection, we should look quickly to David Henry's uncle, Severin Kanute Salting (1805–1865). He was born in Copenhagen to Danish parents, but spent his early working life in London and India, working for Thomas Wilson and Co. In 1833 he married Louisa Augusta Fiellerup (Maria's sister) and they moved to Sydney in 1834. He quickly established himself in business, trading as Flower Salting and Co, was appointed a director of the Union Bank of Australia and trustee of the Savings Bank of New South Wales, and made wide investments in sheep stations and sugar plantations. Severin was granted Letters of Designation (colonial form of naturalisation) by Governor Gibbs, as 'being a gentleman of great respectability'. He founded the Salting exhibition for boys educated at Sydney Grammar School, before dying a wealthy man with the then considerable estates of £90,000 in England and £85,000 in New South Wales. His vast art collection was bequesthed to the British nation, being 2,657 pieces in all, thought to be worth over £5 million in 2016 value.[9]

It's little appreciated that many other Danish people came to Australia in the 19th century, with over 1,000 being on the Victorian goldfields by 1857. The greatest migration occurred to the newly formed state of Queensland under land settlement incentives, with 6,403 Danish people there by 1891. Many successful families around the country have Danish heritage, such as Andersen, Jensen, Jorgensen, Hansen and even the former Queensland Premier, Joe Bjelke-Petersen (the suffix 'sen' being the Danish equivalent of 'son').

2 DAVID – GOIMBLA AND BUSHRANGERS

David Henry Campbell was born at Jellasore, India, on 21 November 1829. His father, Thomas, was a merchant for the Danish East India Company, trading in spices and indigo. The rich blue dye was in high demand in Europe and the Campbells were engaged in its cultivation and harvest (indigo being of the pea family).[10] The Danish time in India was coming to an end, with the Danish East India Co. being ceded to the British in 1845.

David's uncle, Severin Salting, must have 'read the tea leaves' earlier than most, for he moved to the colony of New South Wales in 1834, when the Australian population was about 300,000 ('Natives' not being included for census statistics at the time). The colony stretched from the Port Phillip district in the south to Cape York and the Torres Strait in the north. He arrived at a time of expansion and optimism.

In 1837 William and James Ryrie, together with four convict stockmen, forged an overland route from the Monaro in the Southern Highlands of New South Wales to the Port Phillip district and established Yering as a pastoral run in the Yarra Valley. They arrived with 250 head of cattle and some grape vine cuttings.[11] In 1838 Howden and Bonney opened up a passage along the Murray River to the free colony of South Australia and in 1840 the Leslie brothers pioneered an overland route to the new settlement on the Brisbane River. The colony of NSW was looking to wider horizons beyond the established 19 counties clustered around Sydney.

Salting was already a very successful businessman in NSW and had extensive pastoral holdings, when he wrote to his brother-in-law and family in India, urging them to join him:

India is a crowded place, with less and less opportunity for advancement. NSW, on the other hand, has just reached the point of stability and self-sufficiency, and there are vast areas of good grazing land yet to be settled. Also, there are promising signs of gold, with some prospectors making a good living. Thomas, even if you don't care to leave, at least give your boys the chance to make good in this wonderful new land.

Uncle Severin's words obviously fell on deaf ears, as only David, Walter and William came in the first instance, though Maria was to arrive later. David arrived in 1846 and his first 10 years in NSW are not altogether clear as he apparently spent some time in Sydney but mainly worked on various Salting sheep stations.[12] Severin would have provided good advice to David:

Wool is the future for the colony. It is a compact product once shorn and baled and lends itself to transport both within the colony and for overseas shipping.[13] I have properties in the Southern Highlands and you should make yourself known to some of the successful settlers there – the Powells, Ryries and Brooks – and you have a namesake, the Campbells at Duntroon station. Then you might try the Central West on my other properties near Binalong and Jugong. John Macansh is managing there for me and doing a great job in breeding sheep for better wool production.[14] My advice to you David, is travel freely for a year or two and learn all you can about farming in this magnificent country, but pay particular attention to wool. That's the future, mark my words.

David was gaining the respect of his peers in the colony. He quickly learnt you gained people's trust by what you did, not what you said about yourself. Any Royal Danish connection would cut no ice in Australia!

He learnt you were not judged by the horse you rode but, more importantly, the way you handled it – your riding ability and the look of a well-fed and groomed mount. He realised that in a big wide land, a good 'stayer'[15] was important and he developed a liking for thoroughbreds. He was 'getting an eye' for horses and sheep. The respect must have been widespread and genuine, as he was appointed Magistrate for the Territory of Binalong in the Upper Lachlan in 1854.[16]

Trust and respect was also growing between uncle and nephew. David was benefiting from the steady hand of a businessman and grazier who had already made good in the new, expanding colony. Severin, on the other hand, was being reinvigorated by the enthusiasm and energy of the younger David. This coupling of mentor-financier with the drive and determination of youth was to be a powerful combination in the development of Australian agriculture for generations to come.

David had good reason to be excited, as the volume of wool being exported was increasing at an extraordinary rate: 1.9 million pounds in 1830, 9.7 m lb in 1840 and 39 m lb in 1850.[17] The need for shepherding and folding (penning) of sheep every night was no longer required as the losses to wild dogs and Natives was no longer a serious issue.[18] The use of fencing wire rapidly replaced the labour-intensive role of the shepherd and, as a result, many sheep diseases, such as catarrh, became less of a problem.[19]

The new innovation of wool sorting (classing) at the point of shearing was rapidly expanding, resulting in higher prices for wool. Thomas Shaw was an early proponent of in-shed classing and would have provided inspiration and direction to David in this regard. Wool was being pressed into tighter bales, resulting in more efficient use of bullock wagons for land transport and for overseas clipper capacity.[20]

It was the advent of the clippers, being the pinnacle of sailing ship technology, which allowed Australia to become a trading partner in the global economy, rather than a distant convict settlement of the British Empire. These mighty ships dominated the seas for three decades from 1845 to 1875. Captains ventured ever further south to take advantage of the 'roaring forties' and halved the 12-week sailing time from Europe to Australia, with corresponding cheaper costs of passenger and cargo transport. Freight capacity was limited and favoured high-value commodities, such as wool, at the expense of the more bulky products of lumber, grain and coal. The clippers also opened the way for mass migration to the fledgling colonies.[21]

There were also rapid advances in sheep breeding. The Australian flock was built up from imports from at least 20 different sources, with some less kind commentators claiming it was derived from killers[22] collected by the sailing ships in South Africa and India! For all that, uniformity was slowly emerging, with the Spanish Merinos being improved by the fine wool characteristics of the smaller-framed Saxons and the more robust aspects of the English breeds and Rambouillets.²³ Salting's confidence in his manager, John Macansh, was shared by David in these finer aspects of sheep breeding and he would have been excited by some of the developments in the Riverina and Mudgee regions of NSW and in Tasmania.

And there was gold! Edward Hargraves discovered gold at Bathurst in 1851, followed by nearby areas over the coming years. Australia's population was increasing rapidly: 404,000 by 1850 and more than one million by 1860.²⁴ Severin's business acumen would have been passed on to David:

> Gold's bringing many people to this country, fired up with wild dreams of wealth. While only a few will make it rich, all of them will need feeding – that's where we can make good.

Gold resulted in the need for improved transport and roads. Cobb & Co set up business in 1853 and rapidly expanded to a very efficient network of coach transport for the delivery of mail, passengers and smallgoods.²⁵ Teams of horses and bullocks were transporting the requirements of the gold seekers out from the ports, bringing wool and other produce back on the return journey. All those horses and bullocks were supplied by farmers and, together with their feed requirements, provided a further base for agricultural expansion.

Another aspect of transport was also established. Riverboats! *PS Mary Ann* was the first paddle steamer on the Murray River, working upstream from Goolwa in South Australia in 1853. Later the same year, *PS Lady Augustus* reached Swan Hill, Albury was serviced by 1855 and the Murrumbidgee progressively opened up, with Gundagai being reached in 1858. The less reliable Darling proved more difficult, with Walgett being serviced by 1861 and eventually Mungindi on the Queensland border by 1893.²⁶ A culture of rollicking, rumbustious and tough men plying the rivers was quickly formed. Taking a deckhand job at Hay on the Murrumbidgee and winding up at distant Goolwa in SA, was akin to the overseas travel of today's generation. And of course, station owners' daughters were carefully chaperoned when the boats were loading wool!

The mighty Riverina was rapidly developing, with squatters taking up the valuable frontage country along the rivers and creeks. The region had been landlocked in its early settlement so the focus had been on cattle, as they could be walked to market along the extensive network of stock routes. It was the paddle steamers that allowed wool to quickly become the dominant form

Record load of 1,900 bales of wool on the barge *Kulmine*, towed by PS *Pevensey* (courtesy *Riverine Grazier*)

The Mossgiel bogged wagons. Many stations had wool sheds fronting the rivers, but others had difficulty transporting their wool to a river port (courtesy *Riverine Grazier*)

of production, as sheep thrived on the open saltbush plains. The final surge in river traffic occurred in 1864, when Echuca on the Murray River was serviced by rail from Melbourne. Rather than going downstream to Goolwa, the Darling, Murrumbidgee and Upper Murray now used Echuca and it became the second biggest port in Victoria, with a wharf three quarters of a mile long, 100 boats a day, 500 'wharfies' and 60 hotels. The paddle steamers with their barges in tow were now bringing loads of up to 1,500 and 1,800 bales at a time.[27]

In 1851 the Australian colonies were given the right to govern themselves in most matters, including trade and land allocation, which fired the imaginations of Severin and David. By 1856 the first NSW Parliament was formed with Sir Stuart Donaldson as Premier, the Port Phillip settlement was proclaimed the separate State of Victoria in 1851 and the Brisbane River settlement was agitating for statehood.

There was one final event that must have stirred the interest of uncle and nephew. The colony suffered prolonged drought and recession during the 1840s and the tallow industry (then used in soap, candle and lubricant production) was something of a lifeline to the desperate graziers, with output increasing rapidly: 200,000 sheep boiled down in 1844, 750,000 sheep boiled down in 1845 and 2.5 million sheep boiled down in 1850.[28]

While some good sheep were lost to the boiling down vats, most were inferior types and sheep numbers halved over the decade. (Even though the flock had halved, wool production had doubled, being testament to the rapid advances in sheep breeding.) Many people became so disillusioned by the drought that some started to question whether the colony would ever become anything more than a convict outpost. Severin was more optimistic than the doomsayers and he and David would have agreed that opportunity was there for the taking.

One constraint was the land tenure and occupation laws. The small area around Sydney had been surveyed into 19 counties, which was intended to restrict settlement activity so that roads and policing could keep pace with demand. The thirst for new grazing land was too strong, however, and settlers 'squatted' beyond the boundaries of the counties. The squatters were initially admired and respected for extending the frontiers of settlement, overcoming any problems with 'the Natives', controlling the dingo menace and especially for marking out access tracks and river crossings. Government turned a blind eye.[29]

By 1836 squatting was so widespread that depasturing licences of £10 per year were introduced, property boundaries defined and land divided into districts under the control of a land commissioner. As a result, the practice of squatting was relatively short-lived, though the term 'squatter' remained in common use for another 150 years or so and became synonymous with the wealthy pastoralist or station owner. Early sales from 1836 were termed 'right of station' (hence the origin of 'station' to describe a pastoral holding) and required the approval of one of the commissioners, who were overworked, which often caused delays in land transfers being approved. Living in the regional districts, the commissioners were not always 'beyond a little encouragement' to favour a particular outcome![30]

Severin Salting and David Campbell were ready to take advantage of these favourable times. David acquired Goimbla in 1854[31] and Salting paid £8,800 in October 1855 for Cumbamurra, Beggan Beggan, Cullingra, Bryen and Cunningham Creek, together with 13,400 sheep.[32] All these properties were in the Upper Lachlan district of central NSW.

Goimbla had been grazed by illegal squatters before 1844, but in that year a formal depasturing licence was awarded to Betts and Parton. The renewal licence in 1845 listed 1,865 sheep, four workmen, a slab and bark hut and 20 square miles under management with frontage to Mandagery Creek. Then in 1848, the station was sold to John Walker. David would have been attracted to the property as it had permanent water, good Box, Apple Pine and Myall grazing land and was well situated on the road from Orange to Forbes. The Lambing Flats (later called Young) and Forbes goldfields were rapidly expanding and there was high demand for meat. At auction in 1854, Goimbla was described as:

> being in good repair including a yard with well, mens huts, a three-stall stable with loft, an 80ft x 15ft woolshed and usual homestead paddocks and yards. The residence as a handsome verandah cottage, is shingled and plastered, surrounded by gardens with store, kitchen, tool house etc, attached.[33]

Goimbla was 10 miles from Eugowra and the nearby Murga Inn was a staging post for Cobb & Co on the Orange–Forbes run. The Murga Inn required oats, chaff and hay for the horses and meat for their patrons, providing extra income for the station. And so it was that David Henry Campbell acquired the depasturing licence from John Walker, probably with financial backing from Severin Salting. Two years later in 1856, the Goimbla licence renewal showed the property as 12,800 acres with adjoining grazing lease and turning off 4,000 wethers.[34]

That year was far more important for David for another reason, as he married Amelia Margaret Breillat on 19 February at the then fashionable St Peters Church on Cooks River Road, Sydney (now Princes Highway). She was the 22-year-old third daughter of the wealthy and influential Sydney merchant, Thomas Chaplin Breillat.[35]

David Henry and Amelia (pen and ink drawing by Fiona Craig, the Penzig Collection)

It's difficult to imagine the hardship that Amelia had to overcome as she was now living an arduous three-day carriage journey from Sydney. Her comfortable city life was replaced by the rigours of station activity and the need for self-sufficiency. There was a large vegetable garden and orchard, cows to be milked, butter to be made, sheep to be slaughtered, dripping to be made into soap, daily bread making and visitors to be catered for. While there were servants to undertake these tasks, the responsibility rested with Amelia. There were also children requiring her attention: Thomas Breillat was born on 8 November 1857, David Frances on 17 August 1860 and Percy on 30 October 1861.

Meanwhile, David was steadily improving his sheep flock, working closely with John Macansh, Salting's manager at Cumbumurrah. He also worked with others to establish local agricultural and grazier societies and was successful in winning local awards for his sheep and produce. David was growing oats, wheat and barley and even experimented with Virginian tobacco for three or four years. He was a member of the NSW Acclimatisation Society, which supported the introduction of exotic birds, fish and plants. Fortunately, only two recorded introductions were attributed to David at this time: the release of Toulouse Geese at Goimbla and the use of Schradar Brome grass (*Bromas schraderi*) from the USA as a perennial fodder species.[36]

David and Amelia were now a successful and respected family in the region. However, it was on 19 November 1863, that a single event was to change their lives and, as often happens, a life of hard work and accomplishment is remembered for only one aspect. If you enquire at the Forbes or Eugowra Historical Society and Museum, you will get this initial response: 'Campbell shot O'Meally, one of Ben Hall's notorious gang of bushrangers.'

Bushrangers were causing havoc in the isolated, newly settled regions of inland Australia at the time. Ned Kelly and his gang were the most feared in northern Victoria and southern NSW, while Ben Hall and his followers were equally brazen in central NSW, with resulting loss of life and property. David Campbell had been aiding the police in hunting down the bushrangers and, in retaliation, Goimbla was attacked by Ben Hall and John O'Meally on that fateful night. Gunfire was exchanged and the nearby barn was burnt to the ground before O'Meally was fatally wounded by David. Amelia equally played her part, reloading the guns with powder and percussion caps, and narrowly avoiding being shot herself. The siege was widely reported in the newspapers of the day and was described as the turning point of the bushranger menace.[37]

The Campbells were handsomely rewarded for their bravery: public meetings collected £1,100 to compensate for loss of property; a £500 reward for O'Meally was paid by the government; an electroplated coffee urn was presented to Amelia by 'the ladies of Upper Adelong', which was later donated to the National Museum in Canberra by the family, where it is often on display; and, finally, a Sterling Silver epergne 28 inches high, made by Hardy Bros of London, was presented to the Campbells. The inscription read:

> Presented by the colonists of Australia to Mr and Mrs D.H. Campbell in admiration of their gallant conduct in repelling the attack upon Goimbla, NSW on the night of 19th of November, 1863.

The epergne remained in the family's hands for many years, before being auctioned by Christies in Melbourne on 30 November 1992. The auction catalogue listed it as: 'A national treasure – unique bushranger presentation piece – value $220,000'.[38] It was sold on the day to an undisclosed buyer, though there is no record of the price achieved. It was put up for auction again in 2009 but passed in as not reaching the reserve.[39]

About 25 years after the attack, Banjo Paterson wrote a lengthy poem, *In the Stable*, relating the events of that fateful night. It was supposedly informed by stories he had heard from Alfred (David's son born in 1868) and an old station hand who was present on the night of the siege.[40] The relevant verse reads:

> Ah. We can't breed 'em, the sort that were bred when we old 'uns were young.
> Yes, I was saying, these bushrangers, none of 'em lived to be hung,
> Gilbert was shot by the troopers; Hall was betrayed by a friend.
> Campbell disposed of O'Meally, bringing the lot to an end.

For all the accolades, there was also some 'tall poppy' resentment, as the Irish bushrangers had many relatives in the local towns, which included station hands and shearers of the district. David's son, Alfred, reported later: 'That the lower class people in the district, who were friendly with the bushrangers, made themselves objectionable to the family'.[41]

Life at Goimbla after the siege must have been filled with terrible memories, especially for Amelia, living in the house that still bore marks of the event. There were two more children born at Goimbla following the siege: Eleanor Mary (20 March 1865) and Walter (23 August 1866) but, tragically, both were to die in 1866. Little else is recorded over the final years at the station for David and Amelia, though it's noted David was undertaking work on behalf of the Saltings at Cunningham Plains from at least 1865.[42] John Macansh, the long-serving manager for Salting, wanted to move on and establish his own property and, as neither of Severin's sons had any interest in the hands-on management of the stations, pressure was likely building for David to fill the position. For all these reasons, they decided to leave Goimbla and move to the Salting properties at Murrumburrah, with David as manager. Goimbla was auctioned in 1867, being described as:

> Comprising 150 sq miles of grazing land, 30 miles of dog-proof fencing, a 200-acre two-railed horse paddock, and 600 acres suitable

for cropping. The homestead as seven rooms, including kitchen and store, with nearby stabling, stock yard, and a newly-erected wool shed.[43]

The larger part of the grazing land was sold to Charles Iceley but the 600 acres surrounding the homestead was gifted to Joe O'Brien, 'in appreciation for loyal service'.

Goimbla homestead. It is uncertain as to the identity of the person (courtesy Latrobe Collection, State Library, Victoria)

A visit to Goimbla in 2014 found the crumbling stone chimney, front steps and some old lilac, oak and fruit trees as the only remaining evidence of the early days. With a little imagination, one could picture a shingle-roofed home nestled in the curve of Mandagery Creek, the stables nearby, with sheep and horses grazing in the surrounding paddocks. And maybe even a proud woman with long skirt, standing at the garden gate next to a tall bearded man, holding the reins of his thoroughbred.

3 DAVID – CUNNINGHAM PLAINS AND MERINO SHEEP

The wide open plains were discovered during the John Oxley exploration of the Lachlan River in 1817. Allan Cunningham, botanist and explorer, was one of the party from which the region derived its name. Edward Ryan was the first squatter on the plains, followed by James Manning, who established Cumbamurra in 1835. Ten years later he married Mary Firebrace and together they established 'a residence, built in cottage style sufficiently large for even town comforts'.[44]

Cumbamurra was gazetted in 1848 as being 60,000 acres, with capacity to graze 12,000 sheep and 500 cattle. Many cattle were overlanded to the Port Phillip district, but catarrh badly reduced sheep numbers in 1848–52. Severin Salting purchased the property in 1855, together with the surrounding leases of Beggan-Beggan, Cullinga, Bowyeo and Cunningham Creek, for £8,800, including 13,400 sheep.[45]

John Donald Macansh had been managing Salting's other properties in the Western District of New South Wales since at least 1841[46] and was given the extra responsibility of the new purchases. The Cumbamurra homestead was too far south on the combined properties for efficient management, so it was decided to progressively relocate further north to near the proclaimed town site of Cunningham Plains, on the main road to Murrumburrah. The combined properties were renamed Cunningham Plains, to reflect the new status.

A new woolshed was built in the mid-1860s by John Macansh and reports differ as to the number of shearers it catered for, as some suggested 100 blade shearers, on many occasions shearing 100,000 sheep a year,[47] whereas others refer to only 45 blade shearers.[48] The difference might be explained by blade shearers not being restricted in space by the positioning of mechanical shearing stands.

In addition, some big sheds shore in shifts so that shearing would be completed within a reasonable time and two shifts of 45 could explain the 100-shearer scenario. It was an imposing building, described as:

> a splendid structure, in the form of a 'T' and far too good for the purpose to which it is devoted. The main building is 200 feet in length, and 60 feet across. The top portion, or transept, is 100 feet in length, and about 40 feet in width.[49]

Cunningham Plains woolshed (courtesy Steve and Liz Phillips)

The Robertson Land Act of 1861 allowed for squatters on leased land to apply for conditional purchase, with restrictions to prevent ownership being held in too few hands. John Macansh successfully applied for the land around the Cunningham Plains woolshed, supposedly as a dummy for Salting. (It was later transferred to Salting's legal representative in 1867 for 10 shillings, with David Campbell as witness.) The area totalled 60,000 acres.[50]

David and Amelia formally took over the management of Cunningham Plains in 1867 but it is unclear where they lived, for it took three years to build the new homestead (there would have been cottages scattered over the amalgamated properties). However, it was obviously worth the inconvenience as the completed homestead was both innovative in construction and a very fine home in which to live. It was widely reported in articles of the day, including the Sydney *Town and Country Journal* of 1872:

on a slight eminence is erected, the residence of DH Campbell, esq, JP. This is acknowledged to be the finest pisé house in New South Wales. It is a spacious house, with verandahs and wings for sleeping apartments on one side, and laundry and kitchen on the other. Mr Campbell led the way in pisé work in this and the western part of the colony. The idea was, strangely enough, obtained by Mr Campbell from a Chinaman he had in his employ.[51]

Cunningham Plains homestead 2014, front view from the east (courtesy Steve and Liz Phillips)

During construction of the homestead, David and Amelia had another child, Alfred Walter, born on 18 January 1868, then lost their first born, Thomas, later in the same year. As the house was nearing completion, it was confirmed that Amelia was expecting twins, which provided hope that their fortunes were at last changing for the better. Tragically, their dreams were shattered. On 24 May 1870, Amelia gave birth to a twin girl but died four days later after the stillbirth of a second girl.

Amelia would have to be the most heroic – and stoic – of all the women in the Campbell story. She had already endured the tragedy of losing Eleanor aged 18 months, Walter at two months and then Thomas at 11 years of age. There can be nothing more heart-rending than for a mother to lose a child, let alone four of them, and then to die of childbirth. Amelia's story was typical of so many pioneer women of the day, as can be attested by visiting lonely cemeteries next to isolated churches and seeing the many headstones for young children. Together with her contribution in the siege of Goimbla, she was by any judgement a truly remarkable woman.

The little girl born in such tragic circumstances was christened Amelia in her mother's name, but lived for only 10 months, dying in March 1871. Of eight children, only three survived to adulthood: David, Percy and Alfred, who all went on to contribute greatly to the development of Australia.[52] David snr had little time for quietly grieving the loss of Amelia and the twin girl as he had the other twin to care for and a large new homestead to set up, together with the running of an expanding station. His sister Maria and her husband, Thomas Davies, moved in and helped as best they could, before buying the neighbouring property Nantgwylan, remaining close at hand.

The large stations of New South Wales were just 'hitting their straps':[53] from Belltree in the Upper Hunter; to Coree, Boonoke and Wanganella on Billabong Creek; Tubbo, Burrabogie, Togannain, Uardry, Mungadal and Yanga on the Murrumbidgee; and Booligal, Ulonga and Tupra on the Lachlan, there was tremendous activity. Cunningham Plains was only one of many highly profitable stations of the day that collectively underpinned Australia's prosperity for the hundred years to come.

The stations were largely self-sufficient villages, with the combined rural population far exceeding that of the cities. Cunningham Plains was typical of those large pastoral holdings, employing 80 people at that time.[54] The homestead would have required a cook, kitchen hands, several maids, a tutor for the children, a bookkeeper and storeman, and a head gardener, with assistants (often Chinese), as self-sufficiency in fruit and vegetables was essential, not to mention the formal garden of the house. The yardman's role was to maintain the wood supply and care for a large fowl run. The dairyman and milk maids kept everybody in milk, cream and butter and of course there was a slaughterman, as fresh meat was required daily (at a time before refrigeration was introduced). The homestead would also have employed a groom and stable hands for the horses and vehicles they used.

The working station would have required a blacksmith, leather worker-saddler, fencing teams, boundary riders, windmill men, teamsters for the wagons and ploughing, many stockmen and station hands. There were also outstations, or 'out-camps', as distances were too great from the homestead for the daily checking of stock water and lambing ewes.

As staff aged they would take on the less physical jobs, such as yardmen, and wives of the workmen filled domestic jobs. Children born on a property often went on to work alongside their fathers or the girls would marry somebody employed on the station. The management of all these people and keeping the peace when jealousies and friction erupted was a skill learned only by experience.

Talking of staff, shearing was a major event on these large stations. As noted earlier, the woolshed at Cunningham Plains catered for up to 100 blade shearers with a further 100 men needed as roustabouts, tarboys, wool sorters, penner uppers and wool pressers, not to mention the 28 men employed as sheep washers.[55] In those early days, stations were not obliged to provide accommodation, so a tent town slowly developed leading up to shearing, usually along the nearby creek or river and within walking distance of the shed. The 'bush telegraph'[56] would alert everybody to the due date of a shed starting up and a good shed would attract men from far and wide. Just as a gold find would attract other providers of services, so it was with these tent towns. People would have sold stores, sly grog, snake oil remedies – and 'ladies of the night' were not to be denied an income![57]

Tarwong shearing 1878, similar crowded working conditions as at Cunningham Plains (courtesy *Riverine Grazier*)

David needed to plan well ahead for shearing as bringing in excess of 100,000 sheep into the shed and then back to the paddocks at the rate of over 5,000 a day was no mean feat. He would have said to his overseers: 'Drift the sheep in quietly, make sure they're well watered, but on no account let the shed run short of sheep – nothing causes more strife than an empty shed.'

He would also be giving advice to the permanent employees around the shed and homestead: 'Keep a good look out over shearing – the camp down by the creek attracts a lot of shifty types and we don't want to lose anything to them.'

For all that, a shed of around 200 men and 5,000 sheep in full swing would be poetry in motion! Everybody would be doing their allotted jobs, each relying on the other to keep pace with the demands expected of them. David would have taken his boys down to the shearing shed after their tutor had finished for the day, saying: 'Now just sit up there on those bales and keep out of everybody's way, or you'll soon get a clip under the ear.'

The boys would have been mesmerised by the symphony of activity before them.

Good fortune was at hand as David married Louise Powell on 2 April 1872 at St Phillip's church, Bungendore. She was the daughter of Nathaniel Stephen Powell and Charlotte Sophia (nee Brooks), who were large and successful graziers in the Bungendore–Lake George area.

Louise was able to add the feminine touch to the large house so cruelly denied to Amelia, though David's sister Maria would have been of assistance. David's three surviving sons were aged 12, 11 and six years and there would have been the normal tensions of a second wife gaining the confidence and love of her stepchildren. There is no record of the children attending the local Cunningar public school that David helped establish, so they must have had a private tutor at the homestead before being sent off to boarding school.[58]

Louise and David had four children: Nathaniel Powell in 1874, Charlotte Louise in 1876, Alexander Douglas in 1878 and Henry in 1880. Further good fortune was with them as the four children survived to adulthood. Louise would have been very busy with seven children to care for and a large home to manage. David was continuing to gain recognition as a stud breeder of sheep and for his agricultural practices, which would have resulted in many visitors coming to the station, as well as the normal social functions of the day. All this activity would have added responsibility to Louise as the 'gracious hostess'.

David expanded the cropping area to 3,000 acres, including oats, wheat and kidney beans, which was a huge area in the days of horse-drawn implements. He was winning prizes for his agricultural pursuits as well as for horses he bred and was an early pioneer of improved pastures for stock, as he realised a lot of the natural plants were being eaten out as a result of overgrazing. He had large 50-acre trials of cocksfoot (*dactylis glomerata*), perennial ryegrass (*lolium perenne*) and prairie grass (*bromus wildenowii*).[59] On behalf of the NSW Zoological Society, he introduced English Skylarks, Californian Quail, Goldfinches, Yellowhammers, Green Linnets and stocked the dams and creeks with English Perch during 1880–81.[60] Questionable practices these days, but thank goodness he didn't bring in rabbits, starlings or cane toads!

His greatest interest and success was in sheep breeding and we have already noted his close association with John Macansh, who was the registered joint owner of the sheep stud with Severin Salting. For the best authority, I will quote from the 'bible of sheep breeding' – Charles Massy's *The Australian Merino*:

> JD Macansh, who was managing Cunningham Plains for SK Salting ... was unhappy with the Mudgee blood stock, especially their size, and made an early move to Rambouillets in 1852. Following the influential ram Napoleon, brought from South Africa in 1856, Salting, through Baron Daurier of Rambouillet, obtained a proponent Rambouillet sire named 'Rambouillet' in 1862. He had great influence and, as with the Peppins and a number of South Australian breeders, seems to have come from a drop of rams between 1859 and around 1866 that carried great quality and prepotency. Cunningham Plains made further Rambouillet importations in 1866. Then in 1868 DH Campbell and Sons took over the flock, and immediately introduced Tasmanian-blood rams from Bellevue, Scone and St Johnstone. The result was a slight diminution in size but an improvement in wool quality, lustre and density, as the Tasmanian sheep in the 1860s, 1870s and 1880s had reached their peak for body size, wool quality and productivity. Cunningham Plains then carried on to influence some other important flocks, not the least being Urangeline and Mahonga in NSW, and Canning Downs in Queensland.

David was invigorated by the deeply satisfying experience of developing his sheep flock and breeding thoroughbreds. The sight of a new-born lamb, calf or foal tottering to its feet and seeking its first drink of milk heralds so much promise for the future – and is just reward for past endeavours. This basic cycle of renewal, and observing the steady improvement of the flock or herd, would be the underpinning motivation for commercial and stud breeders for generations to come.

The five grandsons descended from Nathaniel Campbell (David's eldest son with Louise) all have solid silver mugs awarded to D.H. Campbell at various sheep shows, following his taking over the stud in 1868. They are in repousse style, reputedly made by W. Edwards, apprentice to the first Australian silversmith, with the following inscriptions:

> Tim's: Yass P&A Association Challenge Cup – for the champion merino ram
> Alex's: Murrumbidgee Pastoral Association – First Prize, three best colonial bred merino ewes of any age
> David's: Murrumbidgee Pastoral Association – First Prize, for the best ram in the yard
> Andrew's: Murrumbidgee Pastoral Association – First Prize, for best imported ram
> Richard's: Murrumbidgee Pastoral Association – Best three colonial bred two-tooth merino rams

Mugs of this type were valued at £5 when first made, a vast amount compared to the cost of a blue felt ribbon today, and show how important sheep breeding was to the colony's financial wellbeing in the late 1800s. David won many other prizes for his sheep and wool, and really extended his reputation by winning an award at the Philadelphia International Exhibition in 1876.[61] His rams and stud ewes were sold widely in Australia, even as far as Western Australia, sending 100 stud ewes and 150 rams to the Darlot Bros of Beringarra station in the Murchison District.[62]

David was also breeding thoroughbred horses, racing the better ones under his own colours, while providing the station with quality stock horses. His next-door neighbour and brother-in-law, Thomas Davies, raised concerns about David exploiting Cunningham Plains resources for his own benefit, at the expense of Salting's pasture for sheep.[63] It should be remembered that station managers of the

The five silver mugs awarded to D.H. Campbell (now in the hands of the five male grandchildren of Nat, eldest son of David and Louise)

The five grandsons: David, Andrew (Andy), Richard, Alex and Tim Campbell

day were poorly paid by today's standards, but were often given the opportunity to earn extra income 'on the side' as an inducement for continued and loyal service. Under this system, John Macansh and then David were allowed to develop the Merino sheep stud and thoroughbred horse breeding on the basis of supplying the needs for Salting's stations but selling off the surplus in their own names. Proof of the pudding for the effectiveness of this system was Salting's fabulous wealth at the time of his death and the comfortable lifestyle of David, educating his children at private boarding schools and acquiring modest land holdings in his own name.

David Henry's full life was brought to an abrupt end on 23 August 1885 following a short illness. He died at Cunningham Plains, aged only 55. There were many newspaper articles at the time, all referring to the 'attack upon Goimbla' and his two marriages. For example, the article in the *Burrowa News* on 28 August 1885 covered those points and concluded: 'As a large employer of labour, he was kind and liberal, and carries with him to the grave the best blessings of his numerous employees.' Another report stated: 'Such was Campbell's popularity, that a gloom was cast over the town of Murrumburrah on Sunday evening, when the news of Mr DH Campbell's death came to hand.'[64] The gravesite, lot 75 Murrumburrah Cemetery, also carries the headstones of Thomas and Amelia.[65]

There must have been turmoil at Cunningham Plains following David's death. Station management arrangements had to be made with the executors of Severin Salting's estate and Louise had to vacate the house and move to her new home, Douglas, on the west bank of Lake George, near her old family home, Turalla. Before leaving, Louise had other matters to attend to, as the *Cootamundra Herald* reported on 27 February 1886:

> The Golden Fleece Hotel at Cootamundra was sold at auction for £1000 cash to Mrs Agnes Quigley by Mrs L Campbell, executrix for the late Mr DH Campbell of Cunningham Plains.

The Campbell interests had obviously extended to this district as Louise was also presented with a large silver tureen with lid, on which was inscribed: 'Presented to Mrs DH Campbell by the members of the CATC 1886.' There is some confusion about the CATC, as the Cootamundra Trotting Club is referred to as the CTC, but perhaps the 'A' was for 'auxiliary' or 'associate'? (The tureen has come down through the family to Nathaniel's son Pat, grandson David and now my son Jock.)

David Henry's will reads:

This is the last will and testament of me David Henry Campbell of Cunningham Plains, Cunningham, New South Wales. After payment of all my just debts I devise and bequeath all my real and personal property (with exceptions hereinafter mentioned) to my wife Louise Campbell to be enjoyed by her during her life here and at her death to be equally divided amongst my sons and daughter. The exceptions are: I give, devise and bequeath Douglas and all my landed property at Lake George, New South Wales, to my wife Louise Campbell absolutely, £2000 of my life insurance to be devoted to the education of my wife Louise Campbell's children in such manner as she may think fit and £100 to my executors. I hereby appoint Henry George Powell of Bungendore and William Wilson of Cunningham, my son David Francis Campbell and my wife Louise Campbell, executors and executrix of this my will as witnessed this 13th day of January, 1883.

The will had been duly signed and witnessed, and was lodged for probate on 12 November 1885. How much simpler the legal process was in those days!

Douglas was two stories with 20 guest rooms, the larger ones on the upper floor, the smaller ones downstairs: 'all large and airy with fine water views'. The property also included a three-stall stable and coach house.[66] It was certainly a fine house for Louise and her four children, but unfortunately she was not to have a long retirement at Douglas, as she died on 25 March 1892, aged only 51, and was buried in the private Turalla cemetery. Her eldest son, Nathaniel (Nat), was 18 years old and independent, but Charlotte (Bunt), 17, Alexander (Alick), 14, and Henry (Harry), 12, were all in need of care. Her three younger sisters, who remained unmarried, were living at nearby Turalla and took the children in.

Louise is yet another woman in the Campbell story who deserves our admiration as life dealt her a very demanding hand. Being a second wife, responsible for a big home and staff, then to be widowed at an early age and to pass away seven years later, leaving four children to be cared for, was not an easy lot.

4 THE POWELLS OF TURALLA AND LAKE GEORGE

Lake George was discovered by European settlers in 1820. It is the biggest inland lake in New South Wales, being 14 x 6 miles in size with a 29-mile shoreline, and is a little to the northeast of present day Canberra. It has no natural overflow and empties through evaporation, having been dry seven times since 1820, the longest period being 1933–1949. When full, the depth is usually around 12 feet but has been as much as 20 feet on two brief occasions. The original settlers were not aware of it ever drying out and as it was within the boundaries of the 19 counties, there was a rush for land surveying.

Captain Richard Brooks and his wife Christiana were the first settlers to the south of the lake, on properties they called Bungendow and Ashby. Brooks was gored to death by a bull in 1833 and his children inherited the various properties around Lake George and in Sydney.

Charlotte was the sixth of the seven Brooks children and inherited Turalla on the southern end of the lake. The house had been commenced in 1832 and was extended in 1847, with extensive plantings of English trees and shrubs. She married Nathanial Stephen Powell and from that first inheritance to a daughter, it has continued down the female line ever since. It is surely the longest pastoral succession of its kind in Australian history.

The homestead was built in the shape of a quadrangle, with the last extension of the north wing being classic Georgian, comprising three gracious rooms with almost floor-to-ceiling windows. There were heavy wooden shutters on the inside of the windows in case of attack by bushrangers. Charlotte was so concerned about this, she also insisted on having a saddled horse with provisions placed nearby when her husband was away, so that 'would-be villains' would leave the homestead alone. Fortunately, the shutters and saddled horse were never put to the test!

Turalla, 1924. Note the already mature trees and garden of 90 years ago

Nathanial Powell became a highly respected citizen of Bungendore (town gazetted in 1837) and a pillar of the church, school, race and cricket communities: 'a truly fine example of a rural gentleman'. They had eight children, who were all left comfortably off upon Nathanial's death in 1874. Louise, the second eldest, went on to marry David Henry Campbell. Charlotte left Turalla to three unmarried daughters who lived as spinsters until they died: Ada in 1922, Augustus (Gus) in 1924 and Cherrie (Jo) in 1938:

> The sisters made no concession to modern fashions and wore ankle length black skirts and black or striped blouses with high collars and ties, woolly knitted shawls in winter, and always the most sensible boots and shoes.[67]

The three maiden sisters came to the rescue in caring for Louise's children and it must have been difficult on both sides, with the teenagers losing both their parents and no doubt rebelling against life's injustice, the women obviously set in their ways and living in a past age. For all that, it became the children's home, which they came to love.[68]

A visit in 2014 found the charming white house surrounded by ancient deciduous European trees, with lilacs, bulbs, hellebores and English daisies growing randomly under the canopy. There was tranquillity and a sense of permanence about the setting, so I can understand why my father and many other family members had such fond memories of Turalla, thinking of it as 'the ancestral home of their forefathers' – or shouldn't it be 'foremothers'?

We found Louise and Alick Campbell's headstones in the nearby private Turalla cemetery. There could be no more a tranquil resting place for family members than to be in the middle of an open green paddock, with cattle grazing all around.

5 NAT – TRACKSIDE AND SHEARING TEAMS

Nathaniel Powell Campbell was born at Cunningham Plains station near Murrumburrah on 6 September 1874. If it's '20 per cent breeding and 80 per cent feeding', then Nat was dealt a rough paddock. His father, David Henry, died after a short illness when he was only 12 years old and there was the turmoil of leaving the established station, then moving with his mother to Douglas on the west bank of Lake George. Douglas hardly became home for Nat as he was sent off to the Oaklands Boarding School at Mittagong, followed by Kings College at Goulburn.[69]

Only seven years later, his mother Louise died, leaving the 18-year-old Nat to find his own way in the world. And how the world had changed. While he lived at Cunningham Plains, Australia enjoyed good seasons with wool and gold providing wealth for the rapidly expanding nation. The large stations were at the height of their dominance in the community, both in economic and social terms. Being a station owner or manager was the height of personal achievement and social status.

By 1892, when his mother died, Australia was a different place. The British Stock Exchange had collapsed in 1891, depression was gripping the global economy and the Commercial Bank of Australia shut its doors in 1893. Other bank closures followed. There was rapidly growing unemployment and no social welfare to cushion the blow, causing many men to 'hump their bluey'[70] and take to the track in search of work.

Graziers were exerting downward pressure on the shearers' rate of pay, resulting in the 1890s shearers' strike, centred at Barcaldine in Queensland under 'the tree of knowledge' – the foundation of today's Australian Labor Party. Strike action rolled across the country and several large sheds were burnt down in protest, including Uardry's on the Murrumbidgee.

Nat would have been living under the shadow of his father's reputation as a sheep breeder and pioneer of pisé construction, let alone the slayer of bushrangers! His exploits would have been constantly brought up in conversation and how could he ever match those achievements? The memories of his father's fine thoroughbreds and the manner in which he trained them would also be ever present. Nat was so proud when he won his first race on one of David's mounts when only 12 years old, just before his father's death.[71]

Young Nat, having just lost his mother, was desperate for a job and wanted to establish his independence. A position with the NSW Department of Roads and Bridges, based in the Upper Lachlan, provided the opening.[72] After three years, however, the call of the bush was too strong and he worked on several stations, gaining pastoral experience.

Nat was also 'an amateur boxer and footballer of no mean caliber' and 'served as a Lieutenant in the NSW Horse, which was the escort to the Duke of York on the occasion of his visit to that State'. He was gaining a reputation of his own in the world of thoroughbreds:

> Mr Campbell ran horses of his own in NSW, one of them being Gambetta with which he won the Harden Cup in 1893. For three years he participated as an owner-trainer and always rode his own horses when the weight permitted.[73]

It's unclear where he ran his stable, but perhaps the Saltings let him have some space at Cunningham Plains? He then progressed to being the starter at local race meetings, which was very demanding in the walk-up starts of the day (before the advent of the barrier and gates of today's standing starts). He also rode at Randwick and Kensington and, on one occasion, was riding against Banjo Paterson in a steeplechase, when Banjo's horse fell and Nat went on to win the race.[74]

Working on sheep stations during the 1890s brought Nat into direct association with the shearers' strike and resulting turmoil within the industry. Many stations were forced (or chose) to shear their sheep with station hands and labour they employed. Nat wasn't spared the job and learnt to shear with the blades of the day. The turn of the century saw the first mechanical shearing being trialled, with Wolesley and Moffatt-Virtue pioneering the way. As a young man, the advantages of mechanised shearing really appealed to Nat as he believed more

Nathaniel (Nat) Campbell, dressed as a Lieutenant in the NSW Horse

sheep shorn per day should benefit both the shearer and the grazier. At first the unions resisted the innovation, as they thought fewer shearers equated to reduced membership and income to themselves. The fact that a shearer could shear more sheep per day and hence be better off under the piece-work system didn't seem to matter.

The other thing that really struck Nat as he moved around the stations was the constant reference to the Peppin blood line, as most sheep studs in the area were either openly or quietly introducing these rams into their flocks. George Peppin had sold the Wanganella part of his property to Albert Austin and Thomas Millear, and neighbouring Boonoke to F.S. Faulkner in 1878. The new owners built on the pioneering work of the Peppins and these studs have continued to this day. (The properties are all on the Billabong Creek, midway between Deniliquin and Hay.) Other well-known studs, such as Uardry, Haddon Rig, Mungadal, Bundemar, Goolgumbla and Willurah, were founded on the Peppin breeding.[75] The Peppins utilised similar blood lines to those of David Campbell, being Rambouillet and Saxon, and by their sheer skill and persistence, transformed the Australian wool industry. Nat was fascinated by these developments and observed how quickly they were taken up by graziers throughout the country. At last, Australia was developing a uniform Merino style wool for the global market.[76]

The equally important breakthrough of rust-resistant wheat by William Farrer – the beginning of wheat breeding in Australia by Australians – meant very little to Nat. Also, the innovative improvements to farm machinery, such as R.B. Smith's stump-jump plough and Hugh McKay's Sunshine Harvester, did very little to interest a young man focused on thoroughbreds and sheep.

There were three other major events at the end of the century: drought, rabbits and Federation. The drought of 1895–1902 is now referred to as the Federation Drought. As with all dry spells, it sneaks up on you before you realise it, then the insidious grip continues to tighten as each slow month passes. Records set in previous generations were broken: 'permanent' waterholes ran dry; the Darling was dry at Bourke; and riverboat traffic all but ceased, even at Deniliquin and Mildura. The wheat crop was so depleted it was feared Australia might need to import grain. There were enormous stock losses: sheep down from 91 million to 54 million and cattle down from 11.8 million to 7 million.[77] Henry Lawson summed it up in *Song of the Darling River*:

> The skies are brass and the plains are bare,
> Death and ruin are everywhere.

The drought was so devastating, that 26 February 1902 was declared a day of 'humiliation and prayer' by the NSW government.

Stock routes were eaten out and, in any case, where could you move stock to? Lack of water was the harshest blow as there was no means of transporting either water or stock in any meaningful way, and loss by perishing was commonplace. So severe was the Federation Drought that many records set then are yet to be broken. The sobering thought is that, in geological time, Europeans have been in Australia for only 'the blink of an eye'; why should the drought of 100 years ago be the worst we will ever see?

Nat, just as all people on the land ever since, would have the spectre of drought permanently etched into his memory. Bare, windswept paddocks and dust storms assault all your senses: you see it, you hear it, you smell it, you taste it, you feel it on all of your skin. Complete sensory bombardment!

Twenty-four European wild rabbits were released by Thomas Austin at Winchelsea, Victoria, in 1859: 'for sport and a touch of home'. They spread at an unbelievable rate of about 80 miles per year and were well established in the Upper Lachlan district by the 1890s.[78] The depression years and resulting cheap labour helped in their control but the problem continued to grow, and it was evident sheep and cattle numbers were in decline as a result. The combination of drought and rabbits was also having a devastating effect on the environment and native vegetation. Dust storms were becoming commonplace across the Riverina.

The states had been advocating for greater independence from Britain for some time. Sir Henry Parkes, the long-serving NSW Premier, had been promoting Federation and his 1889 Tenterfield Oration was 'a clarion call for action'. Edmund Barton provided inspirational leadership and many conferences were held, including the important Corowa event in August 1893. A Federation League rally held there advocated for Australian people themselves to vote for Federation and a draft constitution was drawn up for consideration.[79]

Federation was proclaimed on 1 January 1901. Later that year, the first Federal Parliament was opened in the Melbourne Exhibition Building by the Duke of York, with Sir Edmund Barton as Prime Minister. The earlier generation had been excited and motivated by the colonies achieving independent statehood, and now Nat's generation embraced Federation and the new century with enormous rejoicing and confidence. King and Empire still prevailed but self-determination provided a sense of national pride and maturity.

Nat Campbell, aged 30 in 1903, would have been seen as a handsome, dashing young man who could handle a horse, was good at all sports and could put his hand to most things in the pastoral industry. Yet many would have thought of him as a rolling stone, not being able to settle down to any worthwhile course of action. It must have been a very nervous young man who approached the formidable Alexander Ryrie at Micalago station to ask for his daughter's hand in marriage. He was a respected member of the NSW Legislative Assembly and the 35,000-acre station had been in the Ryrie family for more than 50 years. Nat was 31 on 9 February 1904 when he married Evelyn Charlotte Ryrie, two years younger than himself.

'... and could handle a firearm': Evelyn at Micalago in 1903

Evelyn was a woman to be admired! She stood 'as straight as a ramrod', was dressed immaculately at all times, could handle a firearm and was a good horsewoman 'with a perfect seat in the saddle'. She was very close to her older brother Granville, who had returned from the Boer War, wounded in the shoulder and a local hero. A hard family pedigree to live up to.[80]

Nat and Evelyn made a very fine couple, but where were they to live and what was Nat to do? Two of Nat's interests came to the rescue: the Federal Sheep Shearing Company, established in Sydney in 1902, was expanding into South Australia and was in need of a manager. The company was very innovative, conducting training courses for mechanised shearing, wool classing and shed work, and also acted as agent for Moffatt-Virtue, which included providing portable plant for the smaller sheds.[81]

The South Australian Jockey Club was also seeking a starter for the Victoria Park, Cheltenham and Morphettville courses, following the retirement of Mr T.F. Wigley. Nat successfully applied for the position.[82] The Campbells moved to Adelaide in 1905 and the Federal Sheep Shearing Company set up its office in the Commercial Chambers in Currie Street with Nat as manager. Within a year it had 24 stations on the books as well as selling Moffatt-Virtue shearing equipment throughout the state.[83]

It was one of those rare times in Australian history, when 'all the stars lined up' for the sheep industry. The Federation drought had broken, the world economy was buoyant with a strong demand for wool, mechanised shearing was now commonplace and organised teams had come of age. Station owners were benefiting from the newly regulated system as no longer were there the tent towns of hopeful workers around the big well-located sheds or the lack of men in the more isolated areas. Teams were put together and moved from shed to shed in an orderly manner, stations could now plan ahead with confidence and good shearers were assured of regular work for the whole season.

The advent of contract teams caused a spate of shed building and, for the first time, on-site shearers' quarters. By today's standards, requirements were somewhat spartan: two men to a room, with wire mesh Cyclone beds; showers and tin washbasins army-style in an open row, one to six men; and a basic kitchen and mess hall. The cook and classer (usually the boss of the team) had their own separate rooms, the cook because of his early rising requirements and the classer so as to do the daily bookwork without interruption.

Many of these grand old sheds and quarters built in the early 1900s are still in operation 100 years on, the exception being the quarters in closer-settled areas with the advent of 'suburban' teams based in regional towns that travel to the sheds each day. The sheds were all equipped with overhead shearing stands, powered by large steam engines or slow-revving kerosene or diesel motors. They all had enormous double-box Ferrier or Hubble & Sons wool presses, requiring the fittest and strongest men to operate them. All teams had an 'expert' who sharpened the shearers' combs and cutters and coaxed the temperamental engines of the day into service.

There are legendary tales about the shearers' cook. If an army marched on its stomach, so it was with the shearing teams – good, plentiful food was the secret to a harmonious team. But spare a thought for the cook 100 years ago: no refrigeration; stores once a week; a freshly killed sheep every morning; and a big Metters 'No 6' stove roaring away in a galvanised iron kitchen in the middle of summer. No wonder many turned to drink, complaints being met with a perspiring, cleaver-wielding man yelling: 'You can eat it, or you'll wear it.' Smokos were taken down to the shed with big billies of hot black tea and plenty of sugar, accompanied by large fruit cakes or scones. Shearers would lay bets as to whether they would score one, two or three sultanas in their slab of cake or scone!

Teams were from 10 to 40 or more shearers, with at least the same number of support staff: roustabouts, skirters, classer, expert and cook. Teams would also be split and amalgamated during the season to accommodate different-size sheds. Stations now negotiated with a single contractor, just as the men negotiated for a stand in the team or other position in the shed. The Federal Sheep Shearing Company was an early exponent of the new contracting system and remained one of the biggest through to the Second World War. Nat Campbell had his hands full as the South Australian manager.

Nat and Evelyn lived in various suburbs during their early years in Adelaide, then in 1919 they bought 177 Barton Terrace, North Adelaide, overlooking the parklands, where they stayed for the rest of their days. Evelyn always retained a maid – 'to which she was accustomed' – and the dashing young couple from New South Wales were quite a hit in the conservative Adelaide of the early 1900s.

The starting of races was proving very demanding, with Nat also officiating for most of the northern race meetings and even Broken Hill for three years.[84] He would have visited his shearing teams on these country trips and was spending more and more time away from home.

Nat was struck by the rapid advances in sheep breeding as he moved around the large sheds in South Australia. The Murray and Koonoona studs were supplying a lot of rams throughout the state, but Bungaree rams were gaining a reputation as 'the best doers' in the station country. Bungaree was first settled in 1840 by three Hawker brothers, but George was credited with the stud's development. Breeding must have been in his blood as he and his wife Bessie had 16 children! By 1880, George had taken up 90,000 acres of freehold land at Clare, built a huge homestead, outbuildings and a church on the property and was employing 139 outside staff, with 23 domestics.[85] However, sheep breeding is his enduring legacy. Together with stud master John Noble, they developed a robust large-framed sheep with medium to strong heavy cutting wool. It's thought the frame and robust characteristics were achieved by careful use of Border Leicesters in the early days. George Hawker died in 1895, being 65 years of age. John Noble retired in 1901 and was widely recognised for his skill in developing the flock.[86]

In 1906 the property was split four ways to accommodate George's sons: East Bungaree to Edmond; Anama to Walter and Edward; North Bungaree to

Michael (who employed Ffloyd Chomley as manager for 34 years); and Bungaree to Richard.[87] The first three of these new entities continued as very influential studs and there were many heated discussions out on the stations as to which was doing the better job. Picture Nat with the station owners on the verandah, late at night, with whisky in hand:

'Those North Bungaree rams I've been using for the past 10 years have lifted my cut by a good pound and a half.'

'Well that's nothing – my East Bungarees have done every bit of that in five years – in only half the time.'

There was another regular item of conversation around the woolsheds and station verandahs: blowflies! The green primary fly (*Lucilia cuprina*) and the brown fly (*Calliphora* spp.) had been observed during the 1800s, but the situation changed rapidly at the time of the Federation Drought. The green fly seems to have gone through a genetic mutation, probably aided by the number of rotting sheep and rabbit carcasses in the drought.[88]

The blowfly problem spread from New South Wales, advancing steadily across the country. Graziers were being forced to spend a lot of time treating blown sheep and jackeroos' standard equipment in the saddle bag now included dagging shears to clip away the affected wool.[89] The verandah talk focused on remedies for treatment and prevention:

'I reckon you can't beat kerosene mixed with tar.'

'Well, you obviously haven't tried oil of rue.'

'You are both barking up the wrong tree – you should try creolin.'[90]

Many other bizarre potions were tried, but sheep losses and costly labour time steadily increased, resulting in the need for crutching,[91] especially in areas of improved pastures. Sheep grazing close to the ground were prone to intestinal worms, with consequent scouring and dirty wool at the sheep's rear end, which attracted the flies. Station sheep grazed saltbush and other plants higher off the ground, and with lower stocking rates, there was not such a problem. The need for crutching provided Nat and the Federal Sheep Shearing Company with extra work, though shearers often objected to the dirty job, so there was a lot of careful negotiation over rates of pay and trade-offs: 'You won't get a stand at shearing time, unless you do the mid-year crutching.'

And there were dogs! There was hardly a late-night session on the verandah that would not cover the subject. It's believed dingoes were introduced to Australia either with the early Aboriginal migration or by Indonesian fishermen.

They quickly developed a taste for sheep which caused their numbers to increase and were a constant problem, particularly to frontier development. There is no more a dreadful sight than to find sheep brutally mauled by dogs, often half alive and suffering awful pain. The Upper Lachlan of Nat's birth had overcome the problem but South Australia's developing pastoral stations had a very long exposed face to the dingo of central Australia. There was vigorous political debate about governments contributing to the cost of dog-proof fences and bounty payments on scalps to aid in their control. As wool was such a dominant export commodity, the station owners had a very strong lobbying position. Discussion always turned to trapping, shooting and poisoning – which were the most beneficial and who was the best at outwitting the crafty dog:

'Old Percy would be hard to beat – he thinks like a dog, has that same sixth sense.'

'What about Fred out west? He goes bush for weeks on end and always comes back with 10 or 12 scalps.'

Slowly and surely, the problem was overcome. Eventually, there were 5,280 miles of continuous dog-proof fencing stretching from central Queensland down through western New South Wales, then out to the Nullarbor in South Australia. (It's only in recent years, with declining sheep numbers and little government assistance, that dogs are once again becoming a serious problem for graziers throughout Australia.)

And, finally, drought. There were very few years that provided widespread good rains across South Australia, especially through the recently developed pastoral country. The Federation Drought had seen the demise of many perennial plants, including some of the saltbushes, as a result of overgrazing and pastoralists were now relying more heavily on annual plants:

'That fellow Goyder knew his stuff – extend beyond his line on the map and you're asking for trouble.' [92]

'What about those cockies trying their luck around Hawker and Burra? They kidded themselves that rain would follow the plough – all you can see now are abandoned stone cottages.'

Nat and Evelyn had four children with two years between each of them: (Kay) in 1905; Donald Henry Alexander (Don) on 31 July 1907; Nat (Bey) on 11 May 1909; and Pat Powell on 10 July 1911. With Nat away from home a lot, Evelyn and the maid provided a strict upbringing for the family, with appearances and good manners the order of the day. The children attended the local state school and the boys went on to St Peter's College for their final years, though money was becoming a problem.

The Great War broke out in 1914 and Nat was appointed Lieutenant as a recruitment officer, then promoted to Honorary Captain on 24 September 1917. Race meetings were abandoned during the war but it appears Nat had an ongoing connection with the sheep shearing company as sheep still had to be shorn. Men had gone to war with a sense of pride and confidence; they had signed up as one, squatter's son alongside blacksmith and shearer, all together for King and Country. Once in uniform, they were all 'cobbers', all in it together.[93] How sobering it was in 1918 when the terrible loss of life at Gallipoli and the Western Front in France were realised. It was the war to end all wars – the Great War, the First World War.

There was hardly a family spared and the fledgling nation took time to readjust and get back to normal. Nat had an ongoing role after the war, dealing with the wounded returned soldiers, finally retiring from military duties on 12 May 1920. He was back on civvy street, the race meetings were again on schedule and the sheep shearing company was back to normal, training a lot of returned soldiers in the art of shearing and shed work.

In 1920, HRH Edward the Prince of Wales made a tour of Australia to thank the nation for its war effort, having sailed out on *HMS Renown* under the command of Admiral Halsey, accompanied by Lord Louis Mountbatten and staff. While the Royal party was in Adelaide, the Tattersalls Club organised a special race meeting on 13 July at Morphettville, in the Prince's honour.

> Before the running of the Jutland Handicap, the Prince raced around the course on High Degree and was accompanied by the starter, Mr N Campbell, on Ferrignite. The Prince's horse was a slow old steeplechaser that won the event, causing the stewards to ring the bells in protest! However, there was a second race – this time the Prince on Ferrignite and Nat on Boomtree, which the Prince won fair and square.[94]

The Morphettville event received wide publicity and was the highlight of Nat's career as a starter, almost akin to his father's shooting of O'Meally. Nat continued as starter until 1924, when the barrier start was introduced. He was a strong advocate of the change as being fairer to horses, jockeys and punters, and believed its introduction a suitable time to retire.

It was about this time that he also retired from the management of the sheep shearing company. He continued to spend a lot of time trackside, drinking ever more heavily. It was one of those chicken and egg situations between husband and wife: did she become more autocratic and domineering because of his heavy drinking and absences from home, or did he turn to drink as an escape from her dominance? Perhaps the answer, as is often the case, was a little of both.

Adelaide was a boomtown in the 1920s, the third-biggest city in the nation. The transcontinental railway line was completed in 1917, when the 1,063-mile link between Kalgoorlie and Port Augusta was bridged. Adelaide benefited at the expense of Perth as most of the mining companies in the WA goldfields had their head offices there, and the wave of pastoral development in Western Australia was largely financed from South Australia. For example, the Hawkers of Bungaree developed Sturt Meadows station at Leonora and the Hawkes family of Koonoona, in partnership with R. McBride, did likewise next door on Tarmoola.

The large pastoral houses of Elder Smiths, Dalgetys and Goldsbrough Mort operated from Adelaide, with only small offices in Perth. The pastoral houses in the 1920s played a pivotal role in Australian agriculture at the time, being wool and stock brokers, merchandise providers, insurers and, beyond all else, bankers. To have a career with one of these firms was considered very favourably in the social pecking order of the day. The loyalty of the firm to the client and client to the firm was deeply embedded. The pastoral houses were sending large numbers of rams from the Bungaree, Koonoona and Murray studs by train to the west.

Many parents from WA pastoral properties, even some from Perth, utilised the train service to educate their children in the better established Adelaide boarding schools. The wealthy South Australian station owners all had town houses in suburbs such as Unley Park, Gilberton and North Adelaide, providing a strong base for the university, the arts, theatre and culture of the city. It should be remembered, the established pastoral families of the day were fabulously wealthy, as compared to professional and business people in the cities. The wealth was matched by social status – to produce wool, earn valuable export income and extend the frontiers of agriculture was highly admired, almost to the point of adulation by many. To be in business or the professions was seen as 'shuffling paper at others' expense'! While some of the wool producers succumbed to drink, gambling and extravagant lifestyles, most were philanthropic or used their wealth to further expand their properties. The term 'squattocracy' was not too far short of the mark.

The contrast between Adelaide's increasing wealth in the 1920s and the Campbells' declining circumstances became ever more apparent. Of equal contrast was Nat's career and that of Evelyn's favourite brother, now Major General, the Honourable Sir Granville de Laun Ryrie, KCMG, CB, VD, JP, Assistant Minister for Defence.

Retirement from the sheep shearing company and starting the races was not going well for Nat and the family. They even considered returning to New South Wales, with the house in Barton Terrace listed for sale in 1925 but later withdrawn. Life at home for the children was becoming more stressful. Kay had travelled overseas to London in 1927 with her friend Betty Morgan but returned home being unwell and 'tripping over a lot'. The local GP was of no help and she steadily deteriorated to become wheelchair-bound and in constant pain; there was never a clear diagnosis but a cyst on the spine was a possible cause. Her health and ever increasing need of assistance put added pressure on the family.

Nat's generation endured two periods of global depression. The earlier 1890s depression occurred when Australia was more rural-based and subsistence from the land played a greater role. By the 1930s the nation was more urbanised and basic social security measures were in place but, for all that, families really suffered and austerity became the norm. Clothes were recycled between children, shirt collars turned, sheets cut down the middle and rejoined by the sides, food was carefully used and waste eliminated, with bread and dripping not uncommon for a meal. Little more is known of Nat through the depression years of the 1930s, though silverware and valuables were being sold off to augment the family's finances. Evelyn put on a brave face to the world at the loss of her possessions, but was resolute in not parting from either her cherished French porcelain clock on the mantelpiece, or the maid![95] The boys were intensely loyal to their mother and put up with the tightening financial circumstances as best they could. Sport was the great outlet, all being very good at cricket, tennis and football. They sent money home to help their mother and sister once they left school but, with depression wage levels, this was of limited assistance.

Nat again joined the services during the Second World War as a recruitment officer. The war years were particularly hard for Nat and Evelyn, as Pat had joined up at the outset and was stationed in Singapore when it fell to the Japanese. He was taken prisoner and put to work on the infamous Burma Railway. The family had no idea if he was alive or dead for most of that time. Kay was now completely paralysed from the waist down and required constant care and assistance. Bey

Pat Campbell, after 'signing up' in 1941

with his wooden leg and Don managing an isolated sheep station in Western Australia were keeping the home front manned.

The rationing and difficulties at home were accepted as 'your contribution to help the boys overseas'. Nonetheless, life would have been very difficult, especially concerning Pat: Where was he? Was he alive? What might have happened? Picture the utter joy and relief when a telegram arrived in August 1945, addressed to Mrs N. Campbell, 177 Barton Terrace: 'Advice has been received that SX10981 Pte PP Campbell, previously reported prisoner of war, is now reported alive in Siam – August 1945 – Minister for the Army.'

Over the following months letters were exchanged, there was hope Pat would be home for Christmas, and the dreadful war years, at least for this family, were coming to a happy end. The family's joy at Pat's safe return was short-lived, however, as the realities of his years of deprivation became ever more apparent. He was formally discharged from the army on 17 January 1946, exactly five years from joining up. His discharge medical certificate makes sober reading:

> Mr Pat P. Campbell: GSW left forearm; Malaria; Avitaminosis; Dermatitis; Tropical ulcers; Sinusitis; Megacolon; Presbyopia; Pneumonia; Osteoarthritis; Neurasthenia caused by alcoholism and peripheral neuritis; Inability to earn a living because of lack of strength and muscular control of legs, greatly reducing locomotion; Reduced power of arms and hands, especially as regards fine movements such as writing.[96]

There was no knowledge or talk of post-traumatic stress disorder in those days; if you were fit enough to walk out of hospital, you were fit enough to get on with life. As a society we are only just starting to understand the 'down the track fallout' of horrific experiences, and the Vietnam veterans have helped us realise the ramifications of military service.

Better fortune was in store for Pat. Delia Rosemarie Woodley (always known as Rie), had been holidaying with her sister Babs at Alice Springs and was introduced to Pat by a mutual friend, Pat Davis. They married in October 1947 and he accepted the overseer's position at Lake Violet, being managed by his brother Don, as a means of recuperation and getting back into station life.

Following the war and Pat's safe return home, Nat moved from Adelaide to work as yardman-gardener on stations in Western Australia. These positions were often given to older men on a 'board and keep' basis, with only light duties expected in return for a low wage and accommodation. It would be easy to say Nat was neglecting his responsibilities, leaving a wife and a disabled daughter to fend for themselves, but perhaps he realised he was not meeting the expectations required of him, both at home and in the post-war Adelaide community. He had done his bit during the war as a recruitment officer and what else did he have to offer? Nat finally died on Wyloo station in WA's North West, managed by Don and Helen Sears, who referred to him as, 'A charming man who always presented well, kept to himself, but did drink a little too heavily.'[97] His headstone, provided by sons Don and Bey, simply reads: 'Nat Campbell – died 26th July, 1952 – in loving memory'. A brief note in the *Adelaide Advertiser* read:

Nat Campbell passes: I am indebted to Noel Beavan of Giralia station, Winning Pool, Carnarvon, WA for letting us know that our old friend Nat Campbell passed on recently at Wyloo station on the Ashburton River. We remember him well here as the starter for the SAJC, ARC and Tattersalls. Nat was on North West stations for some time. He was with me here for 18 months, and was still, verging on 80, a good horseman with a perfect seat in the saddle. Yes, we can hear the jockeys at the barrier saying: 'Let her go Mr Campbell'. And we must not forget what a courteous, helpful officer he was in World War I when wounded were returning.

So ended the life of a man who was given 'a tough paddock in which to feed', did his best, but succumbed to the frailties of man. Evelyn continued to live at 177 Barton Terrace until near her death, on 19 October 1961. Her daughter-in-law Patsy was particularly helpful, while Don and Bey continued to lend financial support. Her three daughters-in-law were always in awe of her and thought her rather formidable, though her sons were very loyal and held her in their deepest respect and affection. She was a woman shaped by the hand dealt to her but she, in turn, helped shape the generations that followed by the example she set. In particular, Don and Bey benefited from her steady and firm influence as they grew from boys to men in a difficult family situation. Kay, and later Pat, were cared for in a home environment that would have otherwise not been available. Another remarkable woman in the Campbell story.

The Campbell family was more fortunate than many, in Pat's safe return home, but his attempt at life back in the pastoral industry was to prove a step too far. It took many years for the family – and the nation – to understand the extent of brutality and deprivation suffered by the POWs on the Burma line. It was slowly brought to everyone's realisation through books and films, including: *Behind Bamboo – Hell on the Burma Railway* by Rohan Rivett, first published in 1946 by Angus and Robertson; *Bridge Over the River Kwai; Weary Dunlop's Diaries; The Railway Man* by Eric Lomax; and more recently, *Narrow Road to the Deep North* by Richard Flanagan.

Historian Eric Wilson, at a public lecture in Perth in 2015, said:

The less well-known aspect of the Burma line is the incredible engineering feat of construction with 205 miles of railway carved out through dense jungle and difficult terrain, including Hell Fire Pass and the bridge over River Kwai – in just 12 months. Today's railway engineers still classify the Burma Line as: 'a wonder of engineering at the global level'. Some 60,000 allied prisoners were forced to work on the project, of which there was a 12 per cent casualty rate for the Australians and 18 per cent for the British – a difference probably explained by the Australians being mainly from the land and physically tougher than the British. There were also 200,000 local indentured labourers who suffered a far higher death rate.[98]

Pat never mentioned his time as a prisoner and wouldn't be drawn on the subject at all. The only brief comment he is known to have made was in response to Rivett's book, when he was asked if he knew of the author: 'Yes, he camped alongside me on the bamboo slats at one stage.' Meanwhile, Pat was doing his best at getting back into station life. After spending 18 months at Lake Violet with Don and Thelma, Pat and Rie returned to South Australia, taking management positions on isolated stations, including: Illawarra at Kapunda; Newlands at Apsley (just over the border in Victoria); Millers Creek at Farina, north of Kingoonya; and Witchelina at Maree, just south of Lake Eyre.

He was not coping well at all. Sympathetic contacts were willing 'to give a returned POW a fair go', but there were shorter times in employment and lengthening intervals at 177 Barton Terrace. His final job was back at Koonamore, north of Yunta, and he was in real trouble, drinking ever more heavily and withdrawing into himself. He wasn't keeping up with the job and when the owner, Alex McLachlan, came by, he told Pat to take the first mail truck off the place and, 'Mrs Campbell, this is none of your doing – take as long as you like to pack up and I wish you well.'

It was a most humiliating experience for both Pat and Rie. Pat must have realised he had reached rock bottom and could never seek employment again in the pastoral country. He must have also felt a failure to Rie and their two children, David and Penny, and knew of only one escape: the bottle. Rie, on the other hand, had two young children to care for. To her absolute credit she was able to move the family back to Adelaide and, with the help of her father, Walter Woodley, slowly rebuild their lives.

Pat became a semi-recluse, went AWL[99] for a while, then moved back to Barton Terrace with his ageing mother. After Evelyn's death, the old run-down house was sold and became a boarding house, with Pat staying on in a little room at the rear – probably the former maid's bedroom. Bey and Patsy came to the rescue and helped Pat as much as they could, but the deprivation of the Burma Railway was too much to bear and took its final toll on 15 September 1968.[100]

Pat's story is typical of so many. There's hardly a rural town or leafy suburb in Australia that has been spared a similar example of someone going off to war 'for King and Country', only to return broken in mind and body, and resorting to the lonely comfort of alcohol.

6 THE RYRIES OF MICALAGO AND THE MONARO

In 'breeding terms', it was the Ryries who provided a true Scottish connection to this branch of the family, although it was the 'feeding' that was much more important to the Campbells.

The Ryries were a fiercely independent clan, with the family crest depicting a clenched fist holding a cross or sword and the motto *Per Mare Per Terras* (by sea and by land). They put the motto to good effect as they came over the sea to Australia and quickly established considerable land holdings!

It was in the 1820s drought years, when squatters ventured further south from the already settled areas in search of feed for their stock, that they discovered some open plain country in the shadow of the Tinderry Hills on the upper reaches of the Murrumbidgee River, which they called the 'Mikelago Plains' – no one knows the origin of the name. The vast high plains to the east of Canberra and around Cooma are now referred to as the Monaro.

Count Rosi squatted on 35,000 acres that he named Micalago and in 1835 built a solid little cottage of box slabs, lath and plaster and with door frames only 5 feet 9 inches high. He must have been big in courage and adventure, but small of frame! Meanwhile, Stewart Ryrie squatted on Jindaboine station (now under the waters of Lake Jindabyne) and his two sons, William and James, took up land at Braidwood in the late 1820s.

It was in 1836 that William, Donald and James, together with four convict stockmen, made the epic overland journey to the Port Phillip district with 250 head of cattle and some vine cuttings. The route they pioneered is similar to that of the present Hume Highway. They squatted on 43,000 acres in the Yarra Valley which they called Yering and established a cattle herd and the first vineyard for the region, now known as Chateau Yering.

While 'down south', they played a key role in the early development of Melbourne. They helped establish the first Presbyterian Church and were foundation members of the Pastoral and Agricultural Society and of the Melbourne Club. In 1857, William bought a block of land on the corner of Queen Street and Flinders Lane for £30.

They stayed down south for only 14 years, before returning to the high country of New South Wales, having sold Yering to Paul de Castella in 1850. Even though their main pastoral holdings were now back in NSW, the Ryries nonetheless maintained ongoing connections to the rapidly expanding city of Melbourne. On their return, Micalago was bought from Count Rosi for the younger brother Alexander, who continued to develop the property. Alexander married Charlotte Faunce, the daughter of Queanbeyan Magistrate, Captain Faunce, and they had nine children: Casells (b. 1861), Edith (b. 1862), Tasker (b. 1864), Granville (b. 1865), Alison (b. 1867), William (b. 1869), Vincent (b. 1871), Stanley (b. 1873) and Evelyn Charlotte (b. 1875). Evelyn was particularly close to Granville and 'followed him around like a shadow' when he was home from boarding school. She went on to marry Nat Campbell.

Alexander and Charlotte extended the homestead complex with solid stone construction and cedar brought in from the coast and compensated for Rosi's low doors by making theirs 8 feet high. Together with bedroom wings, the complex formed a quadrangle. From the outset, an extensive garden was laid out with European trees and what has become a magnificent Chinese Cypress. A level lawned area flows from the extensive verandahs and a long pergola covered in vines leads out to the trees beyond. Micalago was a profitable big station that allowed Alexander to pursue a political career, firstly in the Legislative Assembly, then the Legislative Council through to his death in 1909.

Alexander was a devout Christian and 'conducted services in his own house for many years, before St Thomas's Church was built in the nearby village of Michelago – largely thanks to the efforts of the Ryrie Family'. It is also reported that he liberated 250 young trout into the Murrumbidgee River at Micalago in 1892.[101]

As mentioned, Evelyn was particularly close to her older brother Granville and was influenced by his personality and achievements. He is by far the best known of the Ryries and deserves further mention. As a young man he enjoyed all sports, particularly boxing, and was a natural horseman. He was not a great scholar and, at best, tolerated boarding school. He had piercing grey eyes and sandy-coloured hair, growing into a man of large frame and heavy build, always sporting a moustache. A man of many talents, he had a fine tenor voice, played the piano, banjo and cornet, and could keep an audience enthralled by whistling a wide repertoire of tunes, using an index finger to his mouth. He was also a talented boxer, being twice in the finals for the amateur heavyweight championship of Australia, only losing on points. A favourite pastime was to go to the shearing shed with two pairs of gloves and 'issue a challenge to one and all'.

He joined the local military force, became Captain of the Imperial Bushmen in 1899 and volunteered for the Boer War with his two horses, Sago and Tracker, where he served with courage and great leadership. He was invalided home with a wounded shoulder and later promoted to Lieutenant Colonel of the Third Light Horse Regiment.

He followed in his father's footsteps in standing for Parliament, though he lost the first time he stood. He tried again and in 1906 attended a noisy rally at the rough mining centre of Captains Flat, a known Labor stronghold, and must have made the shortest political address in Australia's history: 'I am the best man at Captains Flat and if I can prove it, will you vote for me?'

There was a loud roar of 'Aye', to which he replied: 'Alright, choose your best scrapper and I will fight him 20 rounds.'

Granville knocked the burly miner out in the 12th round and went on to win the seat of Queanbeyan in the NSW Legislative Assembly. In 1911 he successfully stood for the federal seat of Werrina and in his maiden speech concentrated on defence and support of the nation's military forces. He later moved to the federal seat of North Sydney.

Granville is best known for his efforts in the Great War. In 1914 he was 49 years old, weighed in at 16 stone and was promoted to Brigadier General in Command of the Second Light Horse. His electorate of North Sydney presented him with a large dark thoroughbred stallion, called Plain Bill, and together they made an imposing sight on the parade ground. His wartime exploits are well covered elsewhere, but suffice to say he served with distinction in Gallipoli, played a major role in the cavalry charge of Beersheba, and had absolute loyalty and respect from his men, 'as one who led from the front and fiercely stood up for their rights'. Granville was one of the first Australian-born senior officers to chart a new course of military leadership for the nation's armed forces. He was often at odds with General Chauvel but in the end it was Chauvel who recommended his promotion to Major General. He was also knighted while serving in the deserts of Palestine.

Granville and Plain Bill in Palestine

Following the war, he resumed his parliamentary career as Assistant Minister for Defence and retained the rank of Major General, as commander of the First Cavalry Division. Micalago was always the home base and a place for Granville to keep his feet on the ground. One of his many visitors to the station was the official war artist George Lambert, who painted scenes of his family and countryside, the best known being *The Squatter's Daughter*.

In April 1927, Prime Minister Stanley Bruce announced Granville to be the next (and first Australian-born) High Commissioner to London. In that role, he represented Australia in setting up the League of Nations in Geneva. His term was a little controversial, however, as he criticised British cars as being too underpowered and not as suited to Australian conditions as American cars! He retired to Australia in 1933 and spent his last four years at Micalago in declining health. For all his political and military success, Granville was a devoted husband to Mary (or Mick as he called her) and father to twin girls, Gwendoline and Marjorie, born in 1897 and a son, James, born in 1911.[102]

James went on to be the first hands-on manager of Micalago, as both Alexander and Granville always employed people to run the station. James' second-born son, also James, is now filling the role. It was James senior and wife Dibby who were credited with restoring the homestead to its former glory and

6 The Ryries of Micalago and the Monaro

renovating the garden to become a showcase in the region. Edna Walling, the renowned landscape gardener, visited Micalago and said: 'The garden is quite perfect. I can see no reason to change anything.'

The film *My Brilliant Career* used the homestead as its main setting, causing Dibby to lament:

'It took me 40 years to remove the Victorian influence in the house and now they have reinstated it all.'

On two separate visits to Micalago, I found the old homestead complex nestled into the Tinderry Hills behind, surrounded by mature European trees and the well laid out garden, including the colonnade and long trellis that was of inspiration to Edna Walling. The old Count Rosi cottage with the low door frames forms part of the quadrangle, with the elegant high ceiling additions behind.

If only walls could talk! Evelyn, the youngest of eight children, holding her own in spirited family discussions; the large, imposing frame of Granville as he sang at the piano in his strong tenor voice, or entertaining politicians and the artist George Lambert; the film set of *My Brilliant Career*, as earlier times were rekindled; the two James Ryries, grappling with the realities of Australia's unpredictable seasons and equally unpredictable commodity prices.

All of them Ryries – all of them contributing to Australia as we know it today.

Micalago front garden, 1920s. Note already mature garden

7 DON – CRICKET, KOONOONA AND MILLSTREAM

Returning to the proposition 'its 20 per cent breeding and 80 per cent feeding', you might think Don could have gone one of two ways: the reckless way of his father or the sound path of his mother. It was because of Evelyn's steadfast example and firm, consistent discipline that Don and his brothers and sister chose the 'high road' for their lives. She taught them the art of 'selective grazing': choosing the right role models, friends and activities that would hold them in good stead as they matured into fine young adults.

Don was born on 31 July 1907, while the family was living at Le Fevre Terrace, North Adelaide, and was christened at the local Church of England with his uncle Alfred (Snowy) Campbell as Godfather. His mother had been brought up in a strict Christian tradition though his father was of only nominal faith. The family changed address every three or four years, also living at Glenelg and Walkerville, before returning to North Adelaide when he was 12 years old. The frequent moving caused Don to rely on his older sister and two brothers for company as other friendships came and went with the moving. The final move to 177 Barton Terrace suited the boys very well for it fronted Adelaide's famous parklands, as laid out by Colonel William Light. Cricket and football could now be played with plenty of space around them.

The house in Barton Terrace was typical of the middle-class Victorian houses of the day. There was a long passage running the length of the house, with a formal drawing room and master bedroom at the front, a morning room and dining room on one side of the passage and three more bedrooms on the other. Beyond an archway was a servery room and kitchen on one side, with two servants' rooms and a bathroom on the other. There were full-width verandahs front and back, with a laundry built into the one at the rear. The house was of Adelaide stone and shielded from the street by a high hedge, with some outbuildings in the backyard – originally a stable and coach house – though not used as a garage by the Campbells for they never owned a car. Furnishings were of the heavy Victorian type and Evelyn kept the house well darkened in summer to combat the Adelaide heat.

Don was sent off to St Peter's College, which opened up a whole new world for a budding cricketer and somebody seeking direction and stability in his life. Many of us only endure our time at school but Don relished Saints, making lifelong friends and he spoke often of his fond memories. One of those friends was Ron Halcombe, who at the time of Don's death, recalled their school days:

> It was about 1918 when Don and I came together. We lived in Barton Terrace East, North Adelaide and Don in Barton Terrace West. He used to ride one of the most shocking bikes ever seen at our illustrious college. He used to take a short cut through Christchurch North Adelaide at the top of Pennington Terrace and he used to tell me how Canon Jose objected to Don and others doing so. From there he would fly down the hill past the zoo and through the parklands to school. The bike – as I remember – had a frame and nothing else; no brakes; no bell; no nothing and he had a few mates no better fitted out. I remember Don's home life was not at all happy, and because of this, his development of a high moral standard was all the more remarkable.[103]

Home life was a formal affair. Meals were served in the dining room with a properly laid table, using the dinner sets and silver cutlery of the wedding presents. Manners were strictly adhered to:

'Place the salt on the side of your plate.'
'Don't start until your hostess/mother does.'
'Offer the condiments to others, or ask by saying, "may I have … ?"'
'Take small mouthfuls.'
'Keep your fork upright.'
'Place your knife and fork together when finished.'

'Always thank your hostess/mother for the meal.'

Equally, cleanliness and proper dressing were carefully enforced: shoes cleaned, hair combed, socks pulled up, shirt properly tucked in and so on. Outings were few and far between, with the occasional trip to town: Evelyn wearing hat and gloves, the children properly dressed and formal greetings to those they knew – always Mr, Mrs or Sir from the children. Less frequent, but much more enjoyable, was taking the tram to Glenelg for swimming at the baths. Imagine Evelyn sitting bolt upright, looking straight ahead as they passed the Morphettville racecourse, ensuring the family always offered their seats to elders and were never noisy or disruptive.

A favourite outing with his cricketing mates: Keith Henderson, 'Slinger' Nitschke, C. Sangster, R. Barwell, D. Downey, E. Findlayson and of course Ron Halcombe, was to the Adelaide Oval, an easy bike ride from Barton Terrace. They would sit on the hill and be captivated by the skill of the interstate and test teams, and Don dreamt of the day that he might pad up for South Australia. It was cricket, above all else, that enthralled the developing young man. Not only a game of skill, it was also a model for how to live life – 'that's not cricket' being a powerful rebuke in those days. Don frequently used cricket terminology throughout his life:

'Well, I'll be stumped.'

'Put your best foot forward.'

'He had a good innings.'

'Keep your eye on the ball.'

'Let's call it stumps.'

'Play it with a straight bat.'

In his final year at school, Don was invited to train with the North Adelaide Colts as a promising all-rounder. The absolute highlight of the year was bowling out Jack Hobbs in the nets.[104] The *Adelaide Advertiser* reported:

> For a 17-year-old schoolboy to be able to say that he clean-bowled JB Hobbs, the world-known English champion batsman, is unique. The feat was performed by Don Campbell when the English team was touring Australia and practising in the nets at St Peters College. Campbell was one of the college bowlers privileged to practise with the Internationals.

Don at the Adelaide Oval, 1924

To young Don, it must have been akin to his father riding with the Prince of Wales at Morphettville racecourse or his grandfather's shooting a bushranger! Don achieved his cricket blues (being in the first 11) in his last two years at school and was a prefect for his last year at Saints. There are a number of articles and photos published in the *Adelaide Advertiser* of Don playing for the Colts, which included:

> Halcombe then had 2 for 1 – Campbell bowled at the other end and with his 6th ball accounted for Sangster – the total was then 3 for 5. Campbell is a promising all-rounder, showing improvement with the Colts. He sends down a fast medium length ball, flighting it occasionally. As a batsman he is a right hander with a free, easy style and able to score runs quickly. He takes his place in the field as a slips-man, and like his club mates, is brilliant and reliable. Campbell

is on the threshold of his cricket career and should develop into an all-rounder of a high standard.

Don was obviously pouring his heart and soul into school and cricket as a means of hiding from difficulties at home. His father was drinking ever more heavily and spending increasing time away from home, both as official starter at the racecourses and managing the Federal Sheep Shearing Company. Money was always in short supply, with difficult saving measures imposed regarding food, clothing and maintenance to the house – everything other than doing away with the maid! Arguments between his parents became ever more frequent.

Don was more a sportsman than a scholar. There is no record of academic achievement, though he was known as being 'able to lose himself in a book' – perhaps more a comment on his home life than his studies? Highlights of Don's years at school were holidays back to the family in New South Wales: the Ryries at Micalago; his favourite cousin Beth and Aunty Bunt at Turalla near Bungendore; and the Gordons at Manar, out towards Braidwood. It would have been a lengthy train journey, but obviously worth the effort for the number of times he recalled those holidays. Don would have joined in with station life: riding horses, mustering stock, shooting and socialising - particularly with tennis and cricket. Those holidays were important in sowing the seeds of a future life in the station country of South Australia and Western Australia, while balancing his home life with sound role models that he could call on as he matured into a man.[105]

Following his five years at Saints, Don joined Dalgetys' head office in Adelaide, staying on at Barton Terrace and paying generous board to his mother, establishing a practice that continued for the remainder of her life. This was obviously aimed at furthering his cricket career, but he tired of 'being a pen pusher in coat and tie' and after two years heeded the call of the bush. A brief mention in the *Adelaide Advertiser* summed up his cricketing career:

> Don Campbell, it is reported, will not be available for Colts again this season. He is going to a station at Burra. His position in the team will be hard to fill, for Campbell is one of the best bowlers in the team.

The system of jackeroo training of young men was now well established, being a form of apprenticeship with the youngsters receiving modest pay, full board and keep. The larger properties employed separate cooks to care for them, while on the smaller places a single cook would serve both the homestead and the jackeroos. The young men were not only schooled in station work, but also in presentation and manners: elders were always Mr, Mrs or Sir; dinner dress was coat and tie; and you were always expected to keep your quarters and personal clothing neat and tidy. Owners of stations always sent their sons off to jackeroo elsewhere, while other young men aspiring to management positions started on that path as a means of achieving their goal – and it was always men, the advent of jilleroos being well into the future.

While working for Dalgetys, Don's attention would have been captured by three stud names: Bungaree, Murray and Koonoona. As with the other pastoral houses, Dalgetys would have acted as brokers and provided financing for the purchase of rams for many of their clients. And so it was that Don was accepted as a jackeroo on Koonoona in 1927 and stayed there for two years, the station being 10 miles south of Burra, with 32,000 acres of freehold and 5,000 of leasehold land in marginal cropping country. Burra was a well-established town, based on copper mining and ideal country for wool growing. By the 1920s, Koonoona had become a closed stud under the careful supervision of studmaster and part owner W.G. Hawkes – his first name was Waldemar but he was always known as 'W.G.' or Mr Hawkes. He, along with John Noble of Bungaree and John Murray of the Murray stud, were considered the three outstanding studmasters of the SA wool industry.[106]

The wool type at Koonoona was described as, 'strong and well nourished with long staple length, particularly well suited to harsh pastoral conditions'. In the 1920s, Koonoona was joining 10,000 stud ewes and selling more than 2,000 rams, both locally and as far away as WA, NSW and Queensland. Ardmore station, 80 miles south of Mt Isa, had a standing order of 300 rams for 50 consecutive years. Ardmore was plagued by dingoes, with associated high stock losses, so asked for the cheapest expendable flock rams: 'the horns and balls type!'[107]

Koonoona was still very reliant on horses for most of the station work: all the stock work was carried out on horseback; the limited amount of farming for hay and oats still relied on horses; and dams were silt-scooped by horse teams. Mr Hawkes drove an American car and the station had a one-ton 'Chev Four' truck, which Don admired greatly. Who got to drive the truck was based on seniority and it took some time before he ever had the chance to take control.

Station work was very much focused on sheep, especially the stud flock. Don spent many hours on horseback, watching over the lambing ewes, mustering

Horse teams at Koonoona, late 1920s

and, above all else, checking for fly strike. Standard equipment in the saddle-bag were the dagging shears and treatment for brushing over the affected areas, a common lament being: 'Flies are the curse of the devil on decent wool growers'.

Don became very aware of the devastating impact of rabbits. Teams of men were employed in trapping, various forms of poison were regularly used (which had serious repercussions on native birds and animals) and rabbit-proof fences were built and maintained at huge cost. Remaining patches of bush were cleared and burnt to allow for ripping of burrows. Rabbits were severely impacting both agricultural profitability and the environment, with little prospect of any means of control ever being available. There were stories of Western Australia building three rabbit-proof fences in a futile bid to halt the advancing plagues from the east: the No 1 fence measuring 1,100 miles in 1901; the No 2 fence of 700 miles in 1905; and the No 3 fence of 180 miles in 1907.[108]

'You have to give the Sand Gropers full marks for trying, but there has never been a fence yet that will stop them. At best, you slow them down for a while.'

Koonoona also owned Winnininnie, a station well out towards Broken Hill in 8-inch rainfall country which was used for breeding replacement ewes, running 6,000 head at the time: 'providing a means of natural selection for robust good doers'. They either thrived or perished out there![109] Don went out on several occasions to assist in moving sheep between the two properties and must have been attracted to the more isolated lifestyle of the low rainfall pastoral country. The time spent at Koonoona was greatly appreciated by Don and while he admired the sheep-breeding attributes of the respected stud, it was more the life skills and personal interactions that were to hold him in good stead. W.G. Hawkes was a powerful role model and gained the loyalty of his clients and staff with his honesty, openness and respect for another man's point of view. Don also learnt the skills of working with men from all walks of life, realising 'that given the chance, everybody had something to offer'.

It's not clear why Don left South Australia for outback Western Australia, or why Millstream was the chosen station. In 1929 it was owned by the Cookson brothers and being managed by Leslie Gordon, and perhaps they had been using Koonoona rams or been Dalgety clients, providing an introduction for Don?

Millstream is 90 miles south of Roebourne, 150 miles east of Onslow on the Fortescue River, and it's an interesting geological feature that gave rise to the name. The river is usually dry but a flow estimated at 125 million gallons per day emerges from the riverbed and forms a pool 10 miles long, 200 yards wide and 60 feet deep, before disappearing back into the dry landscape. The pool known as Deep Reach, or Long Reach, is 2 miles from the homestead and a similar feature, though on a smaller scale, provided water for the house and garden.[110] Don later wrote of the local legend, describing the phenomena:

> The old blacks told me that Deep Reach at one time was an extensive dry clay-pan, where they held corroborees. The stamping in rhythm apparently released the underground water supply, and that was the start of the present water flow.

It was quite a journey from Adelaide, changing trains three times to get to Perth, then on the coastal ship *Centaur* to Cossack and being taken ashore by lighter, only to cool his heels for a few days before being taken to the station. Don travelled light with his swag and suitcase, his trusted pipe for company and dreams of a new life to spur him on. He effectively said goodbye to family and his cricketing mates for the distance meant only very infrequent trips back to South Australia. There were only two items to comfort him among his belongings: a new Kodak Brownie box camera and the *Collected Verses of AB Paterson*, given to him by his sister.

Don was immediately struck by the difference of his new surroundings compared to the more established life around Burra, as the stations on the Fortescue had only been established from the 1890s onwards, providing a sense of frontier development. There were no trains and only tracks passing as roads, and all transport south was by the WA Coastal Shipping Service. Stocking rates were lower, meaning bigger properties spread much further apart. Dingoes were a constant problem on Millstream and men were employed to trap and shoot them, whereas they had been eradicated around Burra for many years. At least there were no rabbits or blowflies pestering the sheep!

Social life was minimal and very reliant on individual station communities. For the first time in his life, Don was in close contact with the local blacks, who in turn were adjusting to the intrusion of the pastoral industry. (Koonoona had relied on a largely white workforce.) A police station on Millstream dealt mainly with 'Native issues' and was also used to house the Tableland Road Board office. The stations relied on the fortnightly mail service, which Don used to maintain written contact with his mother and sister (with regular cheques being sent home) and spasmodically with Ron Halcombe and a few other school friends.

Cattle camp, Millstream, late 1920s

It wasn't long before Don was made aware of another very big difference – the stock-camp and out-camp. Because of the long distances, mustering was conducted over many months, with the team changing camp as the sheep were brought in closer to the shearing shed and then taken back to their distant paddocks. These camps were rough affairs, with some permanent shacks, such as Cattle Camp, Middle Creek and James Creek, while others were under canvas.

For the first year at Millstream, Don was the 'offsider' to the camp boss, but in later years he was in charge of the team. Life in the camp was tough: there was no communication of any type (e.g. telephones or wireless); provisions of hard rations were brought out once a week; and Barcoo Rot was prevalent.[111] Don also learnt the bushman's trick of making chutney by mixing Worcestershire sauce with plum jam, and a salve for festering sores and drawing splinters by mixing sugar and soap shavings together into a paste.

The team had two or three whites, but mainly blacks. Don found 'understanding the blacks' somewhat of a challenge, as he confided in a letter to Ron Halcombe.[112] On the one hand he was sympathetic 'to the poor devils losing their free and easy way of life', but then 'you can never tell what they are thinking, or if they will go walkabout and leave you in the lurch'.

It was in his first year at the mustering camp that Don had a serious accident, being dragged by a stirrup iron after his horse shied and threw him. Fortunately, the camp boss saw the incident and brought the horse to a standstill, but not before Don suffered concussion and bleeding from the ears. (He was to suffer severe headaches for the rest of his life, which he attributed to that accident.) As a result he was invalided home to Adelaide, arriving just in time for Christmas, with Leslie Gordon saying: 'Well, he was a promising young bloke, but that's the last we'll see of him.'

Don was made of tougher stuff, and was back on the job early in 1930. The out-camp, known as Cattle Camp, was manned throughout the year. In the days of horses, long distances to check waters necessitated the use of these out-camps. Windmills could break down but more often a sheep or roo would knock a ball valve out of position, or get trapped and die in the trough. Water was the key element determining pastoral success and perishing would quickly occur in summer if proper management was neglected. Water quality was also very important, with the salt content determining wool cut and lambing percentages. Lambing ewes were always given priority for the best available water.

Don and Bill, Millstream, 1930

Long days were spent riding from mill to mill and checking fences along the way, while evenings were spent in solitude and 'gave a man plenty of time to think'. Some men found it too difficult, others would 'go troppo' or become quite eccentric, while people like Don found ways of coping. It was Banjo's poems and other reading that 'kept him on an even keel'. The single men were rotated through the out-camp, unless somebody turned up showing a preference for that lifestyle, often those evading the law or domestic issues!

Millstream was running around 25,000 sheep, breeding horses for local use and sale to other stations, and had only a small milking herd of cattle, even though the main out-camp was called Cattle Camp. The first shearing at Millstream was of interest to Don, as he was used to hearing his father describing the difficulties of providing teams to the outback of South Australia, but they paled as compared to the North West of Western Australia.

Synnot and Dunbar turned up in two Chev Four one-ton trucks, with benches bolted to the tray and loaded to the hilt with men and swags. Two roustabouts sat on the front mudguards, partly because of the crowded vehicle, but also to open and shut the many gates they passed through. The team and trucks were taken to Derby by the Coastal Shipping Service, then they would work their way south over an eight or nine-month period.

The two Chev 4 trucks of the Synnot and Dunbar shearing team, late 1920s (courtesy Mark Synnot jr)

One of the trucks with half of the team (courtesy Mark Synnot jr)

Will Synnot was the wool classer and boss of the board, while Arthur Dunbar was the expert, responsible for the mechanics of the shed, sharpening the shearers' combs and cutters, and most important of all, keeping the old Chevs in running order. Don was told many stories of how the team pushed and pulled the old trucks through flooded or sandy river crossings, how uncomfortable it was on the truck in the heat and dust, how basic many of the sheds and quarters were …

One of Arthur Dunbar's favourite yarns was the certainty some shearers had about the end stand running slower than the others (impossible when they were all driven by a single overhead shaft).[113] There's a story of how Will got his name as he was christened Frederick Synnot. Apparently there was a noisy shearer on an earlier team called Fred and it was confusing, and risky at times, to also have the boss called by the same name, so at smoko one day somebody asked: 'Can we call the boss by some other name – what will we call him?'

To which a quick reply came: 'that's it, we *will* call him Will.' And so it was for the rest of his days![114]

Another later story (when Will's son Mark was running the team) occurred at the Whim Creek pub. Mark was hell-bent on not stopping there as he knew he would never get the men out of the bar, so he thundered past in the 1938 Bedford only to hear somebody yell: 'Swag overboard.'

Mark yelled back: 'It can bloody well stay there.'

To which the reply came: 'But boss, it's yours!'[115]

Back to Don's first shearing at Millstream. It was not only the difficulty of providing shearers, but also how slow and costly it was to market the wool. It had to be carted to Roebourne for shipping south, either by bullock wagons or the small motor trucks that were taking over, then unloaded and auctioned in Fremantle, before being reloaded for overseas shipping. The distances around the north would always be a burden to pastoral activity, compared to the closer-settled areas of southern Western Australia and most of eastern Australia.

The problems of distance and isolation were further driven home to Don when he was part of the droving team taking surplus wethers to Onslow for shipping south in 1931. Once the stations had reached full stocking capacity, the selling of surplus sheep was a costly and difficult business, that also contributed to over-grazing, as often the cost of selling stock exceeded the value achieved at auction. Don took an interesting series of photos along the way to Onslow, carefully labelled: Pannawanacka Hill; Dray broken down, Robe River; Camp at

Dray broken down, Robe River, 1931

Hamersley wool, 1931

Pannawanacka hill, 1931

Yarraloola; Soak well at Peedamulla; and Hammersley wool (under a photo of an old truck and trailer carting 36 bales). How could Don have envisaged the vast mines and infrastructure of today's Pilbara?

It was while at Millstream that Don learnt to shear. There was a shearers' strike in 1930, so stations pooled their resources (just as they had done in the 1890s) to get the job done. The length of the strike is not recorded but the nearby Hooley station clip was taken off that way, which was back-breaking work for the inexperienced station hands: 'You could always count on me for 100 a day, but I was never a 'natural' – it was always damned hard work.'

For the rest of his life, Don always thought well of those 'pushing the hand piece' and could stand and watch 'a natural' shear sheep after sheep:

> Just look at his style, he hardly seems to be moving, but the comb's always full and the sheep are in just the right position. That way sheep don't kick – and look, he hardly has a sweat up.

Don stayed at Millstream for nearly four years, reaching the position of overseer, but always found the out-camps 'very lonely affairs'. Banjo's *Collected Book of Verse* continued to provide solace and how different the back paddocks of Millstream were as compared to the high country of the Monaro or the vast plains of the Riverina, so vividly depicted in those poems. Life back at the homestead was a lot easier, with Bill Cleland as overseer until Don took over and Peter Corbin as a jackeroo, and all were to remain close friends for the rest of their lives. Bill was a champion tennis player and built an ant-bed court that they all enjoyed.[116]

Cricket continued as Don's main social interest. He pored over newspapers that were weeks or even months old, following the progress of some of the Colts players back in South Australia, and was enthralled by the ability of Don Bradman as a newcomer to Australian cricket, being only one year younger than himself. Every summer at Millstream he played for Roebourne in one or two local matches, a highlight being the Roebourne / Port Hedland game in 1932, just before he left the north. Don left Millstream at the end of 1932, only his second trip south since arriving in early 1929. Good fortune was with him as already aboard the ship was Canny Rose from Mount Anderson station out of Derby, also heading south for a once-in-two-years holiday. They quickly struck up a friendship and Don was invited back to meet the Rose family at Wingfield, 3 Albert Street, Claremont.

Don had been missing out on female company so was pleasantly surprised the family consisted of not only Canny's brother Kim, but also four unmarried sisters: Sylvia, Alice, Grace and Thelma. There is no record of him taking out any of the older girls but the 15-year-old Thelma must have made a mark, as he was to return in later years! After a short break in Perth, Don set off by train for Leonora and Tarmoola station, then owned by R. McBride and Rollo Hawkes of the same family as the owners of Koonoona.[117] The SA connections were at work.

Leonora was a thriving town in the 1930s and, together with nearby Gwalia, boasted a population of 7,000, with associated good shopping, medical, schooling and sports facilities, not to mention seven hotels and even a tram service between the two towns. The Sons of Gwalia mine proved to be the third-biggest producer of gold in Australia, operating from 1898 to 1963. Don was told of Herbert Hoover being the first mine manager at Gwalia and, later, President of the USA (1929–33):[118]

'If he could handle a few thousand Aussie miners, a few million Yanks would be a pushover!'

Tarmoola homestead, 1933

Tarmoola was 30 miles north of town in a 10-inch rainfall area, but had rougher country of lower stocking capacity than many other properties in the district. Don was overseer but little is recorded of his time there as far as the station is concerned, though it's known he was able to continue his cricket and relished the grassed Leonora grounds. Don soon got to know Gef Chomley on next-door Sturt Meadows. (Gef was christened George, but always known as Gef, being the initials of his three given names.) Gef had a small shareholding but the majority owners were the Hawkers of North Bungaree, being further SA connections. Sturt Meadows was a bigger station with better grazing flats, turning off 1,000 bales at the time.[119]

Cricket also brought Don into contact with Daniel MacKinnon, the manager of Pinnacles, who was an unashamed cricket tragic and was known to enquire of a jackeroo's cricketing skills, rather than his work experience, when offering a job. Pinnacles was also turning off 1,000 bales a year and both these stations employed a good quota of jackeroos.[120] Bill Cleland was now managing Glenorn so Don was able to pick up on the earlier friendship.[121]

If Millstream appeared 'new and frontier', then the Eastern Goldfields stations were even more so. Gold had been mined since the 1890s, with pastoral development for wool production only taking place in the 1920s. While there were earlier leases, they were used only for supplying meat and milk (mainly from goats) to the mining towns.

The 10-inch rainfall dictated low stocking rates and large leases, resulting in mile upon mile of sheep fencing and numerous water points, one blessing being good stock water at reasonable depth, accessed by wells in those days. While the rest of Australia (and most of the world) was suffering the effects of the Great Depression, the Eastern Goldfields was cushioned to a large degree as gold was always in demand and the recently developed stations were carrying large numbers of sheep. There was still some development work being undertaken in fencing and well sinking, so employment and population remained largely unaffected. That's not to say there wasn't severe belt tightening: replacement of vehicles and other plant was put on hold; holidays restricted or cancelled; food and clothing 'made to go the distance'. Some stations offered managers shares in lieu of wages, as happened for Bill Cleland on Glenorn.[122] It was only the mines that seemed unaffected, attracting a lot of hopeful men to take the train to towns such as Leonora and Wiluna.

8 DON – LAKE VIOLET, WILUNA AND THE GOLDFIELDS

Wiluna had been a large gold mining centre at the turn of the century, but after 20 years the shallow workings had been exhausted. Claude de Bernales came to the rescue. He undertook deep drilling analysis of the ore load, floated a company in London with a £1 million base and commenced mining as the Wiluna Mining Company Ltd in 1926. By 1934, the mine had produced £3 million worth of gold and by its closure in 1947, £12 million. Claude was charming, urbane, always immaculately dressed and known as 'the man with the Midas touch'. He floated many other gold mining companies, many of which 'went bust', costing shareholders millions of pounds. He built Overton Lodge at Cottesloe as his Perth home and had equally lavish homes in Sydney and London. He was the Holmes á Court, Bond and Connell of the day, all rolled into one![123]

Don was now 25 and his station career was about to take off, being offered the position of overseer at Lake Violet, 30 miles east of Wiluna. When he arrived there in 1933 the town was in its heyday, the railway line to Meekatharra and on to Perth had been opened the year before, the mine was in full production and there were 4,000 people in town. Like Leonora, it was well set up with all facilities, even down to the grassed cricket ground, and there were three hotels: the Weeloona, Commercial and Club – the last being preferred by the station people. The Club was owned and run by Barney O'Shaughnessy, who was also a top cricketer, providing Don with a common interest.

Many of the old buildings of the first mining boom were replaced or refurbished, giving the town a fresh new appearance. As well as a hospital and doctor, bakers, ice works and cordial plant, there were Laurie Gerrick's grocery store, Mick Finch's garage, the Union, NSW and Commonwealth banks, a tobacconist/billiard salon, Eric Burgess's legal practice and Ward's butcher shop, to name just some of the businesses. The Canning Stock Route, stretching 1,150 miles to Halls Creek, had been opened in 1910 but was little used. In 1928 the wells had been rebuilt and with the opening of the railway line, 35 mobs of cattle were brought down in the following years, providing further stimulus to the town.[124]

Pastoral families from around Australia, including the Riverina in NSW and the Clare Valley in SA, made false assumptions and thought the goldfields of WA would be as productive as their home properties had been for over 75 years. There was a wave of development following the First World War based on these expectations. Lake Violet was established by the McCaughey family in 1926, though the lease was originally taken up by the Ward and Tweedy families in 1906, then known as Millbillillie. The Wards also owned the butchers shop in town and the lease was not developed beyond supplying stock for the shop.[125]

Lake Violet was based on the grand scale of the Riverina and if anyone could afford such grandeur, it would be the McCaugheys. Sir Samuel McCaughey was Australia's biggest wool producer at the turn of the century, having more than one million sheep and vast land holdings, which included Dunlop in Queensland; Coree on the Billabong Creek; Coonong on the Yanco Creek; and North Yanco, between Narrandera and Leeton on the Murrumbidgee. On North Yanco he constructed 190 miles of irrigation channels that became the catalyst for the government's Murrumbidgee Irrigation Scheme, and the grand old homestead is now the administrative centre for the Yanco Agricultural High School.[126]

Sir Samuel never married but was generous to his family and various charities. It was Sir Samuel's nephew, Sam, who was the managing director of the Coree Pastoral Co Pty Ltd and had the vision for Lake Violet. Sam sent the Coree bookkeeper, Bob MacMillan, over to supervise the station's development and gave him a bold plan for its implementation – along with a very deep chequebook. Sam had ideas of his son, Michael, taking over Lake Violet and instructed Bob to have everything in order for such an outcome: 'Spare no expense, do the job properly' – and he did just that.

A large homestead was built of jarrah with an iron roof. The logistics of getting materials to the site would have been daunting at the time of building as the nearest railhead was then at Meekatharra, with rudimentary roads and vehicles to complete the journey. The homestead was planned on a traditional Riverina design, very similar to Cunningham Plains: it was U-shaped, with formal wood-panelled rooms at the front, a three-bedroom wing down one side and a servery, kitchen, men's dining room and cook's bedroom on the other. At the end of the bedroom wing was the office and next to it the station store. There were two bathrooms, a 'private' one near the main bedroom, with the other at the end of the verandah for general use. Both had indoor 'lavs' – very modern indeed! Verandahs all around, including the central courtyard, provided shade to the homestead.

The three main buildings were set 3 feet above ground level on mulga stumps, partly for coolness, but also in case of flood. In December 1927, the *Geraldton Guardian* reported:

> Near Wiluna, Lake Violet station, under the energetic manager, Mr McMillan, is making a rapid push forward on somewhat of a magnificent scale towards a well-developed sheep station. Its first clip of a few hundred bales came through to the Meekatharra railhead a few weeks ago. A rather pretentious homestead is in course of erection. Though the station may be known by its euphonious name of Lake Violet, it is likely to be referred to in bush land stories as 'the station of three thousand gates'. And that, be assured, is no figment of speech, but indicative of the tremendous system of sheep-proof fencing erected. Indeed so large are the immediate requirements that quite a fleet of motor trucks are kept busy transporting materials from Meekatharra to the station.

Not only was the homestead pretentious in size, it was also set up with quality furnishings, such as the jarrah dining room suite with seating for 10 or 12 and large sideboards. There were complete dinner sets of English fine-bone china, silver-plated cutlery, large serving dishes – all set up for a squatter's son!

Outbuildings included an overseer's cottage, jackeroos' quarters (suitable for eight or so men), a large workshop and a charcoal-lined meat house with water trickling down for coolness. The landscaping featured formal gardens, an orchard of mainly citrus trees, a vegetable garden, poultry run and two grassed tennis courts. Nearby was an elaborately conceived lucerne patch of 5 acres, levelled off for irrigation, with water supplied by four motorised pumps on individual wells.

Front view, Lake Violet homestead, 1933

Lake Violet woolshed, 1933

The site had been chosen because of abundant fresh water at shallow depth on a flood plain running southeast through the property.

The homestead was towards the northwest corner of the one million acre lease and the woolshed was built 12 miles further east to be more centrally located. The shed was typical of its day: eight stands on raised wooden boards and grating, with the Ferrier double-box wool press and bale storage being down on a concrete slab. Yards were of mulga posts standing upright in tight rows. There were the regulation corrugated iron shearers' quarters, cook house, shower rooms and separate quarters for the classer and station manager to share. (It was assumed the manager or overseer would be on hand for shearing as the distance from the homestead in days of poor transport was too great.) The shed was powered by a slow-revving 6-horsepower petrol Lister engine with a trip-action magneto.[127]

Further east was the out-camp, together with a set of yards for lamb marking and other activities. By 1933, there were 40 equipped mills and 37 paddocks, utilising 750,000 acres of the lease. Fencing was of four wires, with the top wire to the out-camp and woolshed being an earth return telephone line. The eastern boundary was 'the last fence this side of Queensland', so dingoes were a constant problem and required a lot of resources, firstly to get them under control, then to combat the ongoing incursions from the hinterland. The station reached 16,000 sheep by 1930 but the drought of that year saw numbers decline to 6,000, before slowly building up again in 1933. Initial stocking was with Bungaree blood-line sheep from SA, the 9,000 ewes being walked from the Leonora railhead and the rams trucked up.[128]

It can be seen Bob MacMillan had been busy from 1926 to 1933 and faithfully completed the huge task given him by Sam McCaughey. Bob was ready to return to his family in the Riverina and the management was given to John Featherstonhaugh, the overseer at Sturt Meadows. John had got to know Don, being next door on Tarmoola, and suggested he come with him to Lake Violet as overseer. Don jumped at the chance to be on a bigger and better established station and being a promotion in his pastoral career.[129]

The social life was very agreeable: the grassed tennis courts were put to regular use and, with good numbers of jackeroos, Don could get some cricket practice in as well. He was also playing regularly in Wiluna for Towns against the seven other local teams and for Wiluna in intertown matches. He became friendly with the mine manager, Bert 'Bull' Carroll, Dr Phipps and other station people in the district. The Club Hotel was the meeting place, Barney O'Shaughnessy also being in the Towns cricket team. Don was a very modest drinker, remembering his father's failings and the harm caused to the family, and noticed overuse of alcohol on many of the stations: 'I've seen too many good men lost to grog and their stations as well. Some of them will knock over a bottle of Scotch a day.'

With crude transport and no refrigeration, bulky beer was not an option. Whisky was the preferred tipple in Western Australia and other southern states, while rum was drunk in Queensland and the Northern Territory.

Those first years at Lake Violet were testing times for the new manager and overseer, and it was almost as though Bob MacMillan had taken the deep chequebook back to Coree with him, for even the McCaughey family were feeling the effects of the depression. 'Keep your eye on the expenditure, don't spend more than you have to' was now the directive. Budgets had to go back to Coree for close scrutiny.

The seasons were again turning against them, with 1934 the first dry year of what would become known as 'the seven-year drought', and sheep numbers were once again in decline. They were able to squeeze more development into the budget, providing a further 32 equipped wells and extra subdivision fencing. This allowed better access to feed for the sheep and helped the station cope with the onset of the drought.

Wiluna, on the other hand, continued to prosper with the mines employing greater numbers of men: by 1937 the population was 7,000, reaching 9,000 by 1939. The hotels couldn't keep up so a syndicate planned for the building of a 'large and suitably luxurious addition', to be known as the Lakeway. (The final cost was £40,000 and it was the only tiled-roof building in town.) Other shops opened and the town even boasted an ice cream cart. Rail patronage steadily increased, with 4,000 passengers and 4,500 tons of freight achieved in 1938. John Featherstonhaugh became a member of the Road Board from 1933 to 1937, followed by Don in 1937–39.[130]

John and Don had a monthly visit by either Ken Mitchell or Peter Creswell, who were developing Granite Peak, a further 100 miles to the north. (Ken had been the bookkeeper on Lake Violet for a time and yearned for the opportunity to go out on his own.) They took it in turns for the fortnightly trip to Wiluna for stores, mail and anything else needed for the station and, because of their humble conditions, left their 'town clothes' at Lake Violet, spending a night each way as part of their only social contact. You couldn't get two more extremes

Granite Peak homestead, 1940

of a development story than between these stations. While Ken and Peter had been educated at Melbourne Grammar and had backing from the Brookes and Lyle families, they were certainly 'doing it the tough way'. They thirsted for conversation so there were many enjoyable late-night sessions between the four men as they passed through Lake Violet.[131]

If Wiluna was the 'town on the edge of the desert', then station development certainly pushed the limits to the extreme. As well as Granite Peak, the Finches were setting up Lorna Glen 70 miles northeast of Lake Violet and the Wards were on Glenayle, between Granite Peak and the Canning Stock Route. Dingoes were a constant threat and there were some tense and difficult times with the desert blacks for these new frontiers of pastoral development. Millrose, immediately north of Lake Violet, was in the suburbs by comparison![132]

These were the outposts of sheep stations, but to the east of Lake Violet and 220 miles east of Wiluna there was the vast Wongawol lease running cattle and breeding horses. Wongawol was later divided three ways, establishing Carnegie and Windidda as separate properties. Spencer Doman owned these stations as well as Billiluna at the top end of the stock route and a large holding at Waroona in the South West of WA. He brought cattle 'down the Canning', cutting southeast to Wongawol before reaching Wiluna, then, as seasons dictated, railed to Waroona for finishing. It was a Sydney Kidman-like concept but very difficult to implement, with distances and seasons the common enemy. Spencer was killed in Belgium by 'hopping out the wrong side of a taxi and being run over', after which the empire was successfully run by his daughter, Margaret, for many years.[133] She was a 'solidly built woman' and as Don said:

'You have to take your hat off to her – she's surviving in a man's world – and teaching them a trick or two.'

The cattle stations were largely unfenced, with stock roaming into the desert in good years, returning to water as seasons dried out. It was therefore true to say, 'The sheep stations were the last fences this side of Queensland'.

Wally Dowling was the legendary drover of the early days, but Ben Taylor and George Lanagan also brought mobs 'down the Canning'. In all, it's believed 35 mobs were brought south to either Wiluna or Wongawol, with several mobs of replacement horses being taken north to Billiluna. Without exception they were epic endeavours, handled by tough knockabout drovers who were exceptional bushmen – the stuff of legends! Australia will never experience these heroic ventures again as today's heroes 'tackle the Canning' in air-conditioned four-wheel-drive vehicles, bristling with two-way radios and 'sat' phones. I wonder if they ever stop to think of Wally Dowling breaking a leg along the way, wrapping it in a moist green-hide splint, cutting the hide off weeks later and always walking with a crooked leg?[134]

Don marvelled at these far-flung outposts of civilisation, enjoying the conversation as the owners, managers and drovers passed through. As tough as the depression was for Lake Violet, he was humbled by how much harder it was for those further out. Don was making good use of his annual fortnight's holiday, with the railhead at Leonora providing ready transport to Adelaide via Kalgoorlie, or the Wiluna line to Perth.

In 1934 he was in Adelaide and it was the last time he would see his sister, Kay (Bub), still able to walk, though in constant pain. The later 1936 trip to Adelaide was an exciting adventure as Don took his first flight in a DC3 for the trip over, then returned by train. His other holidays in the 1930s were spent in Perth, coinciding with Country Week cricket, but also including time at Wingfield with the Rose family.

Kim had married Pat Savage and was managing Liveringa in the West Kimberley, turning off 1,000 bales a year; Canny married Joan Rose and was managing the family property, Mount Anderson; Grace married Bill Henwood, manager of Noonkanbah (another 1,000-bale station in the Kimberley); Alice married Herbert Shields from Glenvar, Wongan Hills; while Sylvia and Thelma were still at home. The 15-year-old Thelma of his first visit was now an attractive, vivacious young woman, employed by Dalgetys as a shorthand typist. Courtship was not easy, with two trips to Perth a year at most and slow return mail via a twice-weekly train to Wiluna and a weekly mail run from town to the station. Don's chance came in 1937 when John Featherstonhaugh said he was planning to leave Lake Violet and would recommend him to the McCaugheys as his replacement. Don became manager later that year and now had the large homestead at his disposal, so was in a position to think of marriage.

Then in 1939 Don was able to convince the McCaugheys that the 1930 'A Model' Ford ute needed replacing, resulting in the purchase of a Ford Roadster utility with the side valve 'flat head' V8. It was one of the first V8 models sold in Australia and a very fine vehicle for a station manager's use, being towards the end of the depression when most others were not so fortunate. Don marvelled at the rhythmic beat of the V8 and would drive around the rough station tracks at no more than a fast idle, rejoicing at the steady throb of the motor under light load. A common saying at the time was: 'If you can't afford a Ford, dodge a Dodge!'

Thelma aged 22 and Don aged 32 were married on 22 November 1939 at Christ Church in Claremont, with his two brothers as groomsmen and his mother in attendance from Adelaide. After a brief honeymoon south of Perth, they headed for Wiluna in the Ford ute. The sealed road came to an end near New Norcia, followed by indifferent roads for most of the 600-mile journey. As Don never exceeded 50 miles per hour, it was a long trip. They broke the journey by staying at a hotel in Mt Magnet and reached Wiluna late on the second day. There were crude 'run-throughs' on subdivision fences but still gates to open and close on the boundaries.[135]

Barney O'Shaughnessy at the Club warmly welcomed Thelma to town, providing ice-cold lemon squash in the cool confines of the Ladies Lounge. They reached the station just on dark and Thelma felt overwhelmed by the size of the house and garden, along with the sense of emptiness and isolation. She was exhausted and couldn't help resorting to tears. In the morning she was introduced to Jack O'Keefe, the old yardman/gardener, and Daisy, the 'black as spades' house girl, who would be her constant companions over the following years. There was also a cook of questionable ability, an overseer and a few jackeroos, who all 'came

Don and Thelma's wedding day, 1939

and went' as the nation geared up for the war – 'went' being the operative word, as fewer came as the young men enlisted.

Thelma felt awkward having meals brought to the sideboard in the dining room and serving from there. She was staggered at the quantity of china and silverware that went with the job. There was hardly a place for the wedding presents and she quickly learnt about polishing the silver – a job that Daisy could never quite understand! She was also dismayed at the lack of variety in the food: eggs and chops for breakfast; cold meat for lunch; a roast or stew for dinner, and as a young bride found it difficult making suggestions to the cook for a more varied diet.

Yet change was all about them, with the drought now in its fifth year and sheep numbers once again down to 6,000. With men joining the armed forces, coupled with low sheep numbers, Don made the decision to put the station on a 'war footing'. The cook and jackeroos were dispensed with and the only

Thelma in the 1939 Ford ute on her first trip to Wiluna, at one of the many gates

permanent white staff were Jack O'Keefe at the homestead, Dan Jones at the out-camp, an overseer and a few casuals from time to time.

Thelma was now the cook and had to quickly come to terms with the large Metters 'No 4' wood stove – and bread making! The extensive garden became more her domain as Jack was taking on other jobs, such as doing the killing for the meat house and servicing the 32-volt lighting plant. Don always ensured Jack was about the homestead, 'as you can never be sure who's roaming about the place these days' and he didn't want Thelma left on her own. The lucerne patch, 'which was always a labour-intensive and doubtful proposition', together with the grass tennis courts, were also done away with.

They both got on with life the best way that they could. Don's only extravagance was his pipe and, while he didn't consume a lot of tobacco, the ritual of stoking, lighting and cleaning was of comfort. The pipe was often hanging from the side of his mouth, unlit, but providing some solace. He refrained from alcohol. Thelma slowly developed a love of gardening: 'At first I planted a few vincas and geraniums – and can still remember the joy I got from the splash of colour.'

Lake Violet garden, with the orchard in the background, 1936

The Lake Violet gardens had been set out formally, with beds surrounded by white-painted stones and planted with shrubs, while the lawns were military-like built-up squares, surrounded by wooden planks. Bob MacMillan certainly lacked the feminine touch! Thelma also gained great pleasure from the vegetable garden, watching the peas, beans, pumpkins and melons rotate through the seasons: 'The common interest of the vegetables with Jack O'Keefe was a Godsend.'

While Don had found it difficult 'understanding the blacks' in his first year at Millstream, he was now appreciative of what they had to offer and worked out a system of mutual dependence, just as most of the stations of the day were doing. Blackfellas were in their first- or at most second-generation contact with Europeans and still retained close links to their traditional ways. The system was based on the station providing basic clothing and rations to the whole camp, such as flour, sugar, tea and hand-me-down clothes. Other more desired items, such as boots, hats, new clothing, tobacco and jam, were dependent on the amount of work being done by the individual, the best rewarded being mustering and various domestic jobs around the homestead. Many of the chores were of only an hour or so a day, but established a concept of reward for effort. Traditional food, such as roo, bungarra and bardie grubs, were still being eaten, with the bush providing local 'tucker' and connection to their country. Regular 'walkabouts' suited both parties, so long as they were not in the middle of mustering, with various means of cajoling and flattery being used to keep a team together until the job was done:

> You fellas did a good job today – I reckon that paddock is good and clean now. Tommy and Billy – you see tracks way up there on horseback that I can't even see from down here on the ground – and you know which way they are going as well!

Don, along with the vast majority of stations, was very strict about not fraternising with the blacks and leaving them to their traditional culture and practices as far as was possible. That is not to say there was 'no crossing the line' by some in the white community, as evidenced by the few 'little bit blackfella – little bit whitefella' offspring. The mothers were all too obvious but the fathers usually open to conjecture (sometimes ribald, but also genuine concern as to who it might be). A jackeroo would be sacked on the spot if caught out, though the itinerant workers, such as fencers and well sinkers, were harder to supervise and severely frowned upon by the wider white community if found out. It was a transitional system that by and large worked well, but couldn't be expected to last for too many generations.

The station store played an important role in the old system and was kept under lock and key, being open for business only a few hours a week. All provisions supplied to the blackfellas were carefully recorded, along with the items used in the homestead, as managers and white staff were employed on the 'found' basis of board and keep. Most of the throughput was tax-deductible expenditure to the station, which required accurate bookkeeping.

Thelma started to take an interest in the store, which included unpacking the supplies and carefully stacking the shelves, while suggesting some extra items that might be added to the orders. Don was a frugal manager and watched the store account carefully so it was a fine balancing act! As Don was almost a teetotaller, the matter of 'entertainment allowance' at the store was not an issue, though other station managers with a heavy thirst were often challenged as to the quantity of whisky being ordered.

Life for Don and Thelma was very difficult in the early stages of the war and the resulting shortage of labour, coinciding with the final two years of

Rear view, Lake Violet – mail truck unloading at the store

drought. Fuel was rationed and Mick Finch's garage was kept busy fitting gas producers to the station utes. The stations were also kept busy producing the charcoal to feed the cumbersome additions, which required filling a pit with mulga logs and, once alight, covering with sheets of iron and dirt, so that the fire burnt with little oxygen. As a result, travel was restricted, with fewer trips to town and neighbouring stations and very few trips to Perth. It was all very demanding:

> My grandfather, David Henry, lobbed in Australia during the 1840s drought – my father cut his teeth in the pastoral country of New South Wales during the dreadful Federation Drought, and here we are in the middle of another confounded war, with yet another big dry! When and where will it all end?

Don hardly left Lake Violet during the war, but Thelma had the occasional trip to Perth by train and there were infrequent visits from her sister Sylvia and other family, utilising the 39-hour service. A highlight was the birth of Alex on 4 August 1941, Thelma having moved to Perth for the birth, staying at Albert Street with the family. Sylvia accompanied her home on the train and Don was presented with his little cross-eyed son, probably thinking: 'The poor little beggar will have trouble on the cricket field.'

They both poured their total love on the baby. Don started to call Alex 'Snow', partly because of his fair hair, but also in memory of his uncle and Godfather, Alfred 'Snowy' Campbell. Two years later, Tim arrived on 20 November 1943 and both parents felt pleased with their lot: two healthy babies, a good home in which to live and as safe a place as could be hoped for in the wartorn world of the day.

Thelma travelled to Perth by train in advance of Tim's birth and Don made a rare trip south with the gas-producer powered ute to collect them. The excitement of a second son must have been overwhelming, for on the way home to Wiluna he left his chequebook at Paynes Find, where they spent the night. The hotel phoned ahead to Wydgee (pronounced Wodgee) and Ian Thom attached a note to the gate near the homestead: 'Don Campbell – please call in at Wydgee'. Jocelyn Thom, who had been at school with Thelma's sister Grace, insisted Thelma stay with her while Don went back for the chequebook, which started a friendship that was to last for the rest of their lives, with every subsequent trip including a stopover at Wydgee with the Thoms.

On their arrival home, Don attended to a matter of importance to him and arranged a £1,000 whole-of-life policy with AMP for Tim, just as he had done for Alex. Even though it was the middle of the war years, he was going to set his sons up for a stable and independent life.[136] Don had little time to enjoy his new family, though, as pressure and expectations were being heaped upon him and he was prevailed on to again serve on the Wiluna Road Board, which he did from 1943 to 1946.

Along with other station people, he joined the Volunteer Defence Corps. This involved a certain amount of training, including recognition of aircraft and various reporting responsibilities, but at least all the station people were proficient in the use of firearms. The commitment was willingly undertaken, though with a healthy dose of realism: 'Heaven help the rest of the country, if we start reporting Jap aircraft over Wiluna!'[137]

Yet it was Granite Peak that put the most pressure on a busy man. Peter Creswell returned to the east in 1937 after suffering a relatively mild polio episode, with Ken Mitchell now being helped by overseer and friend Tom Cartwright. The station was struggling financially and the two single men felt they should sign up and take some pressure off the place. The owners and directors of the company agreed so long as alternative management arrangements could be put in place.

Ken found 'a reasonably reliable bloke' called Archie Hogg to live at Granite Peak who would be answerable to Don as supervisory manager. This was all put in place but proved a real burden as Archie was becoming less reliable and needed a lot of supervision, with precious fuel being used on regular return trips of 200 miles. It all came to a head just before shearing in 1944, when Archie committed suicide. Don had to organise the mustering and shearing, being helped by Mick Finch and the Wards to get the job done. Ken was able to get an early discharge and returned to Granite Peak at the end of the year.[138]

The absolute highlight of the war years was the breaking of the drought in 1942. 'There's nothing like a good flood to break a drought' and so it was for the Eastern Goldfields. Bob MacMillan's decision to build 3 feet above ground level was vindicated as the creek was in full flood and water surrounded all the buildings for several days. Lake Violet and Lake Way joined together and remained full for some years, allowing for dust-covered boats and little yachts to be brought out of sheds, providing some social relief for the local war-frazzled population.[139]

Don was relieved to see the herbage germinate so quickly and evenly, and marvelled at the response of the mulga (*acacia anera*) and saltbushes (*atritlexes*) to the rain. Thelma was overjoyed at the masses of everlastings (*rhodanthe*) and the spectacular Sturt's Desert Pea (*Swainsona formosa*), appearing as if from nowhere. The irregular transformation from bare red soil to fields of green and colour has been a source of constant wonderment to generations of both black and white Australians.

The relief of drought-breaking rain was short-lived as the sheep blowfly had at last reached this outpost of sheep grazing, no doubt helped along by the humidity and moisture. Sheep were very weak so were mustered into temporary yards for treatment and, as labour was very scarce, Don once again picked up the handpiece alongside the two-stand portable shearing plant. Dan Jones and a few of the blackfellas tried their hand as well, but Don said: 'It was one of the most gruelling experiences of all my time in the bush.'

Dan was one of a dying breed of characters who populated the outback in those days and preferred to use a pushbike for his mill rounds, refusing the use of a motorbike or ute, 'as them dangerous new-fangled things'. His annual fortnight's holiday was to Wiluna, 'where he would go on a binge of epic proportions and take a further fortnight to recover'. There's a yarn about one such trip to town, when the local Catholic priest came up to him: 'You are getting on in years my

Mustering plant, Lake Violet, 1930s

Temporary crutching facilities, 1942

son, and perhaps you would care to come to confession and make peace with the Lord?' Dan's lofty reply was: 'I don't like using middle men – I'll deal direct.'[140]

While rain was the highlight of the war years, the bombing of Darwin in February 1942 by 242 aircraft with the loss of 235 lives, then Broome one month later by nine aircraft and 88 lives lost, was certainly the low point. Never before or since has Australia been so immediately threatened by invasion.[141] Women and children were being evacuated from the north and so it was that Grace Henwood and her three young sons, Bill, David and John, came to Lake Violet. They were there for a little under a year before moving to Perth, then back home to the Kimberley. While Thelma was pleased to have her sister and boys with her, it put an extra strain on the understaffed station.

There are many other stories to demonstrate the difficulties of the war years for those left to run the stations and farms: labour difficulties on the shearing teams; rationing; vehicles wearing out; and tyres and tubes almost unobtainable. There are stories of tyres so thin 'that you could read a newspaper through them'; tyres being stuffed with stained wool and vegetable matter when the tubes gave out; rope being coiled around a rim in place of a tyre, and so on. One of Don's contributions to fuel saving was the use of a Triumph motorbike for mill rounds, though it was very temperamental: 'being difficult to start and easy to stop'. It was all borne with stoic reserve, 'as our bit to help the boys overseas'.

The cabinet wireless in the corner of the sitting room, powered by a 6-volt car battery, was the ear to the world, with the ABC news and relays from the BBC being carefully listened to. What relief there must have been when the tide turned in 1945, with ultimate victory for the allies, firstly in Europe, then against the Japanese in the Pacific later that year. A lot has been written about those in uniform and the terrible times endured by our fighting forces, but we should also be very grateful to those who stayed behind to keep the vital food and wool industries operating in those difficult times.

The war had ended, sheep numbers were steadily picking up following the breaking of the seven-year drought in 1942, labour and supplies were becoming more plentiful and surplus army vehicles were becoming available for station use. Don's brother Pat had been a POW on the Burma Railway and wanted to get back to work in the pastoral industry. Don felt some time at Lake Violet might help him readjust and recover from his injuries so offered him the position of overseer. Pat married Rie Woodley at Christ Church, Claremont, on 25 October 1947, with Don as best man and Thelma as matron of honour. They stayed at

Triumph motorbike, 1940

Lake Violet for 18 months and it must have been difficult for both parties, with brothers working alongside each other and two sisters-in-law thrown together on a lonely station. It would test the best of families but the arrangement seems to have worked remarkably well.

Social life was improving, parties were organised on stations in the district and Ken Mitchell married, followed by Tom Cartwright, so they were regular visitors on the way to town from Granite Peak. Herb and Mim Lukin were particular friends on Lake Way, while others were Bob and Alice Adamson on Yakabindie; Len and Hilary Bilston, next door on Barwidgee; the Howards on Albion Downs; Wendy and George Folvig on Yeelirrie; the Greens on Cunyu; and Pattersons on Yandil. Alf Patterson's nickname was 'Dingo' as he was particularly successful in their eradication – and he had plenty of practice on the edge of the sheep country. Bert 'Bull' Carroll the mine manager and his wife, Elsie, became very close friends and a trip to town always included time at their comfortable home, set in a large garden with grass tennis court.

Thelma was fortunate in having 32-volt lighting and an Electrolux kerosene 'fridge', but ironing was still with the heavy Mrs Potts irons – the trial of a petrol iron being quickly abandoned!

Thelma and Rie, outside the overseer's cottage, 1948

Shearing had been a challenge over the drought years, with the difficulties of mustering and yarding weak sheep. In the post-war years and with better seasons, numbers were picking up and shearing was a lot easier to handle, with the shed enlarged to 10 stands and Len Mitchell now the contractor. As Don said: 'It was always a breeze, having Len in charge.'[142]

Don used to share the hut with Len during the week, leaving Thelma at home with Jack O'Keefe and Daisy for company. As always, he was very interested in all the activity in the shed and admired the skill of the 'natural' shearer. Don Munday was shearing during the drought years and remembered:

> Lake Violet was hit pretty hard by drought and I couldn't help feeling sorry for the manager, Don Campbell. He was a pretty quiet, decent sort of bloke and unlike most squatters, would occasionally visit the shearers huts for a bit of a wongi.[143]

Another shearer in the late 1940s was Clem McKenzie, who was developing a small 500-acre farm on the south side of the Porongurup Hills. He spoke well of Don and would have thought you were crazy in those early days if you had said his little farm would be worth more than Lake Violet within 50 years.[144]

Ted Jessop was the local carrier, taking the wool into Wiluna for railing to Fremantle. He was a giant of a man with a wooden 'peg leg', could leap around on top of the bales without any difficulty and was apparently 'a bit of a terror' in the pubs after having more than a few drinks. Wool was loaded on to his truck and trailer through a windlass arrangement, with the station ute going backwards and forwards as the power source. At 35 bales a load, Ted was kept busy.[145]

In 1947, all of Don's dreams came true. He had a long-standing order at Winterbottoms in Perth for a new Chev car and, 18 months later, was advised that 'his turn had come'. The family caught the train to Perth and took possession of a lovely cream-coloured Chevrolet Fleetmaster car, with a six-cylinder engine and column gear shift. What a pride and joy it was for Don!

Far less exciting than a Chev car, was the issue of Alex's education. The men's dining room next to the kitchen was converted into a school room and correspondence courses commenced, with a weekly turnaround of lessons being mailed from Perth. Thelma, along with her other jobs, was now a school teacher and while one or two governesses were tried, they soon tired of the lonely station life. In earlier days, there would have been jackeroos seeking their attention and making life more interesting, but not on post-war Lake Violet.

Sue was born on 2 January 1949 and the curly-headed little girl quickly became the 'apple of their eyes' – a girl after two boys was just the thing to round a family off. When Sue was still a baby, the children all came down with measles, which was a serious illness in those days. Sylvia had been a nurse, so came rushing up by train to lend a hand and insisted on darkened rooms, complete rest and lots of fluids. The boys objected to a fair degree, but her nursing efforts paid off, as there were no lasting side effects.

Don had been sending regular cheques home to his mother but had not been back to South Australia since before the war. Dr Black was an eye specialist in Adelaide who reputedly could straighten the eyes of those with a squint, so in 1949 the family made the train journey from Kalgoorlie (the Chev being left there) with high hopes for the family reunion and a good medical outcome for Alex.

Don was quite upset at seeing his old house at 177 Barton Terrace, which had not been maintained at all: paint was peeling and faded, carpets were threadbare and the garden neglected. Sister Kay was very much bed-bound and, even though putting on a bright face, had aged a lot in the interim. Their mother, Evelyn, was as disciplined as ever and quite unsettled Thelma! The only bright spot was catching up with Bey and Patsy – the intervening years faded away and the two brothers picked up 'as though only yesterday'. Thelma couldn't adjust to Evelyn ringing a bell for the maid when tea or a meal was required and Dr Black didn't live up to expectations. Alex's eye operation was unsuccessful.

Don was presented with one of the most difficult decisions of his life in 1949. Elders offered him Wogarno station, southwest of Mt Magnet, 'if he would take on the debt owing to them'. This was not an unusual happening in those days, as many stations had incurred large debts over the depression and war years and the owners were now 'throwing in the towel'. (In one of life's coincidences, it was the same station bought by cousin David Campbell 40 years later.) The pastoral inspectors had a keen eye for the better managers, knowing they would have the energy and ability to turn the financial situation around. A win–win outcome often resulted, with the chance of ownership for a manager and a debt being serviced for the pastoral house. Don gave it plenty of thought, but his careful and conservative nature won out and he turned the offer down. Life is made up of many 'ifs'. If he had chosen otherwise, wool was to reach a 'pound a pound' and within two years the debt would have been paid off. On the other hand, if he had taken the station on, how would he have responded to the insidious slow decline in wool profitability and the ever reducing carrying capacity of the country? Would he have been like the frog in slowly heating water and not responded in time?

There were regular overnight visits by 'reps' from the pastoral houses, such as 'Tommy' Thompson and 'Shally' Shallcross, who were all fine men and enjoyed for their good company. Friends of Thelma also came to stay, including Marg Monger as a 16-year-old in 1946, then again in 1949,[146] and Peter Atkins in 1945 as a 17-year-old schoolboy, who had just completed his leaving.[147] Both the Monger and Atkins families were long-time friends of the Roses. Ron Halcombe, who was now a sports commentator for the ABC and particularly enjoyed for his insightful cricket commentary, visited several times and he and Don would relive the old South Australian days of their youth.

For all the visitors and outings, Thelma was very lonely on the station, with Don away from home for long hours on mill runs and other business. Teaching the boys by correspondence was a difficult task, the long summers were very trying and it was Marg, Peter and Ron who, in later years, pointed out just how lonely and desperate she had become. Don's health was also starting to suffer as the gruelling war years had taken their toll and he never gave himself time to recover.

Sam McCaughey had lost his son Michael during the war and turned ever more to drink. The family made his brother, Roy, the managing director of the Coree Past Co and he was now casting a very jaundiced eye over Lake Violet. Sam's daughter, Unity, wrote in her diary: 'Family finances were depleted following years of extravagance and the disastrous Lake Violet venture.'[148]

The pressure of running a station is never easy when the owners lose interest in the investment, though Don always had the utmost respect for Roy, 'as a fair and reasonable bloke'. It all came to a head following Ron Halcombe's visit in 1950. On his return to Perth he met up with Fred Waldeck, state manager of Goldsbrough Mort (an old cricketing mate of both Ron and Don back in the SA days), who said there was a pastoral inspector's position available, 'if Don could be prised away from the North'. The upshot was along those lines, with sufficient notice being given to the Coree Past Co, loose ends tidied up and Lake Violet left shipshape for a new manager.[149]

Don undertook a final job for the Coree Past Co, selling off the undeveloped 250,000 acres of the lease around the town of Wiluna, with the smaller area once again being called Millbillillie. Stock numbers recovered, having just reached 20,000, and the wool market was 'taking off'. In July 1951 he put through his final shearing with Tony French, the replacement manager, on hand. As always, Don was very particular about things being done properly so wanted final sheep numbers at handover being beyond doubt, with Len Mitchell the 'umpire' and both departing and incoming managers being present for the count. Don was also careful to sign off on the inventory of household goods and chattels belonging to the station.

Farewell parties were organised with the presentation of a large art book, along with 'a nice little cheque', the station friends having all signed their names inside the front cover. It was a slow and sombre final trip to town in the Chev and then on to Perth. While Don was physically worn out, he could hold his head high: he had brought the station through depression and war, drought and flood, good prices and bad, and handed it over in better shape than ever before. He made as significant a contribution to the pastoral industry as could be expected of any man.

Daisy and her mother farewell Sue, Tim and Alex on leaving Lake Violet

9 THE ROSES OF MOUNT ANDERSON AND THE WEST KIMBERLEY

Robert Henry Rose arrived at Fremantle on the *Merope* on 25 May 1852. He firstly tried farming near Lake Monger, then south of the Peel–Harvey Estuary and finally settled at Parkfield on the Old Bunbury Road, north of the Leschenault Inlet. They farmed dairy and beef cattle, grew crops and had a large vineyard and an olive grove.

Robert married Ann Allnut in the Australind Church on 26 March 1857. They had five children: Robert Henry jr, John Charles, George Canler, James and Edwin. Ann died only five weeks after Edwin was born. Robert then married Elizabeth Teede at the Old Picton Church on 22 July 1865 and had 14 more children: the first unnamed, Maryann, Louisa, Augustus, Arnold, Ada (died young), Ada, Percival, Madeline, Bessie, Florence, Thomas, Ella and Annette.

Without doubt, virtually any Western Australian family back in those early times would have sooner or later married into the Rose family. Many of them went on to farm in the South West of the state, including at Wilgarrup (near Bridgetown), Roelands and Burekup. Madeline (known as Lena) married Maitland Roberts of Yathroo, near Dandaragan.

George Canler (the third son) was to become a pioneer of the Kimberley. He knew that Alexander Forrest was to mount an expedition, so went to Perth and offered himself and horse to the cause. Forrest had gained £10,000 backing from J.A. Game to open up pastoral country in the Fitzroy Valley and appointed George to lead the party.

The 'Heather Bell', a 470-ton barque, was chartered for the purpose and loaded with the requisites for settlement, together with 1,700 sheep, 10 horses

The Grange, Claremont, 1920s

and seven cattle. They landed at Beagle Bay, the closest point to the mouth of the Fitzroy that was free of crocodiles. In early 1883, they made their base at Yeeda near the mouth of the river, before moving inland and marking out the leases for Forrest and Game. George selected Mount Anderson for himself, which remained in the family until 1969. In the following years, various members of the Rose family either owned or managed Quanbun, Yeeda, Liveringa, Myroodah, Cherabun, Mount Anderson and Leopold Downs. The Fitzroy Valley was settled with sheep, while cattle 'came across the top' to the East Kimberley with the Duracks and McDonalds. Family members often wondered at George selecting Mount Anderson for himself when other, better land was still available.

On 20 March 1901, George married Edith Bertha Clarke (always known as Bertha), 16 years his younger. She was the granddaughter of Ephraim Clarke, who arrived at Australind on 19 March 1841. He had 11 children, the seventh of whom was also called Ephraim, who in turn had 12 children, of which Bertha was the oldest. Like the Roses, many early WA families also have a Clarke connection.

George purchased The Grange in Claremont as his Perth base, which was Bertha's home, as she never lived in the Kimberley. The Grange covered the land

Wingfield, 3 Albert Street, Claremont, 1950s

bordered by today's Parry, Albert and Kingsmill Streets, with frontage to Stirling Highway. They had several dairy cows, a large vegetable garden, poultry run and formal gardens, including a croquet green, and employed a permanent gardener to manage the place while George was away in the Kimberley.

They had seven children: George Canler (Canny) (b. 1902), Sylvia Anne (b. 1903), Alice Bertha (b. 1904), Olive who died at birth in 1906, Kimberley Clarke (Kim) (b. 1908), Grace Connor (b. 1913) and finally Thelma Raye (b. 1917), who married Don Campbell.

The Grange tragically burnt down in 1922, when Thelma was only five years old. George had retired from the Kimberley by then, so the family went to live on a small farmlet on the outskirts of York, known as Upalong. After living at York for seven years, the family returned to Claremont, living at Wingfield, 3 Albert Street, being the final half-acre of the Grange land still in George's ownership. Wingfield was a charming wooden cottage, which they extended by

George Canler Rose, then in his 90s

enlarging the drawing room, adding a big dining room and enclosing part of the verandah as a sleep-out. Sylvia used the upstairs attic bedroom as her own while caring for her elderly parents.

Bertha died in 1960 and George in 1959, aged 98. He was widely remembered as a pioneer of the West Kimberley, but not as a businessman as he gained little from the pastoral and other real estate assets that passed through his hands. Other than Sylvia, who remained unmarried, all the other children lived on stations and farms in Western Australia. Wingfield became the base for all the family when holidaying in Perth and she became a 'de facto mother' to her many nieces and nephews.[150]

10 Don – Goldsbroughs and Wydgee Past Co

It was a sombre trip to Perth in the Chev and even the children sensed that life as they knew it was about to change. While Thelma had been lonely at Lake Violet, she realised what true friends she had made in the Wiluna district and wondered how she would readapt to city life. Don had already accepted the pastoral inspector's position at Goldsbroughs but also wondered about being confined to a quarter-acre block. A final meal at Wydgee with the Thoms only accentuated the change that was in store for them all. They moved into Albert Street with the Roses and immediately started looking for a house.

Don had been carefully 'putting a few shares together' over the years, with a particular leaning towards an old cricketing mate, Frank Beaurepaire's Olympic Tyre and Rubber Co (so called because of Frank being an Olympic swimmer in his day). Don quickly realised that his budget was not going to meet the Perth housing market so he made the greatest sacrifice a man could make. He sold the Chev! There was still a waiting list for imported cars and for the new Australian-made Holden, so the Chev was easily sold and replaced by a dark blue 1949 Ford Prefect, which was a 'huge come-down' for the family.

Don was determined to pay cash for their house as he wanted to be self-sufficient in his affairs and never impose a burden on the children. (He and Bey made regular payments to their mother until Kay's death in 1951.) Don and Thelma soon found a small three-bedroom house at 39 Loftus Street, Claremont, which was of weatherboard with an iron roof and reminded them of Lake Violet, with jarrah wood panelling in the entrance and sitting room. The house had been owned by 'Thompson the builder', who had used it as his base, with a storage shed and office in the backyard. Don was pleased to have a workshop and his own office, with settlement taking place on 2 August 1951 for £3,500.

They wanted a separate dining room and used a front bedroom for the purpose, then built on a large extra room for the boys and a back verandah to shade the house. New furniture had to be bought as the station provided so much in the past. Thompson was a builder but no gardener and Thelma immediately set about planting flowers and shrubs at the front of the house and some vegetables in the back yard, with George Rose's vegetable patch being a source of inspiration: 'At last I will be able to grow apple cucumbers, after putting up with the Wiluna heat for all those years.'

39 Loftus Street, Claremont, 1950s

Don's budget precluded any long holiday between jobs so he was soon at work for Goldsbroughs as a pastoral inspector, being presented with an 'L Series' heavy-duty International ute, describing it as: 'a fuel guzzling cow of a thing to drive'. It was a good time to be working for one of the pastoral houses. Wool was in keen demand during the 1949–53 Korean War, being in a cold part of the world and military uniforms still made with wool. The early 1950s was one of those rare times in Australian agricultural history when debt could be repaid, those who wanted to retire did so with dignity and property build-up could take place. Instead of doing battle with 'welded on' debt-laden clients, the emphasis was now on growing market share and providing good service to those already on the books.

Just as Don and Thelma had provided a bed for pastoral inspectors, such as 'Tommy' Thompson and 'Shally' Shallcross, now it was Don's turn to be on the receiving end. He was well known through much of the station country, largely through cricket, not to mention marrying into the Rose family, so found the job was better than he had hoped for.

It's timely to reflect on the importance of wool in those times. The shilling piece, or 'bob', depicted the Uardry ram 101 on the reverse side from 1938 to 1963, and postage stamps had the image of a Merino sheep from time to time. Australia 'riding on the sheep's back' was not too far short of the mark. Farmers equate the price of wool to the number of bales you would need to buy a Holden ute, with the FJ in 1951 costing £750, so two 400-pound bales at a 'pound a pound' would be the starting point. The last of the Holden utes being produced in 2016 at $32,000 for the base model would need 20 bales, with average-styled wool selling for 900c per kilogram in a similar weight bale.

Goldsbroughs' head office was in St Georges Terrace, opposite Newspaper House and next to Foy & Gibson's department store. Don soon became friendly with stock manager Malcolm 'Mac' McLennan, merchandise manager Darby Clifton, Jack Lanyon, Fred Daw and Evan Cresswell, as well as renewing contact with his old cricketing mate, state manager Fred Waldeck. Phil Cullingworth had managed Pardoo (on the coast north of Port Hedland) for the Thompson family and also moved south for health reasons, joining Goldsbroughs at the same time as Don, so they had a lot in common. To have a career with one of the pastoral houses was still viewed very favourably in the social 'pecking order' of the time.

Don eventually persuaded the firm to replace the truck-like International ute with a Holden FJ, so country trips were a lot easier. The downside of the job was extended trips away from home, leaving Thelma alone with the children. He enjoyed the wool sales and meeting clients while in Perth, though some might have been disappointed at his modest drinking habits! A highlight was the Perth Royal Show, when rams would come over from the Riverina and South Australia and shedded at Booths in Fremantle prior to the sales, a good meeting place to mix with stud people and clients in a less formal environment.

The Campbell family was completed on 13 December 1953 with the birth of Elizabeth Rose. She was the only one born in Perth and an important part of the Loftus Street story, firstly as the new baby who everyone doted on but later giving back so much to the family.

In 1954 Alex started at Christ Church Grammar School, followed by Tim in 1957 (Sue and Liz attended St Hilda's in their senior school years). One has to marvel at Don's financial management on a modest salary. Thelma had a fixed weekly housekeeping account which she managed very carefully, with any surplus put aside until she could afford a little treat: usually a piece of china – Spode, Crown Derby or Wedgewood. Don had a carefully prepared budget showing utility charges, vehicle expenses, clothing and so on, and now school fees. He was very frugal on his own account, hardly ever buying new clothing for himself and a modest supply of pipe tobacco being his only indulgence.

As an example of Don's honesty and lack of salesmanship, there's the story of a station sale near Meekatharra when in his final year at Goldsbroughs. Jim Cunningham had come across from Wentworth in New South Wales and was showing interest in the place, so was driven out for an inspection. It's a long return trip from Perth to Meekatharra and they got to know each other quite well. As they neared Perth on the way back, Don said: 'Jim, I think I've got to know you well enough to suggest you forget about stations and look at some farms down south. Anyhow, I think the Eastern Goldfields has seen its better days and farming is the future.'

And that was in 1955! Jim has often quoted the yarn and he and Rosie became very successful Cranbrook farmers, before handing over to son Twynam and retiring to Albany.

A fortunate turn of events brought Don's time at Goldsbroughs to an end in 1955. Ian Thom had built up a diversified pastoral/farming enterprise that comprised Wydgee and Yoweragabbie at Mount Magnet with a combined 750,000 acres, running around 26,000 sheep depending on seasons, and Mungaterra at Mingenew of 6,000 acres, carrying 4,000 sheep and 50 breeders. Yoweragabbie was on the Mullewa–Mount Magnet railway line with its own siding, providing for easy railing of stock. The arrangement allowed for the farm to take surplus stock from the stations and finish them off for the local market, while the farm could also provide oats and hay to the stations in times of drought.

Ian had also taken the lease of Yanchep Estate, a 23,000-acre holding with 12 miles of ocean frontage, adjoining the Yanchep National Park. In 1955 the lease had one year to run and the property was listed for sale. Ian had considered buying it himself, but it was time for the family to move on, so the three properties together with the Yanchep lease were put on the market.[151] The complete package was bought by Pastoral Development Holdings Ltd, with George Henderson as managing director, while all the company's other interests were in Queensland and New South Wales. On completing the sale, George asked Ian if he could recommend somebody to manage the WA amalgamation: 'You couldn't do better than Don Campbell.'

The Thoms' example of pastoral families purchasing farms was typical throughout Western Australia: sometimes it was for 'drought-proofing' and finishing off stock for market, at other times to allow a parent or extra son to leave the station. It was the wealth generated by the stations that allowed for the purchase of the 'side enterprise', which had been going on for 50 years or so. The Hardie, Thompson and Anderson families at Broomehill would be three examples that come to mind. Little did they know that within a generation or two it would be the 'side enterprise' generating the wealth and carrying the stations.

The following year in 1956, Pastoral Development Holdings (now trading in WA as Wydgee Past Co) finalised the purchase of Yanchep Estate from 80-year-old, the Honourable Mary Lindsay. She was a somewhat eccentric woman who, when on a world tour in the 1920s, bought the undeveloped land from the Midland Railway Company and built a homestead behind the first sand hill from the water's edge. She lived a lonely existence, scattering seeds about to contain the shifting sand dunes and to provide some grazing for animals. The army used much of the area as a firing range for many years so there was only limited development when bought in 1956.[152] The use of trace elements was only just being understood, with animals suffering 'coastal disease' if grazed in the area for extended periods.

Don set up his office at Loftus Street for the new job and appointed managers on the four properties: Roger Fraser at Wydgee; Jim Leeds at Yoweragabbie; Jim McAuliff at Mungaterra; and Syd Yeo at Yanchep. (The two Jims had managed for Ian Thom, Syd was an old acquaintance from Depot Springs near Sandstone and Roger had come from Queensland, as part of a company promotion scheme.) The arrangement was for Don to do the bookwork, pay the wages and take care of administration matters and for the property managers to undertake the day-to-day running of the stations.

A monthly trip of a week or so allowed him to oversee the whole operation. The two Mount Magnet stations were straightforward for Don as he had been in that sort of country all his life. Being developed well before Lake Violet, the extra consideration was ageing infrastructure, with fences and waters needing major maintenance or replacement. Declining wool prices and lower carrying capacity couldn't justify replacement so it was a case of 'patching up' and, in some cases, closing down waters or 'letting a fence line go'. The farm at Mingenew continued with the same management, so presented few challenges, and was heavy 'old country', with considerable water erosion/gullying, lending itself more to grazing than cropping.

Typical watering point, Wydgee, 1950s

The real challenge was Yanchep. It was largely undeveloped and, being the largest capital investment, warranted most of Don's attention. Before the war of 1939–45, most of WA's farming development had concentrated on the heavy soils of the ancient inland river systems of Gondwana-land, now reduced to chains of salt lakes. The lighter coastal and mallee soils had been considered worthless and unproductive, so were unoccupied. Rock phosphate had been used since 1905, superphosphate 25 years later and the big breakthrough in the 1950s was the use of trace elements, initially cobalt, copper and zinc, and later on, molybdenum.

Pioneering work by Dr H.W. Bennetts in the 1930s had concentrated on animal health and nutrition, but post-war WA was at the forefront of trace element use for crops and pastures. Don attended field days and read Ag Dept publications, with people such as Noel Fitzpatrick, Mike Carroll, Tom Smith, Jack Toms and George Burvill all becoming known to him (Fitzpatrick and Carroll went on to be successful directors general of the department). Professor of Agriculture at the University of Western Australia, Eric Underwood, was undertaking valuable related research and was well regarded by Don.[153] Most of these men had BSc (Ag.) degrees from UWA.

Don also attended Ag Dept field days related to light land farming and always planned his Mingenew trips to coincide with Eric Smart's private field days. Eric had come to WA from Jamestown in South Australia with £200 and 'a bucketful of ambition' in 1935, then share farmed at Watheroo before purchasing Erregulla Springs at Mingenew in 1949. By 1955, the farm comprised 80,000 acres and employed 120 staff and share farmers, producing 8,000 tons of wheat and more than 1,000 bales of wool.

Smart pioneered a two-stage approach to developing light land, being initial fertility build-up with New Zealand bitter blue lupins and trace element-boosted superphosphate, before a secondary fertility phase using subterranean clovers and cropping rotations.[154] For many years the Ag Dept was opposed to the two-stage approach, but in Don's opinion: 'You have to hand it to Eric – he puts his money where his mouth is – and one look at Erregulla Springs shows he's doing something right.'

In today's jargon, Don would be termed an early adopter, rather than an innovator. After weighing up the best of Eric Smart's ideas, together with recommendations from the Ag Dept, he set about developing Yanchep Estate. Considerable fencing was required to protect the sand dunes from grazing, then strategic clearing of the more fertile inter-dune flats. Blue lupins were used extensively, requiring careful management to avoid lupinosis from the *Phomopis* toxin. With stock still consuming some native vegetation, cobalt, copper and zinc were added to the water points (all being tanks and troughs from bores as no dam sites were available) and care was needed to not over administer the trace elements.

Being schooled through the depression and war, Don was very careful about capital outlays on plant and equipment – no doubt a frustration to the property managers. He kept his Holden utes for 100,000 miles and expected his managers to do likewise, though good use was made of ex-army jeeps, while mustering at Yanchep was still done on horseback to cope with the crossing of sand hills.

All the major development of clearing, seeding, fencing and so on was done by contract: 'that way you can budget ahead and see just where your money's going'. Development work in the 1950s and '60s was greatly encouraged by full tax write-off in the year of expenditure and a generous subsidy of $12 per ton for superphosphate. Super was supplied in jute sacks, 12 to the ton, and the standard application rate was 'a bag to the acre'.

Cleared and pastured areas steadily increased to around one-third developed and two-thirds retained as protected sand hills or shade and shelterbelts. Sheep and cattle were run at conservative stocking of 3 DSEs (dry sheep equivalents per acre) on improved pastures, with Yanchep Estate reaching more than 20,000 DSEs in due course. Don attended sheep and cattle sales at Midland, being particularly pleased when Yanchep stock topped the market from time to time.

Family life was settling down to a comfortable routine. Thelma didn't know whether to be pleased or sad when Liz went to school for the first time in 1959, leaving her at home without children during the day for the first time in 20 years of marriage. Most weekends found Don either at the WACA watching cricket or on the grassy hill at Claremont Oval watching football, often accompanied by a half-interested son or, to his delight, a totally interested daughter. Sue really loved an afternoon at the footy! Social life revolved mainly around family and ex-station people. 'A girl marries a man – a man marries a family' was certainly a truism for the Campbells. All Don's relatives were in South Australia or New South Wales, whereas 'you couldn't shake a tree without a Rose falling out' applied to Thelma. There always seemed to be a Rose, Henwood or Shields holidaying (or later living) in Perth, not to mention cousins and extended family.

The Nor-West cricket matches at the WACA were great social occasions and Thelma particularly enjoyed catching up with her old Wiluna friends as well as other station people. Don was able to relive some of the cricket highlights of his younger days, catching up with his old team mates, while the older children also made the most of the occasion. It was only after they had left the pastoral country that they realised the strong common bond between station people – developed by the shared experiences of isolation, self-reliance and relentless hard work – that forged a mutual unspoken empathy for each other.

Cattle at water, Yanchep Estate, 1958

Meanwhile, Don had traded in the FJ ute at 100,000 miles and taken delivery of a pale green FE model, with the optional extra of a radio! There was nothing he enjoyed more than driving in the country at 50mph, pipe in mouth and listening to Ron Halcombe covering a Sheffield Shield or Test match:

'There's no doubt about these car wirelesses – you get to Wydgee before you know you've left home.'

The Frasers left Wydgee to further their careers back in the eastern states and were replaced by Bob Scott, a sheep station acquaintance of Don's. Syd Yeo also 'hung up his boots' and was replaced by Cecil 'Tiddles' Cockman at Yanchep. (Tiddles gained his nickname because he 'tiddled' his pants as a boy!) The Cockmans were early settlers in the Wanneroo district, Tiddles had friends and connections all over the place and it was never a problem finding a few shearers or contractors for farm development work once he was in charge.

There was a final challenge for Don at Yanchep when it was decided to undertake a beach development of 103 housing lots. Peet & Co were appointed to assist with the planning then to be the selling agents. By today's standards, the approval process was less complex but nevertheless required 'doing battle' with local government, utility providers, road builders and environmental agencies. It was very frustrating for a man from the bush: 'All the bureaucrats in creation have nothing better to do than dream up ways of holding things up.'

Perseverance paid off and in the early 1960s brochures were promoting 'Yanchep Beach Estate – 99 blocks with £5 deposit and 6 per cent reducible interest – bitumen roads to all lots'. Prices ranged from £370 to £750 for quarter-acre blocks, 'with all measurements in links', while four other blocks were set aside as public open space. Sales progressed steadily and with discounts offered for early home building, it wasn't long before people were living there.[155]

Don only had both boys together at Christ Church for two years, which stretched the budget. With a five-year gap to each of the girls, there was then only one school fee per year, being some benefit to a drawn-out family.[156] With the double school fees behind him, Don purchased an EK Holden in 1961 to replace the Ford Prefect, 10 years after having sold the Chev. He was also able to undertake maintenance to the house and had it painted inside and out, with the weatherboards restained in dark oil, the roof painted green and other woodwork in cream. New canvas blinds of yellow and white stripes were used on the front verandah.

The 1960s were difficult times for Australian agriculture. Wool was being challenged by synthetic fibres and manufacturing industries were being protected by high tariffs, raising the cost of inputs for farming. The Pastoral Development Company had expanded into WA on the promise of 1950s wool prices, with financial backing of Dalgety NZ, and now pressure was building on servicing the debt. Don's salary remained unchanged for nine consecutive years as he could obviously 'read the tea leaves' and led from the front in not seeking an increase.

It all came to a head in 1966, with the WA properties being 'sold' to Dalgetys, no doubt to relieve the pressure on the core interests in Queensland and NSW. Don continued to manage for Dalgetys, his main task being selling off individual properties as the market permitted. The two stations then Mungaterra at Mingenew were sold, leaving Yanchep as the final asset. Perth's urbanisation was spreading northwards up the coast, with Wanneroo market gardens slowly being lost to housing. Yanchep was being seen more as outer metropolitan than rural and the 100-lot Yanchep Estate development proved that people were interested in living that far from the city.

Alan Bond was not a man to miss an opportunity! He purchased Yanchep Estate in 1967 with grand visions of urban development along the 20 kilometres of coastline and asked Don to stay on as manager of the farm, which lasted for only a year:

'Alan Bond has different ideas to me on just about everything, so I'll do us both a favour and get out of his way.'

In the 1960s Bond was still 'on the make', largely through property development, and became one of Australia's most prominent businesspeople, attracting numerous investors to his companies. It would be some years before his America's Cup victory, forays into brewing and van Gogh art purchases, not to mention taking on Kerry Packer over the Channel Nine Network. (Packer reputedly sold for $1.05 billion and bought back three years later for $250 million, saying 'you only get one Alan Bond in your lifetime and I've had mine'.) But just as pastoral empires came and went, Bond 'went' in grand style in 1992, being declared bankrupt with a debt of $1.8 billion and serving time in prison.[157]

Don spent the last two and a half years of his working life with Dalgety NZ in their wool department, from 1968 to 1971. It was a client relationship role, checking on sale rosters and clip presentations, taking clients around the wool stores and showing them their clips presented for sale, then attending the auction days with the drinks and nibbles to follow.

There was one event that particularly appealed to Don in his retirement years: the landing on the moon by Neil Armstrong and Buzz Aldrin in July 1969. Don had started his life on horseback, marvelled at driving a 1920s Chev Four truck, been fascinated by the first aircraft flights, enjoyed the early 6-volt cabinet wireless and here he was sitting at home, watching those memorable first footsteps on the moon on his own TV. Without doubt, Don's generation experienced more profound change than any that preceded it – or any to follow?

His final capital purchase was a six-cylinder 1976 Mark III Ford Cortina with a vinyl roof, 'four on the floor' and a radio! Don enjoyed 16 years of retirement from 1971 to 1987 and, with Tim's help, installed air conditioning in the house. Thelma accepted a hand-me-down washing machine from Jocelyn Thom, having done washing by hand and lighting a wood-fuelled copper every Monday of the year. Many of their station friends were getting on in years or 'falling off the perch', so social life became more centred on family and grandchildren. Don was able to enjoy seeing his grandchildren Anna and Jock, Sophie and Becky, Louise and Annie, and Sally arrive in those years. (He missed out on seeing Jillie by four years.)

The many years of comfort and enjoyment from his pipe were taking a toll and the debilitating effects of emphysema started to impact on his life. An open wood fire in the sitting room and a cricket match on the television became his main enjoyment, and he was particularly interested in the outstanding careers of 'the two local boys', Rod Marsh and Dennis Lillee.

After a short illness, Don died on 29 March 1987. He was able to move on with the knowledge 'that he had a good innings': his four children were well established; Thelma was left with a modest and adequate income for her final days; and the pastoral and farming industries had benefited greatly from his tireless efforts over 45 years. Perhaps his life is best summed up by his old school and cricketing mate Ron Halcombe:

> I have always believed that up on that final grandstand, there is a section reserved for sportsmen who played well on the field and off, and I believe that is where Don is. He would have been given a warm welcome, and some may have had to move a bit so he could see what was going on, and I would be surprised if some of his cronies didn't buy him a drink.[158]

Thelma stayed on at Loftus Street until 1990 before moving into a unit at the Salvation Army's Hollywood Retirement Village. Once again, she built a little garden, had many years of enjoying her family and grandchildren, and put up with the sale of the village to a Macquarie Bank entity and the resulting decline in care, with good grace. She enjoyed a hand of bridge or a game of Scrabble into her 90s and, after a year or two of increasing dementia, died peacefully on 27 November 2010, aged 93.

Thelma is yet another woman in the Campbell story who deserves the highest praise for her contribution to future generations. A young woman who dreamed of being a journalist and loved the Perth social life, then went to live on an isolated station and raise four children on modest means, is a tribute to her character and selfless love. There can be no greater reward for a mother than to be remembered with love and gratitude by her four children and eight grandchildren.

Rest in peace. A life well lived.

PART TWO

A PRODUCT OF THE MENZIES ERA

You're braver than you believe, and stronger than you seem, and smarter than you think.
Christopher Robin to Pooh, A.A. Milne

The great vice of democracy is that we have been busy getting ourselves on to the list of beneficiaries and removing ourselves from the list of contributors, as if somewhere there was somebody else's effort on which we could thrive.
Sir Robert Menzies

11 Lake Violet, Through a Boy's Prism

I was born on 4 August 1941 and shortly afterwards christened Alexander David Campbell. My two Godmothers, Aunty Syb and Aunty Kay, both gave me solid silver napkin rings elaborately inscribed 'ADC'. Even though one was bought at Levinson's in Perth and the other at Sheppard's in Adelaide, by good chance they were a matching pair.

Sticking with the adage, 'it's 20 per cent breeding and 80 per cent feeding', I can only say I was raised in a very special paddock. Feed was short at times and I was quickly taught the art of selective grazing. The gate was left ajar and I could explore wider pastures, but always with the security of the home paddock and knowing what was expected of me if venturing further afield. Let me explain …

Lake Violet, 35 miles east of Wiluna, might have seemed isolated to most people, but if it's all you've known, isn't that how everybody grows up?

My earliest memories are of the enormity of my surrounds: the homestead and verandahs went on forever and it was easy to get lost; the sheds and quarters seemed miles away; and the garden offered a huge opportunity for hide and seek and other games. There was Jack O'Keefe, the seemingly very old yardman/gardener, a very tall Uncle Pat (overseer) and kind Aunty Rie, and several bossy governesses. Daisy was the Aboriginal house girl and she belonged to Peter. I have vague memories of the blackfella camp and many dogs, but not of any children. My only recollection is going on bushwalks with Daisy and Peter, when they would point to various plants and animal tracks with brief comments, such as: ''im good fella, 'im proper bad fella.'

As I grew older, I remember going on mill runs with Dad, usually standing up beside him on the seat of the Ford ute for a better view. It was a sense of responsibility to help clean the water troughs, but very concerning if he went up the tower to service the mill or down the well to check on the pump. There was a regular trip to the out-camp taking supplies to Dan Jones, who was a short 'bent over' man with lots of old pushbikes around the place. He had a few dogs for company and, most intriguingly, a pet carpet snake in the mud brick chimneystack!

Mum seldom left the house and garden, but obviously enjoyed getting dressed up for trips to town and outings to neighbouring stations. I was relying on my brother Tim for company and still remember how awkward I felt when sent outside to play with other children on our occasional social visits. Trips to town were more enjoyable, with the treat of an ice cream served from a green canvas bag of dry ice. The day always included time at the Club Hotel, with the women and children gathering in the cool confines of the Ladies Lounge, while the men did their business around town, before joining them for lunch in the hotel dining room.

We often had an evening meal with the Carrolls before heading home in the dark. The only memory I have of mine manager Bert 'Bull' Carroll is of a rather large man sitting back in a huge leather armchair, with an elaborate chrome ashtray and cigarette holder on a stand by his side. (Dad always smoked a pipe so I was interested in the cigarette procedure.) There are memories of Dad playing cricket on the grassed Wiluna Oval, with all the men dressed in white and the women and children under shady trees drinking either iced tea or ginger beer. Mixing with other children was not enjoyed and those days seemed to drag on forever.

I recall coming home from visiting the Mitchells at Granite Peak in the Ford ute and finding a group of blackfellas at one of the many gates that needed opening. They requested – almost demanded – a lift by sign language, which caused some discomfort to Mum. I spent the trip home looking at them through the back window of the ute, while she looked steadfastly straight ahead. They were apparently 'just in from the desert', with little or no English, not to mention clothes. Dad's main concern was trouble that might be caused when they were dropped off at the Lake Violet camp.

There was a more startling occasion when Daisy walked into the kitchen one morning with blood pouring from an open wound on the top of her head. Apparently Peter had taken to her with a lump of mulga (and that was before alcohol was available). Mum was in a flurry and called out for Dad to ring the police and get the ute ready for a trip to the Wiluna Hospital. Meanwhile, Daisy was mumbling: 'Peter orright – 'im good fella.'

Dad appeared and said: 'Let them sort things out their own way – we'll patch her up and see how she looks in a day or two.' Daisy patched up remarkably well, especially when she was able to sit by the wood stove for several wintery days without any chores. Peter was regarded with deep suspicion by Mum until we left the station and it took a week or so for things to get back to normal, both inside the homestead and out in the camp.

I can't remember either Mum or Dad ever referring to Aboriginals as other than 'blacks' or 'blackfellas' – other, cruder names were never used. Equally, Dad never swore in front of women or we children (in fact I doubt he ever swore, even if on his own?) General annoyance and frustration would bring forth 'curse it all'; 'bally fool of a thing'; 'I'll be blowed, what have I done to deserve that?'; 'deuce it all'; 'confounded thing'; 'son of a gun'. Severe provocation: *'blast and damnation'*.

Among the stations we visited were the Lukins at Lake Way, the Folvigs at Yeelirrie, the Adamsons at Yakabindie and the Howards at Albion Downs. A trip to Barwidgee was always appreciated, for Len and Hillary Bilston had no children of their own and always doted on any who visited. An absolute highlight was an overnight stay with the Wards at Millrose, when Tim and I were dropped off while Mum and Dad went on to Granite Peak for some party or other. The Wards made a great fuss of us and we were most impressed with the line-up of Rosella Tomato Sauce, Rosella Green Pickles and Holbrooks Worcestershire Sauce on the table! Dad was very spartan in that respect, even though he drowned his food with salt, then sugar on all puddings. 'Your mother's good cooking needs no other adornment.'

As with all stations, many visitors came and went, including relatives and friends such as Aunty Syb, Marg Monger, Peter Atkins, Ron Halcombe and Aunty Grace, but also stock firm and other business people. As a boy, these visits were tolerated as best as possible but I always looked forward to things getting back to normal.

The big cabinet wireless with attached car battery was a great source of entertainment to Mum and Dad. They had been given a pair of wireless chairs for a wedding present and would sit and listen to the ABC news, cricket, or *Blue Hills*. There would always be a cup of tea on hand, a pipe for Dad and an odd sweet or chocolate for Mum, and I have no memories of any children's programs. The wireless was used sparingly and required the full attention of listeners.

Alex with a 'road train' of toys in front of the Lake Violet meat house. Note Mum's 'splash of colour' Vincas

I clearly recall shearing. Tim and I would be taken to the woolshed as we got older, with firm instructions: 'Keep out of everyone's way and don't make a nuisance of yourselves, or you'll soon get a clip under the ear.'

The novelty of the shed in full swing aroused all our senses with the smell, sounds and visual activity. I was particularly intrigued by the wool presser as he stamped the wool in two wooden boxes, then pulled one above the other, the contents being compressed into a jute bale by heaving down on a long metal lever operating the ratchet and wire rope. The classer in his white apron had such nimble fingers and we could hear the 'snap-snap' of testing a wool staple for strength. The shearers and roustabouts all operated like clockwork: the whir of the handpieces, supported by the rhythmic 'pop-pop-pop' of the Lister engine, and the smell of sheep urine and manure, lanoline in the wool and sweat of the men, completed the sensory medley. As a reward for good behaviour, we could apply the blackening for the Lake Violet stencil on a wool bale.

Perhaps the fondest and most lasting memories are of Mum's valiant efforts to educate Tim and me, not only in school work but also the finer things of life. Mum read to us as we were put to bed: Beatrix Potter's many illustrated stories of Peter Rabbit, May Gibbs' *Snuggle Pot and Cuddle Pie* and A.A. Milne's

Christopher Robin, to name but a few – the exploits of Alexander beetle was a favourite! Sunday's readings were from a children's Bible with black and white illustrations and, whether Milne or the Bible, Mum used to make the stories virtually come to life. There was a final little prayer before the lights were turned off: 'Gentle Jesus, meek and mild, look upon this little child. Bless Mum and Dad, Alex and Tim ...'

Neither Mum nor Dad could sing in tune to save themselves, but they did their best to introduce us to 'God Save the King', 'Jingle Bells' (and other carols) as well as 'Onward Christian Soldiers', when we could stamp around the room in military-like time. Dad for his part would recite Banjo Paterson's poems while doing the mill rounds.

Discipline was quite fair and very predictable. Dad was the main person to watch for and if you crossed the line, he would briefly say: 'You were told not to ...' WHACK.

There was no thought of coming up with a mitigating excuse and a very firm hand on the seat of your pants or the back of bare legs left no doubt as to the boundary you were not to cross. Mum was a lot softer but in sheer desperation would resort to a large wooden spoon. If she came from the kitchen to the school room with the large spoon in hand, she had your undivided attention.

Holidays were few and far between, with vague recollections of trips to Perth and staying with grandparents and Aunty Syb at Wingfield in Albert Street, Claremont. Gran and Syb Rose thoroughly spoilt all their grandchildren, nieces and nephews, so there are only happy memories. The trip to Adelaide by train from Kalgoorlie is more vivid and less happy. Gran Campbell seemed very stern and ruled her large darkened house with authority, while Aunty Kay in her wheelchair was the only bright relief as, when on her own, she gave you her complete attention. The Adelaide trip was organised so that my crossed eyes might be straightened by a Dr Black and my clear memory to this day is the utterly sickening experience of chloroform anaesthetic. The operation was unsuccessful.

Late in our time at the station, we boys had our peaceful lives turned upside down by the arrival of Sue, as if from nowhere. We were no longer the centre of the universe! She being five years younger than Tim, we boys could still play outside without competition, but once inside we were very aware of Sue's presence and the resulting demand of Mum's time.

Formal education was by correspondence, with weekly lessons and marked work coming back by return mail. It must have been absolute torment for Mum and the other station women, doing their best in the classroom as well as running a large homestead and garden. Mum had dreamt of becoming a journalist so she encouraged us to write stories or essays, forgiving of spelling though very particular about punctuation: 'Spelling will come later, but write with the same pauses and exclamations as though you are speaking to somebody.'

Spelling didn't come later, but I think most of the rest must've sunk in. There were two or three governesses who came and went fairly quickly, as the isolation and lack of social activity was not the thing for a young, single woman. On another occasion a cook was taken on but her interest in sweet sherry exceeded that of her cooking!

For most of my time at Lake Violet, there was only Mum and Daisy in the house and Jack O'Keefe, with occasional reluctant assistance from Peter, in the garden. Dad had various station hands or overseers (including Uncle Pat), with Dan Jones always at the out-camp and a group of black stockmen who came and went with the seasons. It was a small, orderly world, halfway between Wiluna and the edge of the desert. Such are the memories of a boy through to 10 years of age, happy and carefree times and, to my parents' credit, with no inkling of Mum's loneliness or Dad's pressure of work. This was to change in 1951 with the decision to leave Lake Violet and move to Perth.

As a boy, I detected the mixed emotions of this big event, with tears from Mum and long periods of silence from Dad. I still recall the final departure in the Chev and we children in the back seat were unusually quiet as the emotions from the front seat swept over us. All of a sudden, for the first time, the future was filled with uncertainty and unanswered questions.

12 THE PERTH SCHOOLBOY

On arrival in Perth, we settled in with the Rose family at 3 Albert Street, Claremont. Mum and Dad were busy looking for a house and making other arrangements, so we children were left with Aunty Syb and the grandparents. We quickly started to sum up the strange new ways of city life – and how different it was!

Milk was left at the back door in pint glass bottles while we slept; the morning paper was thrown over the fence; the baker brought a cane basket of bread to the back door, while on the street his horse kept moving, keeping pace with his deliveries; the rubbish man ran into the backyard and emptied the galvanised rubbish bin once a week (and was always left a bottle of beer at Christmas time); the 'bottle-o' came every week or so; the post boy delivered mail twice a day and blew his whistle when leaving any letters; and the telegram boy would come to the front door. Over the road, children at St Louis school were all dressed in uniform and responded to the ringing of a bell. A trip to Perth with Aunty Syb in the trolley bus meant dressing up and putting on our best manners.

Grandfather Rose turned 90 the year we moved to Perth and quickly recruited a pair of willing hands to help him in the garden! Wingfield was half an acre of mainly vegetable garden, fruit trees and a chook yard. He established a routine of jobs that was to last for six years: pruning the Muscatel grape vines and putting brown paper bags over the ripening bunches; picking the figs as they ripened; cutting lucerne for the chook feed; and digging in the vegetable garden. He had a three-legged stool that he carted around the garden and would point with his walking stick: 'Dig deeper boy – cut the lucerne closer to the ground – that bunch up there boy.'

Tim and I enjoyed walking to Swanbourne with him and carrying the shopping home. He had the same procedure in the shops: at the butcher he would poke a side of mutton with the walking stick, 'Take the leg off there'; and at the greengrocers, 'Not that cabbage, the one behind'. At the store he would watch the scales carefully as sugar, flour and other items were weighed into brown paper bags. The reward for our efforts (and patience with his slow walking gait) was an ice cream.

He had two procedures that were of great interest. A clucky chook would be put under a box covered with several jute sacks, then left without food for three days in total darkness. After the third day, a bewildered chook would appear and stagger around the yard – but not clucky. His other intrigue was to direct we boys to capture a bee in the flower of an Apple Blossom Hibiscus and open it onto his arm so the bee might sting him. After up to six stings at a time, he would say: 'That's fixed the rheumatism for another day or two.'

He had a favourite saying that would come forth for no apparent reason: 'There we go, there we go, now we stop still.'

He read the newspaper every morning, ate at least three eggs a day, loved butter and cream and had a stiff medicinal brandy before retiring. A truly remarkable man and what a wonderful grandfather for a shy boy from the bush.

One day Aunty Syb took me two doors up the street to meet a boy of my age who had come down from Malaya in 1948. Derry Macqueen was also finding his way in a big new world and even though we went to different primary schools, we kept in touch as I regularly attended grandfather's garden. I remember we had one thing in common. He had a large Meccano set of shining red and green parts and Tim and I were given an even larger set of much-used pieces, handed down from the Monger boys. If we combined our stock, we could construct just about anything. His father had been managing a rubber plantation and they had to leave Malaya at the time of the communist insurgency.[1]

Meanwhile, Mum and Dad had found a house, furniture was taken out of storage and we moved to 39 Loftus Street at the end of August in 1951. Albert Street had seemed small after Lake Violet; Loftus Street seemed smaller still as it had only three bedrooms, one bathroom and virtually no garden, but a large Peppermint and a Japanese Pepper tree were good for climbing.

Of more immediate concern, Tim and I were sent off to the East Claremont Practising School – 'The Prac'. We were dressed in shoes and socks, with lunch packed in a little Mills and Wares brown suitcase (from a Royal Show biscuit bag), and delivered to the headmaster's office. He chatted for a while to Mum then sent her off and ushered us to our respective classrooms. Mr Baker was in charge of the combined sixth and seventh grades and had 39 children well organised and under his control. I was told to put my hand up if I had a question and to always call him 'Sir'. The school work was fairly straightforward so Mum's perseverance with correspondence must have paid off.

The social side was another matter as there seemed to be a bewildering number of children, being around 200 in all.[2] Tim and I would seek each other out at lunch and play breaks and we both looked about carefully to work out how we could fit in. A girl in my class took me under her wing (I think her name was Margaret Jones), probably instructed by Mr Baker to 'show me the ropes'. I quickly worked out the tough boys, such as Doug Rowe, went barefooted so I would take my shoes and socks off after leaving home. I lost a lot of marbles to the local 'champs' to start with, but learnt that being a good sport in handing over your prized possessions was the way to get on.

The daily one-third of a pint of free milk was much enjoyed in winter, although a little warm and sickly in summer. To be on inkwell roster was of great importance, but to have a role at school assembly was almost too difficult to consider. Parents were never seen at school unless collecting a sick child or taking one off to the dentist.

For the two and a half years I attended The Prac, it was used as the experimental school for new teaching methods rather than as a practising school for new teachers. Probably because of this, headmasters rotated through on an annual basis: Mr Peterson in 1951, Mr Norham in 1952 and Mr Pirett in 1953. The one constant teacher was Mr Jim Mews in the rural school – the one-teacher, stand-alone building – teaching children from grades one to seven. He was a brilliant teacher and was well liked and respected by all who knew him. In 1954 the school reverted to its role as a practising school. My memories of the The Prac in the early 1950s are confirmed by the official attendance records as, almost without exception, all the kids were of Anglo background.[3]

None of the children wore hats. Games such as 'brandy' and 'dodgem' were played on bitumen or dirt, as the only grassed area was the oval over the road, used for sport. The boys made little boats by joining several foil milk bottletops together, then raced them down the gutters after winter rains. I slowly got to know other boys, such as Dick and Norm Sudlow, Ted and Den Culley, Doug Rowe and Peter Ellis, who have remained friends to this day. After the first week or two, Tim and I rode our bikes to school: 'Always hop off and walk across the highway – don't risk getting hit by a car.'

Social life in Perth was somewhat limited as Dad was away from home a lot with his Goldsbroughs job. Mum used to catch up with station women, such as Jocelyn Thom, Mim Lukin, Alice Adamson and Hope Hancock, as well as Mary McLennan, Molly Cresswell and Claris Cullingworth from Goldsbroughs. For afternoon teas, Mum would prepare apple cucumber or sheeps' brains and crushed walnut sandwiches, with the crusts cut off (which we children would devour), and small meringues with fresh cream.

There were also various country relatives who were at boarding school or holidaying in Perth, while Dad always enjoyed an afternoon at the cricket or football. Highlights were occasional Sundays and most Christmases, with Rupert and Kitty Monger and any of their older family who might be at home: Marg, Adrian, Peter or Henry. They had a large comfortable home in McNeill Street, Peppermint Grove, with a grass tennis court. Rupert had owned the stock and station agency in Derby for many years and became very friendly with all the Rose family. There was a great collection of toys and games we could use, such as the Meccano set and two canoes that were given to us.

Mum had missed the contact of church and religion while on the station, and took to the local St Andrew's Anglican Church on the corner of Napier Street and Stirling Highway with gusto. Dad attended on most Sundays if at home, though I think rather under sufferance, and we children were sent off to Sunday School – definitely under sufferance. Canon Brown, the rector, had jackerooed on a Mount Magnet station in his youth so had a bit in common with Dad. We were all confirmed there at the appropriate time and I was prevailed upon to serve at the altar for communion services. One hot summer's day, dressed in cassock, I fainted in front of the altar. I don't know if Mum thought I had been called by God or was about to die, but I never had to front up again for the job. To Tim's great relief, he was spared his turn at being altar boy.

In my last year at The Prac, I was bundled off to St John of God Hospital for a second eye operation, undertaken by Professor Ida Mann. She successfully straightened the eyes but, after 12 years, I had permanently lost the sight of the right eye, other than peripheral vision. With no straight-ahead vision in that eye, I developed the habit of always having my head turned a little to the left so that my line of sight could cover the right.

Liz was born on 13 December 1953 and Tim and I were better prepared for her arrival than we had been for Sue, as we were now aware of how these things happened! Dad and Aunty Syb had been exhorting the three of us: 'Let your Mum have a rest. It's a big thing having another baby at her age. You'll all have to be very good and help look after the new baby.'

We took to our new little sister in our stride and had fun helping to look after her – the only downside was fitting all six of us into the Ford Prefect.

Meanwhile, largely through Mum's valiant efforts, Loftus Street had been transformed from a bare weatherboard cottage into a comfortable home. A large boys' bedroom and back verandah had been added, with cheerful yellow and white canvas blinds shading the front verandah and some extra furnishing purchased to complement the various rooms. Above all, there was now a colourful garden with green lawns, a lemon tree and a few vegetables, especially apple cucumbers. Dad set up his office and small workshop in the back shed, together with a half rainwater tank for his wood supply. Modern appliances were thin on the ground: there was no washing machine, no clothes dryer, no air conditioning (but an electric fan), no hot water to the kitchen sink or wash house – not even an electric Mixmaster. The 'fridge' was an Electrolux kero' model and the stove was a rather old fashioned Metters 'Early Kooka No 12' gas arrangement. For all that, we were very happy and Mum could still produce country-style roast dinners, pea soup, pies, curries and puddings for Dad's sweet tooth. A wood fire in the sitting room cheered the house in winter and summers were endured by playing under the sprinkler and sleeping with all the doors and windows open, to catch the 'Fremantle doctor'.

We had been introduced to cards while on the station, playing snap and other childish games. Now it was time for bridge. All the Roses played Auction Bridge and we started playing with Aunty Syb and grandfather. Rules drummed in then still resonate to this day: 'Second player plays low – third player, high!' In relation to dummy: 'Through strength to weakness.' In suit play: 'Unless you have a better plan, get all the trumps out.' In no-trumps: 'Lose tricks early while you still have stoppers.'

I progressed to filling in if the 'oldies' needed somebody to make a four and was surprised that grandfather, then in his 90s, still liked to win: 'There you go – you should've got your trumps out early in the game!'

In the final year at The Prac, I was sent off for scholarship exams for entry to either Perth Modern School or Christ Church Grammar School. I failed both but was enrolled to start in the first year of senior school at Christ Church in 1954. School uniforms were organised from the clothing exchange and any new items to complete the kit from Aherns or Boans in Perth. I was taught how to tie my new tie and went off with socks pulled well up to just below the knee, held in place by homemade garters, complementing the shiny black shoes. A very large cap, pulled well down over my eyes, completed the summer uniform of grey cotton shorts and shirt.

Christ Church provided a new start to my life. I was separated from Tim for the first time but had moral support from Derry Macqueen and and Dick Sudlow. By contrast, there were about 16 new boys who knew nobody, especially those who were boarders and away from home for the first time, so at last I was neither the newest nor the shyest one in the class.

The Senior School was very small in 1954, with only 335 students of which 144 were boarders. There were 24 enrolled to sit for their leaving and 11 teaching staff, including the headmaster, who taught history as well as his other responsibilities. There were 58 of us in Year 8, of which 42 had come up from the junior school to join the 16 of us who were new. Many parents of the day gave their children one or two years in the Prep School before entering Senior School, to help them adjust to a new school system, and among these were a number of boarders from the country. As with The Prac, almost all the boys were of Anglo origin, though Irwin Lewis was of Aboriginal heritage. He was two years ahead of me and, as a sergeant in cadets and a talented footballer, was looked up to.[4]

We were divided into different classes: the ones who were aiming for university went into the P for professional class, the rest of us into G for general. The G class included most of the country boarders, who used their forced stay in the city to play cricket and football, while undertaking the bare minimum of study.

Mr 'Blinky Bill' Rucks was our form teacher and we went off to different rooms for various subjects. Other than Mr 'The Boss' Moyes, all the other teachers were of pre-war vintage and showed their age! 'Blinky Bill' took us for some subjects; 'Hoont' Blackwood for P&H (physiology and hygiene); 'Patrick' O'Connor for maths; 'Mad Prof' Richardson for geography; 'Hot Box' Ovens for economics and bookkeeping; 'Horry' Lance for biology; 'Ma' O'Connor for art; 'Octane' Trimby for English; 'Hutchy' Hutchinson for physics; and Arcos Kovacs ruled the gym with an iron fist. Correspondence and The Prac must have served me well as it was not a problem keeping up with the school work.[5]

Talking of 'Blinky Bill', he lived with his family in a little house in the corner of the school grounds on Stirling Highway, next to the MLC entrance.[6] He had two very well-endowed teenage daughters, who often wore revealing blouses, and we day boys never knew if the boarders' stories of after-school shenanigans were true or not. (The stories are repeated at old boys' get-togethers and I still doubt their accuracy.)

Every day started with a chapel service, held over the road and in the same Christ Church that the Rose family attended and where Mum and Dad were married. We all formed into our class groups under the Plane trees and marched over in formation. There would be a hymn, the daily Bible reading by one of the prefects, a word or two about the reading from 'The Boss', then we all marched back to our classrooms.

My first year at a new school was interrupted by the Royal Tour of March 1954. The whole family, and most of our neighbours, all assembled along Stirling Highway with little flags to wave as the Queen and Prince Philip drove majestically by. Robert Menzies's famous quote certainly held true for Mum: 'I did but see her passing by, and yet I love her till I die.'

In the first year at school, cricket and football were the two main sports. With my 'one-eyesight', cricket was not easy and I received a few hard blows from the cricket ball, so was relieved to take up rowing for the rest of my school days. Football was more straightforward but I was always in the bottom team. In the final four years there were schoolboy cadets, which I enjoyed and, having used a rifle before, was one of the better shots on the rifle range with the .303. It was a welcome change to be in the top group.

We had a week's cadet camp at the Northam Army Base every May. The camp was built at the beginning of the Second World War and was now showing its age, and the huts were unlined and freezing cold as we slept on our straw-filled paillasses. We marched to the mess hall at the call of a bugle; we marched up the hill for evening films; we marched to the rifle range and parade ground; we seemed to march everywhere. The first-year cadets were filled with dread of being 'nuggeted' or 'scragged' in initiation rituals, but fortunately I was spared any of that. The two powerful memories were the awe and thrill of firing a Bren gun and of marching on a cold frosty night to the school drum and fife band playing 'Colonel Bogey's March', to which we sang in loud voice:[7]

> Hitler – has only got one ball;
> Goring – has two, but very small;
> Himmler – has something similar;
> But poor old Goebbels – has no balls at all!

In the first few years at Christ Church, I spent a lot of time with Derry and his family, especially at weekends. We would ride our bikes for hours on end and

Alex as a school cadet 1956

spend a lot of time doing modifications, such as painting different colours, fitting wide handlebars, lights and even a three-speed hub with back-pedal brakes. The Macqueens also introduced me to Mah-jong and we had great times playing with his mother, older sister Judy and younger sister Kay. Derry and I often had meals at each other's place – I enjoyed pastas and curries with his family, he enjoyed a Campbell roast and pea soup with mine.

With Mr Dandoe's help next door, I built a table-tennis table, which was set up on the front verandah and provided a lot of fun as we honed our skills at this new game. For some reason I was OK at table tennis but battled on a real tennis court.

Tim and I also undertook some epic bike rides at weekends and holidays, either around Kings Park, out to City Beach or 'around the highways'. This entailed riding along Mounts Bay Road, over the Causeway, along Canning Highway, over the old Fremantle Bridge and home along Stirling Highway. On one of these highway jaunts, Tim came off his bike at Cottesloe, right in front of a doctor's surgery. A concerned passer-by took us in and Tim was given two stitches to his hand before we continued on our way.

We saved our pocket money and, together with grandfather's payments, walked from Loftus Street to the annual Royal Show at the Claremont Showgrounds. We could only afford one or two attractions at Side Show Alley, maybe the boxing tent and a ride, a show bag or two and a hot dog for lunch. We would fill in several days, however, looking over farm machinery, animals and various pavilions and watching ring events. As mentioned earlier, 'the gate was always left ajar' and the way Mum and Dad gave us freedom to roam so widely at that young age demonstrates the point.

At school, hardly any boys dodged the cane. Only 'The Boss' and 'Octane' Trimby were authorised to use it so you were sent to them for the action. Being late for class, not saying 'sir', being seen out of school grounds in an untidy uniform – all were reasons for 'the cuts'. It was usually three but for a serious offence, 'six of the best'. The procedure was quite straightforward:

'I am told you were late for class – is that correct?'

'Yes, sir.'

'Well, we can't have that. Bend over.' WHACK, WHACK, WHACK.

Often there were a few in front of you and it was disconcerting to hear the swish and WHACK coming through the closed door. Once back outside, you were questioned: 'What was he like today?'

Usually bravado ruled: 'Just a bit of a tickle-up.' But a few drama queens would try, 'He must have had a bad weekend – he was *really* savage!'

There were extracurricular subjects, with most boarders doing boxing with Danny Ryan or wool classing with Mr Stone. I did woodwork with Mr Schorer and dancing classes with Miss Linley Wilson. Most boys were enrolled for dancing lessons to equip for times ahead; sullen boys would line up on one side of the hall with shy awkward girls from MLC on the other. Miss Wilson deserves full marks as by year's end we secretly admitted to it being 'not so bad after all'. Many of us were sent off for tennis lessons on Saturday mornings to the Claremont Tennis Club. Derry really shone at tennis (I struggled) and it was probably the start of us drifting off in different directions.

I spent a lot of time riding between Loftus Street and the Rose and Macqueen families in Albert Street, so always had to pass through Claremont. I would usually go via the back way: along the railway line past the Showground subway, the Post Office, Hotel and the large United Bus depot next door. I was intrigued by the activity at the depot, which had a large shed for servicing and repairing buses and always had buses coming and going. The London-style double-decker was a favourite – the only one in Perth – and I hoped it would be hired for school outings. I loved the smell and sound of the Leyland diesel motor, the driver sitting next to it in a cramped cabin, the other side open next to the entry door. The petrol Bedford buses were more modern but not admired at all.

The way home was usually along Stirling Highway, past Christ Church and the Lucknow Hospital to Bay View Terrace and sometimes there was a policeman on point duty, so I rode my bike with correct hand signals. The places of most interest to a boy were Drabbles Hardware and the bike shop. Drabbles had their frontage to Bay View Terrace but had many interesting sheds at the back for all the bulky building supplies. Nails, screws and similar items could either be bought singularly or weighed on scales and paint was in a limited colour range, all oil-based, with no tinting available. I would drool over the tools and slowly started a collection, the little fine-toothed bandsaw being in the workshop to this day. There was an old grumpy, but helpful, man in the bike shop, where we could buy anything to keep our bikes going and get help with tricky things, such as the three-speed hub arrangement.

Grandfather's payment would be spent at the milk bar near the picture theatre and, as there were often older teenagers hanging around, I felt uncomfortable in school uniform. Claremont Drapers were just up the road, surrounded by the normal range of other shops, and Whittles newsagent was opposite the National Bank on the corner of Stirling Highway – where I would try to read a comic without having to pay for it! A ride along St Quentin's Avenue past all the little workers' cottages was interesting because at the Stirling Road end was Boulton's lawn mowing service. They used old 'A model' Ford utes and always seemed to be fixing up mowers and utes in the open shed as I passed by.[8]

School holidays were often spent in the country. An early holiday was with the Bilstons at Kojonup, where I was allowed to drive the tractor, but many were with the Shields at Wongan Hills. Mum's sister Alice married Herbert Shields and would often have Tim and me to stay, with cousin Penny being my age and Virginia a bit older. Aunty Alice's stepson, Hubert, by Herbert's earlier first marriage, was also bringing up a family on Glenvar, with Robin being older than me but Waverley, Christine and Graham fitting in better, while Peter, Elizabeth and Tony were much younger. There was a swimming pool on the farm and many picnics organised, and we always had a lot of fun with such a large extended family. Aunty Alice was also looking after Ben Clarke, a distant cousin, who was share farming on Glenvar. He had a mischievous sense of humour and would take us out to the paddock where he was ploughing or seeding with his old P6 Fordson tractor. Tim and I would sit on the seed box of the drill as he went round and round the paddock.

Dad had changed jobs in 1955 and now managed the four properties comprising Wydgee Pastoral Co. There were two stations at Mount Magnet, Wydgee and Yowergabbie that Tim and I enjoyed visiting. Half the fun was getting there and back as from about age 13, Dad would let us drive once we passed through Wubin and hit the gravel road beyond. The Great Northern Highway was little used in those days so there weren't many vehicles to pass. When the occasional one would come towards us, or come up behind, he would say: 'Slow down and pull well over until it passes.' He would puff away on his pipe while we drove and listened to the cricket or football on the radio, with only an odd exclamation: 'By Joves, that Benaud is shaping up well.' And: 'What the deuce did he think he was doing?'

These trips were very special times for Tim and me and we would usually stop at White Wells (between Wubin and Paynes Find) for lunch: sardines on cracker

Tim and Alex in front of FJ ute, White Wells, 1956

biscuits and billy tea. One trip we camped out on our swags, with an evening meal and breakfast around the campfire. Dad was not a great conversationalist, so you tended to take on board the things he came out with:

> Never judge a farm by the front gate – the back paddocks are very often a disgrace.
>
> Never chase the market – buy a good ram when wool is down and you'll have good progeny on the ground for the next upturn.
>
> See those starving sheep – always sell early if you are heading for a drought, and don't get caught with stock too poor to fetch a reasonable price.
>
> Look at that fence over there – always keep up with maintenance or you'll get to a stage like that when it's beyond repair.

On the rules of the road:

> Look at that fool passing on a blind corner.
>
> What's that galah doing speeding like that?
>
> It's better to arrive late than dead on time.

At other times, he would come out with a verse or two of Banjo Paterson and we would ask for more. Favourites were: *A Bush Christening; Mulga Bill's Bicycle; Clancy of the Overflow; Saltbush Bill; The Man from Snowy River* and *Hay, Hell and Booligal*. They were often followed by a brief geography or history lesson:

> Back in the 1800s there were no organised shearing teams, and men would walk or ride pushbikes for miles in the hope of finding a job at a shed. Hay is in the middle of the vast Riverine plains on the Murrumbidgee and Booligal is to the north on the Lachlan. Halfway between is the One Tree pub, the old staging post for Cobb and Co, and as lonely a place as you could hope to find, which they nicknamed Hell.

Dad also had some favourite bush yarns, such as Henry Lawson's 'The Loaded Dog' and Jack Moses' 'The Dog on the Tuckerbox, Nine Miles from Gundagai':

A dog was often the drover's best mate and a tremendous loyalty would build up between them. Gundagai is on the Murrumbidgee where the flood plains start, and as far inland as the old riverboats could go. It now has the longest wooden road and rail bridges in Australia. By the way, my mother's home was Micalago, way up in the High Country of the Monaro Plains, and on the upper reaches of the same Murrumbidgee.

Alex with his first 'roo, Wydgee, 1956

On one trip, Dad gingerly started to talk about the birds and the bees. I chimed in quickly: 'We have learnt all about that stuff in P&H at school.' With considerable relief he replied: 'Well that's good, if you ever have any questions – just ask.'

John Hamilton's father was more to the point: 'God gave you a cock and a brain – you can't use them both at the same time so make sure you use your brain first.'

John Hamilton had come to Christ Church at the beginning of his junior year. We seemed to 'click' straight away and became very good friends. His father had been a Group Captain in the RAF and the family had come to Australia after the war. There was an unsuccessful attempt at farming near Bridgetown; they then moved to Perth, where his father sold insurance for AMP before retiring on an airforce pension.

Life was progressing well and I achieved a six-subject Junior Certificate,[9] which spoke more for Mum's correspondence endeavours than my own ability. Subleaving year brought a change of interests and all of a sudden, riding bikes and playing table tennis lost their appeal and the prospect of parties and other outings took over. For Mum's part, she did her best and arranged mixed tennis parties at the Mongers and gatherings at home, with jazz music from our few records on a little portable player. She invited mainly offspring of her friends: Trisha McLennan, Elspeth and David Thom, Mary and Roger Day, Derry Macqueen, Diana Cresswell, Bev Cullingworth and various Rose and Henwood cousins. Of more interest were other parties, interschool sports days and Head of the River where girls would be sure to attend.[10] The Hamiltons had a beach camp at Siesta Park near Busselton and summer holidays there were an ideal way of extending our social lives. Of course, there were the formal school dances: the agony of asking somebody to the Christ Church event; the pleasure of being invited to St Hilda's or PLC (so long as it was somebody you liked).[11]

It was while in subleaving that I attended a senior NCOs[12] course at Leighton army camp in December 1957. There were boys from other schools at the course and I became friendly with Robin Kempton from Scotch College. He was a bright, energetic sort of bloke, always just at arm's length from getting into trouble, who arrived with a pack of cards and was intent on gaining some of our pocket money at poker and pontoon. Fortunately, my family's card playing had me well covered and Robin and I did fairly well against some of the others.

In leaving year I was made a corporal and went off to the Northam army camp in May with high spirits – and several packets of smokes. A few of us got busted. I got demoted back to private and had the humiliation of getting Mum to take off the corporal stripes that she had recently sewn on. Not much was said at home as Dad had smoked from a similar age, so the emphasis was all on 'sticking to rules' and 'not smoking too much, or you will run out of puff for your rowing'. Talking of smoking, the Windsor and Claremont outdoor theatres were great venues to have a smoke. After standing for 'God Save the Queen', everybody lit up and we could hardly see the screen for smoke, then after interval and with the main film just started, the same procedure would be repeated. We were now spending all summer weekends at North Cottesloe beach, riding our bikes both ways, smoking Peter Stuyvesants and looking at the girls.

In the final year of school, two big things happened. Steph became my first girlfriend and I obtained my driver's licence. She was 18 months or so younger than me, went to St Hilda's and lived at West Perth. I believe there's a lot of luck in who your first girlfriend might be as those early shared experiences shape the rest of your life in relationship matters and, while it was all very innocent by today's standards, I am grateful for those early few years. I kept a home-knitted jumper Steph gave me for many years, even after marrying and with Jenn's approval!

The driver's licence was obtained in August using the Ford Prefect. As many friends were yet to get their licences, I was quite popular. Nonetheless, they were fairly scathing of the Prefect, calling it the 'Defect'. Mum and Dad were very generous in how much I used the car and it was probably just as well they didn't know my attempts at driving up Mount Street from the Terrace, with five or six of us on board. On another night, a few of us were looking for a parking spot near the Snake Pit at Scarborough when a policeman shone his torch through the open window: 'What are you boys doing at a place like this? Hop it home before you get into trouble.'

I think we were quite relieved to have the excuse to leave as we knew in our hearts that it wasn't for us. While on the subject of cars, even though the Ford Prefect was showing its age, most day-boy parents were still driving Austin A40s, Morris Minors and Hillman Minxes, while it was the boarders who arrived in the Chev 210s, Ford V8 Customlines or current model Holdens. Nobody got dropped off at school by car as we all caught buses or rode bikes, hail, rain or shine.

Mr Moyes must have been trying to keep the school academic record in good shape, for he wrote to several parents to suggest their boys in the G class not sit for their leaving as they weren't looking for university entry. It was one of the few times Dad got involved in school matters. He phoned and asked 'for the headmaster in person' and went on to say, 'I've paid school fees for five years and believe Alex should be given a chance along with the others.' This caused me to

Dad and Liz in front of the 1949 Ford Prefect

put in a burst of last-minute swatting and I passed in seven subjects,[13] which says more for the quality of teaching than any personal effort.

On reflection, I have great appreciation for those five years. We were taught well, given clear direction on how we should lead our lives and, beyond all else, had the opportunity to mix with decent kids with similar hopes and ideals. Peter Moyes was a great headmaster and by his steady guidance Christ Church grew from a small struggling school into one of the great private colleges of Perth.

The 1950s provided a very stable political environment. Bob Menzies had been Prime Minister since 1949 and, together with the wool boom of the 1950s, Australia was enjoying a buoyant post-war recovery. At home, politics was not mentioned a lot, though it was always 'Robert or Mr Menzies' with a respectful tone of voice.

Mum had a very dark view about communists and the threat they posed to our orderly lifestyle. On the one hand, the Royal family represented all that was good and to be admired, while on the other, communists were all that was bad and to be feared. The 'Petrov Affair' of 1954–55 was proof positive to Mum: 'Thank goodness for Mr Menzies – where would we be with Russia and the communists trying to take over the world, if he wasn't prepared to take a stand?'

PART THREE

FROM A MALLEE BLOCK TO LANDCARE

I am a great believer in luck. The harder I work, the more of it I seem to have.
Coleman Cox, 1922

In this world, everyone gets their share of luck. It takes courage to grab it with both hands when it comes your way.
Harry Hodgson, 1963

13 THE WOULD-BE FARMER

After the leaving examination results came out at the end of 1958 (which pleasantly surprised both father and son), Dad came straight to the point: 'Now are you sure about farming as your future career?'

I said that was still the case, based on having enjoyed country holidays and having no better idea at the time. 'Well, how about putting in a year at Yanchep and doing a bit of stock work and try your hand at operating machinery, then see where you would like to go from there?'

Dad had been responsible for 20,000 acres at Yanchep since taking on the management of Wydgee Pastoral Co in 1955, and I had often joined him on day trips to the property. It was arranged that I would spend five nights a week at Yanchep then come home on Friday evenings after work, returning on Sunday evening. Tiddles Cockman was the manager and his son Terry also worked there, who came to Perth every weekend to be with his girlfriend, therefore built-in transport for me.

Looking back, I think Dad had organised the next best thing to a gap year as I was able to experience farming for five days a week, but continue my family and social life in Perth every weekend. I was paid the bare minimum found rate for a farm hand and Mrs Cockman was paid the appropriate rate for keeping me.

John Hamilton had started a journalism cadetship with WA Newspapers; Dick Sudlow was with WD & HO Wills; Barry Cook, Ian Richie and Peter 'Beak' Brazier were doing accounting; and John Schupp was studying geology at UWA. We were still in the same social group, including Jill and Gay Clarkson, Judy and Angela Hampshire – and I was still seeing Steph. Summer holidays continued with the Hamiltons at Busselton and what more could an 18-year-old want for his social life?[1]

Dad must have had a word with Tiddles for I was exposed to the full range of farm activity. All farming work was done by contract, including the new fencing by Greg Christianson, who had an old unlicensed 'A model' Ford ute with oversize tyres for the fencing work, and used to brag: 'This old ute will go anywhere over the sand hills that those ex-army jeeps can!' It was a pleasure spending some time with him, learning how to 'sight' a straight fence line and erect a good end assembly. The tractor work was done by various contractors and I was given time to drive a few shifts, learning the importance of proper maintenance.

Yet the main work was with the sheep and cattle. Yanchep was used for 'finishing' a lot of the sheep from Mingenew and the two stations, so there were a lot of small shearing and crutching jobs. I learnt how to throw a fleece, press a bale in an Ajax press, and brand, drench and dip sheep as well as lamb marking and fly treatment. Likewise with cattle: drafting, weaning and marking. All work was done on horseback and, to start me off, I was given Mickey to ride – a very old stock pony whose one intent was to get home as soon as possible. I learnt the hard way to never let go of the reins when opening a gate! The next mount was Lord Nelson, a thoroughbred who had had his left eye removed after a horse float accident and was getting on in years, but still enjoyed a gallop, holding his head to the right to get a good view of the world. Tiddles and Terry were highly amused: 'Look at those two – Alex with his head turned left, Nelson's head turned right. It's a wonder they don't come to grief.'

Tiddles loved fishing. We would stand waist-deep on the Yanchep or Two Rocks reef and catch tailor and an odd dhufish, summer or winter. During the crayfish season, Tiddles had mates on the boats who would float a bag of undersize crays ashore to where we would have a campfire burning with an old copper of boiling sea water. Freshly cooked crays, dipped in salt and vinegar, fresh bread and a beer on the beach is an experience I am yet to better. (How different then – you would be heavily fined and severely ostracised for such practices these days!)

I was smoking openly and regularly by now, enjoying a smoke rather than using them as a way to look like one of the bunch. An early start on horseback, with a roll-your-own smoke for company, was really quite a pleasant combination. Having disposable income for the first time also meant I could consider alcohol (even though the legal drinking age was still 21). A King Brown bottle of beer was the usual thing to take to a party, but I remember on one occasion somebody arrived with a bottle of port. Having already had a beer or two, the port was not a good idea, causing me to be violently ill. It was a timely lesson for, as much as I enjoy a drink or three, I have always stopped short of reliving that experience.

The year went quickly and I came to a few conclusions: I didn't like horses; only partially enjoyed stock work; really enjoyed fencing and machinery; and thoroughly enjoyed crayfish, but not line fishing. I kept the last of these to myself but had another conversation with Dad. After some discussion he said:

> Well, it's farming for you. I'm glad you are not leaning towards station life as I think most of the sheep stations have had their day. Would you like me to have a word with Mac McLennan to see if he can recommend a Wheatbelt farmer who might take you on?[2]

And so it was arranged. Harry Hodgson at Kulin was the name put forward and Dad suggested I drive out to see for myself. A 400-mile return trip in a 10-year-old Ford Prefect is no mean feat, so the journey required a very early start in order to have a few hours at Kulin. Mr Hodgson (as I always called him) met me in his dirty work clothes with his bristling grey hair in a crew cut, then showed me around the machinery sheds – which impressed me – and finally the quarters: 'They are a bit rough, but I can guarantee you'll get well fed.'

It was arranged he would collect me in Perth at the end of January 1960, after I'd had two or three weeks' holiday. In due course, a green Chev with a KU number plate pulled up at 39 Loftus Street, Mum and Dad provided morning tea and talked to Harry Hodgson, while I packed my swag and suitcase into his car.

Mr Hodgson smoked all the way to the farm and pointed out things of interest, which barely registered at the time. I smoked one for his two. He explained they were fully staffed and for a while I would be sharing the shearers' quarters with Bruno Sorgiovanni but, if I stayed on, would progress up to the cottage with my own bedroom.

The shearers' quarters comprised an unlined room built into the end of the machinery shed with concrete floors, some small louvre windows and an ablution room next to it. This in turn consisted of a wood-fuelled copper, concrete wash trough and a galvanised bucket with shower nozzle under it, hanging from the roof by rope and pulley. Bruno explained we would take it in turns to light the copper for a shower after the evening meal and: 'You go behind the shed for a leak and down to that patch of bush for a shit – unless you want to empty the thunderbox yourself.'

The married couple cooked for all the single men and were given free meat and eggs, so our diet was high in protein: fried eggs and chops for breakfast; cold meat sandwiches for paddock lunches; and a roast or stew for the evening meals. If we wanted hot tea in the paddock, we had to provide our own Thermos flask.

Breakfast was at 7am (earlier during seeding) and we were all at the shed by 7.30 for work. Most days we were out in the paddock, with only a short smoko and untimed lunch break. The evening meal was after dark, so we worked longer days in the summer than winter. We worked five and a half days a week, seven for seeding and six for harvesting, with two weeks' holiday a year.

I was the youngest and most junior of the workforce. Mr Hodgson ran the farm and was referred to as 'The Boss'; his son Geoff filled the role of overseer and was the one in charge out in the paddock. There was a married man, two or three young farm hands and an old pensioner yardman who was a returned soldier and an alcoholic, dubbed 'The General' – the general nuisance. There was also a seasonal employee called Tom Cole who came back each year for seeding and was another returned soldier of short, stocky build, nicknamed 'Khrushchev' for his habit of waving his arms about while talking to you. Another very talkative bloke was called 'Biro' – 10,000 words without a refill.

Being the most junior meant never being the driver as you went out to the paddock, not being in charge of any big machinery, being the roustabout at shearing and doing the killing. We killed a sheep twice a week for meat and The Boss was known for adding any maimed sheep to the killer mob, so it was often difficult selecting one that didn't look too unfit for human consumption. The married man had worked in a local abattoir at one stage and showed me the art of killing: punching the skin off and then cutting up in the morning. I was very grateful for proper tuition before bad habits set in, as many farmers really battled with this job.

The home farm was 2,600 acres of heavy land on the southeast corner of Jilakin Lake, which in earlier years had been four selections of square mile blocks, each of 640 acres – one paddock was called Bowdens, in memory of the original selector. Further east there were 7,500 acres of mallee-based light land, which comprised four stages of development. The last 1,500 or so acres had just been cleared and root ripped, using the farm International TD14 crawler tractor and heavy-duty Pederick root ripper.[3]

The Boss was known for giving everybody a fair go and had a team of Aboriginals heaping and burning the ripped stumps. They had an old 'Maple Leaf' Chev truck, were given the use of an outdated Roads Board accommodation van and had rainwater carted out as required. There were lengthy negotiations every week over how much land had been cleaned up, for payment was by the acre. It seemed to suit all parties as the number working in the paddock varied from day to day and The Boss was dealing with only one of the group, who had taken on the contract.

There were also one or two Aboriginals 'pushing the handpiece' at shearing time, just as on many farms of the day. They received the same rates of pay as the white men and were good at the job, even if a little unreliable in showing up each morning. The 1967 referendum quickly saw Aboriginal shearers succumbing to 'sit down money' and being replaced by New Zealand Maoris. By the year 2000, most shearing teams in Australia and especially those in the east would have 50 per cent or more of the workforce made up of Maori men and women (most shed-hand positions are now filled by women) but seldom any Australian Aboriginals. It begs the question, why should this be the case?

While the initial root picking was done by contract, there were still a lot of roots turned up for years to come as the paddocks were ploughed and scarified. Box poison (*Gastrolobium parviflorum*) was prevalent and any stony ridge that couldn't be cultivated had to be picked by hand. It would have to be the most soul-destroying job known to man! To lift your head and view countless acres of torment yet to be tackled is misery personified. The monotony of the repetitive job causes you to stumble over a root or poison plant without having consciously seen it, referred to as 'picker blindness'. Many dreary days and weeks were spent picking roots and poison, so much so that I quipped: 'I'm picking my way through life.'

In that first year, my tractor work was limited to driving the 'big gear' while others had lunch or heavy harrowing for weed kill after seeding. Likewise at harvest, it was driving a header over lunch, but mainly 'odd jobbing' which involved moving plant from paddock to paddock, picking up the 'seconds' grain that had been bagged off and helping with the regular greasing and servicing. Nobody used earmuffs and the Chamberlain tractors were unbelievably noisy.

I remember The Boss often referring to the devastation caused by rabbits before 'myxo' was introduced in 1950. The old farm had been rabbit-proof fenced and there were heart-rending stories of the endless poisoning and ripping of warrens. Myxomatosis was first observed in Uruguay in the late 19th century, causing skin tumours and fever, with death in 14 days or so, and it was spread by fleas and mosquitoes. One hundred years from the first release of rabbits by Thomas Austin in 1859, Australia was finally able to control the economic and environmental disaster.[4]

Social life was spasmodic. I had no vehicle and relied on lifts from the other single men or Geoff. Junior Farmers was at its zenith, most young men and women were members and Geoff used to take me along, where I started to meet others of my own age, including Rex Noble, Kerry Langey and Christina Magee. There was ram and sheep judging, debating competitions, annual achievement days and social events. Geoff was better at the ram judging, but Christina and I carried the debating team and David Quick was the 'adult adviser'.

I tried tennis but found it attracted the really good players who went off to Country Week and were very competitive. My standard was found wanting so after persevering for the first summer or two, I gave it away. Even so, I got to know Tim Clayton, Bruce Eyres and his sisters, Jill and Joan-Anne, as well as others.

The farm was on the Jilakin manual telephone exchange and it never crossed my mind that you would go to the homestead and ask to use the phone. All correspondence was by mail and there was a weekly exchange from Mum and initially from friends, such as John Hamilton, though the latter became less frequent as our lives and interests took different directions.

The first year at Kulin drew to a close and became a time of reckoning. The first fortnight's holiday back at Loftus Street was difficult, as city friends were busy doing their own thing and forming new groups related to their work or study. It seemed difficult re-establishing family ties with parents and siblings and it was hard picking up where you left off. Half of me wanted to leave farming and re-establish city life, while the other half thought some of the city activity rather shallow. I think 'feeding rather than breeding' took over as my own father, uncles and cousins were not the types to 'throw in the towel', so why should I? The dilemma that I was going through was highlighted by the advice I gave Tim at the time:

> For heaven's sake, try city life first. You will find farming a tough gig
> – you can always go bush after a few years, but you will find it hard
> to come back to the city if country life doesn't suit you.

Kulin, on my return, was familiar and welcoming, whereas 12 months earlier it had been alien and uninviting. As we entered town from the Wickepin road, I recognised: the hall; Kulin Road Board Offices; Jim and Ella Greeve's tea shop; the hotel; post office; railway station; CWA Rooms; National Bank; and

W.H. Butler's Ford and Shell agencies along the main street. A street further back were: D. 'Fred' Honey's International; Mike Terry's Holden; and H.R. and E. (Harry) Watson's Chamberlain dealerships; Elder Smiths; the butcher's; baker's; Watson's General Store; the junior high school; and Anglican, Uniting and Catholic churches completing the picture.[5]

The railway station was manned by a station master, porter and several goods-yard men, with all freight being regulated to rail at the time. The post office was equally well staffed, including the manual telephone exchange 24 hours a day. Kulin was but one of many medium-sized Wheatbelt towns of the time and the majority of farmers bought their cars and tractors in their local town, banked and shopped locally, and supported all the local organisations.

We proceeded over the railway line, past the sporting complex, out to Jilakin Rock and Jilakin Lake and so to the farm. Several single men had moved on and I progressed into the cottage with my own bedroom. John Dainton had left Elders and was the newcomer on the staff, as he was taking out Rae Noble and didn't want to be transferred out of the district.

Mum and Dad had given me a subscription to Reader's Digest condensed books for Christmas, and I bought a portable valve radio that used very large (and expensive) dry cell batteries. I could now lie on my bed and read books or listen to the news in the privacy of my own room. Ablution arrangements at the cottage were the same as at the shearers' quarters, so the patch of bush was favoured against being on thunderbox roster!

John was aware of a local farmer who had a 1926 'Chev Four' ute that was used for root picking and suggested a £10 offer might clinch a deal. This came to pass, so I rigged up a 6-volt headlight and tail light, and The Boss suggested I go to the Kulin Road Board and ask for a licence. This was granted, vehicle unseen, probably in view of Harry Hodgson being chairman of the Road Board at the time. John and I now made regular weekend trips to the Noble farm, bypassing town via the Gnarming siding road. When going to Kulin for the weekly picture show, we would park behind the railway station and walk over the line to avoid the local policeman inspecting the vehicle.

I was in my 21st year, fit and strong and now given responsibility on the 'big gear', wool pressing at shearing and in charge of the fencing work. I had learnt how to tip a 44-gallon drum of fuel to the point of balance and roll it single-handed around the truck tray; could easily handle the '12 to a tonne' jute bags of super; stack bagged wheat as they came off the Hannaford grader;

1926 Chev ute outside workers cottage, 1961

and easily fill the seed and super boxes at seeding time. Tom Cole and Charles Walker, 'the married man', used to provide friendly advice: 'Take it easy – you are only a youngster and you'll burn yourself out, or bugger up your back.' That only spurred me on. I relished the extra responsibility; the year of reckoning had passed and I was now enjoying the prospect of a farming career.

It was during the second year that The Boss said: 'It's about time you had a truck licence. Take the Commer to town for a load of super and drop by the police station.'

I duly drove the truck to town, went straight to the police station and was told: 'I'm busy at the moment, so go and load the truck and come back on your way home.' With 96 bags of super on board, I went back to the police station:

> Well, you can obviously drive a truck and have your driver's licence, so we'll get on with the paperwork. By the way, do you think old Harry would ever buy a semi? Just in case, we'll bung that on as well.

From the second harvest on, I did all the truck work to the CBH[6] sidings, being Kulin from the home farm and Pingaring on the Hyden–Lake Grace line from the new-land blocks. That same year, the first of two 8-ton petrol Bedford

'J' series trucks was bought from Mike Terry, while retaining the Commer. We always had 8 tons or better of grain on board so, together with the bin, were always overloaded, with one truck being filled while I drove the other to town. I was given the truck work as there were often negotiations at the bins over quality issues and, together with other paperwork, was the better educated of the farm hands to handle these issues.

Geoff always drove the 14-foot Horwood Bagshaw168 header and ensured the best outcome from the harvest activity in the paddock, together with the second header, which was an International A81 with a 12-foot comb. The old Kulin CBH bins were directly between the railway line and the main street, so everything was covered in dust when the easterly winds were blowing! There were still a number of farmers carting bags so if such a truck was in front of me, I would hop up and help tip the bags into the elevator hopper, thinking to myself: 'Thank God, The Boss was in full bulk handling before I came along.'

The elevators of the day were powered by single-cylinder Ronaldson Tippet engines and were wheeled alongside the bins as they progressively filled. There was usually a spray of malathion (for weevil control) covering the grain as it entered the hopper. The elevators worked well for the leisurely pace of bagged grain, but care had to be taken in not overloading them when the bulk bins came into service.[7]

The uni students manning the weighbridge in Kulin were fairly well off, but I felt sorry for the ones at Pingaring in their little tin huts with minimum facilities. There were many new-land farmers around Pingaring who were 'doing it tough' and most had 5-ton Austin trucks that didn't handle Australian summers well at all. The bonnets were chocked half open with blocks of wood for better air flow over the engine and both doors were removed to help the driver, as the motor was located halfway back into the cab.

For all the skills and life-moulding experiences gained at Kulin in the early 1960s, two fond memories have remained etched in my mind: the lovely earthy smell of freshly turned ground when ploughing the heavy red soils of the salt lake country; and the sound on a still frosty morning of the first tractors of the day starting up. There are two sounds that were very distinctive: the crackling bark of the Caterpillar petrol starting engine and the whine of a GM two-stroke motor, as used on the Chamberlain Super 70s and 90s. I heard neighbours for miles around and swapped notes as I met them: 'You stole a march on us the other day – I heard you starting the D4 at 5.30.' And: 'You must have slept in yesterday – I fired the Super 70 up at 6.30 and it was still quiet in your part of the world.'

Caterpillar D4, Shearer Culti-trash and International D30 truck, Kulin, 1961

At the end of the second year, I received a £100 bonus and, with two years of savings, was able to buy an eight-year-old FJ Holden ute while on holidays in Perth. (Hire purchase was never considered.) The FJs were very basic: 6-volt electrics; vacuum windscreen wipers; 'rag' tyres; a 'pull and hope' handbrake (that never worked); and, of course, no heating, air conditioning or radio. The motor didn't even have an oil filter, which meant 1,000-mile oil changes. Looking back, there were some other best forgotten aspects of 1950s and '60s vehicles: exhaust systems needed annual replacement; front-end wheel alignments every six months or so; windscreens shattered regularly; frequent punctures in the tyres and tubes of the day; prone to overheating in summer; batteries and radiators only surviving for two or three years. A return trip from the farm to Perth without incident was something to celebrate.

A real vehicle, rather than the 1926 Chev, provided a lot more freedom and even a few weekends in Perth over the coming years. Improved transport didn't help in the girlfriend department, with the few school teachers being in high demand, as was the bank manager's daughter, but all seemed out of my range. Some of the single young men around town used to boast (or fantasise?): 'The barmaid will serve you more than a cold beer if you play your cards right.' And: 'The girl in the telephone exchange will connect the trunk calls while she's at work, then connect your trunk when she knocks off!'

As salacious as these options sounded, neither were tried. The Noble and Magee families were very good to me and often provided Sunday roast dinners, while Junior Farmers continued to be a great social and educational outlet. I was now fully committed to a farming career, taking note of all the seasonal activity and the decision processes involved. I also compared the Hodgson farm to others in the district and worked out the often subtle differences between success and failure. I was keen to learn and Harry Hodgson became a mentor to me, more so than he probably realised.

Over the coming years, there were many valuable farming and life skills that I took on board, which have held true over time. Firstly:

> Buy good plant and machinery and look after it well – it will then look after you. Just look around: the farmers who always have the latest machinery in the paddock are often the first ones to go broke.

Examples of this philosophy were readily to hand: the 1938 International D30 truck; the two 20 run Mackay Sunlea combines; the post-war TD14 International and Caterpillar D4 crawler tractors; the 8-tonne Commer truck with P6 motor; the Shearer bridle-draft scarifiers; and the 1950 Cliff and Bunting wire-tie hay baler, had all been doing their job for many years and remained in service for all the time I was at Kulin. The later purchased Chamberlain Super 70, Super 90 and 9G tractors; the Shearer Culti-trash seeders; the Horwood Bagshaw 168 and International A81 headers were all later additions, but had long service on the farm. I remember The Boss saying of his D30 truck:

> During the war, it was the only reliable vehicle on the farm. We had it fitted with a gas producer and used it for all our social activity and trips to Perth, as well as farm work. I was always worried the Army would commandeer it and swore if they tried, it would be hidden at the back of the salt lake, well out of sight.[8]

The second lesson was: 'Never stint on fertiliser inputs and keep up with your paddock husbandry.' All fertiliser came in bags and trace elements were now widely accepted, particularly copper and zinc. The rule of thumb was 'a bag to the acre', but the role of top dressing pasture paddocks during the clover rotation was less widely adopted. All weed control was by cultivation with fallow on the heavy country still employed. Pre-seeding scarifying, often two or three times in the wet early 1960s, and post-seeding heavy harrowing were carefully considered and undertaken.

Thirdly: 'The benefit of a balanced sheep and cropping enterprise.' Sheep were not only good for weed management but also complemented the crop return, utilising frosted or drought-affected crops and the grain left in the paddock post-harvest. The headers of the time weren't as efficient as those of today. The Boss used to say:

> Look around the district. The successful families have always stuck with their sheep. It's those who do away with sheep after a good crop or two who don't last the distance.

Fourthly: 'Feed your sheep properly.' There were always two large silos of oats on hand and the Hodgsons were very innovative in the use of hay. The wire-tie baler was used every year, with a few laps cut around crop paddocks for extra fire protection as well as conserving pasture hay. The baler had a four-cylinder Wisconsin petrol engine and required a person to sit alongside the bale chamber to tie the bales, which was very dusty work as the rammer thumped the bale along, right in front of your face. Lambing percentages, together with wool weight and quality, were always above the district average as a result of a good all-year-round feeding regime. The Hodgsons bought their rams from Phil Freebairn, who was one of the last studs in the state still based on the Murray blood line from South Australia.

The fifth lesson I learnt, which was to influence my later life, was 'salinity management'. The 2,600 acres of heavy country to the southeast of the Jilakin salt lake had been cleared after the First World War and were now showing the effects of a rising water table, with subsequent bare scalding of the lower parts of the paddock. Sheep would camp on these bare, cooler places, which exacerbated the problem. Bevan 'Blue Bush' Parker from next door, together with The Boss, were working closely with Clive Malcolm from the Ag Dept and hosted several trial plots and field days over the years I was there.[9] As a result, these bare areas were fenced off, following Clive's advice:

> Don't be mean – fence off more than you think. Go out past the barley grass line, well into your good pasture area. That way you won't have to move the fence after a year or two.

Barley grass *Hordeum glaucum* and *H. leponinum* are the most salt tolerant of pasture species and the last plant present before land succumbs to bare salt scald. As there were a number of fenced-off areas, water had to be brought in with the use of polythene piping. The Boss bought up all the rusty water tanks at clearing sales, lined them with rabbit netting, then cement rendered the interior. After a lesson from local contractor John Galloway, I did all the cement work. Water pressure was achieved by installing a 30-foot tank stand at the house dam.

Chamberlain Super 70 tractor and 1950 Cliff and Bunting wire-tie hay baler, Kulin, 1961

Rehabilitation was achieved by ripping on the contour and sowing a combination of old man saltbush (*Atriplex nummularia*), creeping saltbush (*Atriplex semibaccata*) and blue bush *Maireana brevifolia* into the furrows. Sheep were only allowed access after the saltbushes were well established, then monitored carefully to prevent overgrazing. As the saltbushes matured and developed deeper root systems, there was evidence of, firstly, barley grass then other pastures re-establishing in these areas. As Clive said:

> Think of these saltbush paddocks as living haystacks. They provide good feed and shelter at important times of the year, such as freshly off-shears or for lambing.

Finally, I learnt to 'respect fire' – and the need for precautionary measures to limit the threat of its devastating impact. Local brigades regularly burnt the railway reserves in late spring in the days of steam engines, along with other reserves and roadside vegetation. The Boss was meticulous with his firebreaks and regular burning of patches of bush as well as an annual burn of grass around the sheds and homestead. Mrs Hodgson and the 'married man's' wife used to complain bitterly about ash cinders landing on their washing for weeks afterwards. As a farm and in the wider community, the emphasis was on prevention and I believe we have lost a lot of the self-reliance that used to underpin society.

One of the most influential aspects of Harry Hodgson's mentoring was his strongly held views on politics, marketing and community service. He was a great supporter of the Country Party:

> If we don't have a voice in Parliament, we'll get taken for a ride by the ever-increasing city population – and most of them have no idea where the nation's wealth is coming from.

He staunchly promoted the benefits of the Australian Wheat Board. He believed that having confidence in the marketing of your product freed you up to concentrate on the growing and tending of your crops. Farmers could then concentrate on what they did best:

> I clearly remember the indignity of dozens of buyers driving around in flash cars during the depression, all trying to outsmart each other, and you never knew which ones would go broke and leave you out of pocket.

Harry Hodgson was a great example of 'giving back to your community'. This was demonstrated by his policy of buying locally, giving employment to those in need, being Road Board chairman for many years and supporting the Farmers Union, Junior Farmers and other groups around town. Cooperative Bulk Handling was his favourite example of community pulling together to benefit all: he was one of the first to move towards total bulk handling of the harvest and kept pointing out the advantages of efficient storage, quality protocols and insect control.

Now, to the serious matter of my farming future. In 1962 I started quizzing The Boss on his thoughts about either share farming or farm management as a career path. After a few of these conversations, one day he said: 'Have you ever thought of taking on a new-land block? David Brand and Crawford Nalder are opening up a million or so acres a year for selection.'

I said: 'It's never crossed my mind! You realise I have no capital backing, so couldn't do something like that with no income for the first few years.' His response was:

> Well, I've had a word with the accountants. They suggest if you got yourself a block, we could form a partnership to farm the land, with us gaining the tax benefits and you not paying interest until the initial development is completed.

We talked the idea over carefully and felt it could be a win–win for both parties. I could do the initial clearing, burning, ploughing and root raking in the off season, then do the seeding and harvesting at Kulin for a further two or three years. There was an allocation coming up south of Ongerup and east of Borden, so The Boss, Geoff and I went down for a look. There were newly formed dirt roads and we had to guess at likely boundary positions. We liked the look of the two most southern blocks which butted on to established farms, where we chanced upon a Land Rover coming towards us, so stopped to swap notes. An attractive woman with blonde hair, dressed in jodhpurs and work shirt, climbed out:

> Hello, I'm Hazel Pither from over the road. Are you checking out those new blocks? Come on in and meet John and we'll pass on what we know – we've only been here a few years ourselves.

As we followed the Land Rover to the old Oakdale homestead, The Boss muttered: 'If they breed 'em like that down here, the country must have something going for it!'

I applied for either of the two southern blocks, was selected to attend a sitting of the Land Board and duly allocated Kent location 1835, of 2,500 acres, in mid-1963. I was overwhelmed by the rapid unfolding of events and said something to the effect of how lucky I was to have the backing and support of the Hodgson family in giving me the chance of farming. A reply from The Boss has stayed with me to this day: 'In this world, everyone gets their share of luck. It takes courage to grab it with both hands when it comes your way.'

Harry Hodgson died in 1983. In 1974 Geoff married Catherine Kavanagh, an attractive Irish school teacher in town. They have three children: Hilary (b. 1977), Marjorie (b. 1981) and Harry (b. 1983), and now farm 14,000 hectares, having bought the farms belonging to the Tholstrups, Ray Baldock, 'Ten Bob' Dimasi and Freebairn's old block.

Just as Harry sr had expanded to remain viable, so the present generation is doing likewise. Many of the adages of the 1960s are holding true: farm machinery is still being well cared for and gives long service, with the TD14 crawler tractor still being in use; sheep remain very much part of the mix, with renewal of yards and fences taking place; fertilising, including the use of lime, is carefully monitored; and spraying rigs have replaced the tillage machines. New weeds, such as caltrop (*Tribulus terrestris*) and statice (*Limonium perezii*), are creating fresh challenges.

Harry sr can rest in peace, knowing that Geoff and Harry jr are building on the solid foundation he provided for them.

14 Tillgaree, the Mallee Block

In the 1840s and '50s, squatters moved beyond the boundaries of the 19 counties of New South Wales to the Riverina and beyond. At the turn of the century, pastoralists forged ever further inland in South Australia, Queensland and Western Australia. Following the First World War, returned soldiers and other settlers were allocated 640-acre (or one square mile) farms for cultivation. After the Second World War, larger war service farms were provided.

Now it was the turn for my generation. We were all aware that the massive allocation of land in WA from the late 1950s onwards would be the last of its type in Australia. The Brand government was re-elected for a record four terms with the promise of opening up one million acres a year for farming. (Sir David was to become WA's longest serving and last rural-based premier, being in office for 12 years from 1959 to 1971.)

The government established a Land Board to oversee a system of conditional purchase, to provide an opportunity for new entrants to farming. Applicants had to demonstrate practical experience in farming and have modest financial backing, which was a very fine balance. The conditions were clearly spelt out:

> Applicants may be allotted one location only. The selector, or his agent, must take up residence within three years from date of approval and make it his habitual residence for the following five years. The selector shall, in each of the first four years, clear and cultivate 250 acres or one-tenth of the area, whichever is the lesser. In the third year and each of the following three years thereafter, plant to pasture or cereal crop the aforesaid 250 acres or one-tenth of the area. Such clearing, cultivation and pasture shall be properly maintained during the term of the lease. Section 47 provides that the lessee shall expend in prescribed improvements an amount

equal to one-fifth of the purchase money in every year of the first 10 years thereof and shall fence in at least one half of the land within the first five years and the whole of the land during the said period of 10 years.[10]

The land was leased to the successful applicant for up to 10 years at a modest annual payment. Conditions were to be completed by that time, when purchase to freehold the land would take place, or could be done sooner if conditions went ahead of schedule. Blocks varied in price according to land type, with Kent location 1835 of 2,500 acres being set at 10 shillings per acre for purchase and £3/10/05 a year lease.[11]

The land was undulating, with mallee vegetation on shallow, sandy loam over clay soils. The creek lines included well-developed Yate (*Eucalyptus occidentalis*) that would not be cleared and there was some box poison in the southeast corner. The higher country had lovely views over the Pallinup Valley to the Stirling Ranges, which provided a sense of place in the landscape.

Mum and Dad came down to see what I had let myself in for and suggested I contact John and Tony O'Meehan at Borden, who might be able to provide useful information. Dad had known their father, Frank, who from 1921 was a major shareholder in Three Rivers station, out from Meekatharra. The O'Meehans suggested I contact either John and Mary Bryant, Peter Crossing or the Stockwell boys, who were all developing land allocated in 1958, so on various weekend trips down from Kulin I managed to catch up with them. The Bryants were fairly well set up – and married – so I gravitated to the single ones who were 'doing it tougher'.

Peter was a Muresk graduate who had worked at Kojonup for a few years and then taken up residence in 1960 in basic quarters, built into the end of the machinery shed. Graham, Richard and John Stockwell had driven a 3-ton Austin truck over from Wellington in NSW and were also living in the end of the shed. Their mother, Ruth, had recently arrived and was living in a caravan nearby and providing for them.[12]

All of them related tales of woe, concerning their tractor and plough tyres being staked by the sharp mallee spikes, following the burns. They were still having problems with dingoes coming out of the Stirling Range National Park but assured me that my area of North Chillinup was free from dogs. Peter, in his dry laconic way, convinced me that batching was manageable enough:

Just do a big shop up when you go to town, eat your meat and veggies while they're fresh, but have a good reserve supply of tinned stuff like baked beans and sardines on hand, with lots of dry cracker biscuits.[13]

With information gleaned from the Pithers and the three contacts from over the Pallinup River, together with knowledge of Hodgson's development activity, a program was sketched out. Kent location 1835 was divided into three almost equal sections by a creek that forked out in the middle of the farm. It was decided to clear one section a year, burn the following autumn, plough and root rake during that year and crop the next season. In that way, if we cleared the first third in 1963, it would all be cropped by 1967 or 1968. Cropped areas would be followed by pasture establishment and fencing so that sheep could be introduced. It all sounded straightforward!

The Findlay Brothers from Narrikup were contracting in the area and it was arranged they would clear the southwest section as soon as possible, so the scrub could dry out sufficiently for a good burn early in 1964. They completed the clearing using a large karri log behind their 70-horsepower Fiat crawler tractor, then ploughed and raked the fire breaks for a total of £449/4/–.

I clearly recall the intoxicating aromas of freshly logged mallees. The pervading smell of eucalyptus in the air was the smell of progress to a young man on the cusp of his farming career.

I was making regular trips down from Kulin over most weekends in late 1963 and gladly accepted John and Hazel Pither's offer of a bed if I needed to stay overnight. They were still in the old Oakdale homestead built in the 1920s and had five children: John jr, Jenny, Colin, Sarah and Kate. Hazel worked full time in the paddock doing most of the sheep work, while John was flat out doing the cropping and further land development. As a result, the home front was rather chaotic, with house chores a distant last behind the farm work. Hazel continued the tradition of the stock-camp and was ahead of today's trend of the 'slow cooked meal', as at lunch time she would put a roast, stew or casserole in the oven and serve it up five or six hours later for dinner. Depending on the vagaries of the wood being burned, the meals varied from excellent to degrees of overcooked! There was always a comfortable bed, shared by a range of cats and dogs if the door was left open. If I thought the Noble and Magee families were good to me in Kulin, I found the Pither family extraordinarily generous, warm and welcoming.

I had a new farm and thought it was appropriate to name it. I didn't want any run-of-the-mill names used by others, so dreamt up Tillgaree, using syllables from various place names that came to mind. A handpainted sign was erected near the entrance to the block. I was often asked as to the meaning of the name, so in later years added 'home of the contented kangaroo' to the sign, as damage to unfenced new-land crops by roos, emus and even wild brumbies proved to be a considerable problem.

The farm is named, 1964

I was back at Hodgsons for harvest, then headed for Perth and the fortnight's annual holiday. The 11-year-old FJ ute was showing its age and while in Perth I traded it in for a new EH Holden ute with the optional extras of sun visor, heater and radio! I received £170 as a trade and paid a further £840 to complete the deal. It was the first model with the new improved red motor and 12-volt electrics, and was a dream by comparison. I still think it was one of the best Holdens ever made as compared to other vehicles of the time.

The Pithers and my neighbours to the north and west had also cleared bush at the end of 1963, so it was decided we would all work together when the fire season opened in March. Local volunteer fire brigades were at their peak of

Alex's drawing sent home at time of the first harvest 1965, showing invading animals!

effectiveness in the 1960s, all on mobile ex-army radios and not yet hindered by **bureaucracy**. Keith Wellstead was the local captain, operating with authority and almost a sixth sense as to the vagaries of fire activity. His favourite plan was to light up the downwind side first, then quickly race around the whole perimeter so that it would all draw into the centre: 'See how well that went – it created its own wind and that white mushroom cloud up there is always a sure sign of a good burn.'

We were lighting up to 1,000 acres in a single burn and always stayed around for a few beers until the cool evening breeze came in. Keith was a careful operator and, even while we were having a beer, always had one crew patrolling the downwind side in case of any 'hop-overs'. Fire officers of the day were known to 'light up' Crown land abutting farms and did so in the spring and autumn when paddocks were green, often coinciding with thunderstorm activity so not too many questions were asked. It imitated Aboriginal firestick practices and was better for the environment as well as protecting community assets. As Keith said:

> The early Wellstead and Moir settlers always burnt strips back into the bush for a 100 years or so and was what the blackfellas had

been doing for thousands of years. That way, animals and people always had a safe haven of recently burnt bush. There were never any disastrous out-of-control fires in those days.

It was the first time I met my two neighbours. Roy Owens was to the west and I discovered he was a builder 'having a go at farming for a change', planning to build a house on the block before bringing his family to live there. Peter 'Bolo' Ellis to the north was a big, free-wheeling sort of young bloke who had been at 'The Prac' with me in earlier days and was now working at Nungarin with the Herbert family. His plans were similar to mine: a year or two of working on the new block, while doing the seeding and harvesting in the Wheatbelt.

Back at Kulin, the Hodgsons and I discussed the type of plant that would best suit our needs. With some advice from Jimmy McCracken at Watson's Chamberlain dealership, we decided on a Countryman tractor with a six-cylinder Perkins engine and an 18-disc Chamberlain plough. The Stockwell and Crossing tales of woe regarding tyre troubles convinced us to try 'Bomber' tyres on the rear of the tractor, with 'over covers' on the front and plough wheels. Bomber tyres were ex-aircraft tyres that had been retreaded with lug grips and were 14 ply in thickness. It sounded a good idea. The plant was ordered for winter delivery to Kulin – £2,570 for the tractor and £839 for the plough. After seeding was completed at Hodgsons, I drove the plant to the block, down through Lake Grace, Pingrup and Ongerup. It meant leaving in the dark and arriving in the dark, but was achieved within the day. A seven-reel Horwood Bagshaw root rake costing £808 was ordered through Wesfarmers' Gnowangerup branch.

The Pither family came to the rescue and offered me board for the first year's ploughing and root raking, following the burn. How quickly the sense of pride and joy was shattered, as within an hour I had the first rear tyre puncture! At that stage I had no air compressor so went back to the Pithers 'on the sponge'. I persevered for a week, averaging one puncture a day before making some alterations. I set up an air compressor on the tractor, which worked from the power-take-off, and carried the full complement of jack, tyre levers and repair kit with me. A rear tyre could now be fixed in an hour instead of half a day or so if there was a long walk back to the ute. The worst day was three punctures but I continued to average about one a day for the rest of the year.

There was only the ploughing and root raking done in 1964 and a further 700 acres cleared and firebreaks installed, so I spent the rest of the time at Kulin.

Sue and Liz in front of Chamberlain tractor (note bomber tyres and radiator guard)

We decided 1965 would be the year to 'really get into action' and go full-time farming on my own. I organised Roy Owens to build a two-room shack with a verandah and bathroom (similar ablution arrangements as at Kulin) and an outside 'dunny', with a Sani-pan 'thunderbox' for visitors use. A 60 by 40 foot Mills and Hassell machinery shed was ordered through Wesfarmers for £947. As the shack was nearing completion, I headed for Perth to purchase a second-hand truck and put together some furniture for my batching future. Used trucks were hard to find but I finally settled on a 1949 'O model' 8-ton Bedford from Atwood Motors for £385. The Swan Brewery had used it to deliver kegs of beer.

I bought a new Metters 'Insulheat No 2' stove from their Subiaco factory (just north of the railway station), some Tilley lamps and a second-hand Electrolux kerosene 'fridge'. The word was put about by Mum, which caused all the aunts, neighbours and friends to donate the rest, resulting in a bizarre collection of furniture, linen, kitchen utensils and things to hang on the walls. 'I feel ashamed at the truckload of hand-me-downs out there – the neighbours must be wondering what on earth's going on.'

Mum's concern was like water off a duck's back. Tim followed me back to the block in the ute and stayed on for a few days while waiting for a lift back to Perth.

Bachelor's quarters, 1965

Mills and Hassall shed and bachelor's quarters, 1965

A 24-run Shearer Culti-trash seeder with extra urea box was ordered from H.C. Trappitt & Sons in Borden for £1,242. Seed wheat was obtained from the Pithers and bagged super-copper-zinc, at £26/2/6 per ton, was delivered by Southern Transport along with bagged urea. Ploughing, root raking and seeding between 700 and 800 acres a year kept me busy. As I was no longer working at Kulin, I undertook contract ploughing and root raking for Roy Owens in order to keep food on the table.

Peter Crossing's advice about batching was close to the mark. I cooked eggs and bacon for breakfast, cut sandwiches for a paddock lunch and had sausages, chops or baked beans for dinner, depending on how long it was from the last trip to town. Extra grocery opportunities arose with hasty trips to town for spare parts, as the newly prepared mallee country was hard on machinery. In 1964 a further 22 blocks were opened up to the south of mine, down towards the Pallinup River. Successful applicants included: Ian MacMillan, Bill Jenson, Frank Pritchard and Henry Reynolds, who were all single, while Barry and Florence King, together with John and Helen ten Seldam were married. Peter Ellis and I joined in with them all and a real camaraderie developed. When coming home from town late in the day, you would call in on somebody with food and a cold beer and yarn away into the night. The Pithers, Kings and ten Seldams were very hospitable to we single men and, as there were no telephones, they often accumulated unexpected visitors in the evenings.

One memorable day I had run out of fresh meat and while driving the tractor planned a grand meal. I was going to boil potatoes, mash them and mix in a tin of salmon, so as to fry up some fish patties. All went to plan until the first mouthful – in the half light of the Tilley lamp, I had used washing-up detergent instead of cooking oil to fry the patties. Back to baked beans!

A seemingly casual event occurred just before harvest in 1965. I had been going to Perth a few times a year, enjoying family life back at Loftus Street and the odd social outing. On this occasion Tim said: 'It's Tom Hollingsworth's 21st birthday party tomorrow night and I'm sure you'd be welcome.'

A phone call to Tom confirmed the arrangement and it was there that I met Jenny Levinson for the first time. She was an attractive 19-year-old and going out with Tom, so I thought no more about it at the time. Harvest was approaching and there were jobs to be done.

I bought a second-hand 14-foot International A81 header from Felix Berger's agency in Gnowangerup for £1,000, along with several weld mesh silos that were lined with hessian. Southern Transport had a fleet of Foden semi-trailer trucks, equipped with their own augers, which they would drop into these flimsy storage bins. It was dangerous work as the silos would collapse sideways if the grain was not removed equally from the middle. If they cleaned the grain too close to ground level, you would be docked for contamination, and if they left too much behind, you were losing money.

The cropping and development work was now an established routine. Gamenya and Insignia wheat were used for the first crop, with Beecher six-row barley or Prior two-row barley for subsequent crops. The initial crops were followed by pasture establishment, which consisted of Woogenellup and Rose clover with Wimmera ryegrass.

Findlay Bros had put in two 2,000-cubic-yard dams for £550 and it was time to start fencing. Five-line Ringlock prefabricated netting was chosen, with two plain wires above. White gum *E. wandoo* strainer posts were bought and, with some advice from John O'Meehan, I contacted Doug Moir at Sandalwood Farm concerning some jam (*Acacia acuminata*) fence posts that he had on hand:

> There's a stack of 3,000 posts here that I had cut for the Gairdner River War Service people, but they rejected them as being too small in diameter. You can have the lot for £180 if you like.

Jam is a particularly hard wood that lasts well when used for fencing so I wasn't too concerned about the size. With two loads on the Bedford, there were sufficient posts to fence the whole farm. The Pithers had been using contract fencers but decided to go half shares with me in a Pizey 'Rockmaster' post hole digger. I was all set to go and really enjoyed the thrill of a completed fence line: 'Look – it's as straight as a die and will be there for the next 50 years or so.'

Australia converted to decimal currency, weights and measures on 14 February 1966. Conservative farmers found the changes very difficult to understand and were outspoken about bureaucrats and politicians who had nothing better to do with their time:

> This bloody decimal business. My farm is now half the size, I live twice as far from town, my debt has doubled, the wool clip has halved and worst of all, I only get a quarter of the rain!

There was one other, more welcome change in 1966. Olympic introduced wire armour tractor tyres, which comprised a mesh of fine steel cables built into the rubber and were almost puncture-proof, so the 'bomber' tyres were replaced and life became much easier. Wally and Margaret Parnell's Chamberlain dealership provided a Gason tractor cab for £268, along with dual rear wheels and fitted power steering, which overcame the crippling experience of having the steering wheel wrenched out of your hands when hitting a stump. I also bought earmuffs for the first time, quickly realised their benefit and wondered how we had all survived without them. It was now an upgraded and very fine Chamberlain 'Countryman' tractor and, to this day, I can still close my eyes and conjure up the steady rhythmic beat of the Perkins six-cylinder motor.

Mallee roots were a continual problem. They were still being brought to the surface after several crop rotations, but not in the numbers to warrant root raking. The only solution was hand picking, using the Bedford truck, the benefit being a rapidly expanding wood heap near the house. There are about 400 species of mallee, all having a lignotuber, or a submerged trunk. They evolved to burn back to ground level after a fire, then sprout away again from the 'stump', which continues to grow ever larger. It was the blue mallee (*E. pleurocalpa*) that was the bane of our lives, as it was the biggest of all and the toughest to plough out.

'You should've seen the blue mallee root I turned out today – as big as your kitchen table.'

'Yes, I had one the other day – the plough fair lifted off the ground once the discs hooked on to it.'

I was developing a love-hate relationship with the 1949 Bedford truck. Any replacement would have been costly, so I made the decision to stick with it and make some necessary improvements, which included converting to 12-volt electrics. The cooling system was non-pressurised, so overheating was a big problem, especially during the fire season when patrolling sandy fire breaks with 5,000 litres of water on board. The problem was overcome by fitting a temperature gauge to the motor, then a hose from the fire-fighting unit through the cab to the top of the radiator, with a tap under the driver's seat to regulate the extra cooling requirement. Heath Robinson, but effective! It still had a mechanical arm on the driver's door for hand signals and even though it looked old fashioned and out of date, I have often wished we still owned it as a vintage vehicle.

A more significant event occurred later in 1966. The crop was in, the next rotation of ploughing and root raking was completed, so it was time for another trip to Perth. I was swapping notes with Tim and the subject of Tom's 21st birthday party came up: 'Tom was taking Jenny Levinson out, but I don't think it was very serious and they've gone their separate ways.'

That seemed useful information as I recalled the attractive, vivacious girl of eight months ago and, with unusual courage, I phoned her: 'You probably won't remember me, but we met at Tom's 21st and …'

Feminine caution and guile prevailed: 'I'm not sure if I do …'

From then on trips to Perth became more frequent, with letters being the main form of communication. The nearest phone was at the Pithers' – an unreliable single-wire 'earth return' party line with eight subscribers, which was used only as a last resort. The Pithers' number was 10G, with the call sign 'two longs and a short' being the Morse code signal. I can remember the tension of listening for that signal on the few occasions when I was waiting for Jenn to call back for some reason or other.

There were necessary changes made for harvest, as the weld mesh silos were proving to be unsatisfactory and had to be located near good roads for access by Southern Transport. Permanent 'pig pen' storage with cement floors were built near the shed, a new auger bought for $390 and a second-hand 100-bag capacity bin for the truck was $260. The target I set myself was two loads a day in an average crop. There were some interesting times driving the 18-year-old Bedford through the creeks on the farm with 8 tonnes of wheat on board. I often wondered what would happen if I missed the gear change from second to first in the four-speed 'crash' gearbox.

Harvest was completed, the grain delivered to CBH, and now there were more pressing thoughts and dilemmas at hand. I thought I had 'found the right girl for me' but how could I expect anybody to share such basic living conditions? Jenn had been down to visit and, decorum being what it was in those days, had stayed with the Pithers. She met the other new-land farming friends and knew how far from everything we were, but would she ever consider sharing that sort of life with me? To my great relief and surprise, the answer was 'yes'. Formalities were still the order of the day, so I broached the subject with her father, Robert Levinson: 'I suppose I should ask if you can keep her in the manner to which she is accustomed?'

'Well, I have to be completely honest – if I was sold up today, my liabilities would exceed my assets, but I have great confidence in the future.'

'Well, that's alright. Now tell me about that farm of yours.'

Chamberlain 'Countryman 6' Tractor, International A81 Header and 1949 Bedford truck, 1966

Robert was helping Jenn's brother, Barry, establish a new-land farm at Tone River, southwest of Kojonup, so was obviously well aware of the up-front expenditure needed for such a venture and wished us well. We decided on a 12-month engagement so that Jenn could do another year's teaching in Perth, while I would have time to add two more rooms to my bachelor's quarters and install running water and a septic system.

The Levinson family have an interesting Australian story. They moved from Posen, Poland, to Sheffield, England, in 1834 to avoid Jewish persecution of the time. When only 20 years old, the eldest son, Hyman Levinson, moved to Ballarat and set himself up in a tent as a watchmaker and jeweller. It was 3 December 1856 – the day of the Eureka Rebellion! The following year he is reported as saying:

> You ask what it was like at Ballarat last December. It was terrible, terrible! I had only just arrived. That Thursday was the day I opened my tent for business. Then the rioting began. I saw men fighting and soldiers everywhere. I grabbed my stock of watches and stuffed them in my pockets. Then an armed digger – a German man – accosted me.

'Out of my way,' he said.

'What are you going to do?' I cried.

'Shoot that Army Captain over by the road there,' he said.

'How could I stand still and watch a poor man be shot dead, so I called a warning. The soldier took my warning and got away, but now the German miners were after me.'[14]

Hyman was saved by another tent-holder and hid under a stretcher bed until the rebellion ceased. Hyman's brother, Mark, came to join him in 1861 and they soon had two successful jewellery businesses operating in Sturt Street. Mark was very mechanically minded: he invented the first safety lift for underground mining and was involved with the first telephone service in town.[15] The brothers moved to Perth in 1896 as the WA goldfields were attracting men away from the depleted Victorian mines. By 1926, after several earlier locations, they had built Sheffield House in Hay Street and were employing 110 staff in the four-storey building. Levinson and Sons were now the respected jewellers of Perth.

Mark Levinson married Amelia Minowski and their two sons, Eugene and Felix, joined the Perth business. While on a sea voyage, Eugene fell in love with Esther Moss from Dunedin, New Zealand. The Levinsons were no longer practising their Jewish faith, but Esther was from a devout family who were very much observing their faith and traditions. The common bond was music, with Esther being a talented pianist and Eugene a violinist. In the mid-1920s Esther sailed for New Zealand to visit her family and, while away, Eugene and Felix had all their children christened into the Church of England. According to the family story, it was the importation of a Bechstein grand piano from Hamburg, Germany, that saved the marriage!

Eugene and Esther had three children: Robert (Jenn's father), Malcolm and Merle. The boys continued the family business until it was sold to Caris Bros in 1961. So ended three generations of jewellers, spanning a little more than 100 years, in Ballarat and Perth. Robert married May Tindal in 1939 and had four children: Barry (15 September 1941), Ross (15 December 1943), Jennifer (23 August 1946) and Christine (16 March 1949). For most of their married life, Robert and May lived at 53 Archdeacon Street, Nedlands.[16]

Farm development was still demanding attention. I now had 700 acres of pasture on fenced and watered land that was the first cleared, so went into Wesfarmers at Gnowangerup where I had bought all the fertiliser, fencing materials, machinery shed and root rake, but had never used them for credit.

I put the proposition to them of providing the finance for 1,000 ewes and, to my horror and disbelief, was informed that my equity was not sufficient for such an arrangement. I then went down the street to Elders GM and asked to speak to the manager, who I had never met. I was now lacking confidence so started on the long story of new-land development, the 700 acres of pasture that was ready for stocking, and just getting into my stride when Peter Moulton interrupted:

'How many ewes do you want?'

'One thousand.'

'And I suppose a few rams?'

'Well, yes.'

'Good. There's a sale at Katanning next week and I'll get Ross Coole to take you along, then on the way home call in at Keith Richardson's Mianellup stud. He has good Collinsville rams that will suit you down to the ground.'

The Collinsville stud had been established by John Collins in South Australia in 1895. It was his son, A.L. (Art) Collins, who developed the stud, bringing together the best of the Peppin styled wool and the robustness of the local Koonoona and Bungaree blood lines. By the 1960s, it was estimated that one-third of the Australian flock was being influenced by Collinsville, with up to half the flock in WA. In SA, the parent stud was selling more than 3,000 rams a year, rising to 4,000 in the 1980s under Tom Padbury's guidance.[17] (Little did we know that a Gnowangerup farmer, Neil Garnett, would decimate the parent stud some 100 years after its founding.)

There were many daughter studs in WA, with Keith Richardson's Mianellup being the local standout. Fred House established Barloo as a daughter stud to Mianellup. Other well-known Collinsville studs in the area included Glen Garnett's Glenroy, Bill Gaze's Yarrawee and Tom Wellard's Yeadgee. Tom had a soft spot for the war service farmers around Gairdner River and would always 'throw in an extra one' when they came to collect their rams. Another example of generosity arose when John O'Sullivan from Gairdner River lost 1,200 wether hoggets, being off shears in an unusual summer rainfall event. When he went to collect his annual order of 20 rams from Bill Gaze, he was told: 'These are on me. You had a run of bad luck and I am sorry I couldn't get to the busy bee when you were burying the hoggets.'

All those mentioned were fine honest men and great supporters of the local community. With a minimum of paperwork, the deal was done and I was now an Elders client. From that day on, right to the end of our farming life, we have repaid the trust shown by Peter Moulton and remained loyal to the company. It's interesting to reflect on the scale of operation that Elders had in a medium-sized town like Gnowangerup. There were two 'stockies' and a merchandise man on the road and, with the manager, they required four cars – either Fords purchased from Eric Richards & Staff or Holdens from G.S. Hendry & Co. There was a girl and chief clerk in the office, with another merchandise man running the store, making seven full-time staff in all. Elders also owned two houses in town as well as the shop front in the main street.[18]

E.B. (Eddie) Norrish owned and ran the Elders agency at Borden from 1951 to 1986 and 'was as good as any two ordinary blokes put together'. He earned the tremendous loyalty of clients from Borden to Bremer Bay and serviced them well. For example, he would pick up a truckload of jute wool packs from Albany and do a run in autumn and spring, dropping off clients' requirements and, in so doing, locking in the clip for later delivery to the Albany wool stores. In 1965 the Gnowangerup branch opened a satellite office at Jerramungup, with a girl in the office and another car on the road for the 'stockie'. In 1967/68, the Gnowangerup branch (which included the Borden agency) was second only to Moora, with a little more than 26,000 bales of wool delivered to the Elders Albany wool stores.[19]

By coincidence, there was an interesting cohort of 'stockies' who passed through the Elders branch at Gnowangerup in Peter Moulton's time as manager (1966–71). As well as Ross Coole, there were Nick Balfe, Garth Kelso, Jim Turley, Greg Hunt (who became Australasian manager for Elders) and Alan Daddow (Australasian assistant manager). There must have been something in the Gnowangerup water! Peter Moulton went on to become area manager for Elders at Katanning, an area stretching from Albany to Lake Grace with 89 staff, for the nine years from 1971 to 1980. His final 10 years with Elders were as state manager for insurance, based in Perth. Peter is an example of the many fine men who made their life careers with one of the pastoral houses. He operated in an era of mutual respect between client and company, an era slowly fading away as farms and service industries became more corporatised with a focus on the bottom line, rather than the human dimension of eye-to-eye contact, the shake of the hand and 'you are as good as your word'.[20]

Melbourne-based businessman John Elliot played a major part in this change of traditional business practices. In the early 1980s he bastardised the proud company, asset stripped it down to bare bones and slashed staff numbers. It also marked a change in status, with the pastoral houses now being referred to as 'stock firms' and no longer offering the premier career path for many bright young people leaving school. The founding Elder and Smith must have turned in their graves as the 100-year legacy of a great Australian agricultural company was torn apart.

With sheep on hand, it was time to brush up on stock management, as machinery and development work had hitherto been the main priorities and interest. Hazel Pither was a great admirer of Helen Newton-Turner's work at the CSIRO on sheep husbandry, especially increasing lambing percentages. She had all of Helen's papers on file and we often discussed aspects of her findings. Hazel also encouraged me to buy *Sheep Management and Diseases* by H.G. Belschner, which was the 'go to' publication of the day. At the time, we were being serviced by the Katanning office of the Ag Dept. George Halpin was the officer-in-charge, with a dry sense of humour and acidic turn of phrase, being supported by Peter Nelson, Peter Seaman, Gary Kennedy and Peter Rutherford as advisers. The department had trial plots on the Pithers' farm and field days were all well attended by the new-land farmers. Almost without exception, these great people were UWA graduates and were highly regarded by the farming community. The state government of the day has to be applauded for not only opening up vast areas of land for farm development, but also supporting the initiative with a well-resourced Department of Agriculture.[21]

I made early plans with our next-door neighbour, Roy Owens, about house additions. He had just started building a timber-framed four-stand shearing shed for the Pithers, and said:

> I'm a bit pushed for time, but if you lend me a hand building the shed and while we do your job, then I can fit it in – and it'll save you money.

It was one of the best experiences of my life. I really enjoyed the work, marvelling at the logical sequence of timber-framed construction and the way in which measurements were double checked with the 'plumb' of a building. The end result was akin to fencing: you could stand back, be proud of its true proportions and be confident it would be still giving good service for 50 years or more. It was very satisfying.

A 50,000-litre concrete rainwater tank was set up next to the machinery shed and, with Roy's help, we built a 3.5-metre tank stand for two 5,000-litre tanks, one for rainwater and the other for dam water. Jenn and Robert found a second-hand Everhot 240 slow combustion stove, which also operated the hot water system.

Meanwhile, Jenn was scouring the second-hand furniture shops in Perth and undertook the daunting task of building sitting room furniture from scratch. She attended Muriel Collins' upholstery classes and from bare wooden frames completed a three-piece lounge suite, a 'grandmother' style chair and a piano stool. The Sanderson-covered suite was to last us for the next 40 years. There was one final touch of good fortune: the Humphris family from Arthur River gave us an old 32-volt lighting-plant for a wedding present. It was powered by a slow-revving McDonald single-cylinder diesel motor with large flywheels. People were doing away with 32-volt units as the state-owned power network slowly covered the farming areas, so second-hand appliances such as irons, vacuum cleaners and Sunbeam Mixmasters were easy to obtain.

In the lead-up to the 1967 harvest, I was able to rest easy in the knowledge that all was ready for starting married life early the following year: house completed; hot and cold running water; 32-volt power; septic system – everything other than a phone. The lack of telephones was not such a problem for bachelors, but as they married it became a more pressing need. For example, Frank Pritchard had married Zanna Bagshaw in 1966 and they were expecting their first baby as harvest approached in 1967. Zanna had moved nearer to the Gnowangerup Hospital as the birth approached and was staying with the Formbys. Frank was a fire officer and had regular morning radio 'skeds', checking on the weather and other relevant matters. These 'skeds' were not to be used for social matters and, as Frank took these things seriously, it was arranged that a message, 'fire pump ready for delivery', would be the code for him to head to town to be with Zanna. All went to plan, though the message was a little different than he expected: 'Fire pump arrived early – without hose.'

Annabelle was born on 21 November 1967, to the delight of Frank and Zanna.

The 1967/68 harvest progressed well. I had mastered the art of new-land crop production and, with good seasons, subsidised fertiliser and high prices for wheat and wool, felt I had it made.

15 THE MALLEE BRIDE

Fresh stephanotis held Jenny Levinson's full-length veil when she married Alex Campbell yesterday at St Margaret's Church, Nedlands. Jenny is the daughter of Mr and Mrs R.F. Levinson, of Nedlands, and Alex is the son of Mr and Mrs D.H.A. Campbell, of Claremont. The bride was attended by her sister Chris, Alex's sister Sue, Jenny Rankin, of Nedlands and Sue Espie, of Nedlands. The best man was Alex's brother Tim and Ian MacMillan, Bill Jensen, both of Borden and Rex Noble, of Kulin, were groomsmen. The couple will live at Tillgaree, Borden.

These words, with an attached photograph in *The Sunday Times*, gave an accurate record of the day, 20 January 1968, but did little to explain the mixed emotions, ranging from nervous apprehension to pride and excitement. The marriage service was a blur of memory but I clearly recall walking arm in arm down the aisle and out of the church with a beautiful bride, ready to start our lives together. Jenn must have been wondering about the *richer or poorer* vow, but at least I offered robust good health against any concern over the *sickness* part of the contract!

Jenn had been a dedicated and respected teacher at Ardross Primary School, loved by her 45 year 1 and 2 students, and admired by their parents. She was moved to tears at seeing a number of these children in the church, who had come to see 'Miss Levinson dressed up as a bride'.

The reception was held at the Cottesloe Golf Club, with good food, music and the well wishes of family and friends. Speeches were short and sincere and the bridal waltz – which I was dreading – went off without too much damage to Jenn's wedding shoes. Rex Noble and others tied tin cans behind the car and we headed off to the South West for a 10-day honeymoon. Tim had loaned us his

Alex and Jenn leaving the wedding reception

Toyota Corona for the purpose and the days flew by as we enjoyed the beginning of life together and planning for the future. One plan involved the purchase of six pullets. They were put into a hessian sack for the trip home from Albany and on release into the recently built chookyard, one immediately laid an egg right in front of us. Surely it was a good omen?

There were quite a few young married people around us and Zanna Pritchard, Helen ten Seldam, Di Ellis, Florence King and Christabel Bennett all did their best to make Jenn feel welcome. Further afield in the older settled areas, Wendy and John O'Meehan, Les and Tony O'Meehan and Jeanette and Peter Thompson helped us in widening our social group. Trish Grahame, who Jenn had known for many years, had married Barry Witham from Tambellup, who I also knew from school days. They lived an hour or so west of us and became ever closer friends as the years passed. Trisha McLennan, a family friend from the Goldsbroughs days, married Peter Miles and they were developing new country in the South Stirling area, which extended our contacts in that direction. The Pithers were our generous and reliable neighbours, though their social life was being concentrated ever more towards equestrian activity.

There was another way of getting to know people. We had been agitating for a telephone service for the area and the Post Master General's (PMG) Department offered to install two automatic exchanges, so long as the community erected the lines out to the farms. There were about 50 properties to be connected and many meetings held to determine how we could fund and build the infrastructure to the rigid PMG requirements. It was decided we would all pay equally, whether closest or furthest from the exchanges, and the PMG offered second-hand copper wire and insulators from areas that were converting to underground cables. I am sure Jenn's eyes were opened to farm politics as discussion raged: contractors versus busy bees; what type of wooden poles should be used; who owned a reliable truck for carting the supplies; and, of course, whose home for the next meeting?

Another introduction to farm life was the need for contour banking and providing catchments for dams. I was an admirer of P.A. Yeomans' work and had copies of his *Keyline Plan* and *Water for Every Farm,* which had stimulated my interest in conservation practices. The Ag Dept at Katanning had Bob Nulsen and Joe Burdass as soil conservation advisers and David Stanton as an experienced technician for siting the contour banks. The initial fencing was along the boundary and major uncleared creek lines, but further subdivision was needed, so we planned to do this on the contour and to soil type, with further contour banks on the steeper, sloping land.[22] Jenn took her turn holding the staff, moving up or down the slope until the exact position was achieved, with either David Stanton or Joe Burdass manning the theodolite and waving their arms one way or the other. David was Jenn's first cousin and stayed overnight with us when in the area.

The most challenging ordeal for any newly wed young woman coming onto a farm were the sheep yards. The man of her dreams that seemed so charming and at ease with all around him would undergo a metamorphosis, becoming a totally different person and using language that would offend a bullocky. The yards were invariably blistering hot and dusty or freezing cold and nothing short of a quagmire. As new-land farmers, we couldn't afford to employ people, so relied on our wives to help with the drafting and other sheep work. Jenn quickly learnt the art of manning the drafting gate, but couldn't come to terms with my lack of self-control. There was an early test of will when the sheep refused to run through the drafting race and I yelled out: 'For heaven's sake take that bright scarf off, it's baulking the sheep and we'll never get the job finished!'

Jenn quickly told me what I could do with the scarf, sheep and sheep dog if I didn't appreciate her help. At least she didn't go storming off home, as one other wife did at a similar time. For all that, I continued to rely on her help for the rest of our farming days and she became as handy at manning the drafting gate as most of the stock firm blokes. (She was later to prove as adept in the cattle yards, using a length of black 'poly' pipe as her aid.)

The word was passed around that Jenn had been a teacher and she was asked to help set up a kindergarten at Boxwood Hills, to which she readily agreed. It was run on a volunteer basis, with her teaching until pregnancy brought her time there to an end. It was an isolated community, with only the hall, Eddie Norrish's Elders agency and Jim Wellstead's trucking business in the town site. Jim ran a few goats for milking and they would often lend a little interest to any activity at the hall, especially for the children.

A number of people came to stay for a day or two because, as you would expect, family and friends wanted to see just what Jenn had let herself in for. All went well, except for one friend who said: 'You have a sweet little cottage, but where on earth do you go for any social outings?'

'Oh, there are lots of things to do down here and lots of nice people,' was the staunch reply, which probably hid a few lingering home truths!

The run of visitors highlighted the lack of space in the 'sweet little cottage'. After seeding, we decided to close in the back verandah and add a garage and spare room to the side of the house. I had gleaned enough building knowledge from Roy Owens 'to be dangerous' and managed the job myself, without too many problems. Wind was the bane of our lives so open verandahs were never used and a brush fence was added to the back garden to prevent the Hills Hoist clothesline from going into orbit every wash day.

The EH Holden ute had now done more than 100,000 miles (too many trips to Perth over a one-year engagement) so it was traded for a new cream-coloured HT model. If the EH was the stand-out best Holden as compared to its competitors, the HT was surely the worst. From the day we bought it, we wished we had persevered with the old one.

Sheep numbers were steadily increasing and we continued to hire the Pithers' new four-stand shed, which I had helped Roy Owens build. It was rather awkward bringing the sheep the two kilometres to the shed – then to be confronted with a range of ponies in the sheep yards!

Jenn took on the job of collecting the twice-weekly mail from the corner of Oakdale and Toompup roads. We were serviced by the Borden to Bremer Bay mail run, which started its pick-up at Gnowangerup with grocery orders, bread and machinery parts filling the van, alongside the mail and papers collected in Borden. When dropping off the Pithers' assortment, Jenn was always confused by the various names that were dropped into the conversation: 'Rosie O'Grady is getting a bit full of herself – she will have to watch her manners.' And: 'Kenneth is really asserting himself – boys will be boys.'

Rosie was a large Irish terrier and Kenneth a stallion, and they were just as much members of the family as the five children.

Before we knew it, we were harvesting again – a good year, both from a cropping perspective and our first year of marriage. The harvest had been above average in Australia with 14.804 million tonnes, following only 7.547 million tonnes the year before, and there were worrying signs of oversupply bearing down on the market, caused by high global wheat stocks.[23]

In 1969 we were to recrop the first cleared land around the house, which had been in pasture for several years. All started well, with germination after a patchy opening rain allowing for cultivation and weed kill. There was no meaningful rain to follow and the district, indeed the whole of the state's agricultural area, was short of stock feed. Worse was to come as strong winds started to erode cultivated paddocks and dust storms became more frequent. The season continued to deteriorate, sand drifts covered the Hassell Highway in the Gairdner River area, and stories emerged of sheep yards filled with sand and fences buried, as sand built up against debris held by the fence wire. We were experiencing the harsh realities of the Australian climate, as had our great-grandfathers in the 1840s drought, our grandfathers in the Federation drought and our fathers in the 1940s drought. We sheltered in the house as the relentless wind howled outside, but could not escape the noise, sight, smell and feel of the dust that assaulted all our senses.

After the first bad storm, a plan was put in place to 'head for the hills' in future events. A picnic spot deep in the Stirling Range National Park was chosen. Without telephones to coordinate the activity, varying numbers congregated and lamented the wrath of God over a few beers and a grilled chop.

To add insult to injury, wheat quotas were introduced to address the grain oversupply. Quotas were determined against past delivery records, which impacted adversely against new-land farmers as our crops were from smaller areas and of lower yields in the early years of development. The other problem was rapidly falling sheep prices and the escalating cost of stock feed. Barry King and I took turns in providing a vehicle as we drove around the back roads of Albany; if we spotted a paddock with spare feed, we would knock on the farmer's door and enquire about agistment. After several days, we admitted defeat. There was no option but to sell stock so we arranged for Elders to bring a buyer to the farm, given the stories of auction prices not covering the cost of freight. Ross Coole arrived with the Borthwick meatworks buyer to look at 500 cast-for-age ewes, and he ran them through the drafting race into two similar sized mobs: 'I will give you 10 cents a head for that lot, but you will have to keep the others.'

There were dreadful stories of farmers shooting stock as the only option left to them and I didn't relish that solution. Box poison was one of the problems of new-land development, but there was word about that freshly germinated plants were not toxic to sheep. There was a 200-acre corner of the farm, the last to be cleared as it was covered in poison, which had been burnt early in 1969 and was fenced, with poison now germinating in the patchy rain. The 250 worthless ewes and a few old rams had to take their chances, so I 'scratched in' some oats and ryegrass on the fresh burn and hoped for the best. They all survived and even had an extra lamb, being the only good news in a bad year. If ever the adage 'it's 20 per cent breeding and 80 per cent feeding' was to apply to my farming life, 1969 was the year that demonstrated the point.

Box poison is but one of a hundred or so related plants in Australia, known by many local names, such as York Road, narrow leaf, heart leaf and Stirling Range. For more than 150 years they had been the farmer's curse, being highly toxic to introduced sheep, cattle and horses. It's only recently that the active component, *sodium flouroacetate*, has been used as the base for 1080 poison for the control of rabbits, foxes and feral cats. Native animals have evolved to tolerate the poison so are not affected by the use of 1080, resulting in a much needed breakthrough in managing our unique flora and fauna. From curse to saviour!

The cultivated paddocks blowing in the wind needed cover to stop erosion. After a light rain, I sowed the crop at an increased rate of seed, going backwards and forwards against the prevailing wind so that the furrows might contain the blowing sand. One day while on the tractor, a ute came across the paddock and waited at the corner next to the truck. Bill Jensen introduced Darryl Smith and they came straight to the point:

The drought and low commodity prices are affecting all of us – we need to stick together and fight for our future. We are sounding people out about starting a Farmers Union branch at Boxwood Hills and signing up new members.

They suggested a date for the first meeting and I promised to attend. Darryl was really 'doing it tough' and had taken up shearing to keep bread on the table, whereas Bill was better set up than most of us. It provided a valuable early lesson: membership of the Farmers Union attracted a cross-section of the community, from those who had the best interests of agriculture at heart to those who had unrealistic expectations of some form of government assistance to save their farms.

There was another influence on my awakening to farm politics. Big Bill Gunn! He had been promoting a reserve price scheme for wool during the 1960s and was often interviewed on the ABC Country Hour. I attended a meeting at Katanning, where he was guest speaker as chairman of the Australian Wool Board, and was captivated by the drive and enthusiasm of the big man in his crumpled suit, hair parted down the middle and big, booming voice. While his towering 6-foot 5-inch, 15-stone presence dominated the podium, it was his 'take no prisoners' style of delivery that dominated the room. I was particularly attracted to the three main tenets of his proposal: wool is the only globally traded commodity where Australia enjoys a dominant position and we should use that to our advantage; most of our inputs to farming are protected by tariffs so we should have a matching form of assistance; the peaks and troughs of the auction system equally harmed both the growers and end users of wool.[24] While many were pushing for total acquisition to achieve these goals, I was more drawn towards a reserve price mechanism with a modest floor, operating within the auction system, and publicly supported those pushing for that outcome. Looking back, it was the first time I dipped my toe into the water of farm politics, though as one of the troops rather than in any leadership role.

A referendum in 1965 for a reserve price scheme was defeated, but after another five years of barnstorming around the nation, Bill Gunn and others successfully built the case for its introduction in 1970. The Farmers Union was one of the many organisations supporting the changes, which helped motivate me to be an active member. Doug Anthony, the federal leader of the Country Party and minister for agriculture, was able to achieve the necessary parliamentary approval for its establishment without the need for another referendum, and gained widespread support and recognition throughout rural Australia for his efforts. Driving home the need for a change was the nation's wool income declining from close to $1,000 million in 1963 to only $300 million in 1970. The introduction was made possible with objective measurement and sale by sample, innovations that many claimed would not have occurred in the old, 'free' system. Bill, later Sir William, was also credited with the introduction of the Woolmark symbol through his involvement with the International Wool Secretariat.[25]

For all the tribulations of drought, wheat quotas and low wool prices, there was one bright star on the horizon – we were expecting a baby! Jenn had been putting her dressmaking skills to good effect, making ever larger maternity dresses. We spent time converting the spare room–office into a nursery-office and getting together the paraphernalia for a baby. How could a little baby demand such a collection of new furniture and clothing? No matter – there was joy and excitement in getting everything ready. Jenn was under the care of Colin Smith, a gynaecologist in Hay Street, West Perth, and for one check-up she arranged to go to Perth with Hazel Pither. They made an early start in the Rambler with horse float and two horses in tow, only to break down near Broomehill. The first vehicle to stop was one of Kiddles' Gnowangerup stock trucks, heading empty to Perth to collect sheep: 'No worries – I'll stop at Broomehill and get the garage blokes to come back here, and I can give the young lady a lift to Perth.'

And so it was. Jenn's little green case was thrown on board and she was helped up into the cabin. Not many 'bursting at the seams' young women would have been dropped off at Colin Smith's rooms alighting from a smelly semi-trailer stock truck. Jenn went to Perth a week or so before the due date to stay with her parents and, with better luck than Frank Pritchard had with his first born, I arrived in time for the big day.

We set off for St John of God maternity hospital in Subiaco, with all the right indications of imminent birth. In those days husbands were discouraged from being too close to the action, so a waiting room was provided for the men. It was basic, with hard chairs, outdated magazines and a strong smell of stale cigarette smoke. Jenn's labour stretched out for 36 gruelling hours, with only brief visits allowed. She suggested I go home for a shower and change of clothes as there was no indication of a change of pace. While away, the birth happened, but the baby was whisked away without explanation. Sometime later, a doctor stood at the door and said:

I am a specialist who has been brought in to look at your baby. You have a Down syndrome baby. Do you know what that is? She is mongoloid and has a few other problems and we are doing some further tests.

No woman today would have such information given in such a brutally blunt way. Poor Jenn had to telephone home with the news and was left on her own, never having even seen the baby, until I arrived with her mother. The following days were a living nightmare of tests, visits, conflicting information and advice.

We found that we had a little Down syndrome girl with other heart and lung problems. We were told she would need constant care and it would be most inadvisable to take her home, being 80 kilometres from the nearest doctor and hospital. Life expectancy was unclear so the Catholic Sisters advised an immediate christening. Catherine Campbell was duly christened on 23 October 1969, just two days after her birth.

We were told of the Catherine McCaullay Centre, where she might be cared for, and were encouraged to visit and see for ourselves. The sight of all the babies in their little cots was hard to take. In the end, we accepted the decision and arranged for Catherine to be cared for there once well enough to leave the specialist ward at St Johns. Even so, she was regularly in and out of Princess Margaret Hospital for Children.

We had a few weeks in Perth and had to go through the awkward experience of seeing family and friends. They didn't know what to say or do, so it was more up to us, especially Jenn, to ease the embarrassment and move the conversation to more neutral topics. It was while in Perth that Brian Newing called, having made a special trip up from Jerramungup, where he was the recently installed Anglican priest, having been of a Tambellup farming family before his calling. Brian was a great help to us then and became part of our lives over the coming years.

The difficulty of seeing people for the first time was more stressful on moving back to the farm. For example, on the way home we called by the Gnowangerup Hospital to visit Zanna Pritchard, who had just given birth to Simon. Imagine how hard it was for Jenn to show her pleasure at his safe arrival, while hiding her own loss and loneliness. No doubt it was also difficult for Zanna. Everybody seemed to be having babies and trips to town inevitably required Jenn to peer into a pram and make glowing comments about the new offspring.

To ease the emptiness, Jenn's parents gave her Rebel, a mature tricoloured corgi who had been mistreated and desperately needed a new home. It couldn't have worked better as both Rebel and we needed each other. It encouraged us to believe in dogs having a sixth sense as Rebel was able to understand a situation and respond to it. It started a long association with the breed, including several litters of puppies, with Jenn even being referred to as 'the Corgi lady'!

There was still a farm to run, a harvest to take off and a summer shearing program to put through. The South Coast had some light finishing rains in the spring that eluded most of the state, so at least there was a modest harvest of about half a tonne per hectare for barley and a little less for wheat. The clover and ryegrass pastures had set seed so, with reduced sheep numbers, we scraped through the summer.

We were just getting back to routine when I had a serious tractor accident in April 1970. I was root raking along the edge of a creek line, driving into the setting sun with dust all around and didn't see a long dead branch of a tree facing the tractor. It smashed through the front of the cab and caught me in the right upper leg, throwing me over the seat, through the open rear of the cab and into the path of the root rake. Instinct caused me to grab the draw bar and I was pulled along until the tractor hit a tree and stopped with spinning wheels. I switched the motor off, held a handkerchief into the gaping wound and hobbled for home using the fence as a hand-rail. Poor Jenn was horrified at the sight of me! She bound the leg up and we headed for the Pithers to use the phone.

Fortunately, John was at home and used the Rambler as an ambulance for the trip to Gnowangerup Hospital. Dr Winrow was notified and promised to be on hand upon our arrival. There's no doubt about the country GPs of the time as they were presented with all sorts of challenges and tackled them head on – the thought of stabilising and calling the Flying Doctor wasn't considered. Alex Winrow cleaned the wound out, did deep muscle stitching and closed the outer skin. There were some facial cuts, particularly to an ear, which he also stitched up, saying:

> You are a lucky boy. If that stake had got you in the belly instead of your leg you would've been a goner. In any case, you will be in hospital for a week or so and no work on that leg for at least another month.

Tractor with tree branch after the accident, 1970. Note air compressor

Tractor at rest after accident, 1970. Note new wire-armour tyres

15 The Mallee Bride

We were about to start seeding when this happened and I was lying in the Gnowangerup Hospital, trying to think through alternative arrangements. I needn't have worried, as John Pither called after a few days:

It's all arranged. I've been working with the Ellises, MacMillans and Jensens. There'll be a busy bee next week and there are enough tractors, seeding machines and trucks lined up to do the job in a day.

I was home for the big day and how humbling it was to see such a turnout, some arriving in the morning darkness, some hardly known to me, but all there to help out. Jenn and the other girls organised a constant flow of sandwiches and hot tea for the workers in the paddock, and then drinks with hot savouries as they came past the house on their way home. It was a typical example of the resilience and generosity of the farming community, all the more special when you are the one being helped.

In the middle of these setbacks, Catherine died on 10 July 1970. We had been visiting regularly and could see she was not gaining weight, being only 9 pounds at nine months and certainly not looking well. For all that, it was heart-rending seeing the little white coffin being lowered into the ground at Karrakatta Cemetery. If ever we could have our time again, we would have taken Catherine home with us, even if this had resulted in an earlier death. It would have at least allowed us to go through the normal grieving process of firstly having an unwell baby, then losing her, as well as providing a loving home environment for her short life.

There were some social improvements in the district. Henry Reynolds had married Jeannie Pearce in 1968, followed by Ian MacMillan to Gillian Angel and Peter Crossing to Jane Drummond in 1969, then Bill and Lola Jensen a year or so later to complete the circle of friends. The Nalyerlup and Monjebup telephone exchanges were opened in 1970 so at last we could communicate – and commiserate – with each other. The first quarterly telephone bill of $83.36 was a pleasure to pay.

The final drama for 1970 was my rolling the HT ute and writing it off. We were no longer in a financial arrangement with the Hodgson family but were now farming in partnership with the National Bank in Gnowangerup. Max Gairdner was the manager and I knew the budget was stretched to the limit, so we went into Hendry's Holden dealership to see what the insurance payout would provide on the second-hand market. In the end we settled for an HR model car (two years older than the written-off ute) and a very dilapidated EJ ute, only suitable for paddock work or an emergency trip to town. There was only one problem: the car was bright red. Jenn put her foot down: 'We will accept your offer, but you will have to paint the car white at your expense.'

To my surprise they came to the party. They had their own paint shop in those days and I guess had spare capacity. In any case, the HR proved a better model than the HT and we had many years of trouble-free service from it, often pulling a trailer of mallee roots to Perth for Dad's comfort as he battled emphysema. It was also a welcome change having a car instead of being cooped up in a ute.

Our family fortunes took a turn for the better with Anneliese Jane born on 16 February 1971. Anna was the brightest and happiest baby you could hope for, always full of life and enjoying all that was going on about her. She loved her food, she loved her bath and her eyes would light up when anyone came into the room. While a new baby should never be expected to replace one that has been lost, it was nonetheless the start of the family life we had been desperately seeking. We hadn't been home with Anna for long when John and Hazel Pither called:

> Roy Owens has put his farm on the market and we are interested in buying it, but are stretched for funds. We have a 250-hectare undeveloped block over the road from you and wonder if you would like to buy that? Also, our plant is pushed to the limit and would you like to share farm the cropping on Roy's place?

We were also 'stretched' following the 1969 drought so decided to sell the block of land at Goode Beach near Albany, which Jenn had bought with her teacher savings and the sale of her little Morris Mini-Minor, and used the funds to purchase the Pithers' land. The share farming also meant our plant and my time were now being put to maximum use.

There was local excitement in the Farmers Union. Sir Basil Embry had been an air chief marshall in the Royal Air Force and migrated to WA in 1956 to try his hand at farming. He started at Chowerup, southwest of Kojonup, and then Cape Riche, east of Albany. He became state president of the Farmers Union in 1971 and was also one of the founders of the Rural Traders Co-op and its inaugural chairman (1972–75). His strength of character and selfless leadership helped to further kindle my interest in farm politics. He was a man of incredible drive and determination and was described as, 'Small and spare, wiry and strong, "with piercing blue eyes and fierce eyebrows"'.[26]

Brian Newing was continuing to support us and we became good friends. He called one day and said:

> I'm thinking of setting up a house church for the isolated new-land farmers in this area. We could take it in turns using the different homes and have a monthly service. Are you interested in being part of the plan?

So started the most meaningful religious experience of our lives. There were always a lot of children about, the young ones in carry baskets, the older ones playing games on the floor. Brian's sermons were unique, more like a yarn in the shearing shed, but always with a strong take-home message. Jenn and Zanna took it in turns playing the little portable organ, a hymn sometimes 'running out of puff' when one of the foot pedals became dislodged!

The 1971/72 harvest was fraught with difficulties. The South Coast was deluged with two rainfall events as tropical lows hovered over the area. Crops were good but the waterlogged soils caused them to fall over sideways and the moisture also weakened the straw. There were bogged headers and trucks everywhere. We were forced into using Heaslip crop-lifters for the headers and they were tricky things to use at the best of times, but in a new-land situation, they would feed a range of sticks and roots into the header. The sickening 'crunch' as they went through the threshing drum was hard to take and a lot of time was spent adjusting the clearances of the drum and straightening the slats on the broad elevator.

The after-harvest Hannaford grading also proved to be challenging. Alf Hannaford from South Australia had established a nationwide seed grading and pickling service, with the machines mounted on trucks and moving from farm to farm on a contract basis. By 1965 there were 16,000 farmers around Australia utilising the service, with contractors supplying their own trucks and earning a commission on every tonne of grain they handled.[27] A lot of retired or 'gone bust' farmers were attracted to the three-month or so season of activity. This particular year there was a very unwell old fellow on the job, with a heart-rending tale of marriage troubles, losing the farm, financial problems, health problems and who knows what else. His old truck was not much better off: 'Don't dob me

'Harvesting was difficult on a new-land farm – whether raining or blowing – and the good days seemed to be spent repairing machinery!' (series of three sketches by Alex, sent to his parents in 1967 – from Thelma's scrapbook)

15 The Mallee Bride

into the company or I'll lose the contract. I just have to finish the run or I'm in real trouble.'

We all took sympathy, did most of the work for him and would telephone ahead to warn the next farm of the problem, who in return phoned back once he arrived in one piece to put our minds at rest for his welfare. Maybe we were grateful that our perilous financial situation had not yet reached such depths!

Our family was completed with Jock Alexander born on 9 July 1972. After the heartache of Catherine's short life, we now had two healthy children and, while Anna was the perfect first baby, Jock was the ideal second. He was no trouble at all, wouldn't be bamboozled by his older sister, would quietly work things out for himself and then get on with doing whatever had to be done. Jenn was now kept busy with clothing a boy as Anna's outfits couldn't be recycled. The absolute highlight of her sewing skills was a little, fully lined, double-breasted, brown tweed winter coat with leather buttons –Jock seldom wore it though it graced his wardrobe for many years!

Brian Page had taken over the management of the National Bank at Gnowangerup and the new-land farmers were testing his judgement to the limit. We had a small Commonwealth Development Bank (CDB) loan at the time and when we approached him for extra money to develop the newly acquired Pither land, he said: 'Your best bet would be to get an extra loan from the CDB. I'll support you in that direction but you have reached the limit with us.'

All the necessary budgets and forms were completed and sent to the CDB. Some weeks later, in a letter dated 10 July 1972, we received the sobering information:

> On the bank's assessment, income generated from your properties would be insufficient to cover operating and living expenses, as well as making commitments to your proposed loan extension. In the circumstances, your loan request is declined.

There were many of us in the same financial situation, so every effort was made to keep family and social life 'on an even keel.' Summer was the time for tennis. Largely through Keith and Ruth Moir's drive, there was a little three-court club built at Boxwood Hills with an open-fronted clubhouse and small kitchen. Busy bees were held from time to time to keep the asphalt surface in order and to maintain the surrounds. There were no grassed areas at all so the children played in the dirt and surrounding bush. Anna and the other girls would arrive neat and tidy but would quickly join the boys and be filthy within minutes. On one occasion somebody complained the tea didn't taste as it should, so one of the men went around to the back of the clubhouse and came back with a long face: 'The wind must have blown the manhole cover off the tank – and there's a very dead possum floating in the water.'

Country families must be tough! There were no reports of any ill effects, though water was always brought from home in plastic containers for the rest of the season.

Most of us had a disciplined work schedule, my own goal being 10 hours out in the paddock, with an extra hour or so for odd jobs around the house and sheds. Everyone made an effort to have Sundays free from work, other than seeding or harvest, while other days off depended on the weather; a trip to Albany for the day would be taken when it was too wet for outside work. Otherwise, 'we all had our shoulders to the wheel', demonstrated by Ian MacMillan's means of winding up a dinner party if it preceded a working day. They had a little Honda powered generator, which Ian filled with petrol from a calibrated measuring jug, being able to carefully time when it would run out of fuel. At 9.00 pm there would be splutter from the Honda, the lights would fade away and torches switched on.

'Should I go outside and put more petrol in the engine?'

'No, no, it's about time we all headed for home,' would be the grudging response.

On 5 December 1972, Gough Whitlam was elected prime minister of the first federal Labor government for 23 years. He formed a duumvirate (ministry of two) with his deputy, Lance Barnard, holding all 27 portfolios between them. In two weeks they had recognised China, ended conscription; reopened the equal pay case; voted against apartheid in South Africa; and removed sales tax on the contraceptive pill, to name just a few of their directives.[28] It was not so much the merit or otherwise of each decision, it was the haste and lack of due process that rankled. Gough was tall and arrogant, made us cringe by calling everybody 'comrade', and provided further cause for my involvement in farm politics.

Fortunately, the 1972/73 harvest was above expectations. The share-farming venture on Owens' block next door also worked well, so for the first time, we had surplus funds at our disposal. Brian Page at the bank must have been equally relieved! We had wanted to build our own shearing shed for many years and this was the opportunity. Roy Owens was now living in Albany but agreed to join me in building it.

> I'll give you a week. We will get all of the heavy construction part done, iron on the roof and walls, but you will have to do the inside fit out.

That seemed a good deal and the four-stand shed was completed for $2,572. The seasonal good fortune also allowed us to proceed with the development of the new Pither block, so we had it logged for clearing and I undertook the boundary fencing. Who needed an extra CDB loan?

The final expenditure was upgrading the A81 International header to an A84 model with the big 3.5-tonne grain bin, for a changeover cost of $1,000. The A84 had been used on clean Wheatbelt farms so the comb was not all dented and bent from hitting mallee roots. The International 'pull-along' headers were good reliable machines but how different to those of today. Sitting on an open tractor with heat, dust and noise all around you, the relief of driving into the wind rather than the itchy dust blowing all over you, yet the lovely smell of freshly threshed grain to spur you on. The headers didn't have the efficiency and capacity of today's models, but could be maintained and repaired on the farm using only oxy and arc welders, a basic tool kit and occasional assistance with a crowbar or sledge hammer, requiring only average mechanical ability. I was able to replace thresher drum bars, any bearing, shaft, belt or chain, and never needed outside assistance.

Meanwhile, Jenn was busy at her sewing machine. She had been making most of her own clothes but now had two children who seemed to be forever outgrowing their outfits. Back then, real money could be made from home sewing. Jenn relished the trips to Albany where she would spend hours in Wilfe's fabric shop, looking through materials and patterns, then choosing the buttons and zips and so on.

The Whitlam government was moving at a frenetic pace: they abolished university fees; introduced legal aid; were moving towards universal health care; and promised no urban houses were to be unsewered. With their support, the National Gallery bought Jackson Pollock's *Blue Poles* for $1.3 million.[29] Once again, every decision had certain merit but how was it all going to be funded? As farmers, we were thrashing out annual budgets with the banks, yet here was the government making huge forward commitments without offsetting revenue.

Then, to top everything off, our national anthem 'God Save the Queen' was replaced with 'Advance Australia Fair' and the British Honours replaced with an Australian-based system. The world as we knew it was changing at too great a pace!

I was now president and zone delegate for the Boxwood Hill branch of the Farmers Union. I was impressed by the dedication and clear thinking of many of those at this new level, including Tom Atterby and Jim Saunders from Jacup; Tony Gooch, Bill Meyer and Bob Tozer from Bremer Bay; Dick Woodhams, Len Gleeson and Charles and Romi Patterson from Gairdner River; Mel Bungey from Borden; and Graham Jones from Ongerup. Tony Gooch was a particularly talented operator and went on to be the organisation's wool section president as well as serving on the Australian Wool Commission and, importantly, the Australian Wool Corporation from 1982 to 1991. Bill Meyer became the organisation's state small seeds president, then went on to be state junior vice president; Len Gleeson became a CBH director; and Mel Bungey a Liberal member in the House of Representatives. The new-land farming areas of the day produced many leaders, which shows they weren't satisfied with just developing farms but wanted to build strong communities as well. Don Eckersley (later Sir Donald) became state president of the Farmers Union and was showing inspirational leadership in his quiet and steady way, which was particularly needed in the chaotic Whitlam years, when all sorts of rebellious ideas were being promulgated.

The federal government was proposing to scrap the $12 per tonne bounty on superphosphate, which would really hurt in WA as we had less fertile soils that required heavier application rates. Gough was to speak at a rally in Forrest Place on 25 March 1974, so plans were put in hand for farmers to mount a protest against the government and the removal of the super bounty. At branch and zone level we organised car pooling and hiring of buses, and generally motivated all and sundry to attend, resulting in more than 1,000 farmers out of an estimated crowd of 6,000. Gough certainly got us all fired up when, on the back of a truck, he bellowed: 'The rest of you are subsidising these farmers to take a day off. They are bludging on the rest of us.'[30]

Tomatoes, screwed-up balls of paper and an open can of drink were thrown. The noise was unbelievable and tension, frustration and indignation were palpable. While I didn't throw anything, I certainly joined in with yelling! The 1,000 or so farmers then moved on to Subiaco Oval for a meeting to which Gough had been invited though, not surprisingly, failed to attend. The meeting proceeded with a carefully positioned empty chair signifying his absence, to which all speakers addressed.[31] We all headed for home, believing we had got our message across, had given Gough something to think about and that all our efforts had been worthwhile. (We didn't realise then that it would be the last 'on the back of a truck' political rally to be held in Forrest Place.) On more sober reflection in the following days, I was shaken by the power of crowd behaviour, the adrenalin surge that it provoked and the unpredictability of such an event. It was my 'baptism of fire' into the world of farm politics.

In 1974 we bought a second-hand 240-volt, 4.5-kva Start-o-matic power plant with a twin-cylinder Lister engine. With the help of the local electrician, we set it up with a 'slave' line that provided power when the engine was operating but would not be involved in stopping or starting it. This allowed us to buy a large Frigidaire 'fridge' and do away with the kerosene Electrolux. We also bought a large deep freeze that worked off the slave line, along with a heating element in the hot water system so the Everhot needn't be used in summer. This meant we could go away, leaving the fridge to turn the power plant on and off, and have hot water on our return. We always had a high degree of trepidation on coming home: would it all have worked as it should or would there be a fridge and deep freeze of spoilt food? We were lucky to be at home the few times the plant misbehaved.

The 1974/75 harvest was looking good and Eric Richards & Staff were having a model run-out, so we decided on a new XB Ford Fairmont with vinyl roof, for a changeover price of $3,605. It was a beautiful car to drive and made us feel like millionaires. It was plagued with problems, however, and went back for warranty work on a regular basis, the main issue being unable to start it on a damp evening or morning. It got to the point of us carrying an electric fan heater and long extension cord with us at all times, but the problem was never rectified to the day we sold it. As if that wasn't enough, it's the only car we ever owned that sustained major roo damage to the point of being undriveable. Many other roos were hit over the years but we were always able to limp home with the damage, such as having one headlight. Maybe we should have stayed with Holden?

The Whitlam government continued to alarm us. Rex Connor was caught out in the Khemlani loans affair, trying to arrange a $4.6 billion loan through Tirath Khemlani, a Pakistani go-between to Arab oil money. Some of Gough's other ministers were in the news for the wrong reasons, including: Attorney General Lionel Murphy; Jim Cairns (and his girlfriend Junie Morosi); Clyde

Cameron; Moss Cass; and the flamboyant Al Grassby from Griffith, NSW. Where and when would it all end?[32]

The harvest exceeded expectations and it was also the final year of share farming. There was sufficient surplus in the budget for us to consider adding on to the house, so we consulted Roy Owens and he agreed to add three more bedrooms and a new bathroom, built in brick with concrete floors. This was his main building type in Albany and he had all the subcontractors in place for a continued rollout of houses. We agreed to provide board and lodging for the 'subbies' and undertook to do the painting, with the job being completed for $3,377. We, particularly Jenn, had great fun choosing tiles, wallpaper, fabrics for curtains and bed covers – a real home at last! The garden had been progressively expanding in all directions but we had left a vacant spot for the extension, so when completed it nestled into its surrounds as if having been there from the start.

Farming was becoming very routine. The cropping was more straightforward as the mallee roots decreased, development of the new Pither block was completed and Lenny Wright was our shearing contractor, based at Wellstead. His team included mainly young men developing new-land farms, such as Bill Wilson and Rick Swarbrick, as well as farmers' sons just home from school. Lenny brought his own hydraulic wool press and fully catered for the team, who all had a great sense of humour, so shearing and crutching were never a chore.

The Whitlam era came to a head on 17 November 1975 with the dismissal by Governor General John Kerr. Gough's cry of anguish is regularly referred to, particularly by the ABC, and now etched into Australian folklore: 'Well may we say 'God save the Queen', because nothing will save the Governor General.' In rural Australia there was an audible sigh of relief. The rollercoaster madness would come to an end and Malcolm Fraser, with a huge majority, promised to restore everything onto an even keel.

The 1975/76 harvest was another good one, so again we had some surplus funds. It would seem that we should have started easing off a bit, repaying debt and enjoying our fully developed 1,200-hectare farm and recently extended house. Yet I felt restless. I had a growing realisation that what I really enjoyed was the building and development work, rather than actual farming. As 1976 progressed, we started looking at options for the future, which included buying another partially developed new-land block or moving to another district. Anna was at kindergarten at Ongerup and future education was also a consideration. If we moved, it should be before her primary school years so she could continue at one school without interruption.

Anna with Rebel, 1975

Jock with his 'plant' in front of the machinery shed, 1975

To test the water, we sounded out Albany real estate agents and chanced upon Eddie Davis from Merrifields, who said he would show us a range of properties. The first property was beautifully presented, though too expensive, then he showed us a few poorly developed farms with war service infrastructure near Many Peaks. 'There's one last place I'll show you. It's looking a bit tired and needs some work, but I think it has real potential.'

Eddie drove us into Townsend's farm at Narrikup, midway between Albany and Mount Barker, which had been a potato farm on a peat swamp, then a dairy through to the 1950s and was now a beef farm. The main feature was the 1920s stone homestead, overlooking a 10-hectare freshwater lake (the old peat swamp) to the Porongurup Hills beyond. Both Jenn and I were captivated! The farm was 400 hectares, with 80 hectares of jarrah / red gum yet to be cleared; the older dairy farm fencing was derelict, while the disused hay shed and dairy complex could be converted into a small shearing shed. There was a second cottage on the farm, providing some rental income.

We did a few quick budgets and thought we could make it work, especially if we increased our income from contract work. Brief enquiries indicated an opening for contract hay making, with large round bales just starting to replace the labour-intensive small square ones. Our offer was accepted, with a delayed settlement date for 1 February 1977, which was planned so we could have one last harvest at Borden and reasonable time to sell Tillgaree. Fortunately, our farm sold easily, with the two settlements arranged for the same date.

With Ron Townsend's agreement, we added Ringlock prefabricated wire netting to the cattle-type boundary fencing so that sheep would at least remain on the property once delivered after settlement. We had effectively reduced the size of our farming business, having less than half the area of Tillgaree, but were now in a much more reliable rainfall region and closer to town for schooling. And we were debt free!

We put through our last summer shearing and retained the best 1,500 Merino ewes and the small 100-head Poll Dorset stud, established a few years earlier. We also bought 80 Santa Gertrudis–Hereford cross cows from the Townsend family, together with sufficient hay for the first autumn.

The Borden farm was bought by Garry and Marie Taylor from Tambellup, who also agreed to buy most of the remaining sheep, the Bedford truck and Chamberlain tractor and plough. I was particularly sorry to say goodbye to the Countryman as it had provided me with just on 10,000 hours of trouble-free service, proving the Hodgson adage of 'buying good plant, looking after it well, and keeping it for a long life'. H.C. Trappitt & Sons traded the header and some other equipment for a new Leyland 250 tractor. The only major plant retained was the Horwood Bagshaw root rake, which had some further work to do at Narrikup.

On reflection, the time spent at Borden was the most rewarding period of our lives. I don't think there can be a more fulfilling experience than turning virgin bush into a fully developed, viable farm. It provided me with the confidence and self-assurance that no matter how difficult a situation might look, it can be overcome with persistence and hard work.

Just as my parents found on leaving Wiluna, so it was for us, that friends formed in those early years of marriage on isolated stations and farms stayed true to you for the rest of your days. We might not see the Crossings, Reynolds, MacMillans, Stockwells, Jensens, Ellises, Pritchards, ten Seldams, Kings, Pithers, Bryants, Miles or O'Meehans for years at a time, but could always pick up 'as though it were only yesterday'.

Tillgaree as we left it in 1976

16 FROM MALLEES TO RED GUMS

We were sitting on the front steps of our new home, watching the sun setting behind the red gums listening to the unfamiliar evening call of kookaburras and enjoying the faint smell of cattle on the evening breeze. Jenn and I were excited about the move as we sat with glasses of wine in our hands, but Anna and Jock were not so sure: 'Why have we moved to this crummy old-fashioned house?'

The farm had been selected in the 1890s for its 10-hectare peat swamp, suited to growing potatoes. A closed-in barn with wooden floor and a two-roomed cottage that had been dismantled and railed from Coolgardie also dated back to that time. The main stone homestead was built in the 1920s, with a verandah all the way around, which separated the cottage from the main building. When built, the cottage section was used as the kitchen with an adjoining cook's bedroom, while the new house comprised three large bedrooms, sitting room and dining room, with a passage running the full length from west to east. The bathroom-laundry was in a separate building close by and the 'thunderbox' toilet was situated under a pine tree some distance away.

Before our arrival, the dining room had been converted to a kitchen and the old kitchen to a bathroom and septic toilet. The cook's bedroom was now a storeroom and trips to the bathroom necessitated crossing the open verandah. There was a dairy, chaff room and hay shed complex that dated back to the 1920s and, along with the barn, was in poor repair. Another hay shed and a cottage dating back to the late 1940s completed the buildings.

There were no sheep facilities at all, other than boundary fences that we had upgraded. We worked out a plan with strict deadlines: sheep yards to be completed for pre-lambing needle and drenching by April; some of the better

Our new Narrikup house and nearby barn, 1977. (Note lack of garden and large pine trees)

internal fences upgraded with Ringlock prefabricated netting by lambing in May; the dairy complex converted to a shearing shed in time for a late September crutching; hay machinery purchased and a contract program in place by mid-October.

We already had some contacts at Narrikup: Jenn's sister Chris and brother-in-law John Blythe were farming a few kilometres away; Evan and Ian Findlay, who had done most of our contract clearing and dam sinking while at Borden, were also close by; and one of the Findlay drivers, Terry Marden, was just down the road and was in the process of buying the bulldozer business. Within a few days the phone rang:

> Hello, I'm Bob Pugh. Judy and I would like you to come around and have morning tea with us. We've been farming here for years and we might be able to help you out while settling in.

The phone call was typical of country hospitality and the Pugh family have become lifelong friends, especially Bob's son John, his wife Kim and their family of four girls: Alexandra, Clare, Harriet and Georgia. Bob was very generous, offered us the use of any of his machinery and said 'we are only a phone call away if you have any problems'. The only plant we ever borrowed was their heavy-duty stone roller to crush the conglomerate gravel.

We had several early discussions with the Blythes. They had been running cattle but wanted to diversify into sheep, as beef was in a periodic downturn, and were now in a similar process of upgrading cattle infrastructure. In the meantime, they had the use of Bruno Rizzi's shearing shed just down the road. It was decided John would help me convert the old dairy complex into a shearing shed if I would help him build his own shed within a year or so. John was also keen to share in the hay machinery and join me in setting up a hay contracting business. He then suggested we help each other at shearing time, doing all the shed work, so that we only needed to employ two shearers. This arrangement is referred to as 'cocky shearing', rather than contracting with a full team.

Meanwhile, Anna's schooling was upon us. Jenn organised the red and black Mount Barker Primary School uniforms and we were pleased to have the school bus pass the gate. Some of the Findlay children were on the bus, together with the Montgomery girls from just around the corner, so Anna had friendly faces to look out for her. Jock was enrolled at the Mount Barker kindergarten.

In the first year we were very busy settling into the farm and a new district. I joined the local Narrikup Farmers Union branch and Jenn became involved with school activities and other community work. David Murray (Brian Newing's replacement) must have given advance notice of our move as we were quickly welcomed into the All Saints Mount Barker Anglican Church, and it wasn't very long before Jenn was teaching Sunday School. I was also asked to serve on the vestry and later took on the rector's warden job.

The first year at Narrikup I spent as a builder and fencer rather than a farmer, which is the work I enjoyed. The farm had never been called by any name other than 'Townsend's Place' so we used the Tillgaree name again.

John and I looked into hay machinery options, then settled on New Holland and bought a reciprocating mower, side delivery roller-bar hay rake and the recently released '850' round baler. The baler was of chains with pipe slats that made perfect bales, but taxed the 70-horsepower Leyland tractor to the limit. There were very few round balers in use and many farmers wanted only a small paddock done 'to see how they go', while others asked for their full requirement to be contracted. We also did some mowing and raking but found that less profitable, deciding to do only enough to pay for the machines and then concentrate on baling. The first hay season stretched out to six weeks, with pasture hay first, followed by oat crops. Saia oats (*Avena strigosa*) was widely used, being a fine-stalked, bulky crop suited for hay but needing care in its management. Ron McTaggart at the Ag Dept provided sound advice:

> You have to watch Saia – put it in early and, if left ungrazed, it is no better than camel bedding! You need to regularly graze it, then give a shot of nitrogen six weeks before mowing and you will have high-yielding good quality hay.[33]

The change to cocky shearing was interesting. Clive Milton was developing a piggery and 'pushed the handpiece' by day, fed the pigs by night and was in a constant state of exhaustion. He was living on Staminade! Doug Baxter was a war service farmer and a reformed alcoholic, who then became a lay preacher with the Seventh Day Adventist Church – and was also vegetarian. Jenn did a marvellous job in providing suitable meals, making nut rissoles, buying vegetarian sausages and using heaps of vegetables. They appreciated her efforts and shearing was trouble free for many years.

Farming in a higher rainfall area required quite different pasture management, so I attended the Mount Barker Research Station field days and utilised the Albany branch of the Ag Dept. Doug Rowe was the research station manager and a no-nonsense, down-to-earth operator. An example of his practical approach was demonstrated in some canola trial plots, where all the plants were disappearing and he was overheard saying:

> These boffins came down from Perth and were scratching through the duck shit to try and find an answer in the root zone – didn't occur to them that ducks were eating the plants![34]

The Ag Dept was located on Albany Highway, near the roundabout at the top of York Street, and staffed by a group of energetic and dedicated researchers, advisers and vets. I quickly got to know Officer-in-Charge Ron Parkin, Steve Trevenen, Peter Stallwood, Roy Gwyn (vet), Ashley Prout and newly arrived Ron McTaggart, and relied very much on their advice, often via a quick phone call. Once again, most of them were UWA graduates.[35]

We were planning to spend some time renovating the house in our second year, when Mother Nature intervened. The arrival of Cyclone Alby! On 27 March 1978, a tropical low formed off the WA coast, reached category 5 and slowly worked its way south, with wind speeds of more than 200 kilometres per hour. By 4 April, it had accelerated its forward ground speed to 50 kph and passed through the southwest corner of the state, with wind gusts exceeding 150 kph. It's the most damaging cyclone ever recorded in southern WA: 114,000 hectares of land burnt; 10,000 sheep and 50 cattle killed; 1,300 kilometres of fencing destroyed; and damage estimated at $39 million. Albany was one of the worst affected areas, with heavy damage to buildings, power lines and infrastructure.[36]

There was ample warning of impending trouble and we went to bed in trepidation with torches, portable radios and candles on hand. It wasn't long before everything changed for the worse. The power went out, the wind increased and there was a strong smell of dust and smoke in the air. Anna woke at midnight and joined us in bed as we listened to the radio and increasing noise outside. There were some hair-raising bangs and clatters on the roof and we feared the worst. Meanwhile, Jock slept right through the night and woke next morning covered in dust from the ceiling cornice which had opened up above his bed.

The wind was easing by daybreak so it was a time for inspecting the damage. Part of the verandah roof was caved in and the floor and nearby lawn were littered with bricks from the chimney above the kitchen which had blown over. The nearby barn had lost a lot of its roof iron, which had ricocheted across the house roof, accounting for a lot of the noise. The verandah posts were at all angles, indicating we were close to having the verandahs peel off the house. The main hay shed had lost most of its roof but the renovated shearing shed was only slightly damaged, which said something for my building prowess! The old outside laundry was completely gone. Probably the worst damage was to the trees; there had been a row of pine trees planted around the house at the turn of the 19th century and most were now lying on the ground, one narrowly missing the barn. Countless red gums had been completely blown over or had lost large limbs, and many were lying over fences.

There were many different stories from that fateful evening. Ian Robinson, a nearby farmer who was very deaf, had slept right through the night and, as was his normal practice, went out the back door for a 'twinkle' when he woke up:

I opened the door and damn near had a heart attack! The hay shed was gone, the dog kennel and dog were gone, trees were down everywhere. It was devastation – I thought an atomic bomb must have been dropped on Albany!

Once again, a list of priorities was drawn up: set the portable generator in place for the fridge and deep freeze; ensure the boundary fences were stock-proof; make the buildings safe; and collect loose sheets of iron. We discovered all the roads were blocked by fallen trees and it was some days before the shire was able to open them again. The power was off for more than a week, nearly a month for some residents. It took a further year to repair the internal fences and buildings. With round hay bales we didn't need a hay shed, so I built a 15-metre by 7-metre wooden framed machinery shed to house our modest plant, utilising all the salvaged iron from Cyclone Alby.

Later in the year, Terry Marden came down with his bulldozer and pushed all the pine trees into big heaps, well away from the house. It was a blessing in disguise for Jenn as she now had an open palette on which to establish her garden – a task she got into with enthusiasm. The house was surrounded by kikuyu grass (*Pennisetum-clandestinum*), as was most of the older farm that formed the dairy pastures, so she established the garden by marking out the shape of a new bed with a garden hose, then spraying the kikuyu with Roundup (*glyphosate*)!

There had been no time for farm politics, but many of us were very frustrated with the Fraser government, a common lament being:

> What's gone wrong with Malcolm? He won the election with a landslide but hasn't lifted a finger. The best you can say for him is that he's stopped things getting worse.

Gough was tall and arrogant, Malcolm was tall and aloof – but at least he wasn't calling everybody 'comrade'! There was a sense of disappointment and of being let down.

The years started to roll into one, with school holidays dictating our lives as much as the seasonal farming activities. After fixing the damage caused by Cyclone Alby, we contracted Terry Marden to clear the remaining 80 hectares of jarrah and red gum on the farm and then, after it was burnt, push the remaining logs into windrows. We upgraded the Horwood Bagshaw root rake with a

Pederick conversion of heavy-duty fingers to tackle the clean-up, then hired it out to others in the district. It was a three-year process to achieve a reasonably clean pastured paddock.

The building program also continued. John and I built a wooden framed two-stand shearing shed on his farm, using the Roy Owens design of earlier years. At home, we closed in the back verandah between the stone house and detached bathroom with large glass windows, taking in the view over the lake to the Porongurup Hills. The old store room was renovated with built-in wardrobes and wallpaper to become a fourth bedroom. We often wondered why the house was designed to not utilise the view and Ron Townsend, who was now an Elders real estate agent, provided the answer:

> Back in those days they were digging potatoes by hand in the swamp. It was back-breaking work and was the last thing they wanted to look at when they knocked off! Nobody imagined it would become a lake once more of the land was cleared.

We also used part of the closed-in verandah as an office and subdivided the barn into separate areas: I had a workshop and room for the motorbikes; Jenn had a garden shed; and the children had a big games room. There was a lot of pine milled after Alby so the internal walls were lined with these planks, a gas stove and kitchen sink were installed, and the old Metters No 2 Insulheat from Borden was used to heat the room. Many Guides, Cubs and various fundraising events used the games room and adjoining double carport as a venue.

Our social network extended beyond the local area. A number of ex-station people had drifted south to try their hands at farming, including John and Jenny Fisher, Robin and Jenny Kempton, Simon and Sue Keogh from Byro in the Murchison, and John Blythe and his cousin Richard from Mount House in the Kimberley. Simon had three sons from an earlier marriage to Bea Cooke: Kim now managing Byro, Rick on a property in Queensland and Peter leasing a farm at Denbarker. Simon then married Sue Russell and their two girls, Janice and Libby, were of similar ages to Anna and Jock. We saw a lot of the Keoghs, and Simon would have to be one of the most delightful and gregarious men you could ever hope to meet, always insisting: 'The only good beer is on tap – cans and bottles kill the flavour. A party without a keg is always a disaster!'

He put his philosophy into regular practice and the parties were always a success, obviously proving his point. On the station he was renowned for setting up a keg in the cool room, with the tap coming through the wall on to the verandah.

We were also seeing a lot of Barry and Trish Witham at Tambellup and through them became friendly with a growing circle of people in that part of the world. Henry and Jeannie Reynolds had moved back to the family farm at Cranbrook, after having been neighbours at Borden, and we got to know others in their area, then the Miles, Crossings and Stockwells helped expand our contacts south of the Stirling Ranges. Country friendship circles are like ripples in a pond: forever getting bigger and more interesting.

The farm now had increased stocking numbers with the new-land in full production and the Poll Dorset stud doubled in size, with rams being supplied around the district. Much of the internal fencing was renewed, mainly to soil type, with the summer flats under kikuyu and the higher country to annual clovers and ryegrass. Fencing was now five-line Ringlock, an electric 'hot wire' and a plain earth top wire – ideal for sheep and cattle.

Digger and Marg Weir moved south from Ongerup to semi-retire, having bought the farm over the road from us. They were warm and friendly people and became de facto grandparents to the children. Digger wanted us to do all his hay work and also offered other paddock renovation work for our Leyland tractor, plough, scarifier and root rake. The other farm over the road was owned by Mike Trevenen, who lived in Albany with his wife Beth, and we became very good friends. He also wanted his hay making and a few other jobs done by contract. Digger had one weakness: he was a collector, hoarder and accumulator of just about everything! The old outside thunderbox toilet had survived Cyclone Alby and was an eyesore to Jenn's expanding garden, so I backed the tray top ute alongside, tipped it on board and then stood it back upright at the Narrikup tip. On our next visit to Digger's, he exclaimed:

> You just don't know what good stuff people will throw out these days. Look at that perfectly good dunny somebody left at the tip – it makes an excellent garden shed.

We quickly appreciated the benefit of other good neighbours: Evan and Norma Findlay had part of their farm joining ours to the east, hired our shearing shed for a number of years and were very helpful in many other ways; Ian and

Contract hay plant, shared with John Blythe, 1982

Joan Findlay were a little further away, but Jenn and Joan shared a lot of common interests; Murray and Pam Montgomery were just to the southeast and, with similar-aged children, became good friends; Laurie Ecclestone lived with his aged mother, provided us with fruit and did odd jobs for us when needed. He was a tall, gangly bloke of few words and did crutching and shearing work around the district. If anyone looked awkward and miserable pushing the handpiece, it was Laurie. He was well short of being a 'natural'!

In farm politics, I became president of the Narrikup branch of the Farmers Union and represented the branch at zone level. The Mount Barker branch was the strongest in the zone and had wonderful people involved, including Gerry, Terry and Keryl Enright; Bert Henderson; Jim and Pam McGregor; and Ernie and Mike Skinner. The Cranbrook branch had good members, among them Nick Burgess, Henry Reynolds and Clem Addis. The Rocky Gully branch had Munroe White and Sean Cameron, while Albany included Ian Steinhart and Graham Davies, to name but a few. Many of these people represented the organisation at state level, while Terry Enright progressed to become chair of the Grains Research and Development Corporation, followed by other national positions.

Jenn's garden was steadily expanding and with Anna and Jock well into their primary school years, she was kept busy with Guides and Cubs, netball, tennis and hockey. We became very good friends with Max and Lorraine Harrison, owners of the local Narrikup shop. Lorraine was very artistic, opened one of the first craft shops of the time and organised art courses and other functions in the local hall. Jenn was a fellow traveller and joined in with a lot of this activity. Max referred to his business as 'the salt mine' and was not averse to booking out the odd Mars Bar as roofing nails or nuts and bolts, so that diligent wives were none the wiser of their husbands' dietary indiscretions – just ask John Pugh!

The contract hay business had reached its maximum potential. We changed the baler to a Massey Ferguson 1450 belt model, which had higher capacity, required less maintenance and was better suited to a 70-horsepower tractor. The mower had been upgraded to a Tarrup rotary disc model and it was so pleasant to mow all day, without forever having to replace fingers and blades, as on the reciprocating models. Mowing became the most enjoyable of all tractor work I had ever done, with the soft whirring sound of the discs and the intoxicating smell of freshly cut pasture.

I joined the Mount Barker Agricultural Society and soon became steward for the British Breed sheep section. Dad had been a member of the Royal Agriculture Society for many years and now we decided to also become members. There were many enjoyable days spent at both the Mount Barker and Royal Agricultural shows, with socialising up in the members stand.

We realised our budget would be stretched once boarding school fees were upon us, so decided to buy a new car the year before. We bought a silver Volvo 240 with manual gearbox, took a trip to the Kimberley, another to South Australia and almost fortnightly Albany to Perth trips once I became further involved in farm politics. It was totally trouble free for the 450,000 kilometres of service and arguably the best car we ever owned.

There were pivotal political changes in 1983. Brian Burke was elected Labor premier of WA and Bob Hawke Labor prime minister, so from a WA perspective it was wall-to-wall Labor. There was a sense of gloom and despair. If Gough wreaked havoc, how much worse would it be under the watch of a past president of the Australian Council of Trade Unions? Gough and Malcolm were tall and arrogant or aloof; we now had a short, beer-swilling show pony – the silver bodgie! Fraser had famously said, 'life wasn't meant to be easy'. To the disillusioned farmers, he might just as well have said, 'life was meant to be full of disappointment'.

In 1984 our family experienced the upheaval shared by many country families when Anna went off to boarding school in Perth. St Hilda's had been Jenn's school as a day girl, but how different it was leaving your little girl to their care as a boarder. I am sure Jenn shed more tears than Anna and both had to cope with some painful readjustment.

The farm was pretty much on autopilot: development work was completed, we had mastered beef cattle and high-rainfall pasture management, and the contract hay business was now a routine annual event. I was now Albany zone vice president of the Primary Industry Association (PIA), which was the new name of the Farmers Union, changed in 1982. (The word 'union' had unfortunate connotations at the time, even if the original meaning had been the union of several small farm organisations into one single body.) I was also now on the State General Council and the few extra trips to Perth worked in well with visits to see Anna at boarding school.

The mid-1980s was an exhilarating time to be involved in farm politics. Winston Crane was state president of the PIA and membership had reached its highest point of about 10,000 members. Ian McLachlan was National Farmers' Federation (NFF) president and, together with industrial director Paul Hoolihan, was 'taking on the unions' to address the rorts and demarcation follies of the time.

At the national level, the Mudginberri abattoir dispute of 1983–85 in the Northern Territory was the main focus. Mudginberri was a cattle station 290 kilometres east of Darwin that had set up an abattoir to process feral buffalo, and the dispute was over contract employment replacing the tally system. The tally system was a union dreamed-up rort of the highest degree. It was based on an 'average man' being able to kill and process a given number of animals per shift and if they exceeded that number, they received double pay. In addition, if they processed an entire (non-castrated) animal, they received double pay. A single testicle constituted an entire animal so if a complete animal was processed, one of the testicles would be slipped into a pocket for a time and be produced again alongside another carcass! Worse still, once the tally was exceeded on the floor of the abattoir, the same proportion of double time would be given to the casual labourers, such as gardeners and stockies out in the yards. Yet worst of all, it eliminated any incentive for the owners to implement innovative work practices because if the tally could be more quickly achieved, it meant more double-time rates.

The tally system had contributed to the closure of 35 small abattoirs around Australia from 1979 to 1982. The eventual successful outcome of the Mudginberri dispute in 1985 'turned the tide against union power and changed the nature of industrial relations in Australia'. Jay Pendarvis, owner of Mudginberri, was awarded $1.76 million damages.[37] Of interest, the barrister representing Pendarvis and NFF was Peter Costello, later to become treasurer in the Howard government.

Of more interest in WA was the wide combs dispute (the 'comb' being the stationary part of the shearing handpiece, over which the reciprocating cutter operates). New Zealand had been using 3.5-inch combs, while Australia was restricted to 2.5 inches under the industrial award. Many NZ shearers were coming to Australia for the main spring shearing season with their 'wide gear' and WA was the preferred destination, being less likely to come under union scrutiny. The issue came to a head in 1983 with a 10-week national strike, having more consequence in eastern Australia, which had more unionised sheds.[38] It evolved into a four-year dispute between the Australian Workers' Union and the Federal Pastoral Industries Award, represented by the NFF. Once again, Ian McLachlan and Paul Hoolihan were at the forefront of the case. It seemed nothing much had changed in 90 years, as the 1890s dispute over mechanised shearing replacing hand shears was more about unions losing members, rather than the individual shearer being better off. In a similar vein, the 1980s dispute was also about the union losing members, rather than the shearers earning more money by shearing more sheep in a day.

The NFF Fighting Fund was established at the time as a means of financing the high cost of legal representation; farmers (and others) made generous donations and the fund continues to this day. In hindsight, this period was the pinnacle of success for farm organisations. I also believe Ian McLachlan and Winston Crane proved to be better farm leaders than politicians, as both went into federal politics, representing the Liberal Party.

I was now attending PIA annual conferences and what a performance they were! There were more than 300 delegates and others in attendance, a big percentage of whom were 'bush lawyers' with a forensic knowledge of business protocol: minutes were amended to the minutest degree, 'moved and seconded as amended'; the correspondence carefully reviewed with probing questions, then 'inward received and outward endorsed'; reports from the president and executive portfolios followed, with numerous questions, then moved and seconded; then the real business commenced. Motions on the agenda followed and, once moved and seconded, would attract queues of speakers to microphones in the aisles. Careful note was taken of equal speakers 'for and against' with the mover's right of reply, and if there wasn't a clear outcome on the voices or a show of hands, the room split in two, delegates' voting entitlements were checked and an accurate head count was made 'for and against'. All this activity was periodically interrupted with 'points of order', 'machinery motions', 'consequential motions' or even 'dissension from the president's ruling'. The zones weren't much different, though at branch level it was more relaxed, and the earlier experience with Junior Farmers had me fairly well prepared. Exhilarating times for a young farmer 'cutting his teeth' in farm politics.

As I started to chair various meetings, one valuable early lesson proved its worth many times over: never let the noisy person get the better of you personally, then make sure they don't dominate the other, more productive people in attendance. All groups – whether farm organisations, conservation bodies, political parties or the local sports club – always seem to have a rowdy member who dominates at a meeting but is of little benefit elsewhere. The person 'that never walks the talk'. They require early identification then a means of toning them down so that other, more tentative types can have a say. I found a quiet word over a coffee break usually solved the problem, especially if you were able to flatter their ego in the process: 'I need your help to…' It's only occasionally that I've had to 'pull rank' as chair of a meeting to solve the problem, even at the risk of losing the noisy member, but gaining support from everyone else. A further, less than subtle piece of advice was offered by an old campaigner: 'Think of them as being the horse's dick – big when they are out, but not much to them for the rest of the time!'

Meanwhile, Jock was still at the Mount Barker Primary School, so for two years our interests were split between two locations. BMX bikes were the thing of the day and Jock had a dazzling yellow and orange model on which he could ride over and around just about anything. We built a BMX track around the house dam, having collected a ute-load of used tyres from the Beaurepaire shop in town. I remember at a Cubs day, boys from around the district all turned up to try their skills on our BMX track. How things have changed – there were no helmets and the track actually went through water on the edges of a deep dam!

I also undertook the last building job on the farm, closing in another section of verandah and adding a new laundry and second bathroom. We used an electrician but the plumbing, tiling, framing and the rest were all self-done. Jenn was only partially satisfied: 'It's not quite an ensuite. You need a torch and compass in the middle of the night, but at least it's a much needed second bathroom.'

In 1986, I was elected Albany zone president of the PIA. There were two very influential men who became my mentors – Gerry Enright and Bert Henderson – and they were encouraging me to take on more responsibility and 'stretch myself a bit'. In the earlier years I didn't know whether to thank them or not, but later came to realise the importance of older men filling that mentor role, to bring out the best in the next generation.

In the same year Jock went off to board in Perth at Christ Church. Once again, there were very different feelings having a son as a boarder compared to my earlier experience as a day boy. With both children at boarding school, Jenn took on some voluntary and part-time jobs in Albany and, above all else, immersed herself in the ever-expanding garden. My fencing skills were now put to use, regularly moving the garden fence ever further out from the house and extending the 'Heath Robinson' home reticulation system. The area of kikuyu to be mown kept expanding and when Aunty Syb died, leaving a few dollars to her nieces and nephews, we were able to buy a second-hand, heavy-duty ride-on mower, to keep pace with Jenn's efforts in the garden.

The 1980s were tough times on the land, however, with low commodity prices (other than for wool) and some poor seasons. While the value of our Narrikup farm had increased many-fold as a result of the work we had done, we were nevertheless the classic 'asset rich–cash poor' farmers. Boarding school fees were adding to the problem, which led us to look at options to expand our income base.

17 CRYSTAL BROOK – BRACKEN TO VINEYARDS

During 1986 Jenn and I started looking for a semi-developed 'add on' farm in the district so as to increase our scale of farming. Clearing bans had been introduced earlier in the year by the state government, covering the main river catchments of the South West, and there was concern this might be extended more widely. As a result, there was a spate of clearing activity, or farm sales if the owners were unable to afford the task themselves. We looked at several partially cleared blocks on the south side of the Stirling Ranges in the Woogenellup area, but none seemed the right fit. On a trip to Perth, Tim came up with a suggestion: 'If you can find an 'add on' farm with a small holiday cottage, Sally and I would be interested in going half shares with you.'

A short time later in the Narrikup shop, I was surprised to see Ross Thompson from Nardlah, Broomehill, so questioned him on what he was up to in our part of the world:

> We're having a bad season at Nardlah and I have some cattle on agistment just west of here on Crystal Brook. The family have gone bust and the property is up for a mortgagee sale, but in the meantime offering short-term agistment. I haven't seen feed like it for a long time – the cows couldn't believe what they'd chanced upon!

Crystal Brook was a large amalgamation of smaller farms and I thought a look might determine if they would sell off a portion that Tim and I could handle. Richard O'Connor showed me around, but said we would have to speak to the agent on any sale arrangements. (Richard was obviously a very capable farm manager and I felt sorry for him bearing the brunt of the wider family's problems.) The property was quite run down with some poor fencing, about one-quarter covered in bracken, but beautifully situated with double frontage to the Hay River of some 6 kilometres. There was an excellent six-stand shearing shed, two cottages being lived in and some lesser improvements. Once again by chance, Tim and I caught up with Ross in Perth and he questioned me about Crystal Brook, to which I responded: 'I had a quick look. It's on the market at the right price, but the agent wouldn't sell it off in parts, so we will have to leave it alone.' Ross replied:

> I've been thinking of getting a block down that way, as I've been finding it harder and harder to run cattle at Broomehill. I'd come in with you, but it's still too big. I have a friend, Jock Morrison, who has shown interest in farmland and if he came to the party it might work?

In the end, a partnership between Jock and Janie Morrison as the 'anchor partner', Ross and Di Thompson, Tim and Sally Campbell, and Alex and Jenn Campbell was formed. The plan was to arrange our own finance to buy the land, then borrow from the bank to stock the farm and buy plant. It was further agreed that any inputs to Crystal Brook would be at 'the going rate of the day': Ross would supply Merino rams and South Devon bulls from his studs; Tim would undertake the accountancy; I would supply Poll Dorset rams and be paid a management fee; and we would employ one full-time worker. Jock was left 'on the outer' in this regard but expressed a desire to develop a vineyard as his main interest.

We took possession of 1,663 hectares at $550 per hectare on 1 July 1987. John Raeside, brought up on a Scottish dairy farm, came to work for us and proved to be very good with stock, but only tolerated anything to do with machinery. One title was Queen Victoria Grant 30, the 30th land title granted in WA, and while it was of similar vintage to St Werburghs further up the river, it had no old buildings or other historic features. It comprised the most southern stand of white gum (*Eucalyptus wandoo*) on the Hay River with accompanying heavy red soils, was poison free and had only been used for shepherding sheep in the early days.

We agreed to initially stock with 6,000 Merino ewes, mating half to Merino rams for a self-replacing flock and half to Poll Dorsets for crossbred lamb sales.[39] Wool was the only buoyant commodity in 1987. Owing to a very tight season, the average purchase price of ewes was a modest $10 per head for a mixed-age flock of hoggets through to sound mouth. Courtney Wheatley had been classing the Nardlah sheep for some time and agreed to help us in selecting ewes, then the appropriate Nardlah rams.

We started with 67 cows of our own at $900/head and 100 Nardlah South Devons on the basis of free agistment in return for sharing the calves. As we cleared the bracken and improved the pastures, the plan was to keep the sheep-breeding flock constant at 6,000 and increase cattle numbers.

We budgeted on $60,000 for second-hand plant and finished up with a tray top Toyota Landcruiser; two 70-horsepower tractors; a full hay plant (including a Massey Ferguson 1450 round baler); a slasher for the bracken; two motorbikes; and sundries. The Chamberlain plough and Horwood Bagshaw root rake had finished the development work on our own farm, so were taken over to Crystal Brook. Interest rates had now reached 15.75 per cent for farmers with good equity, so we were very careful to keep borrowed funds under control.

Bracken (*Pteridium esculentum*), a native plant in the natural forest, was our immediate concern as it rapidly spreads by creeping rhizomes once land is cleared and disturbed. While it can be poisonous to stock if no other feed is available, the major concern was the almost impenetrable growth that shaded out any existing pasture.

Dupont had just released Brush-off for bracken control, the active ingredient being *metsulfuron methyl*. The recommendation was to slash in late spring, then spray in late summer at 30 grams per hectare, costing $30 per ha. With 400 ha to control, we needed to move quickly and planned for 75 ha in the first year. John undertook the slashing and had some interesting times charging through 1.5-metre tall fronds, with little indication of hidden stumps and stones! I did the spraying as John baulked at the maths of application rates. The first year was 80 per cent successful and, as Crystal Brook was the biggest purchaser of chemical in that first year, Dupont supplied a follow-up application and used the farm as a demonstration site. After some trial and error over the first year or so, we found summer rain was the key to success: no matter how soon or how late rain came after Christmas, you needed to spray a week or so afterwards, while there was active growth of the new fronds. After the fifth year it was all under control, with only small areas of 'patch' control needed afterwards.

About one-fifth of the farm was on the west side of the Hay River, was the last to be cleared and still quite rough. We quickly realised the difficulty of moving stock over the river and were also worried about the fire risk, as the 6-kilometre western boundary butted state forest. After considerable negotiation, we contracted the Department of Conservation and Land Management (CALM) to plant 150 hectares of pines (*Pinus radiata*) at an annual rent of $13,000, indexed for inflation, on the roughest country to the southwest. Once they had an asset to protect, they started to back burn into the state forest, so reducing the fire risk. (The other 150 ha over the river was planted to blue gums some years later.)

Fencing was another immediate priority. Half the existing fencing was in poor condition, paddocks were too big and there were good areas of natural bush that warranted protection. There were good stands of jarrah, so we contracted felling and hydraulic splitting of posts on site, with some 6 kilometres of fencing to be completed every year. It was the first time in my farming career that I was not doing the fencing myself, the self-satisfying job I so much enjoyed!

We quickly developed a hay-making routine, with John undertaking the mowing and raking while I did the baling. There were 600 rolls the first year, with the long-term plan to have 1,000 rolls on hand every year, including any carryover.

It was the first time Tim and I had been in a business together and, with his role as accountant and mine as property manager, we were required to work closely. Tim regularly updated the owners on 'actuals compared to budget' and I provided a monthly report on seasonal conditions and farm activity. There needed to be coordination between these reporting roles and it was rewarding for both of us to be working together.

Crystal Brook started to host owners' get-togethers and a really close friendship developed based on the common interest of the farm. Tim taught Sophie and Beck to drive on the private Crystal Brook roads and Sally bought a pony for the girls, which remained on the farm for some years. For one of these get-togethers, Jenn cooked an enormous chilli con carne and Jock referred to it for years afterwards, which made us wonder whether it was so very delicious or perhaps so very hard to digest?

Ross was always interested in the sheep and South Devon cattle, based on his own blood lines, and I found he was a great mentor in getting the best out of the farm. Jock, on the other hand, was casting his eyes around for a vineyard site and plans started to come together. Crystal Brook was very well watered, with four creeks running from the east into the river; the middle two were spring fed and permanently flowing as well as being fresh. The main creek, called Crystal Brook, was the freshest and had sweet-scented brown boronia (*Boronia megastigma*)

Owners' 'get-together', Crystal Brook

Jock, unknown and Ross in discussion, Crystal Brook

growing naturally. A permanent spring-fed pool at the head of the creek, rather grandly known as Blue Lake by the locals, was 'as fresh as rainwater' and an obvious starting point for a vineyard. There were plenty of well-drained gravelly loams suited to vines throughout the shire, but reliable water for irrigation was in short supply.

From January 1989, vineyard plans were being finalised. Jock made several trips down and met with various local leaders in the industry, including Tony Smith (Plantagenet Wines) and Michael Goundrey (Goundrey Wines). Jock was subsequently invited onto the board of Goundrey Wines and a development company known as Agrilink was set up in order to lease land on which they would develop and manage vineyards. The fruit would be sold to Goundrey Wines for processing.

Under this arrangement, Crystal Brook leased land to Agrilink and plans were put in place to establish 17 hectares of vines on good north sloping soils to the south of Blue Lake. It was planned to plant 10,000 chardonnay, 5,000 merlot, 5,000 malbec, 5,000 cabernet franc, 15,000 cabernet sauvignon and 10,000 sauvignon blanc cuttings in the vineyard. It wasn't long before Agrilink was in trouble raising the funds, with the prospectus only half subscribed by the closing date, so an extension was reluctantly agreed to. Jock could see that Michael's finances would never keep pace with his dreams, so he retired from the board at this point.[40]

The development of the vineyard highlighted the value of the two spring-fed creeks. Don McFarlane was the Ag Dept hydrologist and undertook analysis of these waterways. He identified several saline water intrusions into the second creek and suggested strategic tree plantings would help correct the problem. CALM was just starting to promote blue gums (*E. globulus*) as a potential new industry for the higher rainfall zone of the South West and had developed a share-farming scheme, whereby the landowners provided the land and fencing and CALM the site preparation, planting and ongoing management. The 10-year harvest returns would then be shared, the ratio dependent on each individual site (soil type, rainfall isohyet, distance to port, etc.).

Research work undertaken by the Joint Venture Agroforestry Program[41] demonstrated that up to 15 per cent of a paddock could be planted to trees, without reducing production from grazing animals. Wind protection enhanced the pasture growth and the survival rate of lambs and calves, and there were also improved feed conversion rates for all grazing animals. Bruce Mattinson was the forester working for CALM and, with Don McFarlane, mapped the relevant part of the farm showing beneficial areas to establish the tree plantings. It was planned for a 'win–win' outcome: enhancing the water quality in the creek; providing protection to stock; and a diversified income stream. Don established bores through the area so that water table and salinity levels could be monitored.

The first plantings were celebrated by Minister Bob Pearce and CALM Director General Syd Shea, together with a busload of 'hangers-on' coming on site to promote this new and innovative concept of farming. Syd was a bit of a showman and very adept at providing photo opportunities for his minister. We also planted 15 per cent of our own farm to blue gums in a similar format but under our own self-funded management. It was only later that taxation-driven whole-of-farm plantings took over the industry. I often wonder how much better off we all would have been if the integrated mosaic plantings had continued as the base for a new industry.

As with all farming ventures, a routine of seasonal activity became established. Cattle numbers were steadily increasing, bracken being controlled, the new fencing program and integrated tree plantings continued, new paddocks were cleaned up for hay production and some improvements to both cottages undertaken. The owners continued to enjoy get-togethers on the farm and various people came individually for holidays, using Crystal Brook as a base while exploring the local Albany, Denmark and Mount Barker regions. Dividends were withheld as surplus income was being put into farm and vineyard development. The asset value was steadily increasing – what could go wrong?

To quote Queen Elizabeth, 1991 proved to be our (and most other farmers') *annus horribilis*. The first event to have an impact was Paul Keating's 'recession we had to have', with corresponding high interest rates: urban households were paying 18 per cent and farmers from 20 to 25 per cent, depending on equity and other risk factors. Fortunately, Crystal Brook with high equity was at the lower end of this range, but it was an impost that would impact any business.

The second and more concerning event was the dramatic end to the floor price for wool. The successful scheme of 20 years' duration was overwhelmed in 1989 when an exceptionally buoyant market, with resulting false expectations, allowed the indicator price to increase by 70 per cent over the following two years. The Soviet Union collapsed and its purchase of 30–50 per cent of the clip ceased overnight. February sales were cancelled and frantic negotiations between the government and industry were taking place.[42] (A later chapter further reflects on related farm politics.)

When sales resumed in March 1991, pass-in rates were in the order of 30–40 per cent and the market indicator slumped from 700 cents clean[43] under the previous Reserve Price Scheme to 420c per kilogram in the new 'free' market. At the farm level it was devastating. Farmers and their financiers had grown accustomed to having one budget line assured and not subject to the vagaries of the auction market. To have the price almost halved was very difficult for any business and resulted in the demise of many farms. Crystal Brook had diversified income from crossbred lambs, cattle and trees, so there was less of an impact than experienced by many others, though it was still a huge blow to the budget.

As if that wasn't enough, the season continued to deteriorate and Albany and the surrounding districts recorded the lowest ever rainfall for the first six months of the year. We had ample hay on hand for the cattle but had to buy oats and lupins for the sheep. A series of seminars conducted by the Ag Dept provided information about hand-feeding stock, protecting paddocks from wind erosion and budgeting assistance. Digger Weir was at one such seminar and was interviewed by the ABC Country Hour: 'I've been farming all my life at Ongerup and Narrikup, and have never seen such emancipated sheep!'

The drama of the season must have got the better of him, but it added a light touch of humour for farmers tuning in to the Country Hour while having their lunch. From July onward, the season improved somewhat and with Saia oat-based hay crops, we were able to replenish our hay supplies and finish off the crossbred lambs. The young tree crops and vineyard came through the dry first half of the year with little ill effect, proving the benefit of deep ripping before planting.

The final straw testing the camel's back was the vineyard. The trellising had been progressing very slowly as a result of Agrilink's financial problems and the end of financial year lease to Crystal Brook was not paid by the due date. As the year progressed it became clear that Goundrey's entities were collapsing, so it was decided to take the non-payment of the lease 'on the chin' and resume ownership of the vineyard. As extra funds were needed, Jenn and I opted out of the vineyard at this point. Jock organised Di Davidson, the well-known SA consultant, to provide advice and Carey Saggers from Denmark was employed to manage the vineyard. The other three families were now filling Agrilink's role and leasing the land from Crystal Brook.

There was one piece of good news at the end of the year. A neighbouring farm that was almost surrounded by Crystal Brook was put on the market owing to the pressures of the year. The two fresh flowing creeks mentioned earlier had part of their catchments on this farm, so it was a good opportunity to square off our holding and have the complete creek catchments under our control. We added Curtain's block of 247 hectares to Crystal Brook for $750 per hectare and it was a case of 'when everybody else has slowed to a crawl, it's time to start running', which proved its worth in later years.

After the *annus horribilis* year, the routine fell back into place and, once again, we were all enjoying the shared common interest and periodic get-togethers at Crystal Brook. The only small setback occurred when John Raeside was headbutted by a cow:

> I've worked cattle all my life. It's the first time the front end of a cow has caught me out – it's usually a kick from the back end that gets you.

With cracked ribs and bruising, he was off work for a month. We all got to know his wife, Morag, and their children, Elizabeth, Johnny and Margaret, and enjoyed catching up with their activities. Margaret had been born without eyelids and was coping with other eye problems, but now making amazing progress thanks to plastic surgeons and eye specialists.

We were all shocked in 1994 when Ross was diagnosed with bowel cancer, at a fairly well-advanced stage. He explained he wanted to relinquish his share in Crystal Brook so that his affairs were in order and farming interests more straightforward for when his son Scott might take over. I was personally very upset, for Ross had been a real mentor and friend in so many ways. His good-natured and unassuming personality won him the respect of all who knew him. He was equally at ease and comfortable at the Weld Club, among Perth's top business and professional people, as he was in the saleyards and shearing sheds in the country. There were two employees at Nardlah who had been with him for more than 20 years, further demonstrating the good stead others held him in.

None of us could imagine Crystal Brook without Ross being involved so it was decided to put the farm on the market. Seasons and commodity prices were favourable and it looked as though we would more than double our original investment, so it was planned to sell the farm as one entity and the vineyard separately. Following the demise of Goundrey Wines, the fruit was being sold to Plantagenet Wines. It was our good fortune that, following a restructure of the company, Plantagenet was looking to buy vineyards as they had been too dependent on buying in grapes from external sources. They had been pleased with the Crystal Brook fruit and purchased 100 hectares that included the vineyard, water source and some extra land for expansion. We were all pleased with the outcome, as the four families who owned Crystal Brook received good value for the land and the three families who had taken on Agrilink's role were equally pleased with the value attributed to the vineyard asset.

The remaining 1,810 hectares was listed with Elders in September 1994. We couldn't believe our luck when the asking price of $1,629 per hectare was realised in February 1995, with a deposit of $225,000 and 12 months to settlement. The purchaser was Evenwood Pty Ltd, the entity controlled by Ron McGrath, who was planning to establish paulownias on the property and asked for the use of 'an acre or so' to heel in his cuttings for use in the following year.

We didn't realise he was using the 12-month settlement period to set up a unit trust arrangement for the purpose of establishing paulownia tree plantations, similar to Goundrey's Agrilink. Ron McGrath faced the same problems as Michael Goundrey and was unable to settle on the due date, asking for three extensions of 14 days each. On the third occasion, once 14 days had elapsed, we served notice that he was in default and requested the deposit be made over to us. He refused, claimed we were in dispute and placed a caveat on the property.

With a caveat in place and being 'in dispute', we couldn't proceed with alternative marketing arrangements, so challenged him in court. The argument boiled down to 28 days' notice being required if the purchaser had prior use of the land, rather than 14 days if otherwise. Did his 'heeled in paulownias' on less than 1 hectare of land out of the 1,810 hectares being purchased equate to prior use, and did three 14-day extensions of time not satisfy the 28 days required? To cut a long and expensive story short, we won the case after 12 months and, would you believe it, the legal fees were the same as the deposit we were claiming. Lawyers!

During the 12 months' delay, land prices were decreasing and we quickly realised our asking price was unlikely to be achieved again so decided subdivision would be the better way to go. The Plantagenet Shire allowed for title boundaries to be changed but no new lots created and all had to be of commercial size (this was to prevent pockets of urban-sized lots among rural holdings). John Kinnear and Associates were engaged as surveyors to redesign the 15 titles on the farm so that all had road frontages and access to creeks or dam sites, and existing fencing was utilised where possible. Any new road construction was to be minimal.

John did an exceptional job and we were quickly granted shire and relevant agency approval. Brian Attwell from AD Contractors won the contract for building the 3 kilometres of road required at a cost of $120,000. Brian had a great reputation for community work with his equipment, such as building the Albany Speedway. I found him very obliging and easy to deal with and wonder what could have gone so terribly wrong for him to now be in jail, having organised a hit man to take the life of his daughter-in-law?[44]

Early sales proceeded 'subject to completion of road' and many quick results came to hand. One early sale was further land for Plantagenet Wines, which bought 314 hectares to establish its large Hazard Hill vineyard. As we entered 1998, it was decided to auction the remaining three lots. While no sales were achieved on the day, some potential buyers were identified and final sales completed just before Ross died later that year.

There were a few wind-up parties and get-togethers, with all of us agreeing it was a very special and rewarding time in our lives. We had been through a few highs and lows, but that's agriculture, as experienced by so many families over many generations. Tim probably best summed it up:

> We could have bought Wesfarmers shares in 1987 and probably done as well, but we wouldn't have had anywhere near the satisfaction or sense of achievement as having owned Crystal Brook.

18 FARMER POLITICS

The purchase of Crystal Brook in 1987 heralded several changes on the home front. The number of round hay balers in the district was growing and, because of their high capacity, farmers were offering to do their neighbours' hay to offset the initial purchase price. The result was downward pressure on the contract price of baling and a rapid drop in demand for the service. Accordingly, John Blythe and I decided it was time to retire from what had been 'a good little money earner'.

My management commitment to Crystal Brook added pressure on my time, so we started to employ local people on a day-by-day basis. With the tough times for farming in the late 1980s, a number of neighbours were happy to work on this basis, including David Findlay (who became more like one of the family, rather than an employee), John Steele and Graeme Pederick. The call on these people increased as I became more involved in farmer politics. Jenn's contribution to running the farm also grew, checking cattle out in the paddock and working in the yards with her trusty length of 'poly' pipe.

1987 was an interesting time in state and federal politics. With Labor governments at both levels, we were initially more pessimistic about the Hawke administration, but how wrong this proved to be. At state level, Brian Burke and Julian Grill were engaged in a range of business deals which became known as 'WA Inc'. People such as Laurie Connell and his Rothwells Bank, Alan Bond, Dallas Dempster, Warren Anderson and Robert Holmes à Court became household names, for all the wrong reasons. The WA government lost at least $600 million, or more likely up to $1 billion, of taxpayer funds. Many businesses were bankrupted, the losses being born by 'mum and dad' investors.[45]

By contrast, the Hawke government was going from strength to strength. Bob had 'gone on the wagon' and was addressing many of the union rorts through his accord process. Paul Keating and Peter Walsh were imposing financial rigour and reform, including: slashing spending to achieve three surpluses; reducing tariffs; floating the dollar; and introducing compulsory superannuation, fringe benefits tax and capital gains tax (that excluded the family home), to name but a few initiatives. It should be remembered that many of these reforms were made possible by the support of the opposition, a practice not seen in today's 'dog eat dog' parliaments.

With the benefit of hindsight, the floating of the dollar should have been matched by allowing the floor in the Reserve Price Scheme for wool to float against a basket of currencies, as used by our main trading partners. By separating wool from the newly imposed rigours of the global market, it was probably the first nail in the coffin for 'orderly marketing' of the wool clip, though its final demise was still some way off. The Australian Wool Corporation had carefully considered this option but pressure from Wool Council and the growers prevented that outcome.[46]

There were two other innovative outcomes of the Hawke era: CRCs and RRDCs. Cooperative Research Centres (CRCs) were established to encourage collaborative research between two or more universities which could demonstrate industry or 'end use' support for the proposed activity. The government matched the funding on a dollar-for-dollar basis and an assessment process was used to select suitable research programs in several categories, including agriculture. The concept quickly took off, with up to five or more universities in collaboration per application and the matching funding dropping to 25 cents or so in the dollar because of the 'capped' funding available.

John Kerin, the Minister for Primary Industries, brokered a deal with the agriculture sector to establish Rural Research and Development Corporations (RRDCs), on a similar basis to the CRCs. The farm sector agreed to levy produce at the point of sale for research, which would be matched dollar for dollar by the federal government without a 'cap' or limit to funding. The major commodities, such as wool, grain, meat, dairy, sugar and cotton, would have their own RDCs. Smaller commodities, such as rice and chicken meat, would be managed in a combined entity, the Rural Industries R&D Corporation, which would also cater for new and emerging commodities, such as olives, ti-tree and deer. Finally, the Land and Water Resources R&D Corporation was established to undertake research for Landcare and conservation-related activity, with no requirement of matching funds.

A highlight in 1989 was the launch of the 'Decade of Landcare' by Bob Hawke at Wentworth, where the Darling flows into the Murray River. Rick Farley from the NFF and Phillip Toyne from the Australian Conservation Foundation deserve the credit for brokering the deal that made it all possible. It should be remembered, however, that Rick and Phillip were only able to move as far as their constituents would allow and ground had to be forfeited on both sides. I was involved in the earlier debate at state level and it boiled down to a generational divide, as the younger farmers were more clearly recognising the damage that 'business as usual' was doing to the landscape through wind erosion, salinity, vegetation decline, river health and so on.

The Landcare concept took off like wildfire. Bob Hawke committed $320 million in funding for the decade to be accessed by local Landcare groups that could demonstrate a viable project and matching funds. Two early groups in WA were at Jerramungup, through the drive of Rex Edmondson, and Esperance, with Garry English's leadership. Both groups were formed with wind erosion as their main focus. The Ag Dept responded quickly and appointed Kevin Goss as Landcare branch manager. Within a few years, there were 120 such groups in WA and it 'proved to be a golden era for natural resource management and national engagement'.[47]

In 1989, I was elected state vice president of the WA Farmers Federation (WAFF), as another name change from PIA had taken place to reflect the allegiance and support of the National Farmers' Federation. Peter Lee was elected state president in the same year. As vice president, I represented WA on the NFF Executive along with Peter, and at both levels was allocated the portfolio of 'conservation and land management'. In this capacity, I was appointed to several boards representing the farm sector: state and national boards of Greening Australia; Landcare Australia Ltd; State Soil Conservation Advisory Committee; and the CSIRO Institute of Natural Resources and Environment (INRE) Advisory Committee. Dr Roy Green was the director of INRE, who I was to see more of in the following years. With these appointments, I started to develop an ever-expanding group of contacts in political, agri-business, government agency and research circles.

At this point, I will outline the very democratic but rather convoluted structure of the WAFF, largely unchanged to this day. Every commodity, such as grains, meat, wool and dairy, had elected members at zone, state and national levels. Policy positions were established at annual commodity conferences. Alongside the commodity-based structures was the general section, responsible for industry-wide issues, including macroeconomic settings, transport, conservation and education. The general section also had zone representatives and hosted the State General Council, which developed policy positions for final consideration at the annual conference. In those days, the state president, two vice presidents and the treasurer were elected at the annual general conference. For day-to-day management, there was the General Executive, comprising the commodity presidents, elected general presidents, treasurer and three others nominated by the General Council, being 12 in all. Democratic, but convoluted!

As this book is about 'sheep and other things', I will go into some detail over the final difficult years of the Reserve Price Scheme (RPS) for wool. It should be remembered, that, since its introduction in 1970, there had been almost total industry support, including individual growers, state farm organisations, the Wool Council and Australian Wool Corporation. I certainly had my own colours firmly nailed to the mast of the RPS. Under the structure of WAFF, state presidents had little influence over commodity policy decisions but were often required to explain or defend them. To demonstrate the point, in 1990 the wool crisis was unfolding and as a state vice president, I became involved in many rowdy and confused meetings around the state. The stockpile was rapidly increasing and the Soviet Union was imploding, not buying its traditional 30–50 per cent of the clip. All agreed that decisive action was urgently required, but how, when and by whom were the questions. I remember at one meeting Bob Hall, the Darkan-based farm adviser, accused me and all from WAFF as being 'slavishly addicted to agrarian socialism'.

Lyn Johnson, from the Pastoralists and Graziers Association (PGA), was an outspoken critic of the wool marketing system and one of the first to call for the disbandment of the RPS. Unfortunately, her abrasive style of delivery and overuse of economic jargon grated with many, to the point of her message not receiving the attention it might have. She was regularly interviewed and promoted by Bill McCutcheon on the ABC's rural breakfast program, and it's probably the most blatant and prolonged example of biased reporting I ever experienced.

The aggressive and combative approach employed by Bob and Lyn, supported in similar style by Jim Maple-Brown (NSW grazier) and Wilson Tuckey (Liberal member for O'Connor), often had a negative effect as it caused many to switch off and become disengaged, while others were provoked into bunkering down in a defensive stance for the status quo. Even though the 870 cents per kilogram clean floor price might now appear dangerously high (with the benefit of hindsight), it was nonetheless proportionately set against the prevailing

1,100 cent market of the day and was initially supported by the vast majority of growers, the Wool Council, Wool Corporation and John Kerin.

Tony Gooch, a board member of the Australian Wool Corporation, and Mark McQuire, the WAFF's wool section president who was also serving on the Wool Council, were usually in the hot seat at grower meetings and acquitted themselves very well in what was really a no-win situation for the industry. Alan Cleland was representing the PGA on the Wool Council and, with his measured arguments, was one of the first at the national level to express concern at the direction of the unfolding events.

Once the floor proved to be unsustainable at the 870 cents level, as a result of the government putting a limit on any further funding guarantee, there was furious debate as to whether it should be lowered and by how much (supported by ever-increasing taxes on the growers) or abandoned altogether. The RPS had been widely supported through to 1988 but now there was deep division as to the best way forward and perhaps we should've all taken more notice of Alan Cleland's considered points of view. I often wonder if the debate in WA would have been different if 'we were all in the same tent', rather than bunkered down with opposing positions? It's my experience that at the end of the day, most people are influenced by the steady argument of the more moderate presenters, such as Tony Gooch, Alan Cleland, Mark McQuire and Andrew McNiel, rather than the radical fringe on both sides that gain the initial media attention.

Eventually, under mounting pressure from Treasury, John Kerin was forced to use his statutory powers and lowered the floor to 700 cents per kilogram clean, backed up by an 18 per cent tax on growers. The grower members on the Australian Wool Corporation considered resigning over his decision, as they believed any lowering of the floor would be unsustainable, but realised such an action would be counterproductive and further destabilise the industry. The 700 cents level was akin to 'being half pregnant' and the trade lost faith in Australia ever being committed to holding to a fixed floor price again, with the stockpile continuing to grow at an alarming rate. In February 1991 sales were suspended, the RPS abandoned after agonised industry debate, then sales recommenced in March with an open 'free' market. The stockpile stood at 4.77 million bales, with a debt of $2.8 billion, and it was to be a slow and difficult 10 years of recovery.[48]

John Kerin made one mistake in 1987 (that he later owned up to) in allowing the Australian Wool Corporation to set the annual floor price without receiving ministerial approval. His intention was noble in wanting the industry to be free of 'the dead hand of government', but it removed a safety valve for any future crises, as occurred in 1990. As the RPS disintegrated, he was very patient with the Wool Council, Wool Corporation and wool growers, believing the industry had to have ownership of its own destiny. Too early an intervention by government would have fuelled dissent and left the door ajar for another tilt at 'orderly marketing'. Throughout this very difficult period, he won the respect of most in the industry, both out in the paddock and with the representative bodies.[49]

Following the reintroduction of the free market, many wool producers wasted negative energy blaming the Reserve Price Scheme for wool's demise, rather than facing up to the realities of the present day. Others showed unrealistic optimism for the future, as illustrated by the PGA's 'Wear Wool Wednesday' campaign and the setting up of the Tambellup Wool Foundation through the drive of Jamie Kronborg, the Withams, Hardies, Smiths and many other Great Southern families. Some graziers were so optimistic that they bought wheat belt farms to stock with sheep in order to benefit from the expected rebound under a free market. (While you have to admire them for putting their money alongside their mouths, they were to be sorely disappointed.)

Irrespective of the initial response, there was an irrefutable and fundamental change rapidly taking place in the global wool market. The Soviet Union was the last economy still using wool as a base product for blankets, military uniforms and so on. The rest of the world had embraced synthetics to fill these bulk end uses, with wool now being used for niche high-value consumer goods. For the first time in 150 years and four generations of Campbells in Australia, wool was no longer 'king'. Australia was never again 'to ride on the sheep's back'.

There were two farm organisations in WA: the WAFF and PGA. Originally, one represented farmers and the other pastoralists, but now there was a growing crossover of representation, though the PGA was always the smaller of the two. There was good-natured and, sometimes, more bitter rivalry: 'There's no doubt about the PGA – they're a bunch of right-wing "born with a silver spoon in their mouths" old fuddy-duddies, living in a past era.'; 'The WAFF are nothing but a gaggle of left-leaning agrarian socialists and, look, they even have the Walshes as members.'

In 1989 John Walsh was grains section president and served on the General Executive, of which I was part. It rankled with me that being a known Labor supporter should somehow automatically speak against his ability.

John would have to be one of the most clear-thinking people I have ever known and he prosecuted an argument in a concise and thought-through manner. If ever he had an alternative point of view, it gave me cause to double-check my own position before moving on. As for Peter Walsh, most people would agree, often in hindsight, that he was probably the best minister for finance ever seen in Australia.[50]

Peter Lee was president of WAFF from 1989 to 1992 and he had married Christina Magee from Kulin, my old debating partner in Junior Farmer days, so we shared a lot in common. Peter left his home town of Trayning and was now farming the Magee property with Christina. One of his favourite stories regarding the farm was an occasion when some iron gates were stolen from the roadside and on questioning a neighbour, he was advised: 'You want to be careful asking questions about some missing gates – they might take a-fence!'

All presidents bring their own touch to the job. Peter was one of the better educated office holders, with an eloquent and somewhat quizzical turn of phrase, and is still writing the popular 'View from the Ridge' column in *Farm Weekly*. During Peter's term, the WAFF's financial pressures were escalating. One difficult decision was closing the organisation's official newspaper, the *Farmers Weekly*, which had operated for 78 years. Brian Nelson had been the astute and crusty editor for many years and was a great stalwart of both the paper and wider organisation. Dean Alston was the popular cartoonist and he went on to fill a similar role with *The West Australian* in 1986.

The most dominant issue of the time was the 'wheat war' with the USA, which was dumping grain on to the world market. To highlight the point, WAFF dumped a truckload of wheat in front of the US and British consulates in Perth, with the message: 'We will pick up our dumped wheat, which is more than the US will do with the wheat it has dumped on the world market.'[51]

It appealed to the media and certainly got our message across. I don't know if this incident had anything to do with it or not, but the WAFF was invited on to the USS *Enterprise*, steaming down the WA coast for Fremantle. Peter had NFF commitments so I joined the mayor of Fremantle and some journalists to be flown out, with an arrested landing on deck, shown over the aircraft carrier and catapulted back into flight for the trip home. Talk about 'boys' toys' – I'm still boring people to death telling the story!

Peter stood for NFF president in 1991 against Graham Blight and narrowly lost. He was elected vice president, however, and it gave me an early taste of the harsh realities of elections and public life. I was elected WAFF state president in 1992, heralding the busiest three years of my life. The president was paid an annual allowance plus expenses, intended to equal that of a backbench member of state Parliament. The WAFF never reached that goal but the allowance was nonetheless of great assistance.

The use of casual labour on the farm increased significantly, the cost of which was covered by the allowance, and there was enough remaining for us to consider buying a Perth property for our own use. We would be there for three or more nights a week and had been using both our parents up to then for accommodation. We scraped together a minimum deposit, Jenn went hunting for a suitable unit or townhouse and we finally settled on a duplex half in Dalkeith, at 500 square metres for $210,000. It was sobering to see how much easier it was to arrange finance for a Perth property, as compared to a rural loan, and to realise the risk penalties that farmers were expected to bear on interest rates.

This being a farming odyssey, rather than one based on farm politics, I will abbreviate the three years of being WAFF president as much as possible.

Firstly, it was the greatest privilege to have been elected by 7,000 peers for such a position. Tony Gooch stood against me and would have made a great president but, as Peter found the year before, there is only room for one at the end of the day. I was very fortunate in having excellent commodity presidents on the Executive with me: Laurie Marshall for grains; Andrew (Andy) McNeil, wool; Mike Norton, meat; John Crisp, pastoral; and Barry Oates, dairy. As well as these fine people, Don Sutherland and Tony York were vice presidents and Harold McCashney treasurer, together with Shirley Thorne, Russell Crook, Ian Turton and Kevin McMenemy, appointed by the General Council. (Mike Norton was to become state president in 2008 and Tony York in 2016.)

There were also dedicated senior staff, led by Tim Ryan as executive director and supported by Phil Chidgzey for wool, Colin Mann for meat and Wayne Reynolds for grains. Irene Conwell was the president's secretary and had a photographic memory for faces, names, who was married to whom, which branch and zone they came from, and so on. This was always my weakness and I regularly thanked God and herself for being there. The affable Leslie was on the front desk and there was even a tea lady who came in twice a day! John Blake was the accountant with support staff for membership and Mary-Jo Fisher the talented legal officer, who went on to be the industrial director at NFF, then a Liberal senator for South Australia. Neville Munns joined us after working for the PGA and called everybody Mr so and so, until we weaned him of the habit.

Farm organisations had passed their peak of membership, yet remained very relevant. Membership had fallen from 10,000 to just under 7,000 as a result of wool prices being at the lowest level for many years, farms being amalgamated and fewer people living in the country. Nevertheless, there was still a lot of media interest, so I was sent off to a course on TV and radio interviewing and reading the body language of those about you.

By and large, the rural newspapers and ABC rural department gave us a fair hearing, but the wider ABC, the *West Australian* newspaper and commercial television needed a more careful approach. I had several interviews with Alan Carpenter (later premier) when he was hosting the 7.30 pm ABCTV *Today Tonight* program and found him very fair, as compared to some on today's ABC. I quickly learnt that if you do well, the telephone seldom rings – make 'a blue' and it goes crazy! I could judge the mood of members by the nature and number of telephone calls after any press, radio or TV activity, as there were no texts or emails in those days.

Another communication lesson was served up to the WAFF by Geoff Gair, the media consultant for the PGA. We learnt the hard way that it wasn't the accuracy or detail of a case that mattered – it was the 'spin' you put on it that won the day. Geoff was as great a benefit to their organisation as all their other office staff put together and provided me with a valuable early insight as to the power of effective communication.

A highlight was time spent in the country, attending branch and zone meetings, field days and other public meetings. I came to greatly respect the vast majority of members who were 'doing it tough' with poor seasons, wool income almost halved and generally deteriorating terms of trade. Another highlight was the number of business people and members of allied organisations we met and, in many cases, came to know quite well. For example, John O'Meehan was vice president, then president of the Royal Agricultural Society from 1993 to 1999 and we often served on the same committees or met at various industry functions. Jenn and I enjoyed many dinners with John and Wendy in the councillors' rooms at the Claremont Showgrounds.

Annual conferences were always challenging and interesting. The commodities had their own conferences, followed by two days for the general conference – four days in all. There were more than 300 delegates on the opening day, with many other relevant politicians, allied industry representatives and observers present. The media were well represented, including several TV stations to cover both the president's annual address and the official opening, usually by the minister for agriculture or a similar person of importance. John Anderson, then federal shadow minister for primary industries, officiated at my last conference.

Looking back, I remember the 'characters' that added to the occasion, rather than the better informed people who carried the debate. WAFF was well represented by a broad church of members, ranging from the most successful farmers in a district to the battlers and colourful individuals. Some of the characters were: Stan Lewis, a large man of Churchillian qualities, who had a fine deep voice and eloquent turn of phrase, though his focus on style of delivery sometimes caused him to lose direction in his oratory; Dick De Pledge was a passionate processed vegetable grower, but very long winded; Jim Alexander presented as a large blustering hobo, but could buy and sell all his neighbours if he chose; Duncan Hordacre was the face of the battler, who was very frugal in his habits and refused to attend the annual dinner as being too lavish and extravagant; Colin Richardson, a large 'teddy bear' sort of bloke, was always jovial and could see a humorous angle on any issue; and Peter Wahlsten, the steady face of the Merredin zone.

One interesting visitor to the WAFF office was Murray Kennedy, replete in a loud, 1920s-style three-piece suit, large hat and complaining he had to 'leave his side irons at the Midland police station'! He was known as the 'Roy Hill professional litigant' and came in requesting support for a 'stoush' he was having with a local mining company.

A president seldom takes a public stance without consultation or policy direction, but becomes the recognised spokesperson for the organisation. As such, I will outline the most memorable and difficult issues covered in my three years of holding the office. Shortly after being elected, the telephone rang and Max Johnston from the Rural Action Movement came straight to the point: 'There's a farm at Beverley that the banks are about to repossess. Will you show solidarity and join us in blockading them from gaining access?'

Many farmers were in real difficulty with their banks, following Paul Keating's 'the recession we had to have', with interest rates peaking at 25 per cent for those with a high-risk profile. There had been considerable debate on this subject within WAFF so I was able to reply:

> No we won't. If banks are prevented from taking this ultimate step, the risk factor for all farmers will be affected and result in higher interest rates for everybody.

I was subsequently on the Country Hour explaining our position. Within minutes, the telephones started ringing, with accusations of being 'yellow livered' and 'not worth your salt', all interspersed with shearing shed expletives. Most concluded with: 'and that's the last you'll see of our membership'. All my calls came through Irene and she was often able to call out through the door: 'He hasn't been a member for years. It was his father who used to be a loyal member of the xyz branch.'

It was a good early lesson regarding membership response. It was often only days later that I would see somebody at a meeting or social function and hear the opposite point of view:

Good on you for speaking out against blockading the Beverley farm the other day. We would've all paid the price if you'd gone along with them.

A closely related issue was PIA House. The Farmers Union had received a generous bequest from Thomas Henry Peterson in 1954 for £100,000, 'to establish suitable city premises for the organisation'. In due course, 239 Adelaide Terrace was purchased for the ongoing benefit of the organisation, in a structure known as the Peterson Trust.[52] During Wolf Boetcher's term as president (1979–82), it was decided to redevelop the property and rent out the surplus space as a future income source for the organisation. Many of us canvassed local farmers for debentures to help fund the redevelopment, with the remaining finance provided by the Town and Country Building Society.

Keating's high interest rates had an equally harsh impact on city properties. Vacancy rates increased and the interest on our loan did likewise, to a point that WAFF was no longer able to service its debt. The building was sold for $5.9 million to Singaporean interests, trading as Bonneville Holdings Pty Ltd, with a commitment that WAFF would lease its existing space for a further five years. The Town and Country Building Society, now owned by the ANZ Bank, wrote off its share of the remaining debt and the debenture holders were left 'carrying the can' for the remaining $3 million.[53] (It was only in 2014 that all contingent liabilities had been satisfied and the organisation was left with just over $400,000 in the Peterson Trust, for its future benefit).[54]

In hindsight, I believe the experience of redeveloping the Adelaide Terrace property is akin to a farmer buying the property next door. If seasons and commodity prices are favourable, he is credited for his foresight and ability. On the other hand, if seasons, commodity prices and interest rates go against him, he is 'yesterday's man'. There wouldn't be a district in the state that hadn't seen a well-established and respected farming family 'come to grief' in their effort to expand in the name of long-term viability. Henry Schapper had been advocating 'get big or get out' for some time and his message was beyond argument, but his caustic and confrontational style of delivery rankled with many farmers.[55] I remember at one public meeting, towards the end of Henry's time, a disgruntled bloke at the back of the room stood up: 'I've tried getting bigger – I still have to get out, so what's your next bright idea?'

A more traditional win for WAFF in my time, relating to high interest rates, was stamp duty. In the final year of the Lawrence Labor government, stamp duty was removed when transferring a loan from one institution to another, which opened the way for farmers to test the market and seek better terms for their borrowings. Richard Court's incoming coalition government extended the stamp duty relief to transfer of the family farm, which was particularly important for intergenerational decision-making and adjusting to the recently introduced capital gains tax.

The single most complex and divisive issue in my term was the Mabo High Court decision. WAFF publicly endorsed the Court government's response at state level, but the main debate was at the national level, with NFF responding to the Keating government's preferred position. Many landholders were of the opinion that it was counterproductive negotiating with Keating as there was bound to be a change of government in 1996, and they believed the coalition would reverse any unfavourable aspects and 'sort it all out'.

I had clear memories of disillusionment with the Fraser government 'not sorting it all out' after Whitlam, so I was an advocate of working for the best possible outcome with the government of the day. Keating was proposing coexisting title for the pastoral leases so that Aboriginal native title holders would have equal title to that of the pastoralists, which would have been a disaster for the leaseholders. After protracted negotiation, NFF was able to have the proposal overturned. It's open to conjecture whether the Howard government would have come to the rescue if already enshrined in law, but I stand by the course of action taken by NFF, though I received considerable criticism at the time. One disappointing aspect of the Mabo debate was the personal attacks on Rick Farley, the NFF executive director. It was common knowledge he had links to the Aboriginal community and some chose to use that as proof positive he was working against the interests of the membership. It's my firm belief that Rick always operated with the utmost integrity and I continued to support him for his full term at NFF, then in his subsequent public roles.

An ongoing issue that most incoming presidents were bound to confront was the subject of 'one farmer body in WA', or the amalgamation of the WAFF and the PGA. At the national level, the effectiveness of the NFF taking on the unions and macroeconomic issues was beyond dispute. Why couldn't we achieve that same single voice at state level? On my gaining office in 1992, there was a damning article in *The West Australian* by Liz Tickner, with a cartoon of Tony Boultbee (the PGA president) and myself at loggerheads, claiming 'that relations between the two organisations were at an all-time low'. This had been largely brought about over the differing positions on the Reserve Price Scheme for wool, which had come to a head the year before.[56]

It has always been my strong belief that differences are best sorted out behind closed doors, 'having everybody in the tent', rather than megaphone squabbling through the media. Peter Lefroy and Pell House, both previous office bearers with the PGA, had shown enormous courage and leadership in becoming members of WAFF, that others might follow. Few did, but I came to know both men very

Cartoon of Alex Campbell and Tony Boultbee, *The West Australian*, 28 April 1992 (original cartoon purchased from WA Newspapers, now in Alex's possession)

well and held them in my highest regard as men of integrity, while contributing so much back to their local communities. For example, Peter invented the rotary sheep-handling cradle, known as the Cranmore Cradle, but refused to patent it, saying it should be for the benefit of the whole sheep industry. Pell was a tireless worker for his local Kojonup community.

There were many reasons put forward as to why amalgamation would never take place in WA: differing political preferences (Country Party vs Liberal); opposing views on marketing; pastoral establishment versus farmer 'battlers', and so on. At the regional level, the Esperance zone of WAFF and the district committee of the PGA amalgamated and held joint meetings, reporting to both parent bodies. They showed the way but, once again, others failed to follow. John Clapin and Peter Webb invited me along to several Kojonup PGA meetings, holding out an olive branch, but nothing came of that.

By the end of my term, the hostile differences reported by Liz Tickner had subsided and some meaningful activity was underway, with a joint working group exploring options for amalgamation. I think the vast majority of farmers supported having one organisation but there was a rump on both sides suffering the 'big frog in a small pond' syndrome. It has got to the sad state of affairs today that both groups are withering on the vine to the detriment of the wider rural community.

We had two membership drives during my term as president and reversed the trend of declining membership. The dire predictions of Liz Tickner in 1992, together with the bravado of the Rural Action Movement, had not come to fruition. It was reported in March 1994 'that WAFF had 7,649 members, of which there were 5,187 farm enterprises, the remainder being retired farmers and affiliated members from other sectors'.[57]

A challenging industrial dispute arose in 1994 when workers at the fertiliser plant near Kwinana called a strike at short notice. Farmers' trucks were lined up at the locked gates and management said they would load the trucks if WAFF could broker a deal with the strikers. I went to the plant with a few others and by the time we arrived the farmers were really upset at the delay. Negotiation was going nowhere, when Joe Candeloro in the leading truck called out: 'You climb up here with me – we'll sort it all out.'

Once in the truck he engaged crawler gear, set the throttle to fast idle, then climbed out on the step and yelled: 'I can't stop the truck from here, so open up or look out of the way – we're coming through.'

The gates weren't opened so we crashed into them with the bull-bar, pushed them down and drove over the top – with the strikers clearing a hurried path! Management loaded the trucks and I was concerned about revenge as we drove out, but there was now a police presence and everybody had gone home. So much for my only industrial dispute.

It's interesting to reflect on the various politicians I personally engaged with over the six years as WAFF vice president and president and serving on the NFF Executive. At state level, we regularly met with premiers and ministers for agriculture: Brian Burke was at the end of his time when I started and completely swamped by WA Inc; I was not a supporter of Peter Dowding and found it difficult to establish any meaningful communication; on the other hand, Carmen Lawrence

Joe Candeloro's truck at the locked gates and picket line, 1994 (courtesy WA Farmers Federation)

performed really well under impossible circumstances. Maybe it was being a farmer's daughter from the northeast Wheatbelt, but WAFF always had ready access to her and a sympathetic ear. Richard Court was elected towards the end of my term and we had open and good lines of access to his office. Some said he was living under the shadow of his father, Sir Charles Court, but I felt he rose to the role of premier being very much 'his own man' and served the state with distinction.

There were some interesting state ministers for agriculture. David Evans was a popular and effective minister, but Julian Grill (who had been a successful minister for transport) was preoccupied with other matters of government and appeared to almost resent the agriculture portfolio as not utilising his talents to best effect.

Ernie Bridge, the first Aboriginal person to become a minister of government at either the state or federal level, was one of the most open and accessible ministers I ever dealt with. I recall two occasions when his charm and openness served him particularly well. The first was a WAFF conference dinner, where he was scheduled to make a short address. He must have sensed half the room was against the policies he was outlining, so instead of leaving early as most ministers did at these occasions, he stayed on and produced his guitar at the end of the evening, then won everybody over with his repertoire of bush ballads.

On another occasion, he was at the Perth Zoo officiating to a large group of school children who were participating in a Landcare event. As it was such a large gathering, they couldn't all fit into the venue and those outside were quite disgruntled. Ernie quickly read the situation and rattled through the formalities, then produced his guitar and hosted a lengthy outdoor sing-along for everybody. The undersized venue was totally forgotten.[58]

He loved telling yarns about the Kimberley. A favourite concerned the age-old tradition of 'poddy dodging', where an old fellow was having a meal at a neighbour's property and boasted he had never eaten his own beef, to which the host replied: 'Well, you're eating your own meat tonight.'[59]

His one downside was his inability to make a quick decision as there was a growing mountain of issues demanding attention. I think his main problem was hoping to have everybody on side before taking action – a situation that seldom happens in the real world of politics. He is probably best remembered for his dream of a water pipeline from the Kimberley to the South West; while it was a dream too far, at least it was more plausible than Colin Barnett's 'thought bubble' in 1988, when he proposed an open canal to do the same job!

Monty House became Minister for Agriculture in 1993 – and how different he was to Ernie! While some criticised him for being too forthright and pushing proposals forward with undue haste, I never found that to be the case. He got straight to the point and was not averse to giving you an earful, but was always receptive to a counterview that had been well thought through. Maybe not suffering fools gladly isn't such a bad thing in being an effective minister?

At the federal level, it was NFF presidents who would interact with prime ministers, though in those days it was not unusual for one to address the NFF annual conference. I share the view of many that Paul Keating was an outstanding treasurer but failed to meet expectations as prime minister, a typical farmer comment being:

> You know when a government's in trouble. They start concocting social issues, such as legalising prostitution or daylight saving at state level, and the republic or gay marriage at the federal level.

And so it was for Keating.

Those of us at NFF Executive level would meet with the relevant minister, usually the minister for agriculture. John Kerin was the standout federal Labor minister, as mentioned earlier regarding rural research, Landcare and his handling of the wool crises. Simon Crean was akin to Julian Grill – obviously a person of high intellect, but resenting the agriculture portfolio as being beneath his potential. I remember meeting with him on several occasions and, though notified of the topics to be discussed, he appeared poorly briefed and certainly disinterested. Bob Collins, on the other hand, had very little to offer and you have to wonder about Keating's thinking in appointing him to the ministry. While with the NFF, I also had many constructive meetings with the then shadow minister, John Anderson, and came to respect and admire him.

Talking of politics, the subject would be incomplete without mentioning Wilson Tuckey! Not only did I have to interact with him from time to time in my public positions, but was also in his electorate of O'Connor. The first sharp difference of opinion occurred over Mabo, when Wilson was a member of the opposition and opposed to the NFF negotiating with the Keating government over leasehold titles. Then there were opposing points of view regarding the wool industry. Further points of difference arose over salinity issues, as will be covered later. As the years passed, I had further reason to reject his confrontational way of doing business as a politician and believe he was far better suited to running a country pub. I am totally confident that his view of me was no different and he probably didn't even think I was particularly well suited to being a farmer![60]

I always said a three-year term as WAFF president would be my contribution to rural politics, after which I would go back to the farm. I hold the view that we are best served by farm leaders and politicians who have come from the private sector and have a farm or career to go to back to, rather than being held hostage to the demands of an electorate and having to resort to questionable tactics to get elected, then to keep their job. For that reason, I supported either Don Sutherland or Shirley Thorn as a preferred candidate to Kevin McMenemy at the election in 1995, when I stood down. Kevin had been a beekeeper and was now looking for a job to keep bread on the table – in my book, the wrong motivation and prerequisite for seeking office. The majority of members on the day had a different view of the world! One will never know how different it might have been if the result had been otherwise. Don and Shirley went back to their farms, though perhaps before being given the chance of demonstrating their full potential.

19 PARALLEL LINES OF ENDEAVOUR

Men have evolved to be single-minded, in hunting for woolly mammoths or defending the tribe from sabre tooth tigers. Women have evolved to be multitasked, in caring for offspring while gathering seeds and nuts – and being able to talk and gossip at the same time![61]

And so it was for me, the single-minded focus! From 1987, without any planning or forethought, I realised I was operating on two parallel paths – akin to steel train tracks – and able to keep them completely separate.

When at home, our farm and Crystal Brook were the sole focus. I had complete confidence in Tim Ryan, then Wayne Reynolds, as executive directors at WAFF, together with the staff and elected commodity people to ensure all would be well managed in my absence. Equally, when in Perth or Canberra, I was focused on the issues demanding attention and confident all would be well on the farm. Jenn often stayed at home, especially during calving time, backed up by the various neighbours working for us on the day-by-day basis. John Raeside at Crystal Brook was thoroughly reliable.

If I was travelling on my own from the farm to Perth, I always used Skywest; when together, we drove. It got to the point that once at the airport, I had completely changed focus and the one-hour flight was used to plan the days ahead, whether for meetings and other activity in Perth or for jobs at home on the return flight.

The one constant thing that acted as the sleepers supporting the two train lines was the family. When away, Jenn and I regularly telephoned to keep in touch, while time in Perth helped us keep in contact with Anna and Jock at boarding schools and, later, in Anna's case, nursing. On looking back, it's hard to believe that in the 1980s there were no mobile phones, texting or emails! Both of our mothers were widowed in the 1980s so time in Perth was also useful in helping them as they aged. All Jenn's siblings were away from Perth and she played an especially important role in helping her mother.

I thought I was going back to the farm when I retired from the WAFF presidency in 1995, but that wasn't to be. Before getting to my later roles in the wider community, I will recall the highlights of our family's activity to 2007.

Anna finished her time at St Hilda's in 1988 and was intent on a nursing career. She was just short of the marks needed for a university nursing degree so settled for the enrolled nursing course at TAFE. She was then able to use that as a credit for the nursing degree at Edith Cowan, graduating in 1993 – a slower path to the finishing line but a firm goal and perseverance paid off. Once qualified, Anna spent her first year nursing at Norseman. Jenn accompanied her in the little Hyundai car and it was a special few days together that they still talk about.

Jock finished his six years at Christ Church in 1990 and benefited greatly from the guidance he received and the friendships he made. He enjoyed his sport and was able to go windsurfing on the river, but at best was an average scholar. He was intent on a farming career and undertook some TAFE agricultural courses while at school.

I was seeing Rob Chomley at farmer meetings and, with his background at Sturt Meadows, we had a fair bit in common. He was now farming at Kojonup and offered to take Jock on as a jackeroo for a year. I have the utmost admiration for those taking on first-year jackeroos, and Rob and Carol have our everlasting thanks for setting Jock on the right path. Alistair Pennington was a family friend and a few years older than Jock, had gone over east to jackeroo and was now overseer at Uardry, the renowned Merino stud just east of Hay on the Murrumbidgee. He encouraged Jock 'to go over and look around for a few years'. Jock was attracted to the suggestion, jackerooed at Uardry for three years, then moved to Willurah as overseer for Bill Lamb.

We worked out a way of keeping in touch with Jock. I was flying over east a lot and earning frequent flyer points, and at least twice a year we would use them so that Jenn could come with me. In the earlier NFF days a number of wives, including Christina Lee, Ondi Crawford, Gay Blight and Sheila Douglas, would also come to Canberra. The women would attend part of the annual conference, then go off shopping and do the galleries while we men stayed on at our meetings. We would then hire a car and visit Jock in the Riverina, usually dropping it off in Melbourne before flying home. Jenn despaired of Jock's batching habits: a new iron had never been taken from its box; a tin of shoe-cleaning cream lasted

Jock's ute, swag and dog ready for the trip east

forever; and his house was totally disorganised. The overseer's cottage at Willurah had no curtains or blinds and, to say the least, looked bare. There were some dusty heaps of material in a cupboard so Jenn used the sewing kit we had given Jock on leaving home (totally unused for five years) to kangaroo stitch up some curtains. Jenn was relieved to see a glimmer of hope for Jock, when he said later: 'Those curtains made a real difference. I can now sleep in on Sundays and the house really feels a lot cooler.'

We wanted Jock to go to Muresk but when he phoned to say he would like to go to Marcus Oldham, we were so pleased he was self-motivated that we readily agreed. Bill Lamb said to Jock: 'Leave your dogs and swag here – I want to have a word with you when you finish your course.'

Jock gained a distinction in his one-year course and, on his return to Willurah, was offered the manager's position. A very special relationship built up between the two of them, to the point of Bill Lamb saying Jock was like a son to him. Bill made Jock the managing director of the family company, provided him with full access to the station chequebook and we all had hopes of Jock becoming a part owner of Willurah. I enjoyed having a yarn with Bill each time we visited.

He used to put a lot of ram clients up for the night, all of whom would bring a good bottle of whisky, and as he thought it extravagant drinking the good ones on his own, had accumulated a large store of dust-covered bottles at the back of a cupboard. I was a beneficiary, as he was well into his eighties, saying: 'I suddenly realised I couldn't take the good ones with me when I fall off the perch, so am working my way through them while I have a chance.'

In the meantime, Jenn wasn't letting the grass grow under her feet. Her garden was at its best, having reached nearly two acres in size with vistas over the lake to the Porongurup Hills, while using the old stone homestead as a central focus. She was prevailed upon to be part of the Australian Open Garden Scheme and did so in 1996 and 1997. The first year more than 400 visitors attended and over 700 the next, with the garden featured in the *Albany Advertiser*:

> Jenny Campbell's Narrikup farm, Tillgaree, was a big attraction during last weekend's Open Garden Scheme. The rambling garden with its cottage theme and view of the Porongurups attracted hundreds of visitors from all over the Great Southern. It features rose walks, a hawthorn garden, grafted weeping pussy willow, a secret garden with a camellia backdrop and birch groves.[62]

Noted Australian photo-journalist Trisha Dixon visited the garden and used aspects of it in her work. We became good friends, she returned on several occasions and we also visited Trisha at her charming home, Bobundara, near Cooma in NSW.

Jenn also did a word-processing course at TAFE as she realised I required more and more work to be done at home. She practised her new skills doing part-time work in Albany with John Caldwell MLA as a policy officer, at a local physiotherapist and at the Citizens Advice Bureau. Yet it was her emergency word processing at home, often at short notice, that was most appreciated. Jenn had friends through the Great Southern who also had beautiful gardens, including: Trish Witham, Jane Taylor, Helen Walker, Lee Chadwick, Jeannie Reynolds and Katie Sprigg. They all teamed up and stripped their gardens bare as various family weddings started to come on stream and became known as 'The Green Machine'. The plan was for a marquee in the farm garden, local catering and masses of greenery with flowers in all sorts of different themes, depending on the time of year.

Anna and Hugh, leaving St John's church, Albany,
23 January 1999

Our turn came on 23 January 1999 when Anna married Hugh Roberts from Dandaragan. I always remembered walking out of St Margaret's Church arm in arm with Jenn to start a new life. Walking down the aisle of St John's Church in Albany with Anna on my arm, for her to start a new life with Hugh, was extraordinarily moving.

We had a wet summer that year so the kikuyu paddocks were all green. I had mown a large area around the house so that the formal garden merged into the paddocks beyond. The visitors from Dandaragan must have wondered just what farming was all about in the 'deep south' around Albany!

The Roberts are a long-established farming family at Dandaragan. Hugh's father, Bert, had moved from the family farm, Kayanaba, and set up Yandan, a little to the west of town. They specialise in prime lamb production, selling off more than 6,000 a year, including feedlotting the later drafts. Having established a new-land farm ourselves, we fully appreciated the job Bert and Kerrie had done on Yandan and it would have to be one of the best developed, maintained and operated properties in the region. Hugh and Anna are continuing the high standards established by Bert and are now adding their own innovative ideas to the property.

Jenn had other strings to her bow as well as the garden. She was playing pennant tennis for Narrikup right through the year, with the winter months indoors at the Albany Recreation Centre. She also had bridge lessons in Perth with Peter Smith, at about the time Anna Clapin was teaching some of the girls around Cranbrook. A large group resulted, with the 'Green Machine' girls being joined by Lindy and Anna Clapin and Kate Pollard.

If walking down the aisle with Anna was emotional, the arrival of Lachlan on 2 November 2000 was even more so. To hold a little baby in your arms, the son of the little baby you were holding 30 or so years before, is a truly moving experience. Lachie was soon to have a baby brother, with Angus born on 11 October 2002. We couldn't have asked for better, and trips from Albany to Dandaragan were now very much part of our lives, though we often used our duplex in Perth as a halfway meeting place.

Jock married Lou Lugsdin on 3 July 2004 at the All Saints Winery near Rutherglen, with a Scottish piper up in the turret in full kilt regalia to welcome guests to the function. Lou's parents had owned Apsley, northeast of Hay, but were now semi-retired in Melbourne, with Ken being cricket coach and sports administrator at Caulfield Grammar and later Geelong College. Willurah bought a double-sized transportable home for the newlyweds. Jock and Lou were able to set it up as they chose and made a lovely first home for themselves.

Harriet was born on 26 May 2005. By good chance we were in Deniliquin for her birth and there was that same special feeling seeing Jock as a father. We were equally fortunate to be back in Deniliquin on 31 May 2007 for Jack's arrival and then, by arrangement, to be in Albury to help babysit Harriet and Jack when Penny was born on 29 May 2012. Two grandparents couldn't be happier than to have five lovely grandchildren!

Bill Lamb's death in February 2006 (aged 93) marked the passing of an era as he was the last of the old timers in the Riverina. Jock gave a very moving eulogy and Bill was buried in the little cemetery plot on Willurah, with the Hay plains stretching into the distance all around him. Any thought of Jock staying on at

Jock and Lou, 3 July 2004

Willurah was proving difficult because of concern about an outsider becoming a shareholder in the family company, but a 'tap on the shoulder' provided an opportunity for him to move to Pooginook as manager.

Macquarie Bank had just set up Paraway Pastoral as an entity to purchase grazing properties through eastern Australia, and the Pooginook Merino stud was an integral part of the plan. Jock did a great job there but was probably better suited to commercial sheep management, so when Paraway bought Mungadal just out of Hay in 2010, he jumped at the chance of running the bigger property. Even though Mungadal had been one of the earlier Merino sheep studs in the Riverina, it had been deregistered a few years earlier under the ownership of the Twynam Pastoral Company, which also sold off the irrigation water entitlement, so the station was now a sole commercial grazing property. Before long, two-thirds of next-door Pevensey was added to the property, followed by Ulonga northeast of Hay and finally Rosevale, completing the 'hub' under Jock's management. The

Hay amalgamation now totals 117,000 hectares, running 90,000 DSEs[63] in an average year. The broad objective is to maintain a core breeding flock of 30,000 ewes, with a flexible surplus of dry sheep and stock brought in on agistment to allow for rapid adjustment to seasonal conditions. Ground cover monitoring and rotational grazing have transformed pastoral viability – for both Landcare and financial benefit. The Mungadal amalgamation regularly produces over 1,800 bales of wool a year, together with up to 1,600 hectares of irrigated rice, cotton and barley, subject to water availability in the open market.[64]

It's sobering to see how commercial sheep management has progressed. The compulsory subdivision of properties 100 years ago is being overtaken by amalgamation in the free market, often to larger enterprises than the original holdings. Overseers' cottages, jackaroos' quarters, staff kitchens, gardeners' cottages and so forth all lie empty, with Jock employing only four staff on the combined properties. Local contractors based in the regional towns do all the lamb marking, sheep classing, pregnancy scanning, shearing and crutching, firebreaks and any new fencing or other capital works – a tight ship!

The family farms that underpinned Australian agriculture for so many generations, based on lifestyle and 'the ideal environment to raise a family', are being replaced by corporate entities with a strong business focus. While many of these new amalgamations are still family owned, the emphasis from lifestyle to the realities of a large business has seen the demise of many small rural towns. Empty homesteads litter the farming landscape and schools are closing, to the point of some families relocating to regional centres and operating the farms at arm's length. The regional port of Geraldton and its hinterland is one such example in WA.

Meanwhile, Tillgaree was being kept in good shape. A testing event occurred the year after completing my term as WAFF state president, as the neighbouring property was found to have ovine footrot (*Dichelobacter nodosus*) and it wasn't long before we had it. Even though British Breed sheep seldom show symptoms, they can still carry the infection and we couldn't afford the risk of spreading footrot. We took the difficult decision to close the Poll Dorset stud of 25 years' duration. Treatment is very labour intensive and not always successful so we decided to totally destock the farm of sheep for three months as our preferred control measure.

Back on our Borden farm, a few of us used to comment about Mel Bungey going into politics to the detriment of his farm. Now Jenn was reminding me of those early observations:

Remember how you used to criticise Mel Bungey for neglecting his farm? Well, make sure you don't fall into the same trap, now that you are gadding about all over the country.

It was a timely reminder and with Jenn's help, we managed to keep up with maintenance and prevent things becoming untidy or out of hand. David Findlay and Graeme Pederick had left the district and we were now using Dean Higgins and Doug Stan-Bishop to help us out. Stuart Macaulay was the Elders manager at Mount Barker from 1990 to 1995 and was very helpful, often coming to the farm on weekends to fit in with my travel commitments.

On looking back, I am most grateful for Jenn's forbearance over 20 years or so of my comings and goings. While her garden was obviously a great comfort, she must have had many lonely days and nights. I saw a number of farm leaders and politicians playing up when away from home, as did some of the wives when left on their own, to the detriment of their marriages, and I am grateful ours survived the challenge.

As I said at the beginning of this saga, we Campbells have been blessed with the women we married. I am no exception.

Jenn, looking out to her garden

20 THE WAR ON SALINITY

I hadn't been back at the farm very long after the successful 1995 WAFF annual conference before the phone rang. Monty House, the Minister for Agriculture in the Richard Court government, explained there were mixed messages and false expectations in the related Landcare and farm forestry areas. He was proposing two 'short and sharp' reviews in order to establish community attitudes and expectations and invited me to chair them. As usual, Monty came straight to the point:

> These reviews can be seen as a means of a minister dodging any real action. I don't want that outcome, so bring me some realistic and achievable recommendations that I can implement, so the community won't be disappointed. By the way, it also allows a few disgruntled people to vent a bit of steam, but you'll know how to handle them.

The review of Landcare in Western Australia was set up with a committee of three: Rex Edmondson, who was chair of the Soil and Land Conservation Council; Kevin Goss, executive director of sustainable rural development with the Ag Dept; and myself as chair. We publicly advertised for written submissions, had individual meetings with key people and held 16 public meetings covering the whole state. The review was completed on time in December 1995 with 23 recommendations to optimise the second half of the Decade of Landcare and, more importantly, to set Landcare up as a sustainable activity into the future. The government subsequently implemented the recommendations and I believe the ongoing support of Landcare and 'natural resource management' (NRM) bears testament to the success of the review. Of particular importance were the recommendations advocating a stronger role for regional delivery and assessment (which resulted in setting up the six regional catchment groups); increased research effort by the Ag Dept and other agencies; and for local government to be more actively engaged.[65]

The farm forestry review was established in a similar way but with a bigger taskforce, including: relevant development commissions; government agencies; local government; and the Australian Forest Growers. There were four public meetings. The review was also completed on time in December 1995, with 29 recommendations to foster the integration of farm forestry with traditional agriculture.[66] It's a tragedy that tax-driven 'whole of farm' lease or purchase took over, to the detriment of rural communities and wider conservation objectives. The recommendations were never given a chance to prove their worth or otherwise.

John Howard was elected with a landslide majority on 11 March 1996. There was general relief to see the end of the Keating government, which, at best, had only marked time since the reform agenda of the Hawke–Keating era. John Anderson was sworn in as Minister for Primary Industries and there was an air of optimism following the uneventful tenure of his predecessor, Bob Collins. I had been having considerable interaction with John while he was the shadow minister through my NFF portfolio, and was flattered when he approached me to chair the Land and Water Resources R&D Corporation (LWRRDC) in mid-1996. (John Kerin established LWRRDC in 1990 to underpin research for the Decade of Landcare.)

Dr Graeme Robertson was the inaugural chair, with Dr Phil Price as managing director, and they established a well-balanced portfolio of research programs to support Landcare. There were 15 programs covering a wide suite of activities, including: dryland salinity; agroforestry; river health; groundwater; eutrophication; northern Australia; sustainable grazing; social issues; irrigation; wetlands; and climate variability. Supporting Phil Price was Richard Price (not related), program manager for land resources, and Nick Schofield, program manager for water resources, together with 11 other full and part-time staff.[67]

The annual budget was around $11 million of federal funding. LWRRDC didn't conduct any research itself but managed research undertaken by public and private agencies, which matched the core funding with cash and in-kind contributions. The bigger programs had management committees, while the smaller ones reported directly to the board through the program managers. Under the legislation, the chair is appointed by the minister, while directors are selected through an open and competitive process.

The board of directors comprised: Warrick Watkins as deputy chair; Phil Price as executive director; Charles Wilcox as a government representative; Jason Alexandra; Leith Boully; Stuart Bunn; Sheila Donaldson; and Michael (Mike) Logan. They were a talented group, with a good cross-section of skills and experience.[68] In 1996 it was still considered appropriate for directors to chair committees of the board or research program committees. I feel the pendulum has swung too far away from this practice, as directors today are too neutered by conflict of interest and other restrictions to generate the best outcomes. After discussion of the newly appointed board of LWRRDC, I was allocated the chair of two significant research programs: the National Dryland Salinity Program (NDSP) and the Joint Venture Agroforestry Program (JVAP).

The NDSP had completed groundbreaking research, clearly demonstrating the links between land clearing, rising water tables, dryland salinity and river salinity levels. There were some disturbing predictions as to the area of land that might ultimately be affected and the rivers that may not remain potable. The NDSP had Richard Price as its creative and talented manager. JVAP was a joint venture between LWRRDC, the Rural Industries R&D Corporation (RIRDC) and the Forest and Wood Products R&D Corporation. Under the arrangement, RIRDC managed the program and LWRRDC provided the chair of the management committee.

Salinity quickly became the focus, politically, at community level through Landcare and in research activity. The Howard government established the Natural Heritage Trust in 1997 and started to focus on salinity and water quality. The work of the NDSP was used to inform the Prime Minister's Science Engineering and Innovation Council and either Richard Price or I were invited to speak at forums and conferences around Australia, as appropriate to our differing roles.

Phil Price and I would regularly report to John Anderson in his Parliament House office and he showed particular interest in the salinity research. I remember on the first visit being impressed by the rousing Tom Roberts painting *Shearing the Rams* hanging on his office wall in a magnificent frame.[69] It was a great conversation opener to say: 'I've always loved that painting, and my father also had a copy hanging in his office.'

The WA government was also focusing on salinity. There was a rushed process to develop a WA Salinity Action Plan, with cross-agency collaboration: Kevin Goss, Ag Dept; Kieran McNamara, CALM; Tim McAuliffe, Water and Rivers Commission; and Paul Vogel, Department of Environmental Protection.

Premier Richard Court accepted the report in 1996 and the $10 million plan was launched in November under the auspices of a State Salinity Council, which I was subsequently invited to chair. In accepting the position, I stood down from the Farm Forestry Development Group and Waters and Rivers Commission (to which I had recently been appointed by the WA government) as there were risks of conflicts of interest. I remember having a discussion with Monty House regarding membership of the proposed council and he must have had a few bruising encounters with the 'greenies', because he was opposed to having them represented.

> Salinity is basically a farmers' problem. That's where it has to be addressed – fix it on the farms, then the rivers and bush will also be fixed. We don't need a green voice slowing it all down.

To which I responded:

> I have to disagree with you Monty – salinity has become a whole of community issue. Farmers are the first in the firing line, but it's also affecting rural towns, rivers and native bush. It's my experience, by having everybody in the tent, you get better, long-lasting results and less flak in the media.

As I stated earlier, put an alternative view to Monty and he would give it due consideration. We did have 'the greenies' on the council and I found Rachel Siewert in particular (now a WA Greens senator) somebody who would work positively towards an outcome. Sometimes we would bend a bit her way but, equally, she was able to accept the practicalities of the other point of view.

The council had 12 influential members: John Silby (Alcoa of Australia); Ian Purse (Farm Forestry Development Group); Garry English or Kevin McMenemy (WAFF); Barry Court (PGA); Rachel Siewert or Phil Jennings from the Conservation Council of WA; Rex Edmondson (Soil and Land Conservation Council); Ross Donald (Rural Adjustment and Finance Corporation); Ian Burston (Water and Rivers Commission); Bernard Bowen (Environmental Protection Authority); Tom Day (National Parks and Nature Conservation); Leon Watt (Lands and Forest Commission); and Ken Peck (WA Municipal Association). Relevant state agencies were represented at every meeting by their director general to provide advice, but in a non-voting capacity.[70]

The Salinity Cabinet Standing Committee was also established, chaired by Deputy Premier Hendy Cowan and comprising: Minister for Primary Industries Monty House; Minister for the Environment Cheryl Edwardes; and Minister for Water Resources Dr Kim Hames. The committee met monthly and I was invited to sit at the table, while the directors general sat in a row behind their ministers. It was a real challenge and ego trip for me but, in hindsight, not a good idea. The DGs were rightly put out at having a lower status than me, so perhaps I should have been sitting with them and only responding when invited to do so. As chair of the Salinity Council, I was given simple instructions by Hendy:

> You are chairing a high-profile community-based council. Make your decisions without fear or favour, but I ask one thing of you: always give me 24 hours' notice if you are going to make announcements that might be difficult for the government. I won't be trying to change your mind, I just want time to develop a response.

The Salinity Council was established for policy development. It brought the community, state agencies and research organisations together so that government could proceed with confidence, knowing the proposals were technically sound and widely supported. Don Crawford was seconded from the Water and Rivers Commission to provide executive support for the council and we had media support from the Ag Dept.

The initial rushed Salinity Action Plan was found wanting in two key areas: there was no recognition of the role of perennial pastures and no concept of productive use of saline lands. A formal review of the plan was undertaken in 1998, with Rex Edmondson, Kevin Goss and myself as chair, given the task of seeking community input. A process of written submissions and holding regional meetings was put in place. Michael Lloyd from Lake Grace had established a group, the Saltland Pastures Association, and he was a major contributor to the revision. As a result, the updated Salinity Action Plan launched by Premier Richard Court in late 1998 gained wider community support.

The Howard government was stepping up its response to salinity and Landcare, and proposed a thorough audit of the nation's natural resources. (The proposal for an audit was originally supported by John Kerin, but John Anderson was also showing interest prior to the election.) LWRRDC was initially given the overall management responsibility for the National Land and Water Resources

Audit, but quickly realised that such an enormous task would require its own management structure. Dr Roy Green, with a stellar career in research policy and management with CSIRO, reaching the position of CEO before retiring in 1996, was invited to chair the Advisory Council. Colin 'Crash Through' Creighton was appointed executive director and I was assigned to the Advisory Council as a link back to LWRRDC and also designated 'champion' for the salinity theme of the audit.[71]

There were eight themes in all and it took four frenetic years and more than $30 million to complete the task. The National Land and Water Resources Audit of 1997–2001 remains a lasting monument to the Natural Heritage Trust and to John Anderson's leadership, and continues to underpin resource management and planning to this day. Ideally, a similar audit should be undertaken every 20 years or so, but I wonder if any future government will ever allocate the financial resources for such a worthwhile purpose? There were some talented people on the Advisory Council, including: Geoff Gorrie, Bernie Wonder, Kevin Goss, Roger Wickes and the crusty but brilliant John Radcliffe. Colin Creighton was very ably supported by Warwick McDonald as his deputy, together with six other staff.[72]

The Natural Heritage Trust (NHT) of 1997 was being delivered at state level through a formal process. WA was receiving around $30 million a year and the NHT funding was open to an array of 'takers', ranging from small Landcare groups up to state agencies managing catchment-wide activities, such as the Wellington River and Lake Toolibin. The NHT State Assessment Panel met annually with between 15 and 20 members, including from: relevant state and federal agencies; regional catchment groups; farm and conservation organisations; local government; and Aboriginal interests. Projects were reviewed for technical feasibility and the level of matching funds was a strong consideration. I wound up chairing the NHT Assessment Panel and its successor, the Envirofund Assessment Panel, for eight years through to 2005.

I have many fond memories. In the early days, farmers tended to arrive in sports coats and ties, while the 'greenies' wore sandals – definitely no make-up for the women – and all carrying large plastic bottles of 'natural' water! There was a whole new language: for example, farmers were 'landholders'; pastoralists were 'rangeland managers'; and a patch of bush was a 'biodiversity refuge'. Talking of biodiversity, at one early meeting this relatively new term kept being mentioned: the richness of it; the tipping point and threshold of it; the hot spot of it in the southwest of the state; and so on. A fellow in his sports coat, who had said very little all day, rose to his feet and exclaimed: 'I don't know about all this biodiversity stuff, but I've worked out I don't want it in my rainwater tank!'

I was flattered at the conclusion of the first assessment panel when one member came up to me: 'Well done – you've certainly mastered the art of herding cats!'

The 'open to one and all' assessment process was an effective way of getting funds on to the ground where it was needed and benefited a lot of good work around Australia. Yet there was always a concern that state governments were 'cost shifting' and using federal funds to augment their own traditional areas of responsibility. While this undoubtedly occurred in some cases, I still believe it was a golden era in federal–state cooperation in managing the nation's natural resources and environment.[73] The dominant role of the federal government and its agencies tended to upset some at state level, but Hendy Cowan had a favourite expression to quell the unrest: 'Remember the golden rule – those with the gold, rule!'

The Murray–Darling Basin Commission (MDBC) was also heavily engaged in salinity activity and was headed by the highly skilled and energetic CEO Don Blackmore, with Kevin Goss moving from WA as his deputy. Don was an engineer by profession and Kevin skilled in land management so they made a formidable team. The MDBC released the Basin Salinity Audit in 1999, which was misinterpreted to suggest Adelaide wouldn't be able to use River Murray water for 40 per cent of the year by 2050. The MDBC was to later release the very credible Basin Salinity Management Strategy 2001–2015.[74]

The salinity 'cause' was gathering pace and strength as we moved into the late 1990s. As chair of the State Salinity Council, I was asked to arrange and host a field trip for Deputy Premier Hendy Cowan, the WA Governor, Major General Michael Jeffery, and a media contingent. It was a great success. The governor took a very close interest in all we showed him and he made the most of the people he met and asked questions so that he was fully informed by the end of the trip. At the next Salinity Council meeting, I raised the idea of inviting Michael Jeffery to be patron for salinity management in WA. The invitation was readily accepted and it's interesting to note the ongoing support he demonstrated later as governor general, and then in his semi-retirement. (As an aside, we realised we were both born and bred at Wiluna!)

In 1999 there was a round of formal briefings of parliamentarians. Dr Tom Hatton from CSIRO led the science and, as chair of the State Salinity Council,

I represented the farmer-landholder perspective. We were supported by a range of other speakers, dependent on which state we were in, and during the year we presented to the WA, SA and federal parliaments, as well as a Salinity Summit in Dubbo, NSW, with relevant ministers in attendance.

In 2000, the Howard government launched the National Action Plan for Salinity and Water Quality (NAP-SWQ), with a budget of $1.4 billion over seven years. The prime minister used the term 'war on salinity', which, even though it had been mentioned before by other commentators, was from then on widely used by all and sundry.

Before the launch, Minister John Anderson requested a tour and briefing on dryland salinity in WA. At the time he was acting PM, as John Howard was on holiday, so had the full security detail afforded to the higher office. All venues were thoroughly checked before his arrival, which startled the CWA women preparing meals and morning teas, and women waiting for the school bus on lonely roads were equally startled when a Commonwealth police car drew up alongside them, requesting a reason for them being parked by the road. For all that, the tour went really well and John would have to be the most genuine and sincere politician I have ever dealt with. We were running late for our night's stopover and evening function, so a local farmer on the bus said: 'Leave it to me – I know a short cut that'll save us a quarter of an hour or so.'

With that, he directed the driver down a side road between Dumbleyung and Katanning, only for us to come to a sliding halt in the middle of a salt flat covered in samphire. The bus wasn't bogged as such, but spinning its wheels on the damp, slippery surface. The embarrassed farmer climbed on to the roof of the bus in order to get a mobile phone signal and was heard saying to a neighbour: 'I've got a bus full of bigwigs stuck on the flat just east of you – get your bloody tractor and tow rope here pronto or else I'm in deep shit.'

It was all part of the experience and John referred to the two days spent in WA at many of his media conferences over the launch of the NAP-SWQ. John stood down later in the year and was replaced by Warren Truss, who requested a similar field trip in July the same year. Being winter, we were a lot more circumspect as to the roads we used, so no bogged bus! There was another field trip hosted for eastern states visitors: Minister for the Environment Senator Robert Hill, plus entourage, and the commissioners of the Murray–Darling Basin Commission, together with CEO Don Blackmore and support staff.

At the end of my first three-year term as chair of LWRRDC, Phil Price advised the board he was not intending to renew his contract as managing director. One of the most important roles of a board is the appointment of a CEO or MD and it's equally so in a research organisation. Phil was highly respected in the science community and it was unlikely that anybody would adequately fill his shoes in that regard. The board appointed Andrew Campbell (no relation) as his successor, who was very strong in public relations, 'knowledge brokering' (to use the new jargon) and corporate management. After nearly 10 years of often groundbreaking research, it was time to promote and share the outcomes. Yet many of us missed the steady hand of a master in the research trade.

Under Andrew's guidance, the clunky acronym of LWRRDC was changed to Land and Water Australia and there was a bright new approach to the corporate presentation. 'Knowledge brokering' was put in place with a strong communication team and many of the products are still in use, some 10 years after Land and Water Australia's demise.

There were other areas of business practice, or 'corporate governance' (to again use the new jargon), that I came to terms with. I fully supported the benefits of having a five-year plan that you could judge progress by, and started attending courses hosted by the Australian Institute of Company Directors that gave me the confidence of being fully briefed on current legal and business requirements. The one practice I could never accept, however, was the use of 'vision and/or mission statements', 'core values', 'key objectives' and so on. These were often laboured over at 'corporate retreats' with directors and senior management endlessly 'workshopping' the final wording. It always seemed to me that by the time divisive issues were watered down, gender neutrality and balance addressed, cultural inclusivity ensured, 'in' concepts such as sustainability, intergenerational equity, biodiversity and climate change included, you were left with something akin to custard!

I have demonstrated the breadth of salinity engagement at all levels, covering the politics, research, funding and community aspects of the cause at full strength. You might well ask: what was achieved in those hectic first few years?

Without doubt, the number of people involved reached a level never seen before and probably won't be seen again. As well as Landcare, there were: Coastcare groups; river catchment groups; 'friends of' people protecting local parks and areas of bush; environment centres; and schools participating in many ways – with most using salinity as their main focus. There were also a number of industry-based organisations formed that also used salinity as a driving force, and they fell into two groups: plant-based and engineering. At this mid-point of the salinity cause, there was often a bitter and antagonistic divide between these two approaches to salinity management.

The plant-based groups were motivated by a simple proposition: 'we farm in the driest continent on earth, it may well become drier, so utilise every available drop of rainfall to profitable advantage'.

The WA No-Tillage Farmers Association (WANTFA) was formed in 1992 with a rapidly growing membership, reaching 1,600 by 1998. While the number of members has declined, the percentage of growers in the state has risen, being a reflection of continued farm build-up and amalgamation. While their main focus has always been profitable cropping, they nonetheless have contributed greatly to the management of wind erosion and salinity by maximising the use of annual rainfall. WANTFA has been led by a series of innovative and progressive farmers, including: Ray Harrington, Geoffrey Marshall, Neil Young, Tim Braslin, Toll Temby, Ty Kirby, Wes Baker and Clint Della Bosca. Bill Crabtree was the somewhat controversial scientific officer from 1992 to 2005, driven by huge vision and matching ego! David Minkey is the current highly effective executive officer.[75] The concept of no-tillage, sometimes referred to as minimum or conservation tillage, has spread Australia-wide, with 86 per cent of WA, 70 per cent of SA, 60 per cent of Victoria and 35 per cent of NSW now utilising this method of production.[76]

The development of no-tillage is the second time in my farming career that the Ag Dept was perceived as being slow off the mark, the first time being Eric Smart's 'two stage fertility build up', described earlier. Usually they led the way.

The oil mallee story is an interesting one. Many farmers around Australia have vivid memories of this tenacious member of the eucalypt family being so difficult to clear for cultivation and so ready to resprout for years afterwards. The Joint Venture Agroforestry Program had invested many thousands of dollars into research-related activity for the commercial use of mallees, including the placement and spacing of cultivated mallees in the landscape, oil content of different species and harvest frequencies. In the early 1990s, Don Stanley and a group of innovative farmers from Kalannie started working with John Bartle from the Department of Conservation and Land Management towards commercial plantings of mallees. The benefits to agriculture were: diversified income; management of wind erosion; controlling salinity through lowering the water table; and shelter for livestock.

The Oil Mallee Association (OMA) was formed and membership rose to 900 farmers in six regions of the state. Interest quickly spread to the Eyre Peninsula in SA and the Mallee region of northwest Victoria. Other than Don Stanley, his son Ian, Keith Parnell, Chris Croote and Mike Kerkmans have been important contributors to the industry. OMA is currently chaired by Lex Hardie and still retains 400 members. David McFall has filled an important role as field officer for more than 20 years and Simon Dawkins on the management committee has been of great assistance in recent years.[77]

The industry gained enormous momentum with the establishment of the Integrated Wood Processing demonstration facility at Narrogin. Western Power (now Verve Energy) was a major contributor to the plant, supported by federal government and other research funding. The plant proved the potential for: energy (electricity) production from renewable biomass; multi-uses for industrial-grade eucalyptus oil; and activated carbon for industrial and agricultural end

Aerial view of an oil mallee integrated planting (courtesy Simon Dawkins, Oil Mallee Asc.)

use. The pharmaceutical market for eucalyptus oil is relatively small so the focus was on high-volume uses, such as transport fuels and industrial solvents. Dr Don Harrison was the lead scientist from Western Power and deserves much of the credit for the construction of the facility. While the plant demonstrated the potential, there was further research required for it to become commercially viable.[78]

The use of a wide range of saltbush and other salt-tolerant perennials for productive grazing quickly gained widespread support. While pioneering farmers, such as Harry Hodgson and Bevan Parker from Kulin, had been developing grazing systems since the 1950s with the help of Clive Malcolm from the Ag Dept, there was now a whole new body of researchers and farmers engaged. The NDSP had progressed research into: selection within species of saltbushes; establishment techniques; grazing management; and placement within the farming landscape. Ed Barrett-Lennard was a driving force in the research, based at the WA Ag Dept and supported by Justin Hardy. Warren Mason was also doing great work in his Sustainable Grazing on Saline Land program.

Michael Lloyd deserves the credit for establishing the Saltland Pastures Association, supported by Tony York and the Chatfield family from Tammin, John Walsh from Cranbrook and Lex Stone from Corrigin. Michael's Lake Grace farm was used as a research site and for field trips, and clearly demonstrated the potential for productive use of saltland pastures – he certainly 'walked the talk'. Membership of the association peaked at around 400 members, before it was wound up on 31 October 2010. Glenice Bachelor, a tireless worker in Landcare, was the last president of the group.[79]

There was also widespread interest around Australia, with a group of farmers at Keith in South Australia led by James Darling, showing the way. James had a low-lying farm called Duck Island and was a person who could really think outside the square. One of his favourite stories was about addressing a group of farmers, promoting the benefits of salt-tolerant perennials: 'You only have to reduce the water table by a small amount before annual clovers and grasses can be re-established. An extra inch or two makes a big difference.'

To which a female voice at the back of the room exclaimed, 'Tell me about it!'

There was a series of national conferences, held under the banner of Productive Use and Rehabilitation of Saline Land. Regular contributors were: Richard Price from the NDSP; Ed Barrett-Lennard from the WA Ag Dept; James

Darling, Michael Lloyd and myself as farmers; supported by other state, national and overseas speakers.

The final industry body promoting plant-based solutions was the Lucerne Growers Association. Membership in Western Australia never reached that of the eastern states but they were a strong force in utilising the deep-rooted perennial plant in lowering the water table, to help in the management of dryland salinity.

Those supporting engineering solutions were dominated by two groups: one promoting surface water management and the other, deep drainage.

Keyline farming and the use of contour banks had been a widely accepted means of controlling water in the landscape for more than 50 years, initially for water erosion control and later for water table and salinity management. A Brookton farmer, Harry Whittington, took the concept a giant step further. His idea was to excavate deep banks on the level contour into the clay subsoil, with areas of bank containing no clay being lined with clay or plastic sheeting, to ensure no leakage. The plan was to capture and hold rainfall throughout the sloping land, to build up subsoil moisture where it was needed and to control rising saline water tables in the lower parts of the landscape. A group was formed in 1978 to foster the concept – the Whittington Interceptor Sustainable Agriculture Land Treatment Society, with the clever acronym of WISALTS. There were approved surveyors to map out the placement of banks on a farmer's property and they made good use of 'divining rods' to help identify subsoil movement of water.

There were many respected farmers who became strong advocates, including: Gavin Drew, Noel Powell, John Metcalfe, Lloyd Richards, Lex Hardie and Jim and Pam McGregor. In the early stages of the salinity 'cause', membership reached 1,200, then decreased to a core of 60 in 2015, with Jim Sorgiovanni as president and Pam McGregor as secretary. Harry Whittington was awarded an OAM in the Australian Honours and his papers are now stored at Murdoch University, known as the WISALTS Collection.[80]

On the negative side, many farmers objected to the aggressive construction of the WISALTS banks as they were impassable to stock and machinery and an eyesore in the landscape. Some others considered water divining as quackery. Others claimed that any benefits were short-lived and water tables would continue to rise in the longer term. Lex Hardie had a more objective criticism of the original concept: he proved capillary action or soil recharge was not taking place, therefore level water storage banks were not justified and less aggressive banks on a gradient were a better option.[81]

However accurate the detractors might have been, there is an overriding benefit that cannot be questioned. The controversial method of land management caused people to think and become engaged in what was a growing problem around Australia.

A more radical engineering approach was 'deep drains' in the lowest part of the landscape. The drains were 2 metres or more in depth and often traversed many kilometres through boundary fences, under roads and finally to a creek or salt lake discharge point. A group known as the WA Conservation Drainage Management Association was formed in 2000 to further their aims and gain support. An advertisement in *The Countryman* promoted the group's formation:

> so that results be achieved instead of mindless studies and research programs that haven't been achieving results (sic). Members to be contacted for further information – John Hall, Mick Georgeff, Stuart Toll, John McKay, John Dunne and John Daley.[82]

Deep drains became popular with farmers. They were tax deductible in the year of expenditure, saline water could be seen flowing away from their properties and there were examples of barley growing alongside a drain on hitherto bare, salty land. The Scott brothers from Watheroo were early pioneers of deep drainage but had subsoils more suited to a successful outcome than the typical Wheatbelt dense clays. Once again, there were also detractors. The main argument was: 'you are only moving a problem sideways and discharging onto somebody else's land, public stream or salt lake'. Others objected to the physical scar on the landscape and the complete barrier to stock or machinery, while some claimed the high cost would never be recouped through the slim profits of cropping. My main argument was that, if a nearby dam held water like a bottle, why would a deep drain in the same clay magically accumulate water from hundreds of metres away? I was giving this type of reasoning at a large Wheatbelt gathering, when tall, bearded John McKay called out: 'Why don't you shut up and sit down – you are as much use as an ashtray on a motorbike.'

Fortunately, there was some support for me: 'Give the bloke a fair go – there's always two sides to a story.'

John got the message and sat slumped, arms firmly folded over his chest, for the rest of the meeting. Country meetings were always robust! They became more so when two unlikely allies got together - the Liberal member for O'Connor,

Wilson Tuckey, and the former Labor member for Kalgoorlie, Graeme Campbell, though they were similar in personality and political modus operandi. Both sided with the deep drainers and the media loved it, being seen as having a go at John Howard's NHT package and Richard Court's Salinity Strategy.

One of the more audacious drainage proposals was promoted by Peter Coyne. His plan was to use deep drains over an extensive area of farm land, discharging into Lake Dumbleyung, then down through the upper reaches of the Blackwood River, before being diverted via canal to the edge of the Darling Scarp near Collie. There was then to be a hydroelectricity scheme powered by the water descending the scarp, before it was finally piped across the Swan Coastal Plain and out to sea.

John McKay in one of his deep drains (courtesy The West Australian, 28 December 2000)

The Salinity Council received independent engineering advice, had cost-benefit analysis undertaken and noted the numerous concerns raised by Landcare groups and others, before publicly coming out against the proposal. Graeme Campbell was quoted in a half-page article in *The West Australian,* supporting Peter Coyne:

> government agencies have opposed any engineering solution. There has been a mindset against drainage despite the clear evidence that drainage works. This proposal was constantly ridiculed by Mr Cowan's office and, especially by Alex Campbell, Chairman of the State Salinity Council.[83]

Another example of the drainage mindset was 'the Brinkworth drain' in the Upper South East of SA. Tom Brinkworth had excavated a drain in the Coorong wetlands through crumbly limestone country; some of the cuttings were of Suez proportions and high volumes of water were being discharged. There were dozens of Wheatbelt farmers from WA who went to see this for themselves and returned as if pilgrims from the holy land! Even though the drain was in friable limestone-based soils, totally dissimilar to the WA Wheatbelt dense clays, had been built without all the necessary approvals and safely discharged into the Coorong, didn't seem to register. James Darling from Keith was particularly dark about the drain:

> All that God-given water being moved about. Thousands of years of evolution of the Coorong wiped out overnight. If I had my way, he should be made to fill it in – by hand!

Fortunately, there was one steady voice in WA who could clearly explain the benefits and negatives of drainage in the landscape and when it was appropriate or otherwise. Richard George, the WA Ag Dept hydrologist, deserves enormous credit for his good science and research, but especially for his ability to impart knowledge to a diverse range of stakeholders.

There was a bitter divide between the 'drainers and the plants people'. I have some sympathy for the drainers feeling isolated. It was always easier for the NHT Assessment Panel or the Salinity Council to support a combined drainage–planting proposal or a sole plant-based proposal than one with only drainage as a stand-alone option.

At this midpoint in salinity management, there was one positive example of integrated options being used. Ron Watkins was a self-taught surveyor and land manager who developed an innovative system that was used by a growing number of farmers, one being Bronte Rundle from near Katanning, whose property was often used when hosting field trips. The Watkins plan was based on having well-made contour banks on a slight gradient, filling dams, then picking up any overflow and proceeding down the slope. On the lower side of the contour banks, there were two or three rows of shrubs and trees that needed fencing from stock, often utilising electric 'hot wires' for economy of construction. Depending on seasons and individual sites, perennials such as lucerne were grown between the contours. Careful record-keeping clearly demonstrated a lift in production from a combined sheep and cropping mix and the lowering of water tables for salinity management.

Both Bronte and Ron are quiet, unassuming men and they let the property and results speak for themselves; I can't remember any visitor being less than impressed. This system was obviously ideally suited to the medium-rainfall sheep-cropping zone, but couldn't be expected to appeal to the lower rainfall crop-dominant regions. Perhaps the best example of the Watkins system was Mervyn Hardie's Wallinar property at Broomehill. He had 'before and after' aerial photographs and meticulous record-keeping, demonstrating the cost-effectiveness of the work.

At this midpoint in the salinity story, there were some early signs of disquiet 'that the impact and extent of salinity was being overcooked'. For example, I will quote directly from information provided by Kevin Goss:

> The National Land and Water Resources Audit published the 'Australian Dryland Salinity Assessment 2000' with the headline conclusion that 5.7 million hectares of predominantly farm land had high potential for developing dry land salinity from shallow water tables and, without further intervention, this could increase to 17m hectares in 50 years. It should be noted that this was not an estimate of salt-affected land per se, but of an area in which salinity could potentially occur. Despite this highly qualified statement of salinity hazard, it was immediately interpreted in popular and scientific press as 5.7m hectares of dry land salinity today and 17m hectares into the future.

It suited everybody to use these misinterpreted figures: politicians to be seen as responding to a crisis; research agencies (CSIRO, universities, government agencies) so they could attract extra funding; and community groups, such as Landcare, to attract further members and funding. To demonstrate the point, just after the release of the Audit Salinity Theme in 2000, I was driving with Monty House (WA Minister for Agriculture) and Graeme Robertson (Director General of the Ag Dept) somewhere in the Wheatbelt, when Monty said: 'Don't you think the salinity predictions are being exaggerated? Can you really believe that one-third of all this cropping land will be salt affected?'

There was general agreement between the three of us, that the predictions were being misinterpreted and therefore exaggerated. We also came to a further understanding: the present community interest would turn to other things before too long, so our job was to use the present funding and support to best advantage, while it lasted.

And so it was, that at the beginning of a new century, we all got on with the job of managing dryland salinity and what was now being termed 'NRM'. I was always a vocal critic of the clunky 'natural resource management' replacing the widely accepted 'Landcare' to describe all the good work being undertaken by so many dedicated volunteers. Only Canberra-based bureaucrats and professional green activists could dream up such an uninspiring jumble of words, totally lacking in soul and endeavour! As many people of the day lamented: 'Canberra is nothing but a few square kilometres of political correctness, surrounded by a continent grappling with reality!'

While membership of Landcare and industry groups had peaked, there were still a lot of unanswered questions requiring attention. In April 2000, an updated Salinity Strategy was launched by Premier Richard Court, with the membership of the Salinity Council expanded to now include: the chairs of regional catchment groups, irrigation interests, farm production groups and Greening Australia. The director generals of the relevant state agencies continued as non-voting advisory members. The original 12 members had now increased to 26, which ensured stronger community support and engagement, even if testing my 'herding of cats' chairing skills.

In launching the revised strategy, the premier rejected the concept of a salinity levy to fund activity but pledged extra funding of $3.6 million per year above the budgeted $40 million. The new strategy, enlarged council and modest extra funding were well received by all and sundry. It was also announced the government would establish a 'one-stop shop' for drainage approvals, which would reduce the time and red tape frustrating that sector.[84]

It was early in 2000 that I received a phone call. The voice was quiet, almost hesitant and apologetic, yet with a calm self-assurance:

> Hello, it's Phil Cocks speaking.[85] You mightn't know me but a small group of us have been getting together at the university to look into the possibility of setting up a salinity CRC. We would like you to come along to our next meeting.

I attended the meeting and was impressed by the people involved and the research ideas they tossed about for plant-based management of dryland salinity. I had been attending meetings of the Oil Mallee Association, Saltland Pastures Association, No-Tillage Farmers and the regional catchment groups, so was well aware of the unanswered questions with which they were grappling. I was also well aware of the financial constraints faced by the National Dryland Salinity Program as being only one of 12 or so programs of Land and Water Australia, so the need for an expanded research effort was obvious. Phil then went on to say:

> We have the research area covered but to get a CRC up, we need strong industry support. You are well known among the RDCs and the NFF, so do you think you can help get them on board?

Phil was very generous in his confidence of me 'getting everyone on board' but, with dryland salinity having such a high profile, it would be difficult not to have been engaged. Perhaps I was able to influence the level of financial support? I would personally contact the chair of the relevant group and seek their support of Phil and me meeting with their managing director to flesh out a proposal. This involved several trips around Australia and with good results.

To progress the bid for a cooperative research centre, we established an interim board and arranged mock interviews to prepare us for the formal assessment process. Phil appointed Professor Mike Ewing as his deputy and they both deserve the credit for leaving no research stone unturned, while I helped identify different issues for the interim board to hone up on, to have all the interview possibilities covered. We were successful in our efforts and in late 2001 had the CRC for Plant-based Management of Dryland Salinity up and running, with a budget of around $180 million cash and in-kind contributions for a seven-year life – the highest funded CRC at the time.

We quickly became known as CRC–Salinity, based at the University of Western Australia in Perth, with contact offices around Australia. It was an unincorporated joint venture, a structure that has been steadily losing favour over the years. The benefit of such an arrangement was the high level of engagement by the partners, as they were all represented on the board, but the downside was the overhead costs and the risk of an unbalanced skills base. Furthermore, a large board can be difficult to manage in getting incisive outcomes so once again my experience in 'herding cats' was put to the test!

The core and supporting partners represented a diverse group of interests. Core partners were: UWA; Charles Sturt University; University of Adelaide; CSIRO Land and Water; Department of Agriculture, WA; Department of Conservation and Land Management, WA; Department of Primary Industries and Resources, SA; Department of Primary Industries, Victoria; Department of Sustainability and Environment, Victoria; Department of Water, Land and Biodiversity, SA; and Department of Primary Industries, NSW. Supporting partners were: Australian Wool Innovation; Grains Research and Development Corporation; Land and Water Australia; Wesfarmers Landmark (later AWB Landmark); Meat and Livestock Australia; Murray–Darling Basin Commission; Office of Science and Innovation, WA; the Australian Conservation Foundation; and the National Farmers Federation.[86]

As well as these parties, there was the position of visitor. The visitor's role, as outlined under the legislation, was both to report back to government and offer advice if they saw fit. Many CRCs filled the role in a token way but we decided to really make it work for us. Dr John Radcliffe, former chief of CSIRO Land and Water and later deputy CEO of CSIRO, accepted the position and anybody knowing John would realise 'a token role' was just not in his vocabulary at all. I had been on the Land and Water Resources Audit with John and formed the highest regard for his insightful skills. He was tall, with the presence of Whitlam or Fraser, but in my book a less controversial and more beneficial contributor to the nation's wellbeing. As crusty and daunting as he might have been to some, in his mellow retirement he is a member of the SA Tram Preservation Society and, on occasion, drives the vintage tram between Adelaide City and Glenelg.

The CRC was structured into seven programs with 13 subprograms, covering 46 projects. The main focus was three programs: new and improved plant species, headed by Professor Mike Ewing; new farming systems, by Dr Anna Ridley; and grazing systems, by Dr David Masters. Supporting programs were: education and extension, headed by Dr Ian Nuberg; functions of natural ecosystems, by Associate Professor David Chittleborough; people, land and water, by Prof. David Pannell; and biodiversity, by Dr Vivienne Turner.[87]

I remember on one early field trip, with a large attendance of stakeholders and researchers, I used the expression 'it doesn't pass the laugh test' in regard to a research proposal. Phil Cocks was sitting next to me and visibly paled at my forthright approach so I wasn't surprised when he came up at the morning tea break with Mick Poole: 'You had better tone it down – these research people are a sensitive lot and you have to be careful not to upset them.'

I never used the expression again in public, but behind closed doors I was often asked: '… and does it pass your laugh test?' My so-called laugh test referred to the relevance of any project out in the paddock, either directly or indirectly, in managing salinity. In my view, a number of researchers were trying to hitch a free ride on the salinity bandwagon to fund their pet ideas, even if there was no gain to the overall task. As Kevin Goss would say, 'A nail looking for a hammer!'

The CRC benefited from the careful approach to detail by our business manager, Mark Stickells. He was a bright young man on the cusp of a sound business career and was able to provide accurate reporting, not only to the large group of partners, but also to UWA (the host university), the federal government CRC program and for more general use in regular publications, such as 'Focus on Salt', the bimonthly publication of the CRC.

At the national level, my second term as chair of Land and Water Australia, which involved chairing the National Dryland Salinity Program and the Joint Venture Agroforestry Program, came to an end in mid- 2001. There was much good work achieved over those six years, but as I'm focusing on salinity, I will only outline the outcomes of the NDSP. Without doubt, the program underpinned the activity and direction of the Natural Heritage Trust, the National Action Plan for Salinity and Water Quality, many state-based initiatives and the CRC-–Salinity.

Kevin Goss followed me as chair of the NDSP and the program wound up in 2004. He summed up the 12-year legacy in six key messages: salinity impacts not only farmland but also water resources, vegetation and infrastructure; salinity costs are significant and rising so responses must be strategic; profitable options for management are lacking; integrated catchment management is only part of the answer; vegetation remains the key to managing water resources but requires careful analysis; and lack of capacity (i.e. through Landcare) is important, but a secondary constraint. Kevin concluded: 'These statements may seem less confronting now than they did at the time. However, they were groundbreaking statements then and are no less relevant now.'

Meanwhile, back in WA, the Court government lost the February 2001 election to Labor, with Geoff Gallop becoming premier. The concept of the Salinity Council developing policy and reporting directly to a cabinet standing committee was a step too far for the directors general of the relevant state agencies and they must have lobbied to put an end to it all. The Salinity Cabinet Standing Committee was immediately disbanded by the Gallop government, with the Salinity Council now only reporting to the Minister for the Environment, Judy Edwards. The role was now advisory so the old order of directors general being the main source of policy input to their ministers was now safely back in place. They all retreated into the comfort zone of their departmental silos, to the detriment of formalised cross-agency collaboration, as had been imposed by the Salinity Council model.

I think the Court–Cowan government deserves enormous credit for their brave move towards direct engagement with the community. It worked well but I doubt we will see such courage again from either major party, as the rocking of boats is a hazardous business when midstream in the brutal world of politics.

As my five-year term chairing the Salinity Council was coming to a close, I was pleased that we were able to host the Dealing with Salinity in Wheatbelt Valleys forum at Merredin. Don McFarlane, now with the Water and Rivers Commission, was the convenor of the conference and deserves credit for the successful outcome. Many options for salinity management were canvassed: saltland pastures as the most economic option in the lower rainfall areas, as demonstrated by Michael Lloyd; a combination of saltland pastures and drainage; mallees with contours in the medium-rainfall areas; and trees and shrubs with combined water harvesting from contours in the higher rainfall cropping-grazing zone, as being practised by Ron Watkins. There was one clear message from the forum: no single solution was the magic answer and as each site was different, they had to be managed appropriately for their individual needs.

Peter Trott, a journalist from *The West Australian*, attended the conference and his article occupying one-third of a page had the following subheading: 'To drain or vegetate? Opposing sides on salinity solutions have found middle ground.' The article covered input from several speakers and community groups, concluding with:

> Mr Campbell's optimism followed the historic rapprochement between researchers and farmers who favour engineering solutions and those who see vegetation as the answer. Both approaches were vital and complementary.

We had made good progress from the antagonistic 'silo approach' of only a few years earlier. The Salinity Council was wound up on 30 June 2002 and replaced by an NRM council, as an advisory body to Judy Edwards, chaired by Rex Edmondson. One of the final tasks of the council was to report on its activities for the years 1997–2002. Among the achievements were: the planting of 20,000 hectares of softwoods; 172,000 ha of hardwoods; 50,000 ha of lucerne; 120,000 ha to saltland pastures; 12,000 ha to summer crops; 9,000 ha of mallees; 1,400 kilometres of fencing to protect rivers and riparian zones; and 217,000 ha of privately owned bush protected from grazing. The council hosted numerous field trips, had governors Jeffery and Sanderson as patrons, benefited 37 regional centres through the Rural Towns Program and established six regional catchment groups to coordinate activity.[88]

Many of the achievements were funded through the Natural Heritage Trust of the Howard government and through traditional state agency responsibilities. The role of the council was in policy development, coordination, priority setting and, above all else, bringing the community along towards a common purpose – 'having everyone in the tent'. In this final report, I concluded:

> The State Salinity Council has been an effective force in helping bring about these changes. It has always believed in 'controlled evolution', rather than 'radical change'.[89]

Kim Chance was now the Minister for Agriculture and Food in the Gallop government. While the focus in this chapter has been on salinity, I want to pay tribute to two other important initiatives of Monty House during his term in office. Through his personal drive and persistence, he persuaded Roger Fletcher from Dubbo to establish an abattoir midway between Albany and Mount Barker. Roger agreed to the proposal, on the proviso of dismantling the WA

Lamb Marketing Board. It had been established in 1971 with high hopes and was not living up to expectations, though still required political courage to close it down. More importantly, Monty had to forge a path through all the red tape and environmental concerns to allow for the abattoir's establishment. WA had always suffered from a lack of competition in the meat-processing industry so the new player was of great importance. Monty's other legacy was the development of leadership skills throughout regional WA, with many of the young people who participated in those programs now serving their communities through local government, Landcare and other business activities.

At the national level, the late 1990s and early 2000s proved to be a very stable period in politics. John Howard initially lost some support in the rural community with his gun control laws following the 1996 Port Arthur massacre,[90] but then gained wide respect for his steady leadership and statesman-like qualities. Howard made one great misjudgement in not 'doing a Menzies' and stepping aside while still on top, so no one will ever know how successful or otherwise Peter Costello might have been if given the chance. We were equally fortunate in having Kim Beazley as leader of the opposition, and I share the view of many that 'he was the best prime minister we never had'. I often wonder how much better off Australia would be now if Beazley had been at the helm instead of the dysfunctional Rudd/Gillard/Rudd combination?

A very influential group was formed in November 2002 which helped shape the political and research direction for the coming decade. The Wentworth Group of Concerned Scientists had its first meeting at the Wentworth Hotel in Sydney (hence the name) and initially focused on the over-allocation of water in the Murray–Darling basin. They promoted what was then considered daring and provocative solutions: water property rights; environmental flows (including 'slugs' to mimic flood events); caps on allocation; and buybacks. Much of the data they relied on was closely related to salinity research and the Land and Water Resources Audit in which I had been involved.[91]

Five of the founding members were people I had come to know quite well through my time with Land and Water Australia and the CRC–Salinity: the brilliant Professor Peter Cullen, ecologist, whose life was to end all too soon in 2008; Dr John Williams, hydrologist and ex-CSIRO Land and Water; Dr Denis 'Wheatbelt Birdman' Saunders, ecologist at CSIRO; Peter Cosier, the former policy adviser to Senator Robert Hill when he was Minister for the Environment; and Leith Boully, grazier and former board member of Land and Water Australia.

It was always stimulating to speak with any of these people individually or to read any of their collective papers.

Meanwhile, the CRC–Salinity was bedding down its research programs in a professional and workman-like manner. Phil Cocks and Mike Ewing were very well regarded throughout Australia's research community and the large 19-member board was showing leadership and support to the overall activity. An important early realisation was: 'The large scale of planting required, if vegetation options are to manage salinity. Landcare goodwill and government incentives would never generate the momentum that was needed, so vegetation had to be profitable in its own right if farmers were to use it at a scale to make a meaningful difference.' As a result, the mantra of 'profitable perennials' started to take hold and became a guiding principle in the CRC's work. A secondary realisation was: 'It may never be cost-effective to reverse salinity on low asset value land, so adaptation (or living with salinity) is the practical response.'

For that reason, there was an increased focus on saltland pastures research.

Salt bush trial site, Anameka, Tammin (courtesy Tony York)

We were midway through the six-year term of the CRC when Phil Cocks advised he was intending to stand down, reasoning that at least another six-year 'life' would be required to gain meaningful research outcomes, and he wasn't prepared to see that through. He considered a replacement CEO needed sufficient time to undertake a rebid in their own right so the large board appointed a recruitment committee to undertake the task of finding a replacement. There was considerable interest from all around Australia and, after careful consideration, the committee recommended Kevin Goss to the board as the appropriate choice. Kevin had a very impressive background with the WA Ag Dept, the Murray–Darling Basin Commission and the NDSP. He was competent in research and, being a very capable manager, proved a worthy successor to Phil. There was a moving farewell function for Phil and he could retire to his cottage and garden in Denmark, secure in the knowledge that his legacy would endure through the remainder of CRC–Salinity and beyond. A job well done.

A highlight early in Kevin's term as CEO was a visit by Prince Charles. Before the visit, interested parties were invited to submit proposals that might be included in the Prince's itinerary; land management and salinity were obviously of appeal and were included. I was personally impressed by Charles being so well briefed on salinity issues and the obvious interest he was taking. (His interest may have been heightened in having the vivacious and vibrant Hayley Norman of CSIRO Livestock Industries present on sheep nutrition when grazing saltland pastures!) It was reported in the next day's paper:

> At the university, Charles visited the Co-operative Research Centre for Salinity and talked to Tammin farmer Tony York about the success of his salt bush program for salt affected land. There were even sheep lining up for Royal perusal.[92]

A successful bid or rebid for a CRC takes about two years of planning and preparation so the process commenced in 2005. I made the decision not to be part of the next-generation CRC, believing the present board deserved the single focus of its chair. An interim board for the rebid was formed and Andrew Ingles, a South Australian farmer and previous chair of the Grains Research and Development Corporation, was selected to lead the process. To reflect the 'profitable perennials' mantra, it was decided the successor would be named

Future Farm Industries CRC. The rebid was successful and CRC–Salinity moved on in a seamless transition into the new entity.

Rather than sum up the benefits of the CRC–Salinity, I think it's more appropriate to look at the 13-year life of the two CRCs, as much of the research activity went from one to the other. There was in the order of $300 million cash and in-kind funding for the combined activity, being from the government CRC program and all the supporting partners. ('In kind' is often open to dispute, as organisations use differing 'overhead loadings' to their costings, but nonetheless is a legitimate contribution.) I approached a number of people: 'If a farmer asked you to outline the key findings of 13 years' research, costing millions of dollars, what would you come up with?'

Mick Poole is the only director who served the full 13 years of both CRCs, so his views were important to me:[93]

> The first thing to remember is that a lot of research sits on the shelf until the economic and political settings are right. Take rape (later called canola) and minimum tillage – they both had about 30 years of research before taking off. I put oil mallees in that category. The CRC's research efforts resulted in an efficient harvester that also chipped on the move, so traditional bulk-handling equipment could be used, and the liquid fuel replacement was perfected, with Virgin Airlines proving its product quality. It's now an industry that's ready to go, when political and economic settings change in its favour. The greatest success, however, would be the new pasture plants for the livestock industries.'

I checked with the chair of the Oil Mallee Association, Lex Hardie, who supported Mick's assessment about mallees and added there was ongoing research at Curtin University with Professor Chun-Zhu Li in perfecting a cool process to transform biomass into bio-energy. It would be far more efficient and cost-effective than the current heat-reliant method.[94]

I also talked to Kevin Goss, CEO of both CRCs from 2004 to 2011. He supported Mick in identifying new grazing plants as the greatest achievement. Two in particular, out of a wide selection, have a very large potential footprint and each one of them alone could well justify the research effort of the CRCs. To pick up on Mick's earlier point, the economic settings of wool, beef and sheep meat are currently very favourable to grazing endeavours. Politically, the federal government has completed free trade agreements with Japan, South Korea and China which provide improved long-term access for meat into those markets, and is well advanced in its negotiations with India and Indonesia.[95]

They both mentioned two new grazing plants that have great potential. Messina (*Melilotus siculus*) is a salt and water tolerant annual and would also be very useful in saltland pasture systems once the saltbushes had lowered the water table. Tedera (*Bituminaria bituminosa*) is a drought-tolerant perennial legume; its potential footprint is greater than for messina and holds promise of being very widely used in the future.[96]

Both Kevin and Mick mentioned the saltland pastures work, so I contacted Tony York from Tammin, whose farm was used as a research site. Tony was impressed by the range of new options in the pipeline, but was particularly excited about a new selection of old man saltbush to be known as Anameka – the name of his farm. The selection process was managed by Haley Norman of the CSIRO, which involved 100 sites and 1,000 plants tested for palatability and nutritional value. Anameka was found on some lonely sites within a national park that had never been grazed by livestock and, as Tony said: 'The most palatable strains of native plants would have been eaten out by sheep, cattle and rabbits, so it was fortunate there were refuge sites still available.'[97]

The Evergraze program of the CRC was pivotal in optimising the grazing potential and profitability of existing pasture species as well as supporting the newer entrants about to be introduced. Meat and Livestock Australia (MLA) holds the legacy of this work and, through them, it will be of ongoing benefit to the grazing industry. As with all research, whether it be the many graziers already benefiting from the Evergraze outputs; more profitable cropping through utilising rainfall to optimal advantage; or hitherto 'worthless' salinised land being brought back into profitable saltland pastures production, most farmers are unaware of the origins of the information they are benefiting from.

Regional farm production groups play an important role in retailing, refining and even participating in research, are very often the first port of call for farmers seeking new ideas and will provide an ongoing service in disseminating not only the work of both CRCs, but also all other rural-related activity. There are many of them spread around the nation, including: the Mingenew Irwin Group with their dynamic CEO, Sheila Charlesworth; the Liebe Group (named in memory of pioneer Wubin farmer Wilhelm 'Gus' Liebe); and the South East

Premium Wheat Growers Association based in Esperance, leading the way in WA. The Birchip Group in northwest Victoria, FarmLink Research Ltd in NSW and Mallee Sustainable Farming in the Eyre Peninsular of SA are further examples of the more progressive groups. Farmers still rely on the physical evidence provided by regionally based field days and advice from local people they respect, so it will become ever more important that these groups continue to prosper in order to replace the nationwide decline in Ag Dept extension services.[98]

For all the success of the CRCs, we shouldn't forget three further important outcomes of salinity-related activity that are particularly pertinent when considering today's climate change 'cause': the overcooking of the salinity threat, being the misinterpretation and exaggeration of data to suit political, science and community ends; the early realisation in the CRC–Salinity of profitable perennials if plantings were to occur at a meaningful scale; and adaptation, or living with salinity, as being the most realistic option for much of the salinised landscape.

Bearing these three points in mind, I question today's management of climate change. Is overmodelling occurring at the expense of research for addressing the issue? Are the models being misinterpreted and exaggerated for political, community engagement and science funding convenience? Shouldn't alternative energy sources be competitive in their own right if they are to be implemented at a global scale to make a meaningful difference? Why should Australia suffer some of the highest electricity costs in the world, while enjoying abundant supplies of black coal and natural gas? If low emission targets are *truly* important, why doesn't Australia embrace nuclear technology, with our generous uranium deposits and geologically stable environs for waste disposal? Shouldn't there be more emphasis towards adaptation or learning to live with the outcomes of any climate change? Hasn't the science community prostituted itself to the climate bandwagon with undue haste?

I still marvel at how quickly worthy institutions, such as the CSIRO and 'sandstone universities', were able to change their focus when the Rudd government was elected in 2007 with the catchcry of 'global warming being the greatest moral, economic and environmental challenge of our generation'. The very same scientists who were the public face of the salinity challenge one day were extolling the global warming threat the next.

Also, note the clever change of terminology from 'global warming' in Rudd's time to 'climate change' in today's parlance. The former was too easily open to question – the latter is an absolute certainty of fulfilment for its disciples, as every hot or cold record, flood or drought, bush fire, cyclone or typhoon can now be heralded as proof positive of change. Just as cricket records continue to tumble at every test match, why should it be any different for climate? Keep records and they will be broken. Perhaps it's a comment on the shortcoming of today's politicised funding of science in Australia and globally that scientists have responded as they have. In voicing the above observations, I have been accused of being a climate sceptic, to which I respond:

> To believe humans can release carbon to the atmosphere in 100 years, which took millions to accumulate, without any repercussion is unrealistic. On the other hand, I shouldn't be criticised for claiming data has been exaggerated or manipulated and climate will continue to change, irrespective of political and economic measures. For that reason, greater emphasis should be put towards solutions for living with those changes.

I was heartened by CEO of CSIRO Larry Marshall's decision, in 2016, to move climate investment more towards mitigation and adaptation, rather than measuring and modelling. As you would expect, he is receiving noisy criticism for 'axing the careers of 350 climate scientists' and not enough support for seeking a practical response to climate change.

I wonder which will be the first sandstone university to have the courage to challenge the politicised funding model and accept Bjorn Lomborg's[99] economic perspective of allocating scarce resources towards a more realistic climate outcome? Surely it makes good economic and social sense to ascertain the most beneficial use of finite funding and limited human capital.

With the pendulum swing from salinity to climate change, some observers claim the current drying trend in rainfall has overcome the problem of rising water tables. I don't support that line of argument. Australia has had many dry periods and, while this spell may have been exacerbated by anthropogenic activity, it is nonetheless part of natural variability. Salinity will remain an ongoing challenge in the management of the nation's natural resources and deserves continued political and scientific attention.

The present climate threat will be no different to many other challenges that have beset Australian agriculture over the past 200 years. The hardworking Australian farmer, supported by innovative rural research, will respond and survive.

21 PUT OUT TO PASTURE

Lifetime experiences are often compared to chapters in a book. As one series of endeavours comes to an end, other opportunities come forward to reinvigorate and challenge. And so it was in 2007: the CRC–Salinity had moved on to become the Future Farm Industries CRC, Kevin Rudd had 'waved the white flag' for salinity-related activity and it seemed my role in public life would come to an end.

We were just getting used to the quieter life back on the farm when the Porongurup National Park caught fire in February 2007. Most of the 2,500-hectare park had been unburnt for 25 years or more and there was a huge build-up of fuel. We had friends on the south side of the hills so I set off with the tractor and fire trailer, while Jenn cut sandwiches and followed in the ute. We were stopped at a FESA roadblock, comprising several four-wheel drive vehicles bristling with radios, manned by people in fluoro clothing. My firefighting turnout was not FESA approved and Jenn's sandwiches weren't prepared in a commercial kitchen, so we were advised to go home. Out of control bureaucracy! We eventually talked our way through by promising to remain at Wal and Marlene Anderson's home to help them with their 'stay and defend' decision.[100]

Karri trees (*Eucalyptus diversicolor*) that had survived countless fires over the previous few hundred years had the bark cooked away, leaving a forest of skeletons to remind all and sundry the folly of insufficient protective burning. The local volunteer fire brigades were scathing of FESA's mismanagement, being fed on cold KFC food brought out from Albany (but cooked in a commercial kitchen) and working strict shift rotations, even if at the expense of fire units being withdrawn from service.

'If those bloody greenies really believed in global warming, wouldn't they advocate more protective burns, rather than less? And then to put those textbook boffins in charge of the fire! No wonder the whole park went up in one hit, with no chance of refuge for any of the wildlife.'

It was a sober realisation that the self-reliant community response to fire management no longer prevailed and gave us further reason to reflect on our farming future. Anna and Jock had established themselves elsewhere and had no call on the farm so we started to plan for ways of selling to best advantage. We had four titles totalling 400 hectares and decided to redesign the boundaries to optimise the potential sales.

Jenn and Alex, 2006

It was only 10 years earlier that we had gone through the same process at Crystal Brook. We designed the four lots to take advantage of views of the Porongurup Hills and the central lake, while having frontage to the main bitumen road. Once again, we engaged John Kinnear to survey the titles and went through the red tape of shire and state agency approvals. The design necessitated a considerable amount of re-fencing and, with more time on my hands, I went back to one of the farm jobs that I always enjoyed. We used treated pine posts and made neat and sturdy entrances to the four lots to optimise the presentation for sale. There was the same sense of satisfaction in seeing a good straight fence line as I had when developing the mallee block at Borden all those years before.

A highlight of the year was being awarded life membership of the WA Farmers Federation. Trevor De Landgraffe was state president and said some complimentary things about my contribution in earlier years, but the greatest pleasure was catching up with many old faces that I hadn't seen for a long time. One fellow came up to say hello:

> Do you remember me? I'm Joe Candeloro and we drove over the top of the fertiliser gates to break the strike! Those were the days when you could do things like that, weren't they?

Off-farm activity was now more centred in the local region. UWA established an Albany campus in 1999 and refurbished the historic old post office building as its headquarters. Enrolments were steadily increasing to the point of further accommodation being built on the vacant site next door and the rental of other nearby properties. From the outset, UWA set up a local foundation as a community support group, on which I had been a member for some time and now became its chair.

I was also a member of South Coast NRM and was elected chair in 2008. I still found 'natural resource management' lacked community acceptance so always used to say 'South Coast NRM, the regional Landcare group' in any public forum. (It wasn't until 2016 that Canberra-based politicians and bureaucrats started to reinstate Landcare to its rightful usage.) Rob Edkins was the innovative CEO and we moved to a formal board structure in order to be well placed for the post Natural Heritage Trust world of the Rudd era. Justin Bellanger was the talented operations manager and went on to become CEO in 2016.

There were five other regional NRM groups in WA, which met together every three months or so in Perth, and there was an annual meeting of the 52 regions spread across Australia. Most of the chairs were contributing on a voluntary basis, with only out-of-pocket travel costs being funded by their organisations. I particularly respected the contribution being made by Bill Mitchell from the Rangelands, David Chadwick from the Blackwood–South West, also Barbara

Morrell and Glenys Bachelor from the Avon–Wheatbelt region. There were many others, but all were motivated by their Landcare ethos.

Now that I was not so busy, Tim and I decided it was timely to make a nostalgic trip back to Lake Violet. Chris and Caroline Ward were very good to us and gave open access to all the old records and to the wider station, and we felt it a privilege being able to wander about and piece all our old memories together. On leaving Lake Violet and the Eastern Goldfields, Tim and I were surprised at how deeply moved we were in visiting the home and country of our childhood. The red soil, the blue-green of the mulga and the vast blue skies created an invisible bond that had to be experienced in order to fully comprehend its power and influence. It caused us to reflect on those feelings:

> Are the ties to your birthplace and country directly in proportion to the remoteness of its location? Can urban people ever experience that same sense of connectiveness as those born on isolated farms and stations? And isn't it a human condition that holds true for everyone, whether blackfella or whitefella?

There was a longstanding plan for an international salinity forum, to be held in Adelaide in April 2008. I had been part of the organising committee for the forum and presented one of my last salinity papers: 'From a Farmer's Perspective'. A couple of people approached me while at the evening drinks session:

> You have some spare time now and know your way around the RDCs. RIRDC are having a few problems and could do with you on the board, so why don't you give it a go?

As mentioned earlier, the chair of a Rural RDC is appointed by the minister, while the board directors are selected through an open competitive process. I had been on the Joint Venture Agroforestry Program committee managed by the Rural Industries R&D Corporation (RIRDC) for many years so had an insight into the organisation. There were advertisements in national newspapers seeking interested people to apply for a directorship, being an initial desktop selection and then face-to-face interviews with a final shortlist. In making an application, I suddenly realised I didn't have a formal CV! All the other positions I had held were as a result of an election, such as the WA Farmers

Federation, or more often by invitation. Jenn came to the rescue and typed up a very presentable CV for me.

I subsequently became a director in 2008 and, for the first time in my agri-political career, experienced the dysfunctional downside of a chair and managing director not operating effectively together. As a result, focus was diverted from the main function of the corporation and overheads of program management were escalating, resulting in lesser funds being available for research.

A number of like-minded directors were on the newly appointed board and I am happy to say that, after a few years, there was a completely changed organisation. Professor Daniela Stehlik was now the chair, Craig Burns had taken over the managing director role and together they provided the leadership required. The number of programs and projects were reduced and many of the top-heavy management committees were abandoned, which resulted in a much improved ratio of research versus overheads. I was to remain a director through to 2014, and I pay tribute to Craig Burns' steady hand and good judgement in helping reshape the corporation.

Farm life revolved around preparation for selling off the separate titles of land. Other than re-fencing, there were numerous little tidy-up jobs, such as burning off some of the trees that had blown over and maintenance to buildings. The rented cottage was on a separate title so required alteration to water and power supplies.

In 2009 there was a completely unexpected surprise. UWA awarded me an Honorary Doctorate of Science in Agriculture, being only the second farmer in 100 years to gain the honour. (The other was Terry Enright from Mount Barker who, by coincidence, had a similar background to me, holding senior positions with the WA Farmers Federation and chairing the Grains Research and Development Corporation.)

In receiving the award, I was invited to deliver the occasional address to graduates and their families in a packed Winthrop Hall. It caused me to reflect on my life in agriculture and I highlighted the most significant events that might be of benefit to the graduates. I realised that developing a new-land virgin mallee block into a viable farm was by far the most rewarding achievement of my life. This became the starting point of my address, then I went on to cover the well-balanced approach of the Brand and Charles Court governments in not only opening up one million acres of land a year for farming, but also providing a well-resourced Ag Dept:

The department had a very strong science-based research capability, backed up with an extension service that was the envy of other states. Most of those dedicated people graduated here at UWA. Furthermore, the state government supported Chamberlain Industries that manufactured robust tractors and tillage machinery, suited to the rigours of new-land development.

After telling the story of my farming career, I mentioned some of the research-related activity in which I had been involved – Land and Water Australia, the National Dryland Salinity Program, the CRC–Salinity – then concluded with:

> To put it bluntly, nobody has a mortgage on good ideas. Just as farmers need the benefits of well-managed science-based research, researchers also need the insights and practical realities of those at the coalface of running a complex, modern farm business. Graduation is not an end in itself but the beginning of a rewarding journey of discovery.[101]

There was one benefit of all the off-farm activity in which I had been involved as we were able to pay off the duplex half in Dalkeith with the funds I received for the work. There was a further act of good fortune when the Nedlands Council rezoned our street so that we had a green title to our 500 square-metre block, rather than being tied to the 'non-conforming use' of a 1,000 sqm block shared with the duplex neighbour.

We were now able to demolish our half, so long as we made good the neighbour, then build a stand-alone retirement house. I had learnt enough about building 'to be dangerous' so we decided to design our own house, get quotes from a few builders to properly draw up the plan for council approval and then undertake the building. We selected Buildwise (now trading as Georgio Homes) and needed to work closely with them as the job proceeded as there was no architect or other third party to ensure a proper outcome.

Jenn's mother was nearing the end of her life so we needed to be in Perth a lot, which helped in checking the building activities. It was a shame, on the other hand, because Jenn couldn't properly focus on the house and the many choices of fittings, colours and so on as she would have wished. At the end of it all, we were very pleased we had built on our own, though we also decided 'one house is enough'! Jenn then designed the garden, a far cry from the 2-acre farm garden, but to equally good effect.

The first two of the farm lots sold quickly but the two with cottage and house were proving more difficult. The lot sizes were far too small for a viable farm but seemed too large for the typical hobby farmer. We were therefore still farming but with the completed house in Perth being used as a weekender.

Another surprise from the blue came about in 2011. I was awarded a Member of the General Division of Australian Honours, an AM, 'for services to conservation and the environment and through executive roles in agriculture'.

This, on top of the honorary doctorate, posed the question: 'why me?' Thousands had turned virgin bush into viable farms and many had given back to agriculture by serving on boards and committees. It made me think of the soldiers at Gallipoli and the Western Front, being ordered 'over the top' into the teeth of merciless machine-gun fire, then of Uncle Pat enduring the deprivations of the Burma Railway under the Japanese. Weren't they all as deserving of similar recognition?

At the end of the day, it boils down to somebody taking the effort to nominate and support your case in order to gain such an outcome. I still don't know those behind the honorary doctorate but, by chance, discovered it was Russell Harrison and Chris Gilmour who had gone to considerable effort regarding the AM. It made the award more meaningful as both men were a few years younger than me and very successful people in their own right – Russell as head of a respected accounting practice in Albany (we always used my brother Tim as our accountant, so no business connection) and Chris an innovative mixed sheep and cropping farmer from Wellstead, to the east of Albany.

These awards are presented at Government House and Malcolm McCusker QC had just started his term as Governor. As there were no ACs or AOs to award on that occasion, I happened to be first in line to be presented and as he leant forward to pin the medal in place, he said in a low voice: 'You will have to excuse me if I fumble while doing this – you are the first person I've had to practise on.'

To which I replied: 'Well this is certainly the first time I've had such an award – so it's a first for both of us!'

Everything seemed to be falling into place. The final two lots of the farm were under offer from the Ravenhill family, subject to selling their large dairy to Chinese interests. Our settlement date was listed for a month after the

Ravenhill sale, to allow time for a clearing sale, so we proceeded with the usual advertising and had everything lined up in rows for the big day. The Chinese delayed settlement due to a 'technical detail' and then again 'for want of an appropriate signature', but we were assured all would be well so continued with the clearing sale.

There were more than 700 people in attendance and I am guessing many wanted a final look (or first look) at Jenn's garden. We sold all our plant and machinery and other bits and pieces to good effect. It's very sobering seeing people crawling all over your valued possessions, only looking for a bargain and not recognising them as the valued items they had been to us. Most sold above our valuation at auction, but the blue Leyland tractor only realised $3,000 instead of my hoped for $5,000 and I felt very upset seeing it loaded onto a truck, having served me faithfully for 35 years. In 47 years of farming, I had bought only two new tractors, so well and truly held true to the Hodgson adage, 'Buy the best plant for the job, look after it well, and it will reward you by good service.'

The sale of Ravenhill Dairy eventually fell through and we were left with two farm lots to sell and no plant or stock – not even a lawnmower or chainsaw! Once again, fortune changed for the better as there was a phone call within days:

> I hear you are in a spot of bother. We have been leasing a farm, which is about to terminate and would like to take yours on while trying to find another long-term place. We could take yours on a rolling three-month basis. If you find a buyer, we need three months' notice to leave, but if we find a long-term lease, we will guarantee you three months' payment.

And so it was that the Lyons family came to the rescue. John Blythe lent us a ride-on lawnmower and we bought a smaller size Stihl chainsaw so we were back in business as caretaker farmers while waiting for a sale. We were becoming sceptical of real estate agents as we were paying for all the advertising and doing all the tidying up before an inspection, so we thought: 'why not try and do it ourselves?' We told Anna of our plans and she said: 'Good idea. You're not selling a farm, but rather a lovely home and garden. Why don't you put an advertisement in the *Australian Country Style*?'

We did just that, as well as local advertising, all in a more personal way than formal real estate jargon. Whether it was beginner's luck or not, we were

Front view of the homestead and front garden, 2006

Jenn's garden, 2006

successful. The cottage block went to a local young married couple and the day *Australian Country Style* was posted to subscribers, we had a phone call at 10.00 pm: 'My wife is lying in bed reading her magazine. She likes the way your ad reads, but I want you to assure me it has good water before she comes for a look.'

The next day Cheryl McCorry arrived for a look and liked what she saw. She was a colourful Kimberley identity and had written three books on her eventful life. The next, more formal inspection was with her partner, Michael Dunnit, who was in the process of semi-retiring from a large farm and feedlot west of Kojonup, and they both decided it was what they were looking for. It was December 2012 and we had three months to give notice on the lease, pack our bags and bid farewell to our farming career. Anna and Jock, with their families, came to say goodbye to their childhood home and various farewell functions were held for us.

It's a tough thing driving out the familiar driveway for the last time as a farm is your home and business all rolled into one. We were in separate vehicles heading for Perth and we stopped at the front gate for the last time to say goodbye to the farm. We hugged each other, there were a few tears, but there were no words to adequately express our emotions. It's a strange feeling, knowing you are now being 'put out to pasture',[102] realising you are no longer an active farmer, and unsure of the future in those promised green paddocks of retirement.

There was now the opportunity for a well-deserved holiday. We had become good friends of Patti and Peter Locke, when they retired to Albany after a successful farming career at Bruce Rock, and started to make some plans with them. They used to host many overseas students for farm work experience and their daughter, Kate, wound up marrying Kristoffer (Kris) Seidenfaden from a lovely farm called Dorthealyst, near Knabstrop, not far from Copenhagen. We joined them for part of a European trip in 2013 that included a week in Denmark, which provided an opportunity to reflect on my Danish forebears. It was rather pleasing to experience a touch of Viking culture, rather than whisky, bagpipes and haggis!

Returning to the starting proposition, 'it's 20 per cent breeding and 80 per cent feeding', causes me to reflect on a lifetime of farming. I was part of the last generation to reap the rewards of clearing virgin bush for farming but, on the other hand, part of the first generation to embrace the Landcare ethos – no better demonstrated than by all of us logging vast areas of Mallee, now to see them being used for environmental and commercial benefit. As with saltland pasture systems, we are now working with our native flora rather than overlooking their natural potential.

At a personal level, I was fortunate in having a 'good paddock' in which to start my life. The five years spent with the Hodgson family provided strong ideals to live up to – 'making the most of available feed' The 47 years of farming in my own right were deeply rewarding and, given the chance, I would do it all again. I guess those years can be summed up literally and metaphorically as: 'some difficult seasons with periods of drought, needing supplementary feeding at times, but responsive to hard work and persistence'.

It's Jenn's and my hope, that Anna and Jock will be able to look back when they are put out to pasture, and also believe they were given a good paddock from which to start their lives.

View of bulls, lake and hills, taken from the garden

APPENDIX I: PROPERTY DETAILS

A number of properties mentioned in the text were either owned or managed by various family members and they continue on as farms and stations to this day. Only some have remained in the family but all were nurtured and built, reflecting the timeless ethic: 'live as though you'll die tomorrow, but farm as though you'll live forever'.[1]

GOIMBLA

There is further information regarding the siege by bushrangers on 19 November 1863. At the time of the 100th anniversary of the event, historian Barry Ledger wrote the following summary, printed in the *Central Western Sunday* newspaper:

> Throughout the Western Districts of New South Wales during the 1860s the bush ranging menace was to cause great problems for the police and citizens alike.
>
> By 1863 the tide was beginning to turn with many brave individuals taking up the fight against this menace.
>
> One of the bravest defences of lives and property occurred at Goimbla Station.
>
> Goimbla was owned by squatter David Campbell and his wife. The property which was jointly run with his brother, William, was situated on the banks of Mandagery Creek at Murga, about 10 miles from Eugowra. It was also the coach stop between Forbes and Orange.
>
> As well as a successful squatter, Campbell was a great ally to the police, having on many occasions participated in hunts for bushrangers. Ben Hall and his gang, comprising 'flash' Johnny Gilbert and the notorious John O'Meally, decided to pay David

Campbell a visit in much the same way they had raided Henry Keightly's home at Dunn's Plains near Rockley.

It was during this encounter that Mickey Burke was killed and as a result John Vane, Burke's best mate, surrendered to authorities at Bathurst on the day of the Goimbla raid.

On 19 November 1863, about 8.45pm, the Campbells were seated in their drawing room when they heard footsteps on the verandah at the front of the house.

Suspecting that it could be bushrangers, David Campbell grabbed one of the double barrel fowling pieces he had loaded for such use from beside the chimney. He then went to the adjoining room while his wife went to the bedroom and William Campbell to the back door.

As David Campbell entered the adjoining room he was confronted by one of the gang standing in the doorway opening on to the verandah. The bushranger immediately raised his gun and fired twice, one ball entering the wall on Campbell's right, and another on his left.

The squatter returned the fire and the bushranger retreated from the verandah to join his mates at the front of the building. The bushrangers then began to pour volley after volley into the homestead whilst calling on those inside to surrender. During these exchanges William Campbell was struck in the chest. He then dragged himself out the back of the house.

Mrs Campbell bravely re-entered the room where the second gun had been left. She secured the gun, a powder flask and some percussion caps from the mantle shelf.

In order for her to secure these items she had to pass a window which was lit with a kerosene lamp. As she ran back past the window she was narrowly missed by shots from the bushrangers. When Mrs Campbell returned to her husband's side they took up a defensive position between two slab walls leading to the kitchen. From this position they could cover every corner.

About 150 yards from the homestead were the outbuildings for the employees. At one stage Mrs Campbell made her way in the dark to them in an attempt to seek some help but the workers were too panic-stricken to be of assistance so she returned to the homestead.

Campbell's resistance to the attack was so great that the bushrangers dared not rush the building, so they decided to drive him out of his stronghold. One of the gang called out: 'If you don't surrender, we will burn the place down.'

Campbell replied: 'Come on, I am ready for you.'

Campbell then heard one of the gang say: 'Oh that is it.'

The barn and stables were then set alight. According to Mrs Campbell this was the time she feared most. The district was in a dry period and straw was littered around the house and barn, which was only a road's width away from the house. Had the wind changed the house would have been engulfed. As the fire took hold the gang was forced to retire behind a fence about 40 yards in front of the house because of the increasing light.

As the barn contained a large amount of hay it was quickly engulfed but the most barbaric part was the squatter's favourite horse was trapped inside. The horse ran madly up and down the barn trying to escape. As the heat increased, so did the sounds of the animal's agony as it was roasted alive. Finally, it died under the shouts and taunts of Hall and his two cohorts.

During the burning of the barn no shots were exchanged, so Mrs Campbell crept through the house to the front rooms again and spotted O'Meally standing on the other side of the paling fence in front of the house watching the fire.

She immediately informed her husband who took advantage of the situation and ran to the corner of the house. He took careful aim and fired at O'Meally, the charge striking him under the ear on the right side of his neck. This caused a gaping wound, shattering the vertebrae and killing him on the spot. After this the bushrangers fired a couple more shots then called again on Campbell to surrender. Then all went quiet. About 11.30pm Campbell ventured from the house to where O'Meally had fallen. He found a cabbage tree hat and a Callisher and Terry carbine. He heard rustling in the nearby field and decided not to venture further in case the bushrangers were waiting in ambush.

Mrs Campbell and the cook then cleared the straw from near the house in case it caught fire. The roof of the barn then caved in. The other servants came out of their huts about 3am and Campbell stationed them around the house to keep watch in case of further attacks until morning when a party of police arrived.

The damage was then established. The barn was completely destroyed and inside was the charred remains of the horse, almost twice its normal size. David Campbell and a constable then returned to where O'Meally had fallen. There they found a pool of blood. A track with traces of blood was followed to a clump of oak trees where O'Meally's body was found.

He was clad in corduroy buckskin breeches, high boots with spurs and three Crimean shirts. Beneath his neck lay a white comforter. His hair was dark auburn, and his beard under his chin was saturated with blood. His features were set in a scowl and to be small and coarse, while the body was athletic with muscular arms. His hands were small and delicate as a lady's. The pockets of his clothing had been rifled and a ring removed from his right little finger. Near the body lay a Colt Navy revolver which had five of its six chambers loaded and capped.

The body was then removed to the verandah of the outbuildings and viewed by members of the public, some of whom made souvenirs of locks of his hair and fragments of his clothing. The body was then covered by part of a wool pack and his face by a towel. Mr Farrand, Police Magistrate from Forbes, held an inquiry at Goimbla into the death of O'Meally. His verdict was justifiable homicide. Several people identified the body, including Sir Fredrick Pottinger, Inspector of Police for the Western District.

It was first intended to remove the body to Forbes for internment but the heat of the weather rendered this impossible. The body was then buried coffin-less behind the homestead on the near bank of the creek.

Soon after, the public began to discuss how to reward Mr

and Mrs Campbell's bravery. Public meetings were held and £1100 was collected to reimburse them for their loss. The loss included a new chaff cutter, the horse, harness, wool, hay and buildings. The government also paid David Campbell O'Meally's reward of £500.

At a later date David Campbell was awarded a gold medal by the government. Mrs Campbell was also honoured with an electroplated coffee urn, valued at £15, upon it was inscribed: 'The ladies of upper and middle Adelong present this token of esteem to Mrs Campbell as appreciation of her heroic conduct displayed during the attack on Goimbla by bushrangers on 19th November 1863'.

In April 1935, the homestead at Goimbla was destroyed by fire. Until this time the building still bore the bullet marks from the historic encounter. All that remains today are parts of the chimney and the front steps. In 1989 historian Kevin Passey and the author erected a sign at the site so it would not be lost for future generations as the remains crumble.

There are some extra points that should be noted which are not covered in the above summary. Firstly, there were three young children at home at the time, being comforted by the maid-servant, which would have added greatly to Amelia's concern during that terrible evening.[2]

There is further detail about David's horse lost in the fire. It is believed to have had a similar pedigree to Panic, which ran second in the fifth Melbourne Cup held in 1865, then went on to sire Nimblefoot, winner in 1870.[3] Whether this was the case or not, it can be safely said it was a valuable thoroughbred and the sound of its agonising death would have been hard to bear, especially for David.

There is little recorded of William Campbell following the event, though it's believed he was the one who rode off to Eugowra to alert the police.[4] It is known he went back to India, no doubt shaken by his experiences in the colony, then later returned to Australia and died in Sydney in September 1873.

Joe O'Brien's son, Pat, inherited Goimbla and was owner at the time of the fire which destroyed the homestead in 1935. Joe's grandson (also Pat) revisited Goimbla as an old man in the late 1990s and left a sketch and notes to confirm many details already covered. The notes also refer to 600 acres being gifted to his grandfather.

I have doubts as to gifting, because why would you advertise the 600 acres including the homestead if it wasn't to be auctioned? Maybe it was sold to Joe at a discounted price or maybe that portion was passed in as not reaching the reserve, and then gifted?

The 600 acres gifted in 1867 still remains intact as a farm. Pat O'Brien sold to Joe Veney following the fire, after which it was sold to the Thurtells, followed by the Pengillys, Carmens, Arndells and finally Geoff Parker, the current owner.[5]

CUNNINGHAM PLAINS

For the best description of the wool shed, I quote directly from Peter Freeman's *The Woolshed: A Riverina Anthology*, referring to an 1872 description:

> It is a splendid structure, in the form of a 'T' and far too good for the purpose to which it is devoted. The main building is 200 feet in length, and 60 feet across. The top portion, or transept, is 100 feet in length, and about 40 feet in width. It is principally constructed of colonial wood, the flooring is of American timber, glass windows and skylights are also in the lofty structure. There is accommodation for 45 shearers. Outside is capital drafting yards and huge tanks. Adjoining the shed is a station store, having a stock equal to many country stores. We were told that the pisé fencing outside cost £48 per mile. It is four feet high. Cunningham Plains shed was unique in many ways. Shorn sheep left the central board by way of races beside the catching pens, and emerged into counting pens at the same level outside. Unshorn sheep were washed under spouts at the wash pool in nearby Cunningham Creek. Another feature of the woolshed was the loft area above the wool-room, where locks and skirtings from the board were thrown, to be tumbled down into the wool-press. Fleeces went straight from the blades into the wool-room on the ground floor. Enclosed within a wing of the wool-room was the woolshed manager's residence which exists today. The pisé store mentioned in 1872 still stands hard by the woolshed.

The completed homestead was widely reported in articles of the day and was featured in another Peter Freeman work, *The Homestead: A Riverina*

Anthology. A quote from his work:

> Cunningham Plains homestead was built between 1867 and 1870. The homestead verandahs have gently curved valence boards with tapered, incised verandah posts; simple ornament, but effective. The cedar entrance door has generous sidelights with side and top margin bars. Over the door there is an elegant semi-circular highlight and around this door and at the building corners the render to the pisé is raised to imitate stonework quoins.
>
> The windows are 12-paned, double-hung sashes with brick sills set into the pisé work and rendered to imitate stonework. There are French doors to the bedroom wing only; these doors have side margins to their glazing and are protected by delicate outer louvre doors.
>
> Internally the four-panelled doors are mostly of pine, grained to match cedar, although there is some cedar joinery. The chimney pieces and mantels are of timber.
>
> The original roof covering was timber shingles. These shingles have since been covered with corrugated iron, but they can still be seen under the existing verandahs. Shingles were preferred as a roofing material 'for coolness and economy', and for facility in putting on with the sort of labour which is always available in the bush – a matter of much importance at a distance from town - they help to equalise the temperature, and thus promote both the health and comfort of their inmates. This is a unique building. It is large and has known many owners, but it remains sound, intact, and almost unchanged since 1870 when the Journal reporter so enthusiastically described it: 'It introduced with great success a building material hitherto rarely used. It is a building of great bulk which sits easily and gracefully on its hilltop site overlooking the road on which the squatters and settlers headed west'. In 1872 a special correspondent from the Sydney Town and Country Journal visited Cunningham Plains and reported: 'on a slight eminence is erected, the residence of DH Campbell, esq, JP. This is acknowledged to be the finest pisé house in New South Wales. It is a spacious house, with verandahs

and wings for sleeping apartments on one side, and laundry and kitchen on the other. Mr Campbell led the way in pisé work in this and the western part of the colony. The idea was, strangely enough, obtained by Mr Campbell from a Chinaman he had in his employ. The stables, stores, and walls of the coach house are also of pisé, and the walls which enclose the choice shrubbery, garden, and orchard is of pisé work'.[6]

Following David's death in 1885, Cunningham Plains was managed by various people, with Robert Futter being the last manager for the Salting brothers, when the property was acquired by the government in 1907 for subdivision into smaller farm lots.

The sheep stud, so carefully nurtured by David, was not taken over by the family. Charles Massy has no further records of it, so perhaps it became part of Cunningham Plains and then deregistered?

Meanwhile, the railway line from Mittagong to Young impacted the region from 1877 onwards, when it was found Murrumburrah was on too steep an incline for a railway station, so the nearby site at Harden was used. Slowly Harden became the main focus of the combined centre of Harden–Murrumburrah. Rail overcame the transport constraints of the horse-drawn era as grain could now be cheaply and efficiently carried to the ports for export.

There were other mixed blessings of rail, as bulky products such as beer and flour were more easily transported, causing the demise of many small breweries and flour mills scattered through regional Australia. Passenger movement was quickly taken up at the expense of Cobb & Co and the staging post inns.

It was the advent of rail and effective movement of grain that led the government to acquire the large stations in the higher rainfall areas for subdivision. The remaining 52,700 acres were advertised for auction in 74 blocks. Bear in mind, in those days of horse-drawn implements, one square mile (640 acres) was considered a very adequate family-size farm. The homestead lot was the biggest being advertised, as block 62 of 4,482 acres.[7] The current size of the property is 2,700 acres and it is now owned by Steve and Liz Phillips. When they bought the property, the grand old homestead was rather neglected, but not spoilt by inappropriate renovations. They have done a very commendable job in bringing the home back to its former elegance, while carefully including the trappings of today's modern family home. They are operating a successful Merino stud, keeping the tradition of David's beloved stud of the 1860s alive. One interesting story relates to the woolshed. Stan Davidson, an early owner following the subdivision, was engaged in a heavy game of poker and must have been playing badly, for he ran out of money and put the woolshed up as his stake. He subsequently lost out and three quarters of the shed was dismantled and moved 10 miles down the road to its new home, where it is still in use today. The remaining quarter is still on Cunningham Plains and used for storage, while sheep are now shorn elsewhere.[8]

A visit in 2012 found the homestead on a gentle rise overlooking the plains beyond, the 100ft frontage of the house facing east, surrounded by garden and mature trees. With a little imagination, we could visualise an older David sitting on the verandah at the end of a long day, whisky in hand, Louise by his side and children tumbling about on the lawn. The sounds of busy station life would be fading away, with the faint smell of sheep, horses and hay wafting forth on the evening breeze.

DOUGLAS

There's conflicting advice about Douglas. David's will clearly shows he owned the property, situated on the west bank of Lake George in 1883, yet other reports refer to Daniel Leahy as providing the funds to build a guesthouse that year, to be known as Douglas. Bungendore had been connected to rail by then and it was thought tourists would flock to the area for water sports and recreation; a small steamboat, the *Pioneer*, was also purchased for the purpose. One year later it was reported that Leahy had exhausted his funds and sold to Wakely and then D.H. Campbell took possession in 1885.[9] Confusion arises at the relationship between Leahy, Wakely and David. Were they partners in the guesthouse venture or were they leasing part of David's land? It doesn't matter much as to the outcome of these questions as Douglas became Louise's home following David's death.

When visiting in 2014, we drove around the western shore of Lake George and there was Douglas, nestled into the side of the range with its wide frontage overlooking a dry lakebed. The fresh white paint of the two-storey house with its green roof speaks well of the current owners who, by all accounts, have carefully restored the old homestead. While cattle grazed on green pastures across the vast lakebed, it was still possible to visualise the *Pioneer* puffing black smoke as she chugged across the blue water towards the eastern shore.

LAKE VIOLET

After the Campbells left in 1951, Tony French managed there until 1961. With the wool boom in full swing, he built a new out-camp and at one stage had 23 staff on the books – who knows what they all did?

Richard and Jenny Shallcross then managed, until the Coree Pastoral Company sold out in 1973, for $75,000. Richard was the son of 'Shally', the Elders pastoral inspector who often stayed at the station in earlier years.[10]

Lake Violet was then bought by Bill May and managed by Ben Bahaan for only a year, before selling to Jamie Venn and Keith Biggs for $90,000. (Keith was the butcher at Leonora 'and made a packet dabbling in Poseidon shares'.)[11] Jamie and Jacqueline Venn were the managers and part-owners to 1987 and were among the last station owners to employ Aboriginal labour: 'who were becoming less reliable by the year, to the point of being more of a nuisance than a help'. The old 6-horsepower Lister petrol engine with the trip-action magneto was still in service at the woolshed in 1987.[12]

The Bowler family from Queensland then owned the station, with Peter Bowler as manager. In 1995 the Bowlers sold to Great Central Mines, which destocked the station, demolished the woolshed as an occupational health and safety hazard, painted the homestead in garish Federation colours popular at the time, and appointed Chris and Carolyn Ward as caretakers. The Wards were granted the grazing sublease and then fenced the station into three large paddocks for cattle, refurbished some of the waters and have been running up to 2000 head, once again making the station pay its own way. In 2014 the Wards bought Lake Violet from Newmont Mining, the mining company then in possession, and are now in full ownership.[13]

Good luck to Chris and Carolyn Ward. If anyone can make a go of it in that part of the world, it would have to be the Ward family, as they've been in the district since 1906 and show no sign of moving anywhere else. Chris's children are the fifth generation of Wards at Wiluna.

Tim and I visited in 2007 and had very mixed feelings. It was tragic to see all the sheep fencing and woolsheds through the Eastern Goldfields completely abandoned, as were some of the homesteads. The sheep industry in that part of the world only had a 75-year life span, as low stocking rates could never sustain such large infrastructure and the rangeland natural feed was too quickly overgrazed. Dingoes are once again becoming a menace as government support for their control is being wound back. More conservative stocking with cattle, together with proper rangeland monitoring, provide an opportunity for the northern areas, but a lot of the more southern stations are questionable as to their future.

The Lake Violet homestead was as we remembered it but on a much smaller scale, as childhood memories tend to have places and people bigger than they really are. It was a comfort seeing it being cared for in contrast to other stations in the region. The jackeroos' quarters were still there but the overseer's cottage was looking the worse for wear. We could still recognise parts of the garden layout, including the location of the grass tennis courts, and found the remains of the 'doubtful proposition' lucerne patch.

The office and store are just as they were. Stations traditionally left all records in place as they changed ownership and managers, and so it was for Lake Violet. Ledgers, journals and stock books are still there, filled in with Dad's meticulous handwriting. It was easy to imagine him sitting at the desk, pipe in mouth, keeping the records up to date and preparing the monthly report for the Coree Pastoral Company.

The kitchen and adjoining men's dining room, later the school room, are as remembered. We could picture Mum doing battle with the hot Metters stove in the kitchen, restless boys in the nearby school room, Daisy's quiet presence alongside 'Missus' and Jack O'Keefe pottering about in the vegetable garden outside.

APPENDIX II: THE CAMPBELLS

Further family detail as of April 2017.

DAVID CAMPBELL (of Argyle, Scotland) m Miss Cameron – parents of **John** (no dates or documented detail).

JOHN CAMPBELL (b February 1766 – d 22 February 1826) m **Elisabeth Sophie Berg** (b 1777 – d 15 June 1853) m 21 October 1796. They had eight children: John (b 1798); Robert (b 1800); Henry (b 1802); **Thomas** (b 1804); Julia (b 1806); Louisa (b 1808); Augustus (b 1809); Phillip (b 1811).

THOMAS CAMPBELL (b 8 November 1804 – d 6 December 1871) m **Helena Maria Elizabeth Fiellerup** (always known as Maria) (b 1810 – d 1863). They had 12 children:
- Thomas Campbell (b 10 November 1827 at Jellasore, Bengal, d 28 February 1879) unmarried
- **David Henry Campbell** (b 21 November 1829 at Jellasore, Bengal – d 23 August 1885, at Cunningham Plains)
  m1: 1856 at Sydney, NSW, **Amelia Margaret Breillat**, daughter of T.C. Breillat (b 26 May 1835 – d 28 May 1870); m2: 2 April 1872, **Louise Powell**, daughter of Nathaniel Powell (b 8 October 1841 – d 25 March 1892)
- Walter Campbell (b 22 October 1831 at Jellasore, Bengal – d 16 June 1908). Served in the Indian/British Army before coming to Australia; m 30 June 1860 at Sydney, NSW, Emma Breillat, sister of David's wife. They returned to India and had six children:
  - Maria Helena (b 1861)
  - Edmund Walter (b 1863)
  - Alan Alfred (b 1864)
  - Mabel (b 1869)

> Avice Blanch (b 1871)
>
> Amelia Mabel (b 1882)

John Clemishaw Campbell (b 5 September 1833 at Jellasore, Bengal – d 28 June 1857). 'Our dear son, John Clemishaw Campbell met his death on this date, being cruelly murdered by Ana Sahib and his followers during the Indian mutiny. It happened while he, along with a number of others, was released from the ill-fated garrison at Cawnpore, proceeded down the Ganges in boats. Notwithstanding that the fiendish rebels had promised a safe passage, no sooner had they embarked and dropped down river when they were fired upon and brutally massacred. A Native who escaped told us that poor John died instantaneously without a groan, a musket ball having pierced his heart while gallantly returning the fire of miscreants. Praise be with him, a better or more affectionate son there could not be.'[14]

William Campbell (b 18 May 1835 – d 3 September 1873 in Australia) m Jan Grice. They had one daughter:

> Severin Maude Campbell (b 1873 – d 1954), unmarried.

Henry Fiellerup Campbell (b 22 August 1837 at Jellasore, Bengal – d 1916 in England) m 26 October 1869, to Lina M. Johnson. No children.

Edmund Campbell (b 10 June 1840 at Jellasore, Bengal – d 1 August 1873, of jungle fever) unmarried.

Maria Louisa Campbell (b 14 February 1842 at Jellasore, Bengal – d 28 July 1906 in Sydney, NSW) m 28 November 1864 Thomas Alfred Davies (b 18 February 1839, Isle of Jersey – d 31 May 1908 in Sydney, NSW) Lieutenant of HM Foot, East Devonshire Regiment. After marrying in India, Maria and Thomas went first to the UK, then Sydney in 1870. They had seven children:

> Evan Alfred (b 1865 India – d 1954 Camden, NSW) m Mary (Polly) Richardson, two children.
>
> Helena Maria (b 1869 Plymouth, UK – d 1958 West Midland, WA) m Alex Goyder, four children.
>
> George William Hope (b 1870 at sea – d 1951 Sydney, NSW) m Elizabeth McCarthy, five children; eldest son, Thomas, is the father of Bronwyn Davies (who supplied useful information for this book).
>
> Alice Katherine (b 1872 Sydney, NSW – d Walcha, NSW) m Dr Samual Stephens, five children.

Lillian Gertrude (b 1874 Goulborn, NSW – d 1962, Brisbane, Queensland) m Herman Zillman, five children.

Llewellyn (b 1875 Cunningham Plains – d 1952, Jarrahdale, WA) m Dorinda Clifton, eight children. The seventh was Madeline who married Arthur Few and the eighth was Dorothy who married Gerard Parkinson, now living at Woodlands, WA. (Madeline and Dorothy supplied useful information for this book.)

Madeline Emma (b 1878 Goulborn, NSW – d 1962 Sydney, NSW) m Arthur Fenwick, no children.

Catherine Elizabeth Campbell (Kitty) (b 16 December 1843 at Jellasore, Bengal – d 26 April 1911, in South Africa from enteric, (typhoid)) m William Fowler Fraser (b 1 October 1842 – d 9 May 1880, at Liverpool from enteric (typhoid) when returning to England on leave). Worked in Bank of Bengal, India. Catherine's grandson, Thomas, is referred to in the text as the author of *Danish Bred – A Family Miscellany*.

Robert Campbell (b 5 February 1846 at Jellasore, Bengal – d 21 May 1873, from injuries inflicted by a tiger attack at Dehrdee), unmarried.

Severin Alexander Campbell (b 4 October 1847 at Jellasore, Bengal – d 1880) unmarried.

Louisa Harriet Campbell (b 19 December 1849 – d November 1928) m on 2 November 1871 William Charles Turner, son of Colonel Turner, viceroy staff.

DAVID HENRY CAMPBELL (b 21 November 1829 – d 23 August 1885) m1 **Amelia Margaret Briellat** (b 26 May 1835 – d 28 May 1870) on 19 February 1856. They had eight children:

Thomas Briellat Campbell (b 8 November 1857 – d 29 January 1868).

David Francis Campbell (b 17 August 1860 – d 15 February 1947) m Marcia Jane Wallace on 4 November 1885. David was a surveyor and engineer. He was the 'resident engineer' in charge of building Burrinjuck Dam (also known as Barren Jack Dam, as a corruption of the Aboriginal name), which was under construction from 1909 to 1928. They lived in the construction town 'Barren Jack City', which is now mostly submerged. The drought of 1895–1902 generated interest in building the dam to provide irrigation to the region between the Murrumbidgee and the Lachlan rivers. In 1907 a 2ft gauge railway line was constructed from Goodah, south of Yass, 26 miles to the dam site. In 1925 the biggest flood on record overtopped the dam wall. The dam height was increased in 1937 to 1,956 feet and subsequently in 1986 to 1,994 feet, along with variations to the spillway design. The David Francis Campbells are also recorded as living at Harrow Road, Petersham (Sydney); Broken Hill; Narrandera; Springwood and 11 Parkview Road, Manly. Marcia Jane Campbell died in 1944 and David Francis Campbell died in 1947 (while living at Parkview Road). They had three children, all born at Petersham:

>Charlotte Mary Campbell (b 1887) m Archie Clark in 1911 (their eldest daughter, Marcia, married John Dale – their daughter, Belinda Dale, provided useful information for this book).
>
>Marcia Helen Campbell (b 1889 – d 1981 in Castle Hill, Sydney).
>
>Wallace Campbell (b 1892 – d 1932 in Manly while living at Parkview Road).

Percy Campbell (b 30 October 1861 – d 1951). He studied architecture under William W.D. Wodel of Sydney and was an early architect in NSW of colonial and state note.

Eleanor Mary Campbell (b 20 March 1865 – d 3 September 1866).

Walter Campbell (b 23 August 1866 – d September 1866).

Alfred Walter Campbell 'Snowy' (b 18 January 1868 – d 4 November 1937) m Walterina Jean MacKay, 30 May 1906 (the only surviving daughter of Alexander and Annie MacKay of Wallanbean, adjoining Cunningham Plains). Alfred was the first Australian-born neurologist, pathologist and research worker. His education was from a private tutor, then Oaklands at Mittagong before attending medical school at Edinburgh University (MB and ChM 1889 and MD 1892). He returned to Australia in 1905 and set up a Sydney private practice and became an honorary consultant to the children's hospital and Prince Henry Hospital. He enlisted in the Imperial Medical Corps in 1915 and spent his service in the Brunswick Military Hospital treating soldiers with shell-shock. They had two daughters:

Veda Annie Campbell (b 25 March 1907 – d 22 February 1934) m James Wesley Hope.

Helen Jean Campbell (b 27 April 1909) m Richard Hammer on 26 April 1939. They had a son, David (b 15 August 1940).

Amelia Campbell (b 24 May 1870 – d March 1871).

Unnamed female, stillborn twin (24 May 1870).

m2 **Louise Powell** (b 8 October 1841 – d 25 March 1892) on 2 April 1872.

Nathaniel Powell (b 6 September 1874 – d 26 July 1952).

Charlotte Louise (Bunt) (b 1 March 1876 – d 1966) m William Deuchar Gordon in April 1901. They had four children:

Margaret Louise (b 1902) unmarried.

William Alexander (b ?) thrice married.

Elizabeth Deuchar (Beth) (b 1908) m Dr Ashleigh Osborne Davy. They had two children:

William Ashleigh (b 1941 – d 2010) m Dimity Davis. They had six children: James, Kate, Lindsay, Nathanial, Deuchar and Tamsin. Tragically the twins, Deuchar and Tamsin, and Nathanial, were all killed in aircraft accidents. Lindsay and her family are now living at Turalla. Dimity provided useful information for this book.

Christine (b 1944) unmarried.

Deuchar Forbes (b 1911 – d ?) m Mary McMaster. They had three children: Forbes, Anne and Alexander.

Henry (b 24 July 1877 – d 21 March 1903). His headstone is also in the private Turalla Cemetery at Bungendore.

Alexander (Alick) Douglas (b 1878 – d 3 October 1901, killed in action Boer War, South Africa). His headstone is in the private Turalla cemetery at Bungendore.

NATHANIEL POWELL CAMPBELL (b 6 September 1874 – d 26 July 1952) m **Evelyn Charlotte Ryrie** (b 11 July 1875 – d 19 October 1961) on 9 February 1904. They had four children:

Kathleen Cassels (b 1905 – d 16 October 1951) unmarried.

Donald Henry Alexander (b 31 July 1907 – d 29 March 1987).

Nat 'Bey' (b 11 May 1909 – d 17 November 1983) m Patricia 'Patsy' Giles, 17 October 1942, two children:

Richard Giles (b 19 February 1944 – present)
m1 Anne Heckenberg; two children:
- Ben Alexander (b 29 March 1972 – present)
- Kate Elisa (b 19 May 1973 – present).

m2 Helen 'Helli' Woodhouse.

Andrew Ryrie (Andy) (b 18 October 1946 – present)
m1 Helen Wighton, three children:
- Nat Blackburn (b 8 December 1970 – present)
- George Giles (b 18 May 1972 – present)
- William David (b 17 August 1976 – present).

m2 Allyson Brace.

Pat Powell (b 10 July 1911 – d 15 September 1968) m Delia Rosemarie 'Rie' Woodley, 25 October 1947. Two children;
- David Ian (b 9 May 1949 – d 21 January 2012) m Lesley-Jane 'LJ' Oliver, no children.
- Penelope Ann 'Penny' (b 13 March 1953 – d 4 May 2015) m Antony 'Tony' Henry. Two children:
  - Anna Jane (b 11 February 1983 – present)
  - Samuel John Powell ('Sam') (b 10 July 1989 – present).

Don, Bey, Pat and Evelyn Campbell (Pat's wedding, 1947)

Kay Campbell

DONALD HENRY ALEXANDER CAMPBELL (b 31 July 1907 – d 29 March 1987) m **Thelma Raye Rose** (b 12 January 1917 – d 27 November 2010) m 22 November 1939, four children:

Alexander David Campbell (b 4 August 1941 – present), m Jennifer Robin Levinson (b 23 August 1946 – present) on 20 January 1968. Three children:

Catherine (b 21 October 1969 – d 10 July 1970)

Anneliese Jane (b 16 February 1971 – present) m Hugh Bryan Roberts (b 15 July 1972 – present) on 23 January 1999. Two children:

Lachlan Hugh Alexander (b 2 November 2000 – present)

Angus James (b 11 October 2002 – present).

Jock Alexander (b 9 July 1972 – present) m Louise Catherine Lugsdin (b 26 February 1974 – present) on 3 April 2004. Three children:

Harriet Lily (b 26 May 2005 – present)

Jack William (b 31 May 2007 – present)

Penny Matilda (b 29 May 2012 – present).

Timothy Donald (b 20 November 1943 – present)
m1 Susan Glen Burnard (b 22 January 1947 – present). Two children:
    Sophia Belinda (b 5 February 1974 – present)
    Rebecca Georgina (b 23 January 1976 – present) m Mathew Gleeson, 18 March 2005, three children:
        Cooper (b 13 October 2003 – present)
        Stella May (b 24 January 2006 – present)
        Ginger Rose (b 8 June 2010 – present).
m2 Alison Jane 'Sally' Sewell, 14 January 1986.

Suzanne Ryrie (b 2 January 1949 – present) m John Edwin Horner (b 20 January 1947 – present) on 7 July 1973. Two children:
    Louise Ryrie (b 25 February 1977 – present) m Behan Flaherty, 22 April 2006, two children:
        Elliot Ryrie (b 30 July 2010 – present)
        Harriet Eliza (b 6 June 2012 - present)
    Anne Elizabeth (b 31 January 1979 – present) m Kevin Steele, 9 April 2017.

Elizabeth Rose: (b 13 December 1953 – present) m Ian Maxwell Briggs, 4 March 1977. Three children:
    Timothy (b 12 February 1986 – d 12 February 1986)
    Sally Elizabeth (b 2 January 1987 – present), partner Brett Anthony Rowley. Two children:
        Stella Elizabeth (b 10 March 2014 – present)
        Ted Maxwell (b 12 September 2015 – present).
    Jillian Lucy (Jillie) (b 12 December 1992 – present).

APPENDIX III: TIMELINE FOR ALEX CAMPBELL

FAMILY

1941 born Lake Violet, Wiluna, 4 August
1951 family moved to 39 Loftus Street, Nedlands
1954–58 attended Christ Church Grammar School
1968 married Jennifer Robin Levinson, 20 January
1969 daughter Catherine born 21 October, died 10 July 1970
1971 daughter Anneliese Jane born 16 February
1972 son Jock Alexander born 9 July

FARMING

1959 Wydgee Pastoral Company, Yanchep
1960–65 Hodgson family, Kulin
1963–76 New-land mallee farm – Tillgaree, Borden
1976–2013 Tillgaree, Narrikup
1987–99 part owner and manager, Crystal Brook, Narrikup

COMMUNITY

1969–present member, WA Farmers Federation (WAFF)
1989–92 State Vice President, WAFF and NFF Executive
1992–95 State President, WAFF and NFF Executive
1989–95 Board member, Greening Australia (WA 1989–91, national 1992–95)
1992–95 Board member, Landcare Australia Ltd
1992–96 Member CSIRO Institute of Natural Resources & Environment

Advisory Committee
1995 Chair, State Landcare Review
1995 Chair, Farm Forestry Taskforce
1996–97 Board member, Water and Rivers Commission
1996–2001 Chair, Land and Water Australia (formerly LWRRDC)
1996–2001 Chair, National Dryland Salinity Program
1996–2009 Member, Joint Venture Agroforestry Program (Chair 1996–2001 and 2008–09)
1997–2001 Member, National Land and Water Resources Audit – Champion, Salinity Theme
1997–2001 Chair, State Salinity Council
1997–2005 Chair, State Assessment Panel for the NHT, and then the Envirofund
2001–2007 Chair, CRC–Salinity
2001–2013 Member, UWA Albany Foundation (Chair 2007–2013)
2008–2013 Director, Rural Industries R&D Corporation
2008–2013 Chair, South Coast NRM

AWARDS

2003 Centenary Medal
2007 Life Member, WA Farmers Federation
2009 Hon Doc Science in Agriculture, UWA
2011 Member of the General Division of Australian Honours (AM)

ACRONYMS

ACTU – Australian Council of Trade Unions
ABC – Australian Broadcasting Corporation
Ag Dept – Department of Agriculture WA
AWI – Australian Wool Innovation
AWC – Australian Wool Corporation
AWL – absent without leave
CALM – Department of Conservation and Land Management WA
CBH – Cooperative Bulk Handling
CDB – Commonwealth Development Bank
CEO – chief executive officer
CRC – Cooperative Research Centre
CSIRO – Commonwealth Scientific and Industrial Research Organisation
DSE – dry sheep equivalent
EPA – Environmental Protection Authority WA
FESA – Fire and Emergency Services Authority WA
FU – Farmers Union
GRDC – Grains Research and Development Corporation
JVAP – Joint Venture Agroforestry Program
LWRRDC – Land and Water Resources Research and Development Corporation
MDBC – Murray–Darling Basin Commission
MD – managing director
MLA – Meat and Livestock Australia
NFF – National Farmers' Federation
NDSP – National Dryland Salinity Program
NRM – natural resource management
NSW – New South Wales
NZ – New Zealand
OMA – Oil Mallee Association

PIA – Primary Industry Association
PGA – Pastoralists and Graziers Association
POW – prisoner of war
PS – paddle steamer
RAS – Royal Agricultural Society
R&D – research and development
RIRDC – Rural Industries Research and Development Corporation
RPS – reserve price scheme (for wool)
RRDC – Rural Research and Development Corporation
SA – South Australia
SPA – Saltland Pastures Association
USA – United States of America
UWA – University of Western Australia
WA – Western Australia
WACA – WA Cricket Association
WAFF – WA Farmers Federation
WANTFA – Western Australian No-Tillage Farmers Association
WCA – Wool Council of Australia

ENDNOTES

PART I
1. Dorothea Mackellar: 'My Country'
2. Anne Campbell was married to Richard Campbell, my first cousin (see Appendix II).
3. Madeline Few is the granddaughter of Maria Louisa, David Henry Campbell's sister (see Appendix II).
4. In 1984, Tom Fraser, another distant cousin (see Appendix II), published Danish Bred – A Family Miscellany, which added: 'George, one of the Salting's cousins, writing to the family after attending a function in London at which Queen Alexandra was present, commented on the extraordinary likeness between Maria Augusta Davies (a daughter of Thomas and Helena Campbell) – and the Queen – which he went on to say was not all together surprising as they were cousins. (Queen Alexandra had, of course, been a Princess of Denmark before she married King Edward VII).' Family records, as shown in Appendix II, have Thomas Campbell marrying Maria Helena Fiellerup and their daughter, Maria Louisa, marrying Thomas Davies, so the names differ a little in this account.
5. Morganatic marriage: 'one between man of exalted rank and woman of lower rank, who remains in her former station, the issue having no claim to succeed to possession or title of the father' (Oxford Dictionary).
6. At the end of the 18th century, Christian VII was King from 1766 to 1808 and his son Frederick was heir apparent, later to reign as King Frederick VI for the years 1808–1839. The Prince in question, later crowned Christian VIII, was born in 1786 and was a distant cousin in the line of succession, and when Thomas was born in 1804, would have been 18 years old. He eventually ruled as King in old age (1839–1848). It should also be noted that Denmark was a monarchy, with constitutional change to an elected two-house Parliament not occurring until 1849. Before these changes, the Royal family ruled with complete authority. Henning Dehn-Nielsen, Kings and Queens of Denmark, Narayana Press, Gylling, 2007.
7. Information regarding John and Thomas Campbell provided by Madeline Few and Dorothy Parkinson, after extensive research and study of Danish archives (they are direct descendants of John Campbell – see Appendix II). Madeline is in possession of all the information concerning the ships he sailed on, dates and destinations; the details of the seven children's birth records; and the 10 extramarital children, as summarised in Chapter 1.
8. Denmark had colonies in India for 225 years, finally being ceded to the British East India Company in 1845. Their presence was accepted by the British, Dutch and Portuguese as they proved neither a military or naval threat and were useful

9. A.F. Pike, 'Salting, Severin Kanute (1805–1865)', Australian Dictionary of Biography, National Centre of Biography, Australian National University, http://adb.anu.edu.au/biography/salting-severin-kanute-2626.
10. 'Danish bred – a Family Miscellany' by TW Fraser (grandson of Catherine Elizabeth Campbell, David Henry's sister)
11. 'Chateau Yering – a short history'. There is a later connection between the Ryrie and Campbell families through marriage in 1904.
12. Some records refer to him as managing Salting's properties at this time. He may have been acting as his uncle's representative on some matters but, with no prior knowledge of Australian agriculture, would have relied on local 'hands-on' managers to run the properties and would have learnt from them.
13. 'Snowy Campbell: Australian Pioneer Investigator of the Brain' by Malcolm Macmillan'
14. 'The Australian Merino' – Charles Massy
15. Stayer: A horse with endurance for long distances - 'staying the distance' etc
16. 'Snowy Campbell: Australian Pioneer Investigator of the Brain' by Malcolm Macmillan
17. 'The Australian Merino' – Charles Massy
18. 'The Australian Merino – Charles Massy
19. Catarrh: respiratory infection, aggravated by dust and close contact
20. 'The Australian Merino' – Charles Massy
21. Wikipedia 'The Clipper Ship Era' - Arthur H Clarke 1912
22. 'Killers' are sheep, usually of inferior types, used for slaughter (carried live on ships before the advent of refrigeration)
23. 'The Australian Merino' – Charles Massy
24. 'The Australian Merino' – Charles Massy
25. Wikipedia: 'A Pictorial History of Cobb and Co' - Rigby Ltd, Adelaide
26. Both are on the Barwon River, a northern tributary of the Darling. 'Paddle Steamers on the Murray Darling Rivers' – Rosalind Stirling
27. The record load was eventually achieved in 1932 when PS Pevencey had 600 bales in her holds and the barge Kulnine a further 1,900 bales, taking a fortnight to reach Echuca from Hay. 'Paddle Steamers on the Murray Darling Rivers' – Rosalind Stirling
28. 'The Australian Merino' – Charles Massy
29. Forbes Historical Society (From information provided when visited in 2013)
30. Forbes Historical Society (From information provided when visited in 2013)
31. Forbes Historical Society (From information provided when visited in 2013)
32. 'Snowy Campbell: Australian Pioneer Investigator of the Brain' by Malcolm Macmillan
33. Forbes Historical Society (From information provided when visited in 2013)

34. Forbes Historical Society (From information provided when visited in 2013)
35. 'Snowy Campbell: Australian Pioneer Investigator of the Brain' by Malcolm Macmillan
36. 'Snowy Campbell: Australian Pioneer of the Brain' by Malcolm Macmillan
37. See Appendix I for a newspaper report from the time of the attack on Goimbla.
38. Christies Catalogue, November 1992
39. 'Snowy Campbell: Australian Pioneer Investigator of the Brain' by Malcolm Macmillan
40. 'Snowy Campbell: Australian Pioneer Investigator of the Brain' by Malcolm Macmillan
41. 'Snowy Campbell: Australian Pioneer of Investigator the Brain' by Malcolm Macmillan
42. 'Snowy Campbell: Australian Pioneer Investigator of the Brain' by Malcolm Macmillan
43. Forbes Historical Society (From information provided when visited in 2013)
44. 'The Homestead – A Riverina Anthology' – Peter Freeman, Oxford University Press, Melbourne 1982
45. 'Snowy Campbell: Australian Pioneer Investigator of the Brain' by Malcolm Macmillan;
46. 'The Australian Merino' – Charles Massy
47. 'Snowy Campbell: Australian Pioneer Investigator of the Brain' by Malcolm Macmillan
48. 'The Woolshed – a Riverina Anthology' – Peter Freeman, Oxford University Press, Melbourne
49. 'The Woolshed – A Riverina Anthology' – Peter Freeman, Oxford University Press, Melbourne 1982
50. 'Snowy Campbell: Australian Pioneer Investigator of the Brain' by Malcolm Macmillan. Severin and Louisa Salting had retired to England in 1858 and as their sons, George and William, had no interest in the stations, management was left very much to Macansh. Salting died on 14 September 1865, from which time the managers reported to the executors of the estate, a practice that continued for all of David's time on Cunningham Plains, and then until the property was compulsorily acquired by the government in 1907 for subdivision into smaller farms. It's known David had some involvement with the station before taking over management in 1867. For example, he met the Albury District Inspector of Schools in 1865 to arrange a school for Cunningham Plains, largely to benefit the station's employees. It's thought he was also engaged in the planning for a new homestead during 1865–67, as the Macanshes were living some distance away.
51. Extract from the Sydney Town and Country Journal, as cited in The Homestead – A Riverina Anthology – Peter Freeman, Oxford University Press, Melbourne 1982
52. See Appendix II.
53. An expression describing horses in harness taking up the load of the wagon or implement behind them
54. 'Snowy Campbell: Australian Pioneer Investigator of the Brain' by Malcolm Macmillan

55. 'The Woolshed – a Riverina Anthology' – Peter Freeman, Oxford University Press, Melbourne
56. Word of mouth that rapidly spread news though rural areas.
57. 'North Tuppal shed re-enactment with 72 stands operating – Outback magazine 2010'
58. 'Snowy Campbell: Australian Pioneer Investigator of the Brain' by Malcolm Macmillan
59. 'Snowy Campbell: Australian Pioneer Investigator of the Brain' by Malcolm Macmillan
60. 'Snowy Campbell: Australian Pioneer Investigator of the Brain' by Malcolm Macmillan. The Zoological Society, formed in 1879, was an offshoot of sorts of the Acclimatisation Society (Royal Zoological Society of New South Wales, 'RZS NSW History', http://www.rzsnsw.org.au/history).
61. 'Snowy Campbell: Australian Pioneer Investigator of the Brain' by Malcolm Macmillan
62. 'Snowy Campbell: Australian Pioneer Investigator of the Brain' by Malcolm Macmillan
63. Research undertaken by Bronwyn Davies, Thomas Davies's great-granddaughter (see Appendix two)
64. 'The Homestead – A Riverina Anthology' – Peter Freeman, Oxford University Press, Melbourne 1982
65. Harden–Murrumburra cemetery records
66. 'Magnificent Lake George – The Biography' – Graeme Barron
67. 'Magnificent Lake George – the Biography' by Graeme Barron was the source for information used in this chapter
68. For further family detail, see Appendix II.
69. 'The Cyclopedia of South Australia'
70. 'Bluey' was slang for swag, or roll of blankets.
71. 'Adelaide Advertiser' 1925 – (on Nat's retirement as a starter)
72. 'The Cyclopedia of South Australia'
73. 'The Cyclopedia of South Australia'
74. 'Adelaide Advertiser' 1925 – (on Nat's retirement as starter)
75. 'The Australian Merino' – Charles Massy
76. 'The Australian Merino' – Charles Massy
77. Bureau of Meteorology - website
78. 'For the complete story of rabbits in Australia, refer to "Those Wild Rabbits" by Bruce Munday, Wakefield Press.'
79. A.W. Martin, 'Parkes, Sir Henry (1815–1896)', Australian Dictionary of Biography, National Centre of Biography, Australian National University, http://adb.anu.edu.au/biography/parkes-sir-henry-4366/text7099.
80. 'My Darling Mick – the Life of Granville Ryrie 1865-1937' – by Phoebe Vincent
81. 'The Cyclopedia of South Australia': Nataniel Powell Campbell
82. 'Adelaide Advertiser' 1925 – (on Nat's retirement as starter)
83. 'The Cyclopedia of South Australia' Nataniel Powell Campbell
84. 'Adelaide Advertiser' 1925 – (on Nat's retirement as starter)

85. 'Bungaree Land, Stock and People' – Frankie Hawker and Rob Linn
86. 'The Australian Merino' – Chales Massy
87. 'Bungaree Land, Stock and People' – Frankie Hawker and Rob Linn
88. 'The Australian Merino' – Charles Massy
89. A blown sheep is infested with maggots by the 'blowfly'. A 'dag' is a clot of wool impregnated with faeces; a dirty sheep would have many dags, be daggy, and so attract flies.
90. 'The Australian Merino' – Charles Massy
91. 'Crutching': shearing urine and faeces-stained wool from the rear end of a sheep.
92. G.W. Goyder was a botanist and SA Surveyor General in the 1850s. He drew a line depicting the limit of the safe rainfall area suited to farming, based on his observations of the local flora. It roughly follows the 10-inch rainfall isohyet (a line on a map or chart connecting areas of equal rainfall).
93. 'Goodbye Cobber – God bless' – John Hamilton
94. 'Adelaide Advertiser' 1925 – (on Nat's retirement as starter). Edward later became King, before abdicating to marry the American divorcee Wallis Simpson.
95. Clock made by Japy-Freres for exhibition at the Paris Exposition Universelle 1889 (when the Eiffel Tower was built), bought by Evelyn's mother and given as a wedding present, handed down through Pat, then Rie to Alex.
96. Information regaurding Pat Campbell, supplied by Rie Saxton
97. Personal comments by the Sears, after retiring to Mount Barker
98. 'The Burma Line' – A lecture by Eric Wilson, historian, March 2015 to the Claremont-Cottesloe Probus Club
99. AWOL: An Army term: 'Absent Without Leave'
100. Information regarding Pat Campbell supplied by Rie Saxton
101. There are three sources for this summary: 'National Highlands Group of the National Trust'; 'A Short History', Chateau Yerring; 'William Ryrie (1805-1856)', by Alan Gregory, for the Melbourne Club
102. Information regarding Granville from Phoebe Vincent, 'My Darling Mick – the Life of Granville Ryrie (1865-1937)'
103. From a letter written by Ron Halcombe in 1987
104. Jack Hobbs' career spanned 29 years, scoring 61,670 runs and 197 centuries. He played in 61 tests for England, toured Australia five times and was the only Englishman named in Wisden's top five cricketers of the century. Wikipedia, 'Wisden Cricketers of the Century', https://en.wikipedia.org/wiki/Wisden_Cricketers_of_the_Century.
105. It is known Don went to NSW in 1923 and 1924, as well as some earlier trips.
106. 'The Australian Merino' – Charles Massy
107. 'The Australian Merino' – Charles Massy
108. Wikipedia: 'The Rabbit Proof Fence", Library of Western Australia
109. 'The Australian Merino' – Charles Massey
110. Wikipedia: 'Millstream Water Reserve', Government of Western Australia
111. Barcoo Rot: festering skin sores in association with minor trauma and a diet chronically deficient in fresh fruit and vegetables.
112. Letter from Ron Halcombe to Thelma, shortly after Don's death in 1987, referring

to the Millstream days.
113. Stories related by Mark Synnot jr – January 2015
114. Stories related by Mark Synnot jr – January 2015
115. Stories related by Mark Synnot jr – January 2015
116. As related by Alan Cleland – January 2015
117. As related by Rob Chomley – January 2015
118. 'The Australian Miners Handbook', Louthean Media Pty Ltd – Editor, Ross Louthean
119. As related by Rob Chomley – January 2015
120. As related by Dan MacKinnon – 2008
121. As related by Alan Cleland – January 2015
122. As related by Alan Cleland – January 2015
123. John H. Laurence, 'de Bernales, Claude Albo (1876–1963)', Australian Dictionary of Biography, National Centre of Biography, Australian National University, http://adb.anu.edu.au/biography/de-bernales-claude-albo-5935/text10117. Overton Lodge was sold to the Cottesloe council in 1950 and is now known as the Cottesloe Civic Centre, while his London home on the Strand was used as Western Australia House for many years. Claude died in England in 1963, after living the last 15 years of his life in obscurity.
124. P.R. Heydon, Wiluna, Edge of the Desert, Hesperian Press, Perth, 1996.
125. Murray T. Pheils, The Return to Coree: The Rise and Fall of a Pastoral Dynasty, Allen & Unwin, Sydney, 1998.
126. 'Sir Samuel McCoughey - a brief history' – Yanco Agricultural High School
127. Memories of Alex and Tim Campbell, together with a return trip in 2007; Information provided by Kip Venn – February 2015 (Kip was the son of Jamie Venn who owned Lake Violet from 1974-1987)
128. 'The Return to Coree – the rise and fall of a pastoral dynasty' – Murray T Pheils
129. 'Granite Peak 1929-1979' – PB Creswell
130. 'Wiluna – Edge of the desert' – PR Heydon
131. 'Granite Peak 1929-1979' – PB Creswell
132. 'Wiluna – Edge of the desert' – PR Heydon
133. 'Wiluna – Edge of the desert' – PR Heydon
134. 'Wiluna – Edge of the desert' – PR Heydon; 'Droving with Ben Taylor' – Len Hill
135. A 'run through' or 'cattle grid' is a vehicle access way through fences.
136. These policies were handed over as 21st birthday presents and, at a cost of $16 per year, stand to benefit the boys' estates in the order of $9,500 upon their deaths. The modest final payout demonstrates the corrosive powers of inflation on what seemed a generous bequest in wartime Australia.
137. 'Wiluna – Edge of the desert' – PR Heydon
138. 'Granite Peak 1929-1979' – PB Creswell
139. 'Wiluna – Edge of the desert' – PR Heydon
140. 'Wiluna – Edge of the desert' – PR Heydon
141. 'The Encyclopedia of Australia's Battles": Allen and Unwin
142. The Mitchell family had owned Laverton Downs, just north of Laverton, providing meat and milk to the local mines, but had to 'walk off' during the depression. The

station later became home to the famous Poseidon nickel mine. After 35 years of contract shearing, the Mitchell family bought Muggon in the Murchison district, which was run by Len's son, Bill. As related by Bill Mitchell, 2015

143. 'Tin dog, Damper and Dust' – Don Munday
144. Personal story related to Alex by Clem McKenzie in 1977.
145. 'Wiluna – Edge of the desert' – PR Heydon
146. Information from Marg Monger – January 2015
147. 'No sequel – the life and times of Peter Henry Atkins' – Peter Atkins
148. 'The Return to Coree – the rise and fall of a pastoral dynasty' – Murray T Pheils
149. Letter from Ron Halcombe to Thelma, shortly after Don's death in 1987
150. Research on the Rose family undertaken by Brian Rose and Frank Slee
151. Information provided by Jim Thom – February 2015
152. Wanneroo Shire Council historical notes
153. 'In response to Need' – E.N. (Noel) Fitzpatrick
154. 'Eric Smart 1911-1973' – John Gladstones
155. Peet & Co Ltd sales brochure
156. When Alex started at Christ Church in 1954, the annual fee was £250 ($500), providing a stark indication of the corrosive effects of inflation, with fees now being $25,000 for a day boy and $50,000 for a boarder.
157. Paul Barry 'The Rise and Fall of Alan Bond' Bantam Press
158. A letter from Ron Halcombe to Thelma, shortly after Don's death in 1987

PART II

1. Shared memories with Derry Macqueen April 2015
2. 'Prac – East Claremont Practising School 1905-1985', by Michael Bearson
3. 'Prac – East Claremont Practising School 1905-1985', by Michael Bearson
4. Christ Church Grammar School archives, with assistance from Andrew Baird and Deborah Hill. By 2016 there were 14 Aboriginal boys boarding at Christ Church, benefiting from a range of scholarships, so perhaps Irwin paved the way that others might follow?
5. Christ Church Grammar School archives, with assistance from Andrew Baird and shared memories with the class of 1958.
6. MLC: Methodist Ladies College
7. Memories shared with Derry Macqueen in 2015
8. Shared memories with Derry Macqueen 2015
9. English, history, geography, maths A, physiology and hygiene, and commercial methods and bookkeeping. I failed physics.
10. Memories shared with Trisha Miles (nee McLennan) 2015
11. PLC – Presbyterian Ladies College
12. NCO: non-commissioned officer
13. English, history, geography, economics, physiology and hygiene, biology and art.

PART III

1. Memories shared with Dick Sudlow 2015
2. Malcolm McLennan was the state stock manager for Goldsbrough Mort.
3. Memories shared with Geoff Hodgson 2015
4. Rabbits slowly developed resistance to 'myxo' and by 2000 the virus was only half as effective. The CSIRO released Calicivirus in 1995 which is now contributing to the control measures. See https://www.csiro.au/en/Research/BF/Areas/Invasive-species-and-diseases/Biological-control/Controlling-those-pesky-rabbits
5. Memories shared with Geoff Hodgson 2015
6. CBH: Cooperative Bulk Handling
7. Memories shared with Geoff Hodgson 2015
8. Memories shared with Geoff Hodgson 2015
9. Clive Malcolm was the WA Ag Dept salt land Agronomist from 1955 and remained active in this area of research well into his retirement
10. Department of Lands and Surveys publication 1963
11. Department of Lands and Surveys publication 1963
12. As related by Richard Stockwell 2015
13. As related by Peter Crossing 2015
14. 'The Golden Dream' – Nancy Keesing (William Collins 1974)
15. 'The Golden Dream' – Nancy Keesing (William Collins 1974)
16. Family tree compiled by Gordon and Ralph Levinson
17. 'The Australian Merino' – Charles Massy
18. Information provided by Peter Moulton, Elders branch manager, Gnowangerup 1965-70
19. Information provided by Peter Moulten, Elders branch manager, Gnowangerup 1965-70
20. Information provided by Peter Moulten, Elders branch manager, Gnowangerup 1965-70
21. Information provided by David Stanton
22. Information provided by David Stanton
23. Australian Bureau of Statistics (cat. 7124.0)
24. 'Memories shared with Tony Gooch, 2016 (Board Member, Australian Wool Corporation, 1982-91)
25. 'Memories shared with Tony Gooch, 2016 (Board Member, Australian Wool Corporation, 1982-91)
26. 'Australian Dictionary of Biographies'
27. John Miels, Historical Society of SA (article)
28. National Archives of Australia – Australian Prime Ministers
29. National Archives of Australia – Australian Prime Ministers
30. Memories shared with Peter Lee 2015
31. Memories shared with Peter Lee 2015
32. Memories shared with Peter Lee 2015
33. Shared memories with Ron McTaggart 2015
34. As related by Kevin Goss 2015

35. Shared memories with Ron McTaggart 2015
36. Bureau of Meteorology Web Site: Summary of information under 'Cyclone Alby'
37. Wikipedia, quoting many sources over the NFF activity in the dispute
38. Memories shared with Peter Lee, 2016
39. 'Crossbred': usually a British-bred ram such as Poll Dorset or Borden Leicester mated to Merino ewes.
40. Memories shared with Jock Morrison 2015
41. Joint Venture Agroforestry Program (JVAP) managed by the Rural Industries R&D Corporation.
42. Shared memories with Tony Gooch, 2016 (Board Member, Australian Wool Corporation 1982-91)
43. 'Clean' relates to weight after scouring out the grease, dust, vegetable matter etc.
44. ABC News 28 Jan 2014 3.37 pm
45. Wikipedia, quoting numerous sources under 'WA Inc'
46. Shared memories with Tony Gooch, 2016 (Board member, Australian Wool Corporation 1982-91)
47. A quote from Kevin Goss 2015
48. Shared memories with Tony Gooch, 2016 (Board Member, Australian Wool Corporation 1982-91)
49. Shared memories with Tony Gooch, 2016 (Board Member, Australian Wool Corporation 1982-91)
50. Shared memories with Peter Lee 2015
51. Shared memories with Peter Lee 2015
52. 'The 100 years of WA Farmers' – WA Farmers Federation 2011
53. Steve Manchee The Countryman 1993
54. Information from Mike Norton, a trustee for the Peterson Trust 2015
55. Dr Henry Schapper, head of agricultural economics at UWA, 1959–1984, and founder of the Farm Management Foundation.
56. L. Tickner, The West Australian, 28 April 1992.
57. The Countryman March 17, 1994
58. Memories shared with Kevin Goss 2015
59. Memories shared with Peter Lee 2015. 'Poddy dodging': branding and ear marking a calf that does not belong to you (usually from a neighbouring property).
60. Before entering politics Wilson Tuckey had been a publican in Carnarvon, where he earned the nickname 'Ironbar' after using a length of heavy steel cable to control an unruly patron. (Wikipedia)
61. Author's quote (when being provocative while having a second whisky!)
62. Albany Advertiser, 7 November 1996.
63. DSE – Dry Sheep Equivalent (dry sheep is a wether or a non-lactating ewe)
64. Paraway Pastoral website: Mungadal Station homepage
65. Landcare Review Committee, A Review of Landcare in Western Australia: the report of the Landcare Review Committee, Perth, 1995.
66. Farm Forestry Task Force, Farm Forestry in Western Australia: report of the Farm Forestry Task Force, Perth, 1995.
67. Land and Water Resources RDC Stakeholder Report 1997

68. Land and Water Resources RDC Stakeholder Report 1997
69. Painted in 1890 at an outstation on Brocklesby near Corowa in the Riverina. The original is housed at the National Gallery of Victoria.
70. As reported in The Countryman February 14, 2002
71. John Kerin had supported the need for a comprehensive audit of the Nations natural resources, as a base line of information for future investment in this politically charged area of growing public concern. Prior to the election and subsequent change of Government, John Anderson also spoke to a number of people as to the need and benefits of an audit, including Peter Cosier, Don Blackmore, Prof Peter Cullen and Prof Mike Young. Once in Government, and with the proceeds of the partial sale of Telstra in hand, Anderson consulted with various people as to the most cost effective structure for such a task. He wanted an 'open and competitive model', rather than 'handing it to CSIRO on a plate' and discussed the matter with Dr Phil Price and myself, re LWRRDC undertaking the responsibility. We said it was too large a task to be considered under the existing structure, but suggested a co-hosting arrangement with the Audit operating under LWRRDC's legislative umbrella, having its own management committee and staff, while sharing other office overheads. This was agreed to, and as Chair of LWRRDC, I also served on the Audit Advisory Council as a common link to both parties.
72. The National Land and Water Resources Audit, 1997-2001
73. Memories shared with Kevin Goss 2016
74. Memories shared with Kevin Goss 2016. Murray–Darling Basin Commission, 'Basin Salinity Management Strategy 2001-2015', Australian Government, 2001, <https://www.mdba.gov.au/sites/default/files/pubs/BSMS-full.pdf>.
75. Shared thoughts with Geoffrey Marshall, WANTFA president 1998-2000 and now a board director, September 2015
76. Information from WA No-Tillage Farmers Association's website and past president, Geoffrey Marshall
77. Oil Mallee Association website and discussions with Lex Hardie 2015 (president of OMA)
78. Oil Mallee Association website and discussions with Lex Hardie 2015 (president of OMA)
79. Information supplied and memories shared with Tammin farmer, Tony York
80. Discussion with Pam McGregor 2015
81. Discussion with president of Oil Mallee Association Lex Hardie, also a member of WISALTS, September 2015
82. The Countryman April 6, 2000
83. The West Australian February 28, 2000
84. State Salinity Council Newsletter April 2000
85. Emeritus Prof Phillip Cocks, WA Institute of Agriculture, University of WA
86. CRC Salinity Annual Review 2004-2005
87. CRC Salinity Annual Review 2004-2005
88. The Salinity Council – Report on Activities 1997-2002
89. The Salinity Council – Report on Activities 1997-2002
90. On 28 April 1996, Martin Bryant shot dead 35 people and wounded 23 others

in the worst ever such event in the nation's recent history. Howard responded by legislating for strict gun ownership controls. (Wikipedia)
91. Memories shared with Denis Saunders 2016
92. The West Australian August 4, 2001
93. Prof Michael (Mick) Poole, formerly with WA Ag. Dept. and CSIRO. Director on CRC-Salinity and Future Farm Industries CRC boards 2001-2014
94. Discussion with president of Oil Mallee Association Lex Hardie September 2015
95. Kevin Goss, CEO of CRC-Salinity then Future Farm Industries CRC 2004-2011
96. In discussion with Kevin Goss, CEO of CRC-Salinity then Future Farm Industries CRC 2004-2011
97. Tammin farmer Tony York, September 2015
98. In discussion with Kevin Goss, CEO of CRC-Salinity then Future Farm Industries CRC 2004-2011
99. Bjorn Lomborg is a Danish environmental economist
100. FESA: Fire and Emergency Services Authority
101. Alex Campbell, Occasional Address, Natural and Agricultural Science graduation ceremony, UWA, 18 March 2009
102. 'Put out to pasture' – Usually referring to a favoured work horse, no longer fit for work, but deserving a retirement on the farm. (Less respected animals would be sent off to the knackers)

APPENDICES

1. From the famous 'learning' Mahatma Gandhi quote, as modified for 'farming' by John Marsden
2. *Snowy Campbell: Australian Pioneer Investigator of the Brain* by Malcolm Macmillan.
3. 'Snowy Campbell: Australian Pioneer Investigator of the Brain' by Malcolm Macmillan
4. Forbes Historical Society: Verbal information provided when visiting in 2013
5. Notes from Pat O'Brien (Joe's grandson) in the late 1990s
6. *The Homestead – A Riverina Anthology* by Peter Freeman, Oxford University Press, 1982.
7. Information and photos provided by the present owners of Cunningham Plains – Steve and Liz Phillips in 2012
8. Information and photos provided by the present owners of Cunningham Plains – Steve and Liz Phillips in 2012
9. 'Magnificent Lake George – The Biography' – Graeme Barron
10. Information provided by Kip Venn – February 2015 (Kip was the son of Jamie Venn who owned Lake Violet from 1974-1987)
11. Poseidon NL (nickel) shares were 80 cents in 1969, rising to $280 in February 1970, then the company was wound up in 1976. Fortunes were made and lost in those hectic years
12. Information provided by Kip Venn – February 2015 (Kip was the son of Jamie Venn who owned Lake Violet from 1974-1987)
13. Information provided by Kip Venn – February 2015 (Kip was the son of Jamie Venn who owned Lake Violet from 1974-1987)
14. Contained in a letter written by Maria Campbell, Thomas's eldest daughter

Acknowledgements

It was cousin Richard Campbell who was the first to provoke my interest in family matters with his trunk full of memorabilia, collected with Anne over many years. He issued the challenge: 'sift through it all and see if you can make a story out of it'. From then on he has been most helpful, firstly in providing information then in proofreading for accuracy and detail.

My brother-in-law John Horner, with help from sister Sue, have been absolute Trojans in converting my longhand to digital format, then initial preparation for publication. It involved many versions and refinement of text and it wouldn't have happened without their help.

My brother Tim and sisters Sue and Liz have shared their family records, photo albums and scrapbooks with the many pasted-in newspaper cuttings. Unless showing alternative sources, all photos are out of family albums and scrapbooks, mainly taken by Don and Alex. Rie Saxton has been very helpful regarding Pat and Evelyn Campbell, and Dimity Davy with information about Louise Campbell (nee Powell) and providing the opportunity of visiting Turalla, 'the ancestral home of our foremothers'.

The venture has unearthed four distant cousins: Madeline Few, Belinda Dale, Bronwyn Davies and Dorothy Parkinson, who have all provided further detail of the early history, particularly relating to John and Thomas Campbell. I am also grateful for Tom Fraser's work (being another distant cousin) with his 1980s publication, *Danish Bred – A Family Miscellany*.

Particular appreciation goes to Malcolm Macmillan, who provided much of the early information after carefully researching the life of Alfred Walter, son of David and Amelia Campbell. His finished work, *Snowy Campbell: Australian Pioneer Investigator of the Brain* (Australian Scholarly Publishing), would also be of interest to readers of this story.

I have referred extensively to Charles Massy's *The Australian Merino*, published by Random Press Australia in 2007, which is truly the bible of sheep breeding in Australia. I thank him for allowing me to reference his work as it's without doubt the most comprehensive source of information on the subject.

I am very appreciative of Steve and Liz Phillips' hospitality and support in welcoming us to Cunningham Plains and then providing follow-up information that has been of great help; also for James Ryrie's generosity on two separate visits to Micalago when we were able to 'add flesh to the bones' of my father's earlier tales of his childhood. Lastly, to Geoff Parker for his assistance when visiting Goimbla and for providing further information regarding the station's early history.

There were two other valuable sources of information: Phoebe Vincent's *My Darling Mick: The Life of Granville Ryrie (1865–1937)* (National Library of Australia), covering the life and times of my grandmother's family in the High Country of the Monaro in New South Wales and Granville's contribution to Australian military history; and unpublished research by Brian Rose and Frank Slee regarding my mother's family, the Roses.

Many other people have been contacted in order to double-check my memory on more recent events and they have been shown by attribution as appropriate. Of these, I particularly thank Kevin Goss, whose career has been interwoven with much of my work, also Rob Chomley, Alan Cleland, Kip Venn, Mark Synnot, Geoff Hodgson, Peter Lee, Tony York, Tony Gooch, Trisha Miles, Lex Hardie, Ron McTaggart, David Stanton, Peter Moulten, John O'Meehan, Peter Crossing, Ian Macmillan, Richard Stockwell, Mick Poole, Dick Sudlow and Derry Macqueen, who all contributed that 'little bit extra' to help in background research.

My brother Tim has been really encouraging and helpful over several years, which included a joint trip back to Wiluna and assistance with collating family information, then in contributing to the cost of publication. We both thank Chris and Caroline Ward for their hospitality at Lake Violet, providing access to all the old records and to the wider station.

I am also deeply appreciative of the final editorial assistance provided by Kelly Somers (with her deft hand on the drafting gate of trivia vs substance), the design input of Margaret Whiskin and the publishing assistance from Rushelle Lister of Lightning Source / Ingram. They have all been very helpful and long-suffering in dealing with a novice in the world of authorship!

Finally, to my immediate family – for Anna and Jock encouraging me 'to have a go and put it all down on paper' and, most importantly, I thank Jenn for once again supporting me in one of my endeavours. She always rises to the occasion, even to a final detailed proofreading of this work, but I have overheard her say on the phone: 'I thought we were retiring to Perth for a quieter life, but Alex might just as well be in Canberra once he gets engrossed in that book of his.'

For all that, I couldn't have done this without her encouragement and forbearance.

INDEX OF PEOPLE AND PLACES

PEOPLE

A
Aboriginal
  Daisy 93, 94, 104, 108, 126, 127, 128, 131
  Peter 126
Adamson, Bob and Alice 103
Addis, Clem 215
Alexander, Jim 241
Alexandra, Jason 261
Alston, Dean 238
Andersen, family 18
Anderson
  family 117
  John 241, 248, 260, 261, 263, 264, 266
  Wal and Marlene 289
  Warren 232
Anthony, Doug 189
Atkins
  family 106
  Peter 106, 128
Atterby, Tom 201
Attwell, Brian 231
Austin, Thomas 48, 153

B
Bachelor, Glenice 270
Baker, Wes 268
Baldock, Ray 164
Balfe, Nick 180
Barnard, Lance 199
Barnett, Colin 247
Barrett-Lennard, Ed 270
Bartle, John 268
Barton, Sir Edmund 48

Baxter, Doug 210
Beazley, Kim 282
Bellanger, Justin 291
Bennet, Christabel 184
Berg
  Elisabeth Sophie 16
Bilston, Len and Hilary 103, 128, 141
Blackmore, Don 265, 266
Blake, John 239
Bligh, Kevin 268
Blight
  Gay 251
  Graham 238
Blythe, John and Chris 208 209 213 232 296
Bond, Alan 122, 123, 232
Boully, Leith 261, 282
Boultbee, Tony 244
Bowen, Bernard 262
Brand. David (Sir) 163
Braslin, Tim 268
Brazier, Peter 149
Bridge, Ernie 247
Brinkworth, Tom 274
Brooks
  Ada 42
  Augustus (Gus) 42
  Capt Richard 41
  Charlotte 41
  Cherrie (Jo) 42
  Christiana 41
  family 20
  Nathanial Stephen 41
Bryant
  family 206
  John and Mary 166
Bungey, Mel 201, 257, 258

Burdass, Joe 185
Burke, Brian 216, 232, 246
Burns, Craig 293
Burston, Ian 262
Burvill, George 119

C
Cairns, Jim 202
Caldwell, John 253
Cameron
  Clyde 202
  Sean 215
Campbell
  Alexander (Alick)
    Douglas 35, 40
  Alexander David (Alex)
    9, 37, 38, 98, 99,
    105, 106, 108,
    116, 129, 130,
    139, 142, 144,
    146, 150, 169,
    183, 184, 197,
    222, 244, 274, 290
  Alfred Walter 28, 32, 33, 67, 99
  Amelia Margaret (nee
    Breillat) 26, 27,
    31, 32, 33, 35, 39
  Andrew (Andy) Ryrie 38
  Andrew (not related) 267
  Anne 14
  Anneliese (Anna) Jane
    9, 123, 195, 198,
    199, 203, 207,
    209, 211, 213,
    215, 217, 250,
    251, 254, 255,
    290, 296, 298, 299
  Beck 123, 224
  Catherine 191, 194, 198

Index of People and Places 337

Campbell (*continued*)
  Charlotte. *See* Charlotte Brooks
  Charlotte Louise (Bunt) 35, 40, 71
  David Frances 26
  David Henry 9, 18, 19–29, 30–40, 42, 44, 45, 47, 98
  David Ian 60, 106
  Delia Rosemarie (Rie, nee Woodley) 58, 60, 102, 104, 126
  Donald Henry Alexander (Don) 9, 53, 60, 67–84, 85–108, 111, 113–124
  Eleanor Mary 28, 32
  Elizabeth Rose (Liz) 116, 120, 171
  Evelyn Charlotte (nee Ryrie) 48, 49, 51, 53, 56, 59, 60, 63, 66, 67, 68, 69, 106
  Graeme 273, 274
  Harriet 255
  Henry 16
  Jack 255
  Jennifer (Jenny and Jenn, nee Levinson) 5, 146, 173, 176, 177, 178, 182, 183, 184, 185, 186, 187, 190, 191, 192, 194, 195, 196, 198, 200, 203, 205, 207, 208, 209, 210, 212, 214, 215, 216, 217, 220, 221, 222, 224, 228, 232, 239, 240, 250, 251, 252, 253, 254, 255, 257, 258, 289, 290, 293, 294, 295, 296, 297, 299
  Jock Alexander 5, 9, 39, 123, 198, 204, 207, 209, 211, 213, 215, 219, 220, 222, 224, 225, 226, 228, 250, 251, 252, 255, 256, 257, 290, 298, 299
  John 9, 14, 16, 17
  Kathleen Cassells (Kay and Bub) 53, 56, 59, 92, 106, 113, 126, 130
  Louise (nee Powell) 35, 37, 38, 39, 40, 42, 43, 44, 123
  Nat (Bey) 53
  Nathaniel (Nat) Powell 9, 35, 40, 44–61, 63
  Pat Powell 39, 53, 56, 57, 58, 59, 60, 61, 92, 102, 126, 131
  Patricia (Patsy, nee Giles) 59, 61, 106
  Penny 255
  Percy 26, 33
  Richard Giles 37, 38, 52
  Sally 123, 221, 222, 224
  Sophie 123, 224
  Suzanne Ryrie (Sue) 105, 108, 116, 120, 130, 135, 171, 183
  Thelma (nee Rose) 60, 82, 93, 94, 95, 96, 97, 98, 99, 100, 102, 103, 104, 105, 106, 111, 113, 114, 115, 116, 120, 123, 124, 197
  Thomas 9, 14, 16, 17, 18, 19
  Thomas Chaplin Breillat 26
  Timothy Donald (Tim) 37, 38, 99, 108, 116, 123, 127, 128, 129, 130, 132, 133, 134, 135, 137, 139, 140, 141, 142, 154, 171, 173, 176, 183, 221, 222, 224, 231, 239, 250, 261, 268, 292, 295
  Walter 20, 28, 51
  William 20
Candeloro, Joe 245, 291
Carpenter, Alan 240
Carroll
  Bert (Bull) 89, 103, 127
  Elsie 103
  Mike 119
Cartwright, Tom 99, 103
Cass, Moss 203
Chadwick
  David 291
  Lee 253
Chance, Kim 281
Charlesworth, Sheila 286
Chatfield family 270
Chidgzey, Phil 239
Chittleborough, Prof. David 279
Chomley
  Ffloyd 52
  George (Gef) 83
  Rob 251
Chun-Zhuli, Prof. 285
Clapin
  Anna 255
  John 245
  Lindy 255
Clarke
  Ben 142
  Ephraim 110
Clarkson, Jill and Gay 149
Clayton, Tim 154
Cleland
  Alan 236
  Bill 82, 83, 84
Clifton, Darby 115

Cockman
  Cecil (Tiddles) 121, 149
  Terry 149, 150
Cocks, Prof Phil 277, 279, 283
Cole, Tom 152, 156
Collins
  A.L. (Art) 179
  Bob 248, 260
  John 179
  Muriel 182
Connell, Laurie 85, 232
Conwell, Irene 239
Cook, Barry 149
Coole, Ross 179, 180, 188
Corbin, Peter 82
Cosier, Peter 282
Costello, Peter 218, 282
Court
  Barry 262
  Charles (Sir) 246, 293
  Richard 243, 246, 259, 262, 263, 273, 276
Cowan, Hendy 263, 265, 274, 280
Coyne, Peter 273, 274
Crabtree, Bill 268
Crane, Winston 217, 218
Crawford
  Don 263
  Ondi 251
Crean, Simon 248
Creighton, Colin 264
Cresswell
  Diana 145
  Evan 115
  Molly 135
Creswell
  Peter 90, 99
Crisp, John 239
Crook, Russell 239
Croote, Chris 269
Crossing
  family 170, 206, 214
  Jane (nee Drummond) 194
  Peter 166, 173, 194
Cullen, Prof. Peter 282
Culley, Ted and Den 134
Cullingworth
  Bev 145
  Claris 135
  Phil 115
Cunningham
  Allan 30
  Jim 116
  Rosie 116
  Twynam 116

D

Daddow, Alan 180
Dainton, John 155
Daley, John 272
Darling, James 270, 274
Darlot, Bros 37
Davidson, Di 228
Davies
  Graham 215
  Maria 33
  Thomas 33, 37
Davis, Eddie 205
Daw, Fred 115
Dawkins, Simon 269
Day
  Roger 145
  Tom 262
De Bernales, Claude 85
De Landgraffe
  Trevor 291
Della Bosca, Clint 268
Dempster, Dallas 232
De Pledge, Dick 241
Dixon, Trisha 253
Doman
  Margaret 92
  Spencer 91
Donald, Ross 262
Donaldson, Sheila 261
Douglas, Sheila 251
Dowling, Wally 92
Drew, Gavin 271

Dunbar, Arthur 77, 78, 79
Dunne, John 272
Dunnit, Michael 298
Durack, family 110

E

Ecclestone, Laurie 215
Eckersley, Don 201
Edkins, Rob 291
Edmondson, Rex 234, 259, 262, 263, 281
Edwardes, Cheryl 263
Edwards, Judy 280, 281
Elliot, John 180
Ellis
  Di 184
  family 194, 206
  Peter 134, 170, 173
Embry, Sir Basil 195
English, Garry 234, 262
Enright
  Gerry 215, 220
  Keryl 215
  Terry 215, 293
Espie, Sue 183
Evans, David 247
Ewing, Prof. Mike 277, 279, 283
Eyres
  Bruce 154
  Jill and Joan-Anne 154

F

Farley, Rick 233, 243
Faulkner, F.S. 46
Featherstonhaugh, John 89, 90, 93
Few, Madeline 14, 16
Fiellerup
  Louisa Augusta 18
  Maria Elizabeth 18
Finch, Mick 86, 98, 100
Findlay
  Brothers 167, 174
  children 209

Index of People and Places 339

David 232, 258
Findlay (continued)
  Evan 208, 214
  Ian 208, 214
  Joan 215
  Norma 214
Fisher
  John and Jenny 213
  Mary-Jo 239
Fitzpatrick, Noel 119
Fletcher, Roger 281
Folvig, Wendy and George 103
Fraser
  Malcolm 203, 216, 278
  Roger 117
Freebairn, Phil 160
French, Tony 107

G

Gair, Geoff 240
Gairdner, Max 194
Gallop, Dr Geoff 280
Garnett
  Glen 179
  Neil 179
Gaze, Bill 179
George, Richard 274
Georgeff, Mick 272
Gleeson, Len 201
Gooch, Tony 201, 236, 239
Gordon, Leslie 74, 76
Gorrie, Geoff 264
Goss, Kevin 234, 259, 261, 263, 264, 265, 275, 279, 284, 285
Goundrey, Michael 226, 230
Grassby, Al 203
Green
  Dr Roy 234, 264
  family 103
Grill, Julian 232, 247, 248
Gunn, Bill (Sir William) 189
Gwyn, Roy 210

H

Halcombe, Ron 68, 69, 75, 76, 106, 107, 121, 124, 128
Hall
  Ben 27
  Bob 235
  John 272
Halpin, George 181
Hames, Dr Kim 263
Hamilton, John 145, 149, 154, 327
Hampshire, Judy and Angela 149
Hancock, Hope 135
Hansen, family 18
Hardie
  family 117
  Lex 269, 271, 285
  Mervyn 275
Hardy, Justin 270
Harrington, Ray 268
Harrison
  Dr Don 270
  Lorraine 216
  Max 216
Hawke, Bob 216, 232, 233, 234
Hawker
  Edmond 51
  Edward 51
  George 51
  Michael 52
  Walter 51
Hawkes
  Rollo 82
  Waldemar (W.G.) 72, 74
Henderson
  Bert 215, 220
  George 117
  Keith 69
Henwood
  Bill 93
  family 120
  Grace (nee Rose).
    See Grace Rose

Herbert, family 170
Higgins, Dean 258
Hill, Robert 266, 282
Hobbs, Jack (J.B.) 69
Hodgson
  Catherine 164
  family 194
  Geoff 164
  Harry 148, 151, 152, 155, 159, 162, 164, 270
  Harry jnr 164
  Hilary 164
  Marjorie 164
Hogg, Archie 100
Hollingsworth, Tom 173, 176
Holmes à Court, Robert 232
Honey, Fred 155
Hoolihan, Paul 217, 218
Hordacre, Duncan 241
House
  Monty 247, 259, 262, 263, 276, 281
  Pell 244
Howard,
  family 155
  John 260, 266, 273, 282
Humphris, family 182
Hunt, Greg 180

I

Iceley, Charles 29

J

Jeffery, Major General Michael 265
Jennings, Phil 262
Jensen
  Bill 183, 188, 194
  family 18, 194, 206
  Lola 194
Jessop, Ted 105
Johnson, Lyn 235
Johnston, Max 241

Jones
  Dan 95, 100, 127, 131
  Graham 201
Jorgensen, family 18

K

Keating, Paul 227, 232, 241, 242, 243, 248, 260
Kelly, Ned 27
Kelso, Garth 180
Kempton
  Jenny 213
  Robin 145, 213
Kennedy
  Gary 181
  Murray 241
Keogh
  family 213
  Janice and Libby 213
  Simon 213
  Sue 213
Kerin, John 233, 236, 248, 260, 263
Kerkmans, Mike 269
King
  Barry 173, 188
  family 173, 206
  Florence 173, 184
Kinnear, John 230, 290
Kirby, Ty 268
Kronborg, Jamie 237

L

Lamb, Bill 251, 252, 255
Lanagan, George 92
Langey, Kerry 154
Lanyon, Jack 115
Lawrence, Carmen 243, 246
Lee
  Christina 251
  Peter 234, 238
Leeds, Jim 117
Lefroy, Peter 244
Levinson
  Barry 177
  business 126

Christine (Chris) 178, 183, 208
Eugene 178
Felix 178
Hyman 177
Jennifer (Jenny and Jenn). *See* Jennifer (Jenny and Jenn) Campbell
Malcolm 178
Mark 178
May 178
Merle 178
Robert 176
Ross 178
Lewis
  Irwin 137
  Stan 241
Liebe, Wilhelm (Gus) 286
Lindsay, Mary (Hon) 117
Lloyd, Michael 263, 270, 271, 280
Locke
  Kate 298
  Patti 298
  Peter 298
Logan, Michael (Mike) 261
Lomborg, Bjorn 288, 332
Lugsdin, Lou 255
Lukin, Herb and Mim 103
Lyons, family 296

M

Macansh, John 20, 22, 26, 28, 30, 31, 36, 39
Macaulay, Stuart 258
MacKinnon, Daniel 83
MacMillan
  Bob 86, 89, 90, 96, 100
  family 194, 206
  Gillian (nee Angel) 194
  Ian 173, 183, 194, 199
Macmillan
  Malcolm 334
Macqueen
  Derry 133, 137, 145, 329, 335
  family 140

Magee, Christina 154, 238
Malcolm, Clive 160, 270
Mann, Colin 239
Maple-Brown, Jim 235
Marden, Terry 208, 212
Marshall
  Dr Larry 288
  Geoffrey 268, 332
  Laurie 239
Mason, Warren 270
Massy, Charles 36, 334
Masters, Dr David 279
Mattinson, Bruce 226
McAuliff, Jim 117
McCashney, Harold 239
McCaughey
  family 86, 90
  Michael 107
  Roy 107
  Sam 89, 107
  Samuel (Sir) 86
  Unity 107
McCorry, Cheryl 298
McCracken, Jimmy 170
McCusker, Malcolm (QC) 295
McCutcheon, Bill 235
McDonald
  family 110
  Warwick 264
McFall, David 269
McFarlane, Don 226, 227, 280
McGrath, Ron 230
McGregor
  Jim 215, 271
  Pam 215, 271
McKay, John 272, 273
McKenzie, Clem 105
McLachlan
  Alex 60
  Ian 217, 218
McLennan
  Malcolm (Mac) 115, 151
  Mary 135
  Trisha 145, 184

McMenemy, Kevin 239, 249, 262
McNamara, Kieran 261
McNiel, Andrew 236, 239
McQuire, Mark 236
McTaggart, Ron 210
Metcalfe, John 271
Mews, Jim 134
Meyer, Bill 201
Miles
    family 206, 214
    Peter 184
Millear, Thomas 46
Milton, Clive 210
Minkey, David 268
Mitchell
    Bill 291
    Ken 90, 99, 103
    Len 104, 107
Moir
    Doug 174
    Keith and Ruth 198
Monger
    Adrian 135
    boys 133
    family 106
    Henry 135
    Kitty 135
    Marg 106, 128, 135
    Peter 135
    Rupert 135
Montgomery, Murray and Pam 215
Morosi, Junie 202
Morrell, Barbara 292
Morrison, Jock and Janie 222–231
Moulton, Peter 179, 180
Moyes, Peter 137, 146, 147
Munday, Don 104
Munns, Neville 239
Murphy, Lionel 202
Murray
    David 209
    John 72

N

Nalder, Crawford 163
Nelson
    Brian 238
    Peter 181
Newing, Brian 191, 196, 209
Newton-Turner, Helen 181
Noble
    John 51, 72
    Rae 155
    Rex 154, 183
Norman, Dr Hayley 284
Norrish, E.B. Eddie 180, 186
Norton, Mike 239
Nuberg, Dr Ian 279
Nulsen, Bob 185

O

Oates, Barry 239
O'Brien, Joe 29, 304
O'Connor, Richard 221
O'Keefe, Jack 93, 95, 96, 104, 126, 131
O'Malley, John 28
O'Meally, John 27
O'Meehan
    family 206
    John 174, 184, 240
    Les 184
    Tony 166, 184
    Wendy 184
O'Shaughnessy, Barney 85, 90, 93
O'Sullivan, John 179
Owens, Roy 170, 171, 173, 181, 186, 195, 199, 200, 203, 213

P

Padbury, Tom 179
Page, Brian 198, 199
Pannell, Prof. David 279
Parker
    Bevan (Blue Bush) 160, 270
    Geoff 305, 335
Parkes, Sir Henry 48
Parkin, Ron 210
Parnell
    Keith 269
    Margaret 175
    Wally 175
    Wally and Margaret 175
Paterson, Banjo 28, 45, 130, 143
Patterson
    Alf (Dingo) 103
    Charles and Romi 201
Pearce, Bob 227
Peck, Ken 262
Pederick, Graeme 232, 258
Pendarvis, Jay 218
Pennington, Alistair 251
Peppin
    family 36, 47
    George 46
Peterson, Thomas Henry 242
Phillips, Steve and Liz 31, 32, 307, 335
Pither
    Colin 167
    family 173, 206
    Hazel 163, 167, 181, 190, 195
    Jenny 167
    John 163, 167, 194, 195
    John jnr 167
    Kate 167
    Sarah 167
Pollard, Kate 255
Poole, Prof. Mick 279, 285
Powell
    family 20, 41–43
    Henry George 40
    Louise. *See* Louise Campbell
    Nathaniel Stephen 35
    Noel 271
Price
    Dr Phil 260, 267
    Richard 261, 270
Prince Charles, 284

Pritchard
  Annabele 182
  family 206
  Frank 173, 182, 190
  Zanna 184, 191
Prout, Ashley 210
Pugh
  Alexandra 208
  Bob 208
  Clare 208
  family 208
  Georgia 208
  Harriet 208
  John 208, 216
  Kim 208
Purse, Ian 262

R

Radcliffe, Dr John 264, 278
Raeside
  Elizabeth 229
  John 222, 229, 250
  Johnny 229
  Margaret 229
  Morag 229
Rankin, Jenny 183
Ravenhill, family 295, 296
Reynolds
  family 206
  Henry 173, 194, 214, 215
  Jeannie 214, 253
  Wayne 239, 250
Richards, Lloyd 271
Richardson
  Colin 241
  Keith 179
Richie, Ian 149
Ridley, Dr Anna 279
Roberts
  Anna. *See* Anneliese (Anna) Jane Campbell
  Angus 255
  Bert 254
  family 254
  Hugh 254

Kerrie 255
Lachlan (Lachie) 255
Tom 261
Robertson, Dr Graeme 260, 276
Robinson Ian 211
Rose
  Alice 111, 141, 142
  Canny 82, 92, 111
  Edith Bertha (Bertha, nee Clarke) 110
  family 82, 92, 109–112, 120
  George Canler 112
  Grace 82, 93, 99, 102, 111
  Kimberley (Kim) 82, 92, 111
  Robert Henry 109
  Sylvia 93, 98, 105
  Thelma. *See* Thelma Campbell (nee Rose)
Rowe, Doug 134, 210
Rucks, Bill 137
Rudd, Kevin 282, 287, 289, 291
Rundle, Bronte 275
Rutherford, Peter 181
Ryan, Tim 239, 250
Ryrie
  Alexander 48
  Charlotte 63
  Donald 62
  Evelyn Charlotte 48
  family 20, 62–65
  James 62
  Sir Granville 49, 56, 63, 64, 65, 66
  Stewart 62
  William 19, 20, 62, 63

S

Saggers, Carey 228
Salting, Severin Kanute 18, 20, 25, 28, 30, 36
Saunders

Dr Denis 282
Jim 201
Schapper, Dr Henry 243
Schofield, Nick 260
Scott, brothers 272
Seaman, Peter 181
Sears, Don and Helen 58
Shallcross, Shally 106, 115
Shea, Dr Syd 227
Shields
  Alice 111, 141, 142
  Christine 141
  Elizabeth 141
  family 120, 141
  Graham 141
  Herbert 93, 141
  Hubert 141
  Penny 141
  Peter 141
  Tony 141
  Virginia 141
  Waverley 141
Siewert, Rachel 262
Silby, John 262
Skinner, Ernie and Mike 215
Smart, Eric 119, 268
Smith
  Colin 190
  Darryl 188
  Tom 119
  Tony 226
Sorgiovanni
  Bruno 151
  Jim 271
Sprigg, Katie 253
Stallwood, Peter 210
Stan-Bishop, Doug 258
Stanley
  Don 268, 269
  Ian 269
Stanton, David 185
Steele, John 232
Stehlik, Prof. Daniela 293
Steinhart, Ian 215
Steph, first girlfriend 146, 149

Index of People and Places   343

Stickells, Mark 279
Stockwell
  boys 166
  family 170, 206, 214
  Graham 166
  John 166
  Richard 166
Stone, Lex 270
Sudlow
  Dick 134, 137, 149
  Norm 134
Sutherland, Don 239, 249
Swarbrick, Rick 203
Synnot
  Frederick (Will) 77, 78, 79
  Mark (jr) 78

T

Taylor
  Ben 92, 328
  Garry and Marie 205
  Jane 253
Temby, Toll 268
ten Seldam
  family 173, 206
  Helen 173, 184
  John 173
Terry, Mike 155
Thom
  David 145
  Elspeth 145
  Ian 99, 116, 117
  Jocelyn 99, 123, 135
Thompson
  Di 222
  family 115, 117
  Jeanette and Peter 184
  Ross 221, 222–231
  Tommy 106, 115, 117
Thorne, Shirley 239
Tickner, Liz 244, 245
Toll, Stuart 272
Toms, Jack 119
Townsend
  family 205
  Ron 205, 213

Toyne, Phillip 234
Tozer, Bob 201
Trevenen
  Beth 214
  Mike 214
  Steve 210
Trott, Peter 280
Truss, Warren 266
Tuckey, Wilson 235, 248, 273
Turley, Jim 180
Turner, Dr Vivienne 279
Turton, Ian 239

V

Vogel, Paul 261

W

Wahlsten, Peter 241
Waldeck, Fred 107, 115
Walker
  Charles 156
  Helen 253
  John 25
Walsh
  John (from Cranbrook) 270
  John (Peter's brother) 237
  Peter 232, 238
Ward
  Chris and Caroline 292, 309, 335
  family 86, 91, 100, 128
Watkins
  plan 275
  Ron 275, 280
  Warrick 261
Watson, Harry 155, 170
Watt, Leon 262
Webb, Peter 245
Weir
  Digger 214, 228
  Marg 214
Wellard, Tom 179

Wellstead
  Jim 186
  Keith 169
White, Munroe 215
Whitlam, Gough 199
Whittington, Harry 271
Wickes, Roger 264
Wilcox, Charles 261
Williams, Dr John 282
Wilson, Bill 203
Winrow, Dr Alex 192
Witham
  Barry 184
  Trish 214, 253
Wonder, Bernie 264
Woodhams, Dick 201
Wright, Lenny 203

Y

Yeo, Syd 117, 121
York, Tony 239, 270, 283, 284, 286
Young, Neil 268

PROPERTIES

Albion Downs 103, 128
Anameka 283, 286
Apsley 60, 255
Ashby 41
Barwidgee 103, 128
Beggan Beggan 25
Belltree 33
Beringarra 37
Billiluna 91, 92
Bobundara 253
Booligal 33, 143
Boonoke 33, 46
Bowyeo 30
Bryen 25
Bundemar 47
Bungaree 51, 52, 55, 72, 83, 89, 179
Bungendow 41
Burrabogie 33
Carnegie 91
Chateau Yerring 62
Cherabun 109
Coree 33, 86, 90, 107
Coree Past Co 107
Crystal Brook 7, 221, 221–231, 222, 223, 224, 225, 226, 227, 228, 229, 230, 231, 232, 250, 290
Cullingra 25
Cumbamurra 25, 30
Cunningham Creek 25, 30
Cunningham Plains 6, 28, 30–40, 44, 45, 87
Cunyu 103
Depot Springs 117
Douglas 39, 40, 44
Duck Island 270
Erregulla Springs 119
Glenorn 83, 84
Glenroy 179
Glenvar 93, 141, 142

Goimbla 6, 19–29, 33, 39
Goolgumbla 47
Granite Peak 90, 91, 99, 100, 103, 127, 128
Hooley 81
Kayanaba 254
Koonamore 60
Koonoona 6, 51, 55, 67, 72, 73, 74, 75, 82, 179
Lake Violet 6, 58, 60, 85, 86, 87, 88, 89, 90, 91, 92, 93, 96, 98, 100, 101, 102, 103, 104, 105, 107, 108, 113, 118, 126, 127, 129, 131, 133, 292
Lake Way 100, 103, 128
Leopold Downs 109
Liveringa 92, 110
Mianellup 179
Millbillillie 86, 107
Millstream 6, 67, 74, 75, 76, 77, 79, 81, 82, 83, 96
Mount Anderson 6, 82, 93, 109, 110
Mudginberri 217, 218
Mungadal 33, 47, 256, 257
Mungaterra 116, 117, 122
Myrooda 109
Nantgwylan 33
Nardlah 221, 223, 229
Noonkanbah 93
North Yanco 86
Oakdale 163, 167, 187
Pardoo 115
Parkfield 109
Pevensey 256
Pinnacles 83
Pooginook 256
Quanbun 109
Rosevale 256
Sandalwood 174
Sturt Meadows 55, 83, 89, 251

Tarmoola 55, 82, 83, 89
The Grange 110, 111
Three Rivers 166
Tillgaree 7, 165, 165–182, 168, 183, 205, 206, 209, 253, 257
Togannain 33
Tubbo 33
Tupra 33
Turalla 6, 39, 40, 41, 42, 43, 71
Uardry 33, 44, 47, 115, 251
Ulonga 33, 256
Wallinar 275
Wanganella 33, 46
Willurah 47, 251, 252, 255, 256
Windidda 91
Wingfield 82, 92, 111, 112, 130, 132
Winnininnie 73
Wogarno 106
Wongawol 91
Wydgee 6, 99, 113, 116, 117, 118, 121, 142, 144, 149
Wydgee Past Co 6, 113, 117
Wyloo 58, 59
Yakabindie 103, 128
Yanchep Estate 116, 117, 119, 120, 121, 122
Yandan 254, 255
Yandil 103
Yanga 33
Yarrawee 179
Yeadgee 179
Yeeda 109
Yeelirrie 103, 128
Yering 19, 62, 63
Yoweragabbie 116, 117

Index of People and Places

TOWNS AND RIVERS

Adelaide 49, 51, 54, 55, 56, 58, 60, 67, 68, 69, 70, 71, 74, 76, 92, 93, 105, 126, 130, 242, 265, 278, 292
Albany 116, 180, 184, 188, 195, 199, 200, 203, 205, 210, 211, 212, 214, 215, 216, 217, 220, 227, 228, 231, 253, 254, 255, 281, 289, 291, 295, 298
Arthur River 182
Billabong Creek 33, 47, 86
Blackwood River 273
Borden 163, 166, 173, 180, 183, 187, 201, 205, 206, 208, 213, 214, 257, 291
Boxwood Hills 186, 189, 198
Bremer Bay 180, 187, 201
Brisbane River 19, 24
Broomehill 117, 190, 221, 222, 275
Bruce Rock 298
Bungendore 35, 40, 42, 71
Burra 53, 71, 72, 75
Canberra 27, 41, 62, 250, 251, 276, 291
Cape Riche 195
Chowerup 195
Collie 273
Cooma 62, 253
Cossack 74
Dandaragan 109, 254, 255
Darkan 235
Deniliquin 47, 255
Denmark 227, 228, 284, 298
Denmark (Europe) 9, 15, 16, 17, 18
Derby 77, 82, 135
Dubbo 266, 281
Esperance 234, 245, 287
Eugowra 25, 27
Fitzroy Valley 109
Forbes 25, 27
Fortescue River 74, 75
Gairdner River 174, 179, 187, 201
Gnowangerup 170, 173, 178, 179, 180, 182, 187, 190, 191, 192, 194, 198
Gwalia 82
Harden 307
Hay 22, 47, 143, 178, 190, 222, 223, 251, 255, 256, 257
Jacup 201
Jerramungup 180, 191, 234
Jilakin Lake 152, 155
Jilakin Rock 155
Katanning 179, 180, 181, 185, 189, 266, 275
Keith 69, 169, 179, 198, 269, 270, 274
Kulin 151, 154, 155, 156, 157, 158, 159, 161, 163, 166, 167, 170, 171, 173, 183, 238, 270
Lachlan River 30
Lake George 6, 35, 39, 40, 41, 44
Lake Toolibin 264
Leonora 55, 82, 83, 84, 85, 89, 92
Leschenault Estuary 109
Mandagery Creek 25, 29, 300
Meekatharra 85, 86, 87, 116, 166
Melbourne 24, 28, 48, 63, 180, 251, 255
Mingenew 116, 118, 119, 122, 150, 286
Mount Barker 205, 209, 210, 215, 216, 219, 227, 258, 281, 293
Mt Magnet 93, 106
Murga Inn 25
Murray River 19, 22, 24, 233, 265
Murrumbidgee River 22, 24, 33, 37, 44, 62, 63, 86, 143, 144, 251
Murrumburrah 28, 30, 39, 44
Narrikup 167, 205, 206, 208, 209, 214, 215, 216, 220, 221, 228, 253, 255
Nungarin 170
One Tree 143
Ongerup 163, 170, 201, 203, 214, 228
Onslow 74, 79
Orange 25, 300
Pallinup River 167, 173
Paynes Find 99, 142
Perth 6, 55, 59, 74, 82, 85, 92, 93, 98, 99, 102, 105, 107, 109, 110, 112, 113, 115, 116, 120, 122, 124, 126, 130, 131, 132, 134, 135, 136, 141, 145, 146, 147, 149, 151, 158, 159, 168, 171, 173, 176, 177, 178, 180, 182, 186, 190, 191, 195, 210, 216, 217, 220, 221, 222, 229, 238, 239, 247, 250, 251, 255, 278, 291, 294, 295, 298
Porongurup Hills 105, 205, 213, 253, 290
Porongurups 253
Port Phillip 19, 24, 30, 62
Roebourne 74, 79, 82

Stirling Ranges 166, 214, 221
Sydney 10, 18, 19, 20, 24, 26, 31, 41, 49, 64, 85, 92, 282
Tambellup 116, 184, 191, 205, 214, 237
Wellington River 264
Wiluna 6, 84, 85, 87, 89, 90, 91, 92, 93, 95, 99, 100, 105, 107, 113, 114, 120, 126, 127, 128, 131, 206, 265
Wongan Hills 93, 141
Yanchep 149, 150
Yanchep National Park 116
Young 25
Yunta 60

Index of People and Places

Index of People and Places

Index of People and Places

Index of People and Places

Index of People and Places

Index of People and Places

Index of People and Places

Index of People and Places

Index of People and Places

Index of People and Places

Index of People and Places

Index of People and Places

Index of People and Places

Index of People and Places